Sams Teach Yourself HTML and CSS in 24 Hours, Ninth Edition

ISBN-13: 978-0-672-33614-0
ISBN-10: 0-672-33614-6

Library of Congress Control Number: 2013954119

Printed in the United States of America

First Printing December 2013

Trademarks

All terms mentioned in this book that are known to be trademarks or service marks have been appropriately capitalized. Sams Publishing cannot attest to the accuracy of this information. Use of a term in this book should not be regarded as affecting the validity of any trademark or service mark.

Warning and Disclaimer

Every effort has been made to make this book as complete and as accurate as possible, but no warranty or fitness is implied. The information provided is on an "as is" basis. The author and the publisher shall have neither liability nor responsibility to any person or entity with respect to any loss or damages arising from the information contained in this book.

Special Sales

For information about buying this title in bulk quantities, or for special sales opportunities (which may include electronic versions; custom cover designs; and content particular to your business, training goals, marketing focus, or branding interests), please contact our corporate sales department at corpsales@pearsoned.com or (800) 382-3419.

For government sales inquiries, please contact governmentsales@pearsoned.com.

For questions about sales outside the U.S., please contact international@pearsoned.com.

Acquisitions Editor
Mark Taber

Managing Editor
Sandra Schroeder

Senior Project Editor
Tonya Simpson

Copy Editor
Krista Hansing Editorial Services

Indexer
Ken Johnson

Proofreader
Sarah Kearns

Technical Editor
Jennifer Kyrnin

Editorial Assistant
Vanessa Evans

Interior Designer
Gary Adair

Cover Designer
Mark Shirar

Compositor
Mary Sudul

Table of Contents

About the Author

Julie Meloni is a software development manager and technical consultant living in Washington, D.C. She has written several books and articles on web-based programming languages and database topics, including the bestselling *Sams Teach Yourself PHP, MySQL and Apache All in One*.

We Want to Hear from You!

As the reader of this book, *you* are our most important critic and commentator. We value your opinion and want to know what we're doing right, what we could do better, what areas you'd like to see us publish in, and any other words of wisdom you're willing to pass our way.

You can email or write to let us know what you did or didn't like about this book—as well as what we can do to make our books stronger.

Please note that we cannot help you with technical problems related to the topic of this book, and that due to the high volume of mail we receive, we might not be able to reply to every message.

When you write, please be sure to include this book's title, edition number, and author, as well as your name and contact information.

Email: feedback@samspublishing.com

Mail: Sams Publishing
            800 East 96th Street
            Indianapolis, IN 46240 USA

Reader Services

Visit our website and register this book at **informit.com/register** for convenient access to any updates, downloads, or errata that might be available for this book.

Introduction

In 2012, more than 2.8 billion people had access to the Internet, including 255 million people in the United States alone. Throw in 567 million Chinese users, 69 million German users, 54 million British users, 76 million Russian users, and 99 million Brazilians, and you can see the meaning of the word *world* in the term *World Wide Web*. Many of these Internet users are also creating content for the web—you can be one of them! Although accurate measurements of the total number of web pages are difficult to come by, Google surpassed the 1 trillion mark of indexed pages in the middle of 2008.

In the next 24 hours, hundreds of millions of new pages will appear in accessible areas of the Internet. At least as many pages will be placed on private intranets, where they will be viewed by businesspeople connected via their local networks. Every one of those pages—like the billions of pages already online—will use Hypertext Markup Language (HTML).

As you complete the 24 one-hour lessons in this book, your web pages will be among those that appear on the Internet. These lessons also provide you with a foundation for developing one of the most valuable skills in the world today: mastery of HTML.

Can you really learn to create top-quality web pages yourself, without any specialized software, in less time than it takes to schedule and wait for an appointment with a highly paid design consultant? Can this relatively short, easy-to-read book really enable you to teach yourself state-of-the-art techniques for developing and publishing web content?

Yes. In fact, within the first two lessons in this book, someone with no previous HTML experience at all can have a web page ready to go online.

How can you learn the language of the web so quickly? By example. This book organizes lessons on the basics of HTML and CSS into simple steps and then shows you exactly how to tackle each step. Many of these HTML code examples are accompanied by pictures of the output produced by the code. You see how it's done, you read a clear and concise explanation of how it works, and then you immediately do the same thing with your own page. A few minutes later, you're on to the next step.

Soon you'll be marveling at your own impressive pages on the Internet.

Beyond HTML

This book covers more than just HTML because HTML isn't the only thing you need to know to create web content today. The goal of this book is to give you a solid foundation in the skills you need to create a modern, standards-compliant website in just 24 short, easy lessons. This book covers the following key skills and technologies:

▶ HTML5 is the most current recommendation for web page creation. Every example in this book is validated HTML5.

▶ All the examples in the book have been tested for compatibility with the latest version of every major web browser. That includes Apple Safari, Google Chrome, Microsoft Internet Explorer, Mozilla Firefox, and Opera. You'll learn from the start to be compatible with the past, yet ready for the future.

▶ The book has extensive coverage of the most current recommendation of Cascading Style Sheets (CSS), which allows you to carefully control the layout, fonts, colors, and formatting of every aspect of your web pages, including both text and images. When it comes to creating eye-popping web pages, CSS goes far beyond what traditional HTML pages could do by themselves.

▶ The technical stuff is not enough, so this book also includes the advice you need when setting up a website to achieve your goals. Key details—designing an effective page layout, posting your page to the Internet with FTP software, organizing and managing multiple pages, and getting your pages to appear high on the query lists at all the major Internet search sites—are all covered in enough depth to get you beyond the snags that often frustrate beginners.

Attention to many of these essentials are what made the first eight editions of this book bestsellers, and this updated edition is no different. All the examples have been updated, and significant portions of the content have been revised to match new examples and new technologies, fully embracing HTML5 and CSS3.

Visual Examples

Every example in this book is illustrated in two parts:

▶ The text you type to make an HTML page is shown first, with all HTML and CSS code highlighted.

▶ The resulting web page is shown as it will appear to users who view it with the world's most popular web browsers.

You'll often be able to adapt the example to your own pages without reading any of the accompanying text at all (although it is highly recommended that you read the rest of the text!).

All the examples in this book are standards compliant and work with Apple Safari, Google Chrome, Microsoft Internet Explorer, Mozilla Firefox, and Opera. Although all the screenshots were taken in Chrome, rest assured that all the code has been tested in all other browsers.

You will also find colors used within code examples and references to elements of code in the explanatory text. These colors highlight the different bits and pieces of code, both to enhance your familiarity with them and to call attention to their use.

- ▶ HTML tags appear in `dark blue`.
- ▶ HTML comments appear in `grey`.
- ▶ CSS elements appear in `green`.
- ▶ HTML attribute names appear in `light blue`.
- ▶ HTML attribute values appear in `magenta`.

Please note that the color of an item can change, depending on its context. For instance, when CSS elements are used within the style attribute of an HTML tag, they are color-coded as HTML attribute values (`magenta`) instead of CSS elements (`green`).

Special Elements

As you complete each lesson, margin notes help you immediately apply what you just learned to your own web pages.

Whenever a new term is used, it is clearly highlighted. No flipping back and forth to a glossary!

TIP	NOTE	CAUTION
Tips and tricks to save you precious time are set aside in "Tip" boxes so that you can spot them quickly.	Note boxes highlight interesting information you should be sure not to miss.	When you need to watch out for something, you're warned about it in Caution boxes.

Q&A, Quiz, and Exercises

Every hour ends with a short question-and-answer session that addresses the kind of "dumb questions" everyone wishes they dared to ask. A brief but complete quiz lets you test yourself to be sure you understand everything presented in the hour. Finally, one or two optional exercises give you a chance to practice your new skills before you move on.

HOUR 1
Understanding How the Web Works

Before learning the intricacies of HTML (Hypertext Markup Language) and CSS (Cascading Style Sheets), it is important to gain a solid understanding of the technologies that help transform these plain-text files to the rich multimedia displays you see on your computer or handheld device when browsing the World Wide Web.

For example, a file containing markup and client-side code HTML and CSS is useless without a web browser to view it, and no one besides yourself will see your content unless a web server is involved. Web servers make your content available to others who, in turn, use their web browsers to navigate to an address and wait for the server to send information to them. You will be intimately involved in this publishing process because you must create files and then put them on a server to make them available in the first place, and you must ensure that your content will appear to the end user as you intended.

A Brief History of HTML and the World Wide Web

Once upon a time, back when there weren't any footprints on the moon, some farsighted folks decided to see whether they could connect several major computer networks. I'll spare you the names and stories (there are plenty of both), but the eventual result was the "mother of all networks," which we call the Internet.

Until 1990, accessing information through the Internet was a rather technical affair. It was so hard, in fact, that even Ph.D.-holding physicists were often frustrated when trying to swap data. One such physicist, the now-famous (and knighted) Sir Tim Berners-Lee, cooked up a way to easily cross-reference text on the Internet through hypertext links.

This wasn't a new idea, but his simple Hypertext Markup Language (HTML) managed to thrive while more ambitious hypertext projects floundered. *Hypertext* originally meant text stored in electronic form with cross-reference links between pages. It is now a broader term that refers to just about any object (text, images, files, and so on) that can be linked to other objects. *Hypertext Markup Language* is a language for describing how text, graphics, and files containing other information are organized and linked.

By 1993, only 100 or so computers throughout the world were equipped to serve up HTML pages. Those interlinked pages were dubbed the *World Wide Web (WWW)*, and several web browser programs had been written to allow people to view web pages. Because of the growing popularity of the web, a few programmers soon wrote web browsers that could view graphical images along with text. From that point forward, the continued development of web browser software and the standardization of the HTML—and XHTML—languages has led us to the world we live in today, one in which more than half a billion websites serve billions of text and multimedia files.

NOTE

For more information on the history of the World Wide Web, see the Wikipedia article on this topic: http://en.wikipedia.org/wiki/History_of_the_Web.

These few paragraphs really are a brief history of what has been a remarkable period. Today's college students have never known a time in which the World Wide Web didn't exist, and the idea of always-on information and ubiquitous computing will shape all aspects of our lives moving forward. Instead of seeing web content creation and management as a set of skills possessed only by a few technically oriented folks (okay, call them geeks, if you will), by the end of this book, you will see that these are skills that anyone can master, regardless of inherent geekiness.

Creating Web Content

You might have noticed the use of the term *web content* rather than *web pages*—that was intentional. Although we talk of "visiting a web page," what we really mean is something like "looking at all the text and the images at one address on our computer." The text that we read, and the images that we see, are rendered by our web browsers, which are given certain instructions found in individual files.

Those files contain text that is *marked up*, or surrounded by, HTML codes that tell the browser how to display the text—as a heading, as a paragraph, in a red font, and so on. Some HTML markup tells the browser to display an image or video file rather than plain text, which brings me back to the point: Different types of content are sent to your web browser, so simply saying *web page* doesn't begin to cover it. Here we use the term *web content* instead, to cover the full range of text, image, audio, video, and other media found online.

In later hours, you learn the basics of linking to or creating the various types of multimedia web content found in websites. All you need to remember at this point is that *you* are in control of the content a user sees when visiting your website. Beginning with the file that contains text to display or codes that tell the server to send a graphic along to the user's web browser, you have to plan, design, and implement all the pieces that will eventually make up your web presence. As you will learn throughout this book, it is not a difficult process as long as you understand all the little steps along the way.

In its most fundamental form, web content begins with a simple text file containing HTML markup. In this book, you learn about and compose standards-compliant HTML5 markup. One of the many benefits of writing standards-compliant code is that, in the future, you will not have to worry about having to go back to your code to fundamentally alter it. Instead, your code will (likely) always work for as long as web browsers adhere to standards (hopefully a long time).

Understanding Web Content Delivery

Several processes occur, in many different locations, to eventually produce web content that you can see. These processes occur very quickly—on the order of milliseconds—and occur behind the scenes. In other words, although we might think all we are doing is opening a web browser, typing in a web address, and instantaneously seeing the content we requested, technology in the background is working hard on our behalf. Figure 1.1 shows the basic interaction between a browser and a server.

FIGURE 1.1
A browser request and a server response.

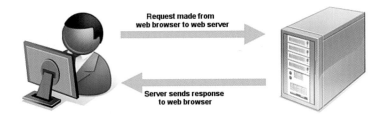

However, the process involves several steps—and potentially several trips between the browser and the server—before you see the entire content of the site you requested.

Suppose you want to do a Google search, so you dutifully type `http://www.google.com` in the address bar or select the Google bookmark from your bookmarks list. Almost immediately, your browser shows you something like Figure 1.2.

FIGURE 1.2
Visiting www.google.com.

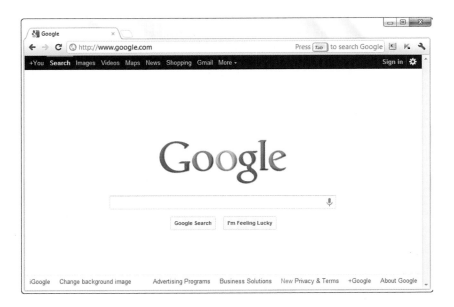

Figure 1.2 shows a website that contains text plus one image (the Google logo). A simple version of the processes that occurred to retrieve that text and image from a web server and display it on your screen follows:

1. Your web browser sends a request for the `index.html` file located at the www.google.com address. The `index.html` file does not have to be part of the address that you type in the address bar; you learn more about the `index.html` file further along in this hour.

2. After receiving the request for a specific file, the web server process looks in its directory contents for the specific file, opens it, and sends the content of that file back to your web browser.

3. The web browser receives the content of the `index.html` file, which is text marked up with HTML codes, and renders the content based on these HTML codes. While rendering the content, the browser happens upon the HTML code for the Google logo, which you can see in Figure 1.2. The HTML code looks something like this:

   ```
   <img alt="Google" src="/images/srpr/logo4w.png" width="275"
   height="95" />
   ```

   The tag provides attributes that tell the browser the file source location (`src`), width (`width`), height (`height`), border type (`border`), and alternative text (`alt`) necessary to display the logo. You learn more about attributes throughout later lessons.

4. The browser looks at the `src` attribute in the `<img/>` tag to find the source location. In this case, the image logo3w.png can be found in the `images` directory at the same web address (www.google.com) from which the browser retrieved the HTML file.

5. The browser requests the file at the http://www.google.com/images/srpr/logo4w.png web address.

6. The web server interprets that request, finds the file, and sends the contents of that file to the web browser that requested it.

7. The web browser displays the image on your monitor.

As you can see in the description of the web content delivery process, web browsers do more than simply act as picture frames through which you can view content. Browsers assemble the web content components and arrange those parts according to the HTML commands in the file.

You can also view web content locally, or on your own hard drive, without the need for a web server. The process of content retrieval and display is the same as the process listed in the previous steps, in that a browser looks for and interprets the codes and content of an HTML file, but the trip is shorter: The browser looks for files on your own computer's hard drive rather than on a remote machine. A web server would be needed to interpret any server-based programming language embedded in the files, but that is outside the scope of this book. In fact, you could work through all the lessons in this book without having a web server to call your own, but then nobody but you could view your masterpieces.

Selecting a Web Hosting Provider

Despite just telling you that you can work through all the lessons in this book without having a web server, having a web server is the recommended method for continuing on. Don't worry—obtaining a hosting provider is usually a quick, painless, and relatively inexpensive process. In fact, you can get your own domain name and a year of web hosting for just slightly more than the cost of the book you are reading now.

If you type **web hosting provider** in your search engine of choice, you will get millions of hits and an endless list of sponsored search results (also known as *ads*). Not this many web hosting providers exist in the world, although it might seem otherwise. Even if you are looking at a managed list of hosting providers, it can be overwhelming—especially if all you are looking for is a place to host a simple website for yourself or your company or organization.

You'll want to narrow your search when looking for a provider and choose one that best meets your needs. Some selection criteria for a web hosting provider follow:

> ▶ **Reliability/server "uptime"**—If you have an online presence, you want to make sure people can actually get there consistently.

> ▶ **Customer service**—Look for multiple methods for contacting customer service (phone, email, chat), as well as online documentation for common issues.

> ▶ **Server space**—Does the hosting package include enough server space to hold all the multimedia files (images, audio, video) you plan to include in your website (if any)?

> ▶ **Bandwidth**—Does the hosting package include enough bandwidth that all the people visiting your site and downloading files can do so without you having to pay extra?

▶ **Domain name purchase and management**—Does the
package include a custom domain name, or must you purchase
and maintain your domain name separately from your hosting
account?

▶ **Price**—Do not overpay for hosting. You will see a wide range of
prices offered and should immediately wonder, "What's the difference?" Often the difference has little to do with the quality of
the service and everything to do with company overhead and
what the company thinks it can get away with charging people.
A good rule of thumb is that if you are paying more than $75
per year for a basic hosting package and domain name, you are
probably paying too much.

Here are three reliable web hosting providers whose basic packages
contain plenty of server space and bandwidth (as well as domain
names and extra benefits) at a relatively low cost. If you don't go with
any of these web hosting providers, you can at least use their basic
package descriptions as a guideline as you shop around.

▶ **A Small Orange (www.asmallorange.com)**—The Tiny and
Small hosting packages are perfect starting places for the new
web content publisher.

▶ **DailyRazor (www.dailyrazor.com)**—Even its Rookie personal
hosting package is full-featured and reliable.

▶ **LunarPages (www.lunarpages.com)**—The Basic hosting
package is suitable for many personal and small business websites.

One feature of a good hosting provider is that it provides a "control
panel" for you to manage aspects of your account. Figure 1.3 shows
the control panel for my own hosting account at Daily Razor. Many
web hosting providers offer this particular control panel software, or
some control panel that is similar in design—clearly labeled icons
leading to tasks you can perform to configure and manage your
account.

NOTE

The author has used all these
providers (and then some)
over the years and has no
problem recommending any of
them; predominantly, she uses
DailyRazor as a web hosting
provider, especially for advanced
development environments.

FIGURE 1.3
A sample control panel.

You might never need to use your control panel, but having it available to you simplifies the installation of databases and other software, the viewing of web statistics, and the addition of email addresses (among many other features). If you can follow instructions, you can manage your own web server—no special training required.

Testing with Multiple Web Browsers

Having just discussed the process of web content delivery and the acquisition of a web server, it might seem a little strange to step back and talk about testing your websites with multiple web browsers. However, before you go off and learn all about creating websites with HTML and CSS, do so with this very important statement in mind: Every visitor to your website will potentially use hardware and software configurations that are different than your own. Their device types (desktop, laptop, netbook, smartphone, iPhone), screen resolutions, browser types, browser window sizes, speed of connections—remember that you cannot control any aspect of what your visitors use when they view your site. So just as you're setting up your web hosting environment and getting ready to work, think about downloading several different web browsers so that you have a local test suite of tools available to you. Let me explain why this is important.

Although all web browsers process and handle information in the same general way, some specific differences among them result in things not always looking the same in different browsers. Even users of the same version of the same web browser can alter how a page appears by choosing different display options and/or changing the size of their viewing windows. All the major web browsers allow users to override the background and fonts the web page author specifies with those of their own choosing. Screen resolution, window size, and optional toolbars can also change how much of a page someone sees when it first appears on their screens. You can ensure only that you write standards-compliant HTML and CSS.

Do not, under any circumstances, spend hours on end designing something that looks perfect only on your own computer—unless you are willing to be disappointed when you look at it on your friend's computer, the computer in the coffee shop down the street, on your iPhone.

You should always test your websites with as many of these web browsers as possible:

NOTE
In Hour 15, you'll learn a little bit about the concept of responsive web design, in which the design of a site shifts and changes automatically depending on the user's behavior and viewing environment (screen size, device, and so on).

- ▶ Apple Safari (http://www.apple.com/safari/) for Mac and Windows
- ▶ Google Chrome (http://www.google.com/chrome) for Windows
- ▶ Mozilla Firefox (http://www.mozilla.com/firefox/) for Mac, Windows, and Linux
- ▶ Microsoft Internet Explorer (http://www.microsoft.com/ie) for Windows
- ▶ Opera (http://www.opera.com/) for Mac, Windows, and Linux/ UNIX

Now that you have a development environment set up, or at least some idea of the type you'd like to set up in the future, let's move on to creating a test file.

Creating a Sample File

Before we begin, take a look at Listing 1.1. This listing represents a simple piece of web content—a few lines of HTML that print `"Hello World! Welcome to My Web Server."` in large, bold letters on two lines centered within the browser window. You'll learn more about the HTML and CSS used within this file as you move forward in this book.

LISTING 1.1   Our Sample HTML File

```
<!DOCTYPE html>
<html>
<head>
<title>Hello World!</title>
</head>
<body>
<h1 style="text-align: center">Hello World!<br/>Welcome to My Web
Server.</h1>
</body>
</html>
```

To make use of this content, open a text editor of your choice, such as Notepad (on Windows) or TextEdit (on a Mac). Do not use WordPad, Microsoft Word, or other full-featured word-processing software because those programs create different sorts of files than the plain-text files we use for web content.

Type the content that you see in Listing 1.1 and then save the file using `sample.html` as the filename. The `.html` extension tells the web server that your file is, indeed, full of HTML. When the file contents are sent to the web browser that requests it, the browser will also know that it is HTML and will render it appropriately.

Now that you have a sample HTML file to use—and hopefully somewhere to put it, such as a web hosting account—let's get to publishing your web content.

Using FTP to Transfer Files

As you've learned so far, you have to put your web content on a web server to make it accessible to others. This process typically occurs by using *File Transfer Protocol (FTP)*. To use FTP, you need an FTP client—a program used to transfer files from your computer to a web server.

FTP clients require three pieces of information to connect to your web server; this information will have been sent to you by your hosting provider after you set up your account:

▶ The hostname, or address, to which you will connect

▶ Your account username

▶ Your account password

When you have this information, you are ready to use an FTP client to transfer content to your web server.

Selecting an FTP Client

Regardless of the FTP client you use, FTP clients generally use the same type of interface. Figure 1.4 shows an example of FireFTP, which is an FTP client used with the Firefox web browser. The directory listing of the local machine (your computer) appears on the left of your screen, and the directory listing of the remote machine (the web server) appears on the right. Typically, you will see right arrow and left arrow buttons, as shown in Figure 1.4. The right arrow sends selected files from your computer to your web server; the left arrow sends files from the web server to your computer. Many FTP clients also enable you to simply select files and then drag and drop those files to the target machines.

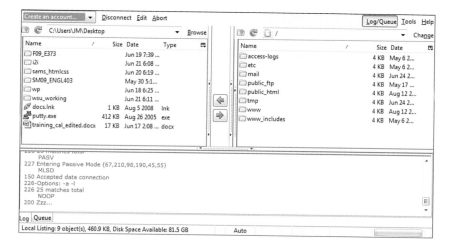

FIGURE 1.4
The FireFTP interface.

Many FTP clients are freely available to you, but you can also transfer files via the web-based File Manager tool that is likely part of your web server's control panel. However, that method of file transfer typically introduces more steps into the process and isn't nearly as streamlined (or simple) as the process of installing an FTP client on your own machine.

Here are some popular free FTP clients:

▶ Classic FTP (http://www.nchsoftware.com/classic/) for Mac and Windows

▶ Cyberduck (http://cyberduck.ch/) for Mac

▶ Fetch (http://fetchsoftworks.com/) for Mac

▶ FileZilla (http://filezilla-project.org/) for all platforms

▶ FireFTP (http://fireftp.mozdev.org/) Firefox extension for all platforms

When you have selected an FTP client and installed it on your computer, you are ready to upload and download files from your web server. In the next section, you see how this process works using the sample file in Listing 1.1.

Using an FTP Client

The following steps show how to use Classic FTP to connect to your web server and transfer a file. However, all FTP clients use similar, if not exact, interfaces. If you understand the following steps, you should be able to use any FTP client.

Remember, you first need the hostname, the account username, and the account password.

1. Start the Classic FTP program and click the Connect button. You are prompted to fill out information for the site to which you want to connect, as shown in Figure 1.5.

FIGURE 1.5
Connecting to a new site in Classic FTP.

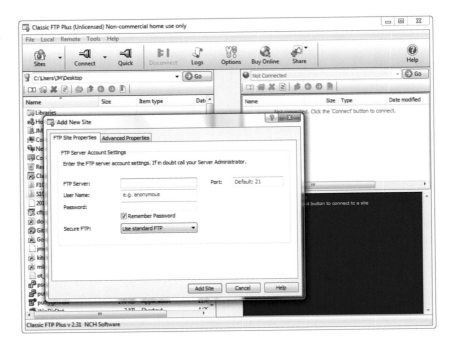

2. Fill in each of the items shown in Figure 1.5 as follows:

- ▶ The FTP Server is the FTP address of the web server to which you need to send your web pages. Your hosting provider will have given you this address. It will probably be yourdomain.com, but check the information you received when you signed up for service.

- ▶ Complete the User Name field and the Password field using the information your hosting provider gave you.

3. You may switch to the Advanced tab and modify the following optional items, shown in Figure 1.6:

- ▶ The Site Label is the name you'll use to refer to your own site. Nobody else will see this name, so enter whatever you want.

- ▶ You can change the values for Initial Remote Directory on First Connection and Initial Local Directory on First Connection, but you might want to wait until you are accustomed to using the client and have established a workflow.

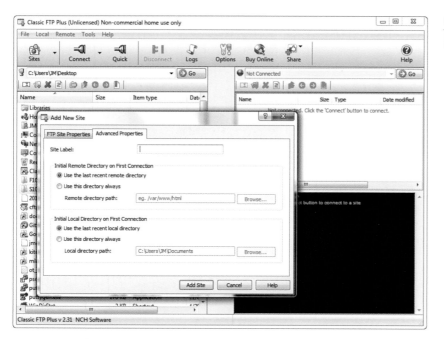

FIGURE 1.6
The Advanced connection options in ClassicFTP.

4. When you're finished with the settings, click Add Site to save the settings. You can then click Connect to establish a connection with the web server.

You will see a dialog box indicating that Classic FTP is attempting to connect to the web server. Upon successful connection, you will see an interface like the one in Figure 1.7, showing the contents of the local directory on the left and the contents of your web server on the right.

FIGURE 1.7
A successful connection to a remote web server via Classic FTP.

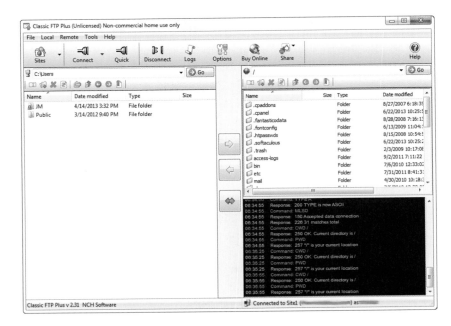

5. You are now *almost* ready to transfer files to your web server. All that remains is to change directories to what is called the *document root* of your web server. The document root of your web server is the directory that is designated as the top-level directory for your web content—the starting point of the directory structure, which you learn more about later in this hour. Often, this directory is named `public_html`, www (because www has been created as an alias for `public_html`), or htdocs. You do not have to create this directory; your hosting provider will have created it for you.

Double-click the document root directory name to open it. The display shown on the right of the FTP client interface changes to show the contents of this directory (it will probably be empty at this point, unless your web hosting provider has put placeholder files in that directory on your behalf).

6. The goal is to transfer the `sample.html` file you created earlier from your computer to the web server. Find the file in the directory listing on the left of the FTP client interface (navigate, if you have to), and click it once to highlight the filename.

7. Click the right arrow button in the middle of the client interface to send the file to the web server. When the file transfer completes, the right side of the client interface refreshes to show you that the file has made it to its destination.

8. Click the Disconnect button to close the connection, and then exit the Classic FTP program.

These steps are conceptually similar to the steps you take anytime you want to send files to your web server via FTP. You can also use your FTP client to create subdirectories on the remote web server. To create a subdirectory using Classic FTP, click the Remote menu and then click New Folder. Different FTP clients have different interface options to achieve the same goal.

Understanding Where to Place Files on the Web Server

An important aspect of maintaining web content is determining how you will organize that content—not only for the user to find, but also for you to maintain on your server. Putting files in directories helps you manage those files.

Naming and organizing directories on your web server, and developing rules for file maintenance, is completely up to you. However, maintaining a well-organized server makes your management of its content more efficient in the long run.

Basic File Management

As you browse the web, you might have noticed that URLs change as you navigate through websites. For instance, if you're looking at a company's website and you click on graphical navigation leading to the company's products or services, the URL probably changes from

http://www.companyname.com/

to

http://www.companyname.com/products/

or

http://www.companyname.com/services/

In the previous section, I used the term *document root* without really explaining what that is all about. The document root of a web server is essentially the trailing slash in the full URL. For instance, if your domain is yourdomain.com and your URL is http://www.yourdomain.com/, the document root is the directory represented by the trailing slash (/). The document root is the starting point of the directory structure you create on your web server; it is the place where the web server begins looking for files requested by the web browser.

If you put the `sample.html` file in your document root as previously directed, you will be able to access it via a web browser at the following URL:

http://www.yourdomain.com/sample.html

If you entered this URL into your web browser, you would see the rendered `sample.html` file, as shown in Figure 1.8.

FIGURE 1.8
The `sample.html` file accessed via a web browser.

However, if you created a new directory within the document root and put the `sample.html` file in that directory, the file would be accessed at this URL:

> http://www.yourdomain.com/newdirectory/sample.html

If you put the `sample.html` file in the directory you originally saw upon connecting to your server—that is, you did *not* change directories and place the file in the document root—the `sample.html` file would not be accessible from your web server at any URL. The file will still be on the machine that you know as your web server, but because the file is not in the document root—where the server software knows to start looking for files—it will never be accessible to anyone via a web browser.

The bottom line? Always navigate to the document root of your web server before you start transferring files.

This is especially true with graphics and other multimedia files. A common directory on web servers is called `images`, where, as you can imagine, all the image assets are placed for retrieval. Other popular directories include `css` for stylesheet files (if you are using more than one) and `js` for external JavaScript files. Alternatively, if you know that you will have an area on your website where visitors can download many different types of files, you might simply call that directory `downloads`.

Whether it's a ZIP file containing your art portfolio or an Excel spreadsheet with sales numbers, it's often useful to publish files on the Internet that aren't simply web pages. To make available on the web a file that isn't an HTML file, just upload the file to your website as if it *were* an HTML file, following the instructions earlier in this hour for uploading. After the file is uploaded to the web server, you can create a link to it (as you learn in Hour 8, "Using External and Internal Links"). In other words, your web server can serve much more than HTML.

Here's a sample of the HTML code that you will learn more about later in this book. The following code would be used for a file named `artfolio.zip`, located in the `downloads` directory of your website, and link text that reads `Download my art portfolio!`:

```
<a href="/downloads/artfolio.zip">Download my art portfolio!</a>
```

Using an Index Page

When you think of an index, you probably think of the section in the back of a book that tells you where to look for various keywords and topics. The index file in a web server directory can serve that purpose—if you design it that way. In fact, that's where the name originates.

The `index.html` file (or just *index file*, as it's usually referred to) is the name you give to the page you want people to see as the default file when they navigate to a specific directory in your website.

Another function of the index page is that users who visit a directory on your site that has an index page but who do not specify that page will still land on the main page for that section of your site—or for the site itself.

For instance, you can type either of the following URLs and land on Apple's iPhone informational page:

> http://www.apple.com/iphone/
>
> http://www.apple.com/iphone/index.html

Had there been no `index.html` page in the `iphone` directory, the results would depend on the configuration of the web server. If the server is configured to disallow directory browsing, the user would have seen a "Directory Listing Denied" message when attempting to access the URL without a specified page name. However, if the server is configured to allow directory browsing, the user would have seen a list of the files in that directory.

Your hosting provider will already have determined these server configuration options. If your hosting provider enables you to modify server settings via a control panel, you can change these settings so that your server responds to requests based on your own requirements.

Not only is the index file used in subdirectories, but it's used in the top-level directory (or document root) of your web site as well. The first page of your website—or *home page* or *main page*, or however you like to refer to the web content you want users to see when they first visit your domain—should be named `index.html` and placed in the document root of your web server. This ensures that when users type `http://www.yourdomain.com/` into their web browsers, the server responds with the content you intended them to see (instead of "Directory Listing Denied" or some other unintended consequence).

Distributing Content Without a Web Server

Publishing HTML and multimedia files online is obviously the primary reason to learn HTML and create web content. However, there are also situations in which other forms of publishing simply aren't viable. For example, you might want to distribute CD-ROMs, DVD-ROMs, or USB drives at a trade show with marketing materials designed as web content—that is, hyperlinked text viewable through a web browser, but without a web server involved. You might also want to include HTML-based instructional manuals on removable media for students at a training seminar. These are just two examples of how HTML pages can be used in publishing scenarios that don't involve the Internet.

This process is also called creating *local* sites; even though there's no web server involved, these bundles of hypertext content are still called *sites*. The *local* term comes into play because your files are accessed locally and not remotely (via a web server).

Publishing Content Locally

Let's assume that you need to create a local site that you want to distribute on a USB drive. Even the cheapest USB drives hold so much data these days—and basic hypertext files are quite small—that you can distribute an entire site *and a fully functioning web browser* all on one little drive.

Simply think of the directory structure of your USB drive just as you would the directory structure of your web server. The top level of the USB drive directory structure can be your document root. Or if you are distributing a web browser along with the content, you might have two directories—for example, one named `browser` and one named `content`. In that case, the `content` directory would be your document root. Within the document root, you could have additional subfolders in which you place content and other multimedia assets.

It's as important to maintain good organization with a local site, as it is with a remote website, so that you avoid broken links in your HTML files. You learn more about the specifics of linking together files in Hour 8, "Using External and Internal Links."

NOTE

Distributing a web browser isn't required when creating and distributing a local site, although it's a nice touch. You can reasonably assume that users have their own web browsers and will open the `index.html` file in a directory to start browsing the hyperlinked content. However, if you want to distribute a web browser on the USB drive, go to http://www.portableapps.com/ and look for Portable Firefox or Portable Chrome.

Publishing Content on a Blog

You might have a blog hosted by a third party, such as WordPress, Tumblr, or Blogger, and thus have already published content without having a dedicated web server or even knowing any HTML. These services offer *visual editors* in addition to *source editors*, meaning that you can type your words and add presentational formatting such as bold, italics, or font colors without knowing the HTML for these actions. Still, the content becomes actual HTML when you click the Publish button in these editors.

However, with the knowledge you will acquire throughout this book, your blogging will be enhanced because you will able to use the source editor for your blog post content and blog templates, thus affording you more control over the look and feel of that content. These actions occur differently from the process you learned for creating an HTML file and uploading it via FTP to your own dedicated web server, but I would be remiss if I did not note that blogging is, in fact, a form of web publishing.

Tips for Testing Web Content

Whenever you transfer files to your web server or place them on removable media for local browsing, you should immediately test every page thoroughly. The following checklist helps ensure that your web content behaves the way you expected. Note that some of the terms might be unfamiliar to you at this point, but come back to this checklist as you progress through this book and create larger projects:

▶ Before you transfer your files, test them locally on your machine to ensure that the links work and the content reflects the visual design you intended. After you transfer the pages to a web server or removable device, test them all again.

▶ Perform these tests with as many browsers as you can—Chrome, Firefox, Internet Explorer, Opera, and Safari is a good list—and on both Mac and Windows platforms. If possible, check at low resolution (800×600) and high resolution (1920×1080).

▶ Turn off auto image loading in your web browser before you start testing so that you can see what each page looks like without the graphics. Check your alt tag messages, and then turn image loading back on to load the graphics and review the page carefully again.

▶ Use your browser's font size settings to look at each page in various font sizes to ensure that your layout doesn't fall to pieces if users override your font specifications with their own.

▶ Wait for each page to completely finish loading, and then scroll all the way down to make sure that all images appear where they should.

▶ Time how long it takes each page to load. Does it take more than a few seconds to load? If so, is the information on that page valuable enough to keep users from going elsewhere before the page finishes loading? Granted, broadband connections are common, but that doesn't mean you should load up your pages with 1MB images.

If your pages pass all those tests, you can rest easy; your site is ready for public viewing.

Summary

This hour introduced you to the concept of using HTML to mark up text files to produce web content. You also learned that there is more to web content than just the "page"—web content also includes image, audio, and video files. All this content lives on a web server—a remote machine often far from your own computer. On your computer or other device, you use a web browser to request, retrieve, and eventually display web content on your screen.

You learned the criteria to consider when determining whether a web hosting provider fits your needs. After you have selected a web hosting provider, you can begin to transfer files to your web server, which you also learned how to do, using an FTP client. You also learned a bit about web server directory structures and file management, as well as the very important purpose of the `index.html` file in a given web server directory. In addition, you learned that you can distribute web content on removable media, and you learned how to go about structuring the files and directories to achieve the goal of viewing content without using a remote web server.

Finally, you learned the importance of testing your work in multiple browsers after you've placed it on a web server. Writing valid, standards-compliant HTML and CSS helps ensure that your site looks reasonably similar for all visitors, but you still shouldn't design without receiving input from potential users outside your development team—it is even *more* important to get input from others when you are a design team of one!

Q&A

Q. I've looked at the HTML source of some web pages on the Internet, and it looks frighteningly difficult to learn. Do I have to think like a computer programmer to learn this stuff?

A. Although complex HTML pages can indeed look daunting, learning HTML is much easier than learning actual software programming languages (such as C++ or Java). HTML is a markup language rather than a programming language; you mark up text so that the browser can render the text a certain way. That's a completely different set of thought processes than developing a computer program. You really don't need any experience or skill as a computer programmer to be a successful web content author.

One of the reasons the HTML behind many commercial websites looks complicated is that it was likely created by a visual web design tool—a "what you see is what you get" (WYSIWYG) editor that uses whatever markup its software developer told it to use in certain circumstances (as opposed to being hand-coded, in which you are completely in control of the resulting markup). In this book, you are taught fundamental coding from the ground up, which typically results in clean, easy-to-read source code. Visual web design tools have a knack for making code difficult to read and for producing code that is convoluted and not standards compliant.

Q. Running all the tests you recommend would take longer than creating my pages! Can't I get away with less testing?

A. If your pages aren't intended to make money or provide an important service, it's probably not a big deal if they look funny to some users or produce errors once in a while. In that case, just test each page with a couple different browsers and call it a day. However, if you need to project a professional image, there is no substitute for rigorous testing.

Q. Seriously, who cares how I organize my web content?

A. Believe it or not, the organization of your web content does matter to search engines and potential visitors to your site. But overall, having an organized web server directory structure helps you keep track of content that you are likely to update frequently. For instance, if you have a dedicated directory for images or multimedia, you know exactly where to look for a file you want to update—no need to hunt through directories containing other content.

Workshop

The Workshop contains quiz questions and exercises to help you solidify your understanding of the material covered. Try to answer all questions before looking at the "Answers" section that follows.

Quiz

1. How many files would you need to store on a web server to produce a single web page with some text and two images on it?

2. What are some of the features to look for in a web hosting provider?

3. What three pieces of information do you need to connect to your web server via FTP?

4. What is the purpose of the `index.html` file?

5. Does your website have to include a directory structure?

Answers

1. You would need three: one for the web page itself, which includes the text and the HTML markup, and one for each of the two images.

2. Look for reliability, customer service, web space and bandwidth, domain name service, site-management extras, and price.

3. You need the hostname, your account username, and your account password.

4. The `index.html` file is typically the default file for a directory within a web server. It allows users to access http://www.yourdomain.com/somedirectory/ without using a trailing filename and still end up in the appropriate place.

5. No. Using a directory structure for file organization is completely up to you, although using one is highly recommended because it simplifies content maintenance.

Exercises

▶ Get your web hosting in order—are you going to move through the lessons in this book by viewing files locally on your own computer, or are you going to use a web hosting provider? Note that most web hosting providers will have you up and running the same day you purchase your hosting plan.

▶ If you are using an external hosting provider, then using your FTP client, create a subdirectory within the document root of your website. Paste the contents of the `sample.html` file into another file named `index.html`, change the text between the `<title>` and `</title>` tags to something new, and change the text between the `<h1>` and `</h1>` tags to something new. Save the file and upload it to the new subdirectory. Use your web browser to navigate to the new directory on your web server, and see that the content in the `index.html` file appears. Then, using your FTP client, delete the `index.html` file from the remote subdirectory. Return to that URL with your web browser, reload the page, and see how the server responds without the `index.html` file in place.

▶ Using the same set of files created in the previous exercise, place these files on a removable media device—a CD-ROM or a USB drive, for example. Use your browser to navigate this local version of your sample website, and think about the instructions you would have to distribute with this removable media so that others could use it.

HOUR 2
Structuring an HTML Document

In the first hour, you got a basic idea of the process behind creating web content and viewing it online (or locally, if you do not yet have a web hosting provider). In this hour, we get down to the business of explaining the various elements that must appear in an HTML file so that it is displayed appropriately in your web browser.

In general, this hour provides a quick summary of HTML basics and gives some practical tips to help you make the most of your time as a web page author and publisher. It's not all theory, however; you do get to see a real web page and the HTML markup behind it.

Getting Prepared

Here's a review of what you need to do before you're ready to use the rest of this book:

1. Get a computer. I used a Windows laptop to test the sample web content and capture the figures in this book, but you can use any Windows, Macintosh, or Linux/UNIX machine to create and view your web content.

2. Get a connection to the Internet. Whether you have a dial-up, wireless, or broadband connection doesn't matter for the creation and viewing of your web content, but the faster the connection, the better for the overall experience. The Internet service provider (ISP), school, or business that provides your Internet connection can help you with the details of setting it up properly. Additionally, many public spaces such as coffee shops, bookstores, and libraries offer free wireless Internet service that you can use if you have a laptop computer with Wi-Fi network support.

WHAT YOU'LL LEARN IN THIS HOUR:

▶ How to create a simple web page in HTML

▶ How to include all the HTML tags that every web page must have

▶ How to organize a page with paragraphs and line breaks

▶ How to organize your content with headings

▶ How to use the semantic elements of HTML5

▶ How to validate your web content

CAUTION
Although all web browsers process and handle information in the same general way, some specific differences among them mean that things do not always looking the same in different browsers. Be sure to check your web pages in multiple browsers to make sure that they look reasonably consistent.

NOTE
As discussed in the first hour, if you plan to put your web content on the Internet (as opposed to publishing it on CD-ROM or a local intranet), you need to transfer it to a computer that is connected to the Internet 24 hours a day. The same company or school that provides you with Internet access might also provide web space; if not, you might need to pay a hosting provider for the service.

3. Get web browser software. This is the software your computer needs to retrieve and display web content. As you learned in the first hour, the most popular browser software (in alphabetical order) is Apple Safari, Google Chrome, Microsoft Internet Explorer, Mozilla Firefox, and Opera. It's a good idea to install several of these browsers so that you can experiment and make sure that your content looks consistent across them all; you can't make assumptions about the browsers other people are using.

4. Explore! Use a web browser to look around the Internet for websites that are similar in content or appearance to those you'd like to create. Note what frustrates you about some pages, what attracts you and keeps you reading others, and what makes you come back to some pages over and over again. If a particular topic interests you, consider searching for it using a popular search engine such as Google (www.google.com) or Bing (www.bing.com).

Getting Started with a Simple Web Page

In the first hour, you learned that a web page is just a text file that is marked up by (or surrounded by) HTML codes that tell the browser how to display the text. To create these text files, use a text editor such as Notepad (on Windows) or TextEdit (on a Mac)—do not use WordPad, Microsoft Word, or other full-featured word-processing software because those create different sorts of files than the plain-text files we use for web content.

Before you begin working, you should start with some text that you want to put on a web page:

1. Find (or write) a few paragraphs of text about yourself, your family, your company, your softball team, or some other subject in which you're interested.

2. Save this text as plain, standard ASCII text. Notepad (on Windows) and most simple text editors always save files as plain text, but if you're using another program, you might need to choose this file type as an option (after selecting File, Save As).

As you go through this hour, you will add HTML markup (called *tags*) to the text file, thus making it into web content.

When you save files containing HTML tags, always give them a name ending in `.html`. This is important: If you forget to type the `.html` at the end of the filename when you save the file, most text editors give it some other extension (such as `.txt`). If that happens, you might not be able to find the file when you try to look at it with a web browser; if you find it, it certainly won't display properly. In other words, web browsers expect a web page file to have a file extension of `.html` and to be in plain-text format.

When visiting websites, you might also encounter pages with a file extension of `.htm`, which is another acceptable file extension to use. You might find other file extensions used on the web, such as `.jsp` (Java Server Pages), `.asp` (Microsoft Active Server Pages), or `.php` (PHP: Hypertext Preprocessor), but these file types use server-side technologies that are beyond the scope of HTML and the lessons throughout this book. However, these files also contain HTML in addition to the programming language; although the programming code in those files is compiled on the server side and all you would see on the client side is the HTML output, if you looked at the source files, you would likely see some intricate weaving of programming and markup codes.

Listing 2.1 shows an example of text you can type and save to create a simple HTML page. If you opened this file with Chrome, you would see the page shown in Figure 2.1. Every web page you create must include a `<!DOCTYPE>` declaration, as well as `<html></html>`, `<head></head>`, `<title></title>`, and `<body></body>` tag pairs.

LISTING 2.1 The `<html>`, `<head>`, `<title>`, and `<body>` Tags

```
<!DOCTYPE html>
<html lang="en">
  <head>
    <title>The First Web Page</title>
  </head>

  <body>
    <p>
      In the beginning, Tim created the HyperText Markup Language. The
      Internet was without form and void, and text was upon the face of
      the monitor and the Hands of Tim were moving over the face of the
      keyboard. And Tim said, Let there be links; and there were links.
      And Tim saw that the links were good; and Tim separated the links
      from the text. Tim called the links Anchors, and the text He called
      Other Stuff. And the whole thing together was the first Web Page.
    </p>
  </body>
</html>
```

CAUTION

We reiterate this point because it is very important to both the outcome and the learning process itself: Do not create your first HTML file with Microsoft Word or any other HTML-compatible word processor; most of these programs attempt to rewrite your HTML for you in strange ways, potentially leaving you totally confused. The same holds true when you use Microsoft Word and "Save As" HTML—you are likely to get a verbose and noncompliant file full of HTML that will not validate and will cause you headaches to edit.

Additionally, I recommend that you *not* use a graphical, what-you-see-is-what-you-get (WYSIWYG) editor, such as Adobe Dreamweaver. You'll likely find it easier and more educational to start with a simple text editor while you're just learning HTML.

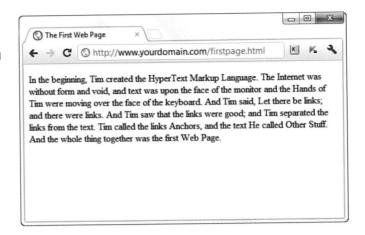

FIGURE 2.1
When you save the text in Listing 2.1 as an HTML file and view it with a web browser, only the actual title and body text are displayed.

> The First Web Page
>
> http://www.yourdomain.com/firstpage.html
>
> In the beginning, Tim created the HyperText Markup Language. The Internet was without form and void, and text was upon the face of the monitor and the Hands of Tim were moving over the face of the keyboard. And Tim said, Let there be links; and there were links. And Tim saw that the links were good; and Tim separated the links from the text. Tim called the links Anchors, and the text He called Other Stuff. And the whole thing together was the first Web Page.

In Listing 2.1, as in every HTML page, the words starting with < and ending with > are actually coded commands. These coded commands are called *HTML tags* because they "tag" pieces of text and tell the web browser what kind of text it is. This allows the web browser to display the text appropriately.

The first line in the document is the document type declaration; you are *declaring* that it is html (specifically, HTML5) because html is the value used to declare a document as HTML5 in the <!DOCTYPE> tag.

▼ TRY IT YOURSELF

Creating and Viewing a Basic Web Page

Before you learn the meaning of the HTML tags used in Listing 2.1, you might want to see exactly how I went about creating and viewing the document itself. Follow these steps:

1. Type all the text in Listing 2.1, including the HTML tags, in Windows Notepad (or use Macintosh TextEdit or another text editor of your choice).

2. Select File, Save As. Be sure to select plain text (or ASCII text) as the file type.

3. Name the file firstpage.html.

4. Choose the folder on your hard drive where you want to keep your web pages—and remember which folder you choose! Click the Save or OK button to save the file.

TRY IT YOURSELF ▼

Creating and Viewing a Basic Web Page
continued

5. Now start your favorite web browser. (Leave Notepad running, too, so you can easily switch between viewing and editing your page.)

In Internet Explorer, select File, Open and click Browse. If you're using Firefox, select File, Open File. Navigate to the appropriate folder and select the `firstpage.html` file. Some browsers and operating systems also enable you to drag and drop the `firstpage.html` file onto the browser window to view it.

Voilà! You should see the page shown in Figure 2.1.

If you have obtained a web hosting account, you could use FTP at this point to transfer the `firstpage.html` file to the web server. In fact, from this hour forward, the instructions assume that you have a hosting provider and are comfortable sending files back and forth via FTP; if that is not the case, please review the first hour before moving on. Alternatively, if you are consciously choosing to work with files locally (without a web host), be prepared to adjust the instructions to suit your particular needs (such as ignoring the commands "transfer the files" and "type in the URL").

HTML Tags Every Web Page Must Have

The time has come for the secret language of HTML tags to be revealed to you. When you understand this language, you will have creative powers far beyond those of other humans. Don't tell the other humans, but it's really pretty easy.

The first line of code is the document type declaration; in HTML5, this is simply

```
<!DOCTYPE html>
```

This declaration identifies the document as being HTML5, which then ensures web browsers know what to expect and prepare to render content in HTML5.

Many HTML tags have two parts: an *opening tag*, which indicates where a piece of text begins, and a *closing tag*, which indicates where

NOTE

You don't need to be connected to the Internet to view a web page stored on your own computer. By default, your web browser tries to connect to the Internet every time you start it, which makes sense most of the time. However, this can be a hassle if you're developing pages locally on your hard drive (offline) and you keep getting errors about a page not being found. If you have a full-time web connection via a LAN, cable modem, Wi-Fi, or DSL, this is a moot point because the browser will never complain about being offline. Otherwise, the appropriate action depends on your breed of browser; check the options under your browser's Tools menu.

the piece of text ends. Closing tags start with a / (forward slash) just after the < symbol.

Another type of tag is the *empty tag*, which is different, in that it doesn't include a pair of matching opening and closing tags. Instead, an empty tag consists of a single tag that starts with < and ends with / just before the > symbol. Although the ending slash is no longer explicitly required in HTML5, it does aid in compatibility with XHTML—if you have a pile of old XHTML in your website, it will not break while you're in the process of upgrading it.

Following is a quick summary of these three tags, just to make sure you understand the role each plays:

▶ An *opening tag* is an HTML tag that indicates the start of an HTML command; the text affected by the command appears after the opening tag. Opening tags always begin with < and end with >, as in `<html>`.

▶ A *closing tag* is an HTML tag that indicates the end of an HTML command; the text affected by the command appears before the closing tag. Closing tags always begin with </ and end with >, as in `</html>`.

▶ An *empty tag* is an HTML tag that issues an HTML command without enclosing any text in the page. Empty tags always begin with < and end with />, as in `<br />` and `<img />`.

NOTE

You no doubt noticed in Listing 2.1 that there is some extra code associated with the `<html>` tag. This code consists of the language attribute (`lang`), which is used to specify additional information related to the tag. In this case, it specifies that the language of the text within the HTML is English. If you are writing in a different language, replace the `en` (for English) with the language identifier relevant to you.

For example, the `<body>` tag in Listing 2.1 tells the web browser where the actual body text of the page begins, and `</body>` indicates where it ends. Everything between the `<body>` and `</body>` tags appears in the main display area of the web browser window, as shown in Figure 2.1.

The very top of the browser window (refer to Figure 2.1) shows title text, which is any text that is located between `<title>` and `</title>`. The title text also identifies the page on the browser's Bookmarks or Favorites menu, depending on which browser you use. It's important to provide titles for your pages so that visitors to the page can properly bookmark them for future reference; search engines also use titles to provide a link to search results.

You will use the `<body>` and `<title>` tag pairs in every HTML page you create because every web page needs a title and body text. You will also use the `<html>` and `<head>` tag pairs, which are the other two tags shown in Listing 2.1. Putting `<html>` at the very beginning of a document simply indicates that the document is a web page. The `</html>` at the end indicates that the web page is over.

Within a page, there is a head section and a body section. Each section is identified by `<head>` and `<body>` tags. The idea is that information in the head of the page somehow describes the page but isn't actually displayed by a web browser. Information placed in the body, however, is displayed by a web browser. The `<head>` tag always appears near the beginning of the HTML code for a page, just after the opening `<html>` tag.

The `<title>` tag pair used to identify the title of a page appears within the head of the page, which means it is placed after the opening `<head>` tag and before the closing `</head>` tag. In the upcoming hours, you'll learn about some other advanced header information that can go between `<head>` and `</head>`, such as stylesheet rules for formatting the page.

The `<p>` tag in Listing 2.1 encloses a paragraph of text. You should enclose your chunks of text in the appropriate container elements whenever possible; you'll learn more about container elements as the book moves forward.

Organizing a Page with Paragraphs and Line Breaks

When a web browser displays HTML pages, it pays no attention to line endings or the number of spaces between words. For example, the top version of the poem in Figure 2.2 appears with a single space between all words, even though that's not how it's entered in Listing 2.2. This is because extra whitespace in HTML code is automatically reduced to a single space. Additionally, when the text reaches the edge of the browser window, it automatically wraps to the next line, no matter where the line breaks were in the original HTML file.

TIP

You might find it convenient to create and save a bare-bones page (also known as a *skeleton* page, or *template*) with just the DOCTYPE and opening and closing `<html>`, `<head>`, `<title>`, and `<body>` tags, similar to the document in Listing 2.1. You can then open that document as a starting point whenever you want to make a new web page and save yourself the trouble of typing all those obligatory tags every time.

FIGURE 2.2
When the HTML in Listing 2.2 is viewed as a web page, line and paragraph breaks appear only where there are `<br />` and `<p>` tags.

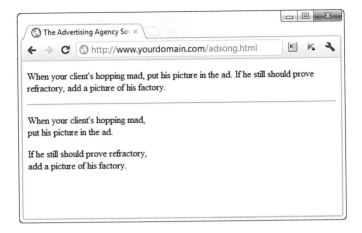

LISTING 2.2   HTML Containing Paragraph and Line Breaks

```
<!DOCTYPE html>

<html lang="en">
  <head>
    <title>The Advertising Agency Song</title>
  </head>

  <body>
    <p>
      When your client's    hopping mad,
      put his picture in the ad.

      If he still should    prove refractory,
      add a picture of his factory.
    </p>
    <hr />
    <p>
      When your client's hopping mad,<br />
      put his picture in the ad.
    </p>
    <p>
      If he still should prove refractory,<br />
      add a picture of his factory.
    </p>
  </body>
</html>
```

NOTE

If a closing slash isn't required for empty elements, you might ask why it's used throughout this book. One reason is that over the years, closing tags went from not being required, to required, to not being required (again), and your author is simply stuck in her ways using the perfectly valid but no longer required closing slash. Another reason is that because that middle period was relatively long, a *lot* of code editors, code generators, and templates use the closing slash, so you will see it used more often than not. It doesn't matter which way you choose to write because both are valid; just be sure that whatever coding style you follow, you are consistent in its use.

You must use HTML tags if you want to control where line and paragraph breaks actually appear. When text is enclosed within the `<p></p>` container tags, a line break is assumed after the closing tag. In later hours, you learn to control the height of the line break using CSS. The `<br />` tag forces a line break within a paragraph. Unlike the other tags you've seen so far, `<br />` doesn't require a closing `</br>` tag—this is one of those empty tags discussed earlier.

The poem in Listing 2.2 and Figure 2.2 shows the `<br />` and `<p>` tags used to separate the lines and verses of an advertising agency song. You might have also noticed the `<hr />` tag in the listing, which causes a horizontal rule line to appear on the page (see Figure 2.2). Inserting a horizontal rule with the `<hr />` tag also causes a line break, even if you don't include a `<br />` tag along with it. Like `<br />`, the `<hr />` horizontal rule tag is an empty tag and, therefore, never gets a closing `</hr>` tag.

TRY IT YOURSELF ▼

Formatting Text in HTML

Try your hand at formatting a passage of text as proper HTML:

1. Add `<html><head><title>My Title</title></head><body>` to the beginning of the text (using your own title for your page instead of `My Title`). Also include the boilerplate code at the top of the page that takes care of meeting the requirements of standard HTML.

2. Add `</body></html>` to the very end of the text.

3. Add a `<p>` tag at the beginning of each paragraph and a `</p>` tag at the end of each paragraph.

4. Use `<br />` tags anywhere you want single-spaced line breaks.

5. Use `<hr />` to draw horizontal rules separating major sections of text, or wherever you'd like to see a line across the page.

6. Save the file as `mypage.html` (using your own filename instead of `mypage`).

7. Open the file in a web browser to see your web content. (Send the file via FTP to your web hosting account, if you have one.)

8. If something doesn't look right, go back to the text editor to make corrections and save the file again (and send it to your web hosting account, if applicable). You then need to click Reload/Refresh in the browser to see the changes you made.

CAUTION

If you are using a word processor to create the web page, be sure to save the HTML file in plain-text or ASCII format.

Organizing Your Content with Headings

When you browse web pages on the Internet, you'll notice that many of them have a heading at the top that appears larger and bolder than the rest of the text. Listing 2.3 is sample code and text for a simple web page containing an example of a heading as compared to normal paragraph text. Any text between `<h1>` and `</h1>` tags will appear as a large heading. Additionally, `<h2>` and `<h3>` make progressively smaller headings, and so on, as far down as `<h6>`.

LISTING 2.3   Heading Tags

```
<!DOCTYPE html>

<html lang="en">
  <head>
    <title>My Widgets</title>
  </head>

  <body>
    <h1>My Widgets</h1>
    <p>My widgets are the best in the land. Continue reading to
    learn more about my widgets.</p>

    <h2>Widget Features</h2>
    <p>If I had any features to discuss,  you can bet I'd do
    it here.</p>

    <h3>Pricing</h3>
    <p>Here, I would talk about my widget pricing.</p>

    <h3>Comparisons</h3>
      <p>Here, I would talk about how my widgets compare to my
      competitor's widgets.</p>
  </body>
</html>
```

NOTE

By now, you've probably caught on to the fact that HTML code is often indented by its author to reveal the relationship between different parts of the HTML document, as well as for simple ease of reading. This indentation is entirely voluntary—you could just as easily run all the tags together with no spaces or line breaks, and they would still look fine when viewed in a browser. The indentations are for you so that you can quickly look at a page full of code and understand how it fits together. Indenting your code is another good web design habit and ultimately makes your pages easier to maintain, both for yourself and for anyone else who might pick up where you leave off.

As you can see in Figure 2.3, the HTML that creates headings couldn't be simpler. In this example, the phrase "My Widgets" is prominently displayed using the `<h1>` tag. To create the biggest (level 1) heading, just put an `<h1>` tag at the beginning and an `</h1>` tag at the end of the text you want to use as a heading. For a slightly smaller (level 2) heading—for information that is of lesser importance than the title—use the `<h2>` and `</h2>` tags around your text. For content that should appear even less prominently than a level 2 heading, use the `<h3>` and `</h3>` tags around your text.

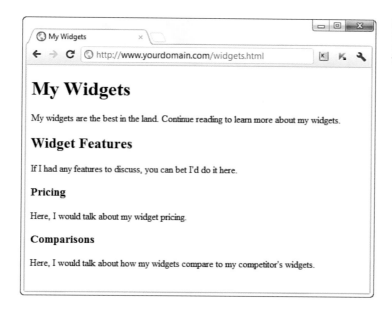

FIGURE 2.3
Using three levels of headings
shows the hierarchy of content on
this sample product page.

However, bear in mind that your headings should follow a content hierarchy; use only one level 1 heading, have one (or more) level 2 headings after the level 1 heading, use level 3 headings directly after level 2 headings, and so on. Do not fall into the trap of assigning headings to content just to make that content display a certain way. Instead, ensure that you are categorizing your content appropriately (as a main heading, a secondary heading, and so on), while using display styles to make that text render a particular way in a web browser.

Theoretically, you can also use `<h4>`, `<h5>`, and `<h6>` tags to make progressively less important headings, but these aren't used very often. Web browsers seldom show a noticeable difference between these headings and the `<h3>` headings anyway—although you can control that with your own CSS—and content usually isn't displayed in such a manner that you'd need six levels of headings to show the content hierarchy.

It's important to remember the difference between a *title* and a *heading*. These two words are often interchangeable in day-to-day English, but when you're talking HTML, `<title>` gives the entire page an identifying name that isn't displayed on the page itself; it's displayed only on the browser window's title bar. The heading tags, on the other hand, cause some text on the page to be displayed with visual emphasis. There can be only one `<title>` per page, and it must appear within the `<head>`

and `</head>` tags; on the other hand, you can have as many `<h1>`, `<h2>`, and `<h3>` headings as you want, in any order that suits your fancy. However, as I mentioned before, you should use the heading tags to keep tight control over content hierarchy; do not use headings as a way to achieve a particular look, because that's what CSS is for.

Peeking at Other Designers' Pages

Given the visual and sometimes audio pizzazz present in many popular web pages, you probably realize that the simple pages described in this lesson are only the tip of the HTML iceberg. Now that you know the basics, you might surprise yourself with how much of the rest you can pick up just by looking at other people's pages on the Internet. You can see the HTML for any page by right-clicking and selecting View Source in any web browser.

Don't worry if you aren't yet able to decipher what some HTML tags do or exactly how to use them yourself. You'll find out about all those things as the book moves forward. However, sneaking a preview now will show you the tags that you do know in action and give you a taste of what you'll soon be able to do with your web pages.

Understanding Semantic Elements

HTML5 includes tags that enable you to enhance the semantics—the meaning—of the information that you provide in your marked-up text. Instead of simply using HTML as a presentation language, as was the practice in the very early days when `<b>` for bold and `<i>` for italics was the norm, modern HTML has as one of its goals the separation of presentation and meaning. While using CSS to provide guidelines for presentation, composers of HTML can provide meaningful names within their markup for individual elements not only through the use of IDs and class names (which you learn about later in this book), but also through the use of semantic elements.

Some of the semantic elements available in HTML5 follow:

▶ `<header></header>`—This may seem counterintuitive, but you can use multiple `<header>` tags within a single page. The `<header>` tag should be used as a container for introductory information, so it might be only once in your page (likely at the top)—but you also might use it several times if your page content is broken into sections. Any container element can have a `<header>` element; just make sure that you're using it to include introductory information about the element it is contained within.

▶ `<footer></footer>`—The `<footer>` tag is used to contain additional information about its containing element (page or section), such as copyright and author information or links to related resources.

▶ `<nav></nav>`—If your site has navigational elements, such as links to other sections within a site or even within the page itself, these links go in a `<nav>` tag. A `<nav>` tag typically is found in the first instance of a `<header>` tag, just because people tend to put navigation at the top and consider it introductory information, but that is not a requirement. You can put your `<nav>` element anywhere (as long as it includes navigation), and you can have as many on a page as you need (often no more than two, but you may feel otherwise).

▶ `<section></section>`—The `<section>` tag contains anything that relates thematically; it can also contain a `<header>` tag for introductory information and possible a `<footer>` tag for other related information. You can think of a `<section>` as carrying more meaning than a standard `<p>` (paragraph) or `<div>` (division) tag, which typically conveys no meaning at all; the use of `<section>` conveys a relationship between the content elements it contains.

▶ `<article></article>`—An `<article>` tag is like a `<section>` tag, in that it can contain a `<header>`, a `<footer>`, and other container elements such as paragraphs and divisions. But the additional meaning carried with the `<article>` tag is that it is, well, like an article in a newspaper or other publication. Use this tag around blog posts, news articles, reviews, and other items that fit this description. One key difference between an `<article>` and a `<section>` is that an `<article>` is a standalone body of work, whereas a `<section>` is a thematic grouping of information.

▶ `<aside></aside>`—Use the `<aside>` tag to indicate secondary information; if the `<aside>` tag is within a `<section>` or `<article>`, the relationship will be to those containers; otherwise, the secondary relationship will be to the overall page or site itself. It might make sense to think of the `<aside>` as a sidebar—either for all the content on the page or for an article or other thematic container of information.

These semantic elements will become clearer as you practice using them. In general, using semantic elements is a good idea because they provide additional meaning not only for yourself and other designers and programmers reading and working with your markup, but also for machines. Web browsers and screen readers will respond to your semantic elements by using these elements to determine the structure of your document; screen readers will report a deeper meaning to users, thus increasing the accessibility of your material.

Throughout this book, you make use of these and other semantic elements for page structure, in addition to the standard types of block elements that HTML provides.

Validating Your Web Content

In the first hour, I discussed ways to test your pages; one very important way to test your pages is to *validate* them. Think of it this way: It's one thing to design and draw a beautiful set of house plans, but it's quite another for an architect to stamp it as a safe structure suitable for construction. Validating your web pages is a similar process; in this case, however, the architect is an application, not a person.

In brief, validation is the process of testing your pages with a special application that searches for errors and makes sure your pages follow the strict XHTML standard. Validation is simple. In fact, the standards body responsible for developing web standards, the World Wide Web Consortium (W3C), offers an online validation tool you can use. To validate a page, follow this URL: http://validator.w3.org/. Figure 2.4 shows the W3C Markup Validation Service.

FIGURE 2.4
The W3C Markup Validation Service enables you to validate an HTML (XHTML) document to ensure that it has been coded accurately.

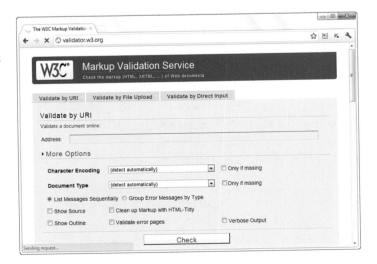

If you've already published a page online, you can use the Validate by URI tab. Use the Validate by File Upload tab to validate files stored on your local computer file system. The Validate by Direct Input tab enables you to paste the contents of a file from your text editor. If all goes well, your page will get a passing report (see Figure 2.5).

FIGURE 2.5
If a page passes the W3C Markup Validation Service, you know it is ready for prime time.

If the W3C Markup Validation Service encounters an error in your web page, it provides specific details (including the line numbers of the offending code). This is a great way to hunt down problems and rid your pages of buggy code. Validation not only informs you when your pages are constructed properly, but it also assists you in finding and fixing problems before you post pages for the world to see.

Summary

This hour introduced the basics of what web pages are and how they work. You learned that coded HTML commands are included in a text file, and you saw that typing HTML text yourself is better than using a graphical editor to create HTML commands for you—especially when you're learning HTML.

You were introduced to the most basic and important HTML tags. By adding these coded commands to any plain-text document, you can quickly transform it into a bona fide web page. You learned that the

TIP

Some web development tools include built-in validation features you can use in lieu of the W3C Markup Validation Service. Some examples include browser extensions such as Firebug (http:// getfirebug.com/) and HTML Validator (http:// users.skynet.be/mgueury/ mozilla/), but many other programs offer similar functionality—check your user documentation.

first step in creating a web page is to put a few obligatory HTML tags at the beginning and end, including adding a title for the page. You can then mark where paragraphs and lines end and add horizontal rules and headings, if you want them. You also got a taste of some of the semantic tags in HTML5, which are used to provide additional meaning by delineating the types of content your pages contain (not just the content itself). Table 2.1 summarizes all the tags introduced in this hour.

TABLE 2.1   HTML Tags Covered in Hour 2

Tag	Function
`<html>...</html>`	Encloses the entire HTML document.
`<head>...</head>`	Encloses the head of the HTML document. Used within the `<html>` tag pair.
`<title>...</title>`	Indicates the title of the document. Used within the `<head>` tag pair.
`<body>...</body>`	Encloses the body of the HTML document. Used within the `<html>` tag pair.
`<p>...</p>`	A paragraph; skips a line between paragraphs.
` `	A line break.
`<hr />`	A horizontal rule line.
`<h1>...</h1>`	A first-level heading.
`<h2>...</h2>`	A second-level heading.
`<h3>...</h3>`	A third-level heading.
`<h4>...</h4>`	A fourth-level heading (seldom used).
`<h5>...</h5>`	A fifth-level heading (seldom used).
`<h6>...</h6>`	A sixth-level heading (seldom used).
`<header>...</header>`	A page or section header.
`<footer>...</footer>`	A page or section footer.
`<nav>...</nav>`	The navigational links for a page or an entire site.
`<section>...</section>`	A thematic grouping of content.
`<article>...</article>`	A standalone piece of content such as a news story.
`<aside>...</aside>`	Secondary content related to the content with which it is contained.

Finally, you learned about the importance of validating your HTML and how to do this using online validation tools.

Q&A

Q. I've created a web page, but when I open the file in my web browser, I see all the text, including the HTML tags. Sometimes I even see weird gobbledygook characters at the top of the page. What did I do wrong?

A. You didn't save the file as plain text. Try saving the file again, being careful to save it as Text Only or ASCII Text. If you can't quite figure out how to get your word processor to do that, don't stress. Just type your HTML files in Notepad or TextEdit instead, and everything should work just fine. (Also, always make sure that the filename of your web page ends in `.html` or `.htm`.)

Q. I've seen web pages on the Internet that don't have `<!DOCTYPE>` or `<html>` tags at the beginning. You said pages always have to start with these tags. What's the deal?

A. Many web browsers will forgive you if you forget to include the `<!DOCTYPE>` or `<html>` tag and will display the page correctly anyway. However, it's a very good idea to include it because some software does need it to identify the page as valid HTML. Besides, you want your pages to be bona fide HTML pages so that they conform to the latest web standards.

Workshop

The Workshop contains quiz questions and exercises to help you solidify your understanding of the material covered. Try to answer all questions before looking at the "Answers" section that follows.

Quiz

1. What five tags does every HTML page require?

2. What HTML tags and text do you use to produce the following body content:

   ▶ A heading with the words `We are Proud to Present...`

   ▶ A secondary heading with the one word `Orbit`

   ▶ A heading of lesser importance with the words `The Geometric Juggler`

3. What code would you use to create a complete HTML web page with the title `Foo Bar`, a heading at the top that reads `Happy Hour at the Foo`

`Bar`, and then the words `Come on down!` in regular type? Try to use some of the semantic elements you just learned.

Answers

1. Every HTML page requires `<html>`, `<head>`, `<title>`, and `<body>` (along with their closing tags, `</html>`, `</head>`, `</title>`, and `</body>`), plus `<!DOCTYPE html>` on the very first line.

2. The code within the body would look like this:

   ```
   <h1>We are Proud to Present...</h1>

   <h2>Orbit</h2>

   <h3>The Geometric Juggler</h3>
   ```

3. Your code could look like this:

   ```
   <!DOCTYPE html>

   <html lang="en">
     <head>
       <title>Foo Bar</title>
     </head>

     <body>
       <header>
         <h1>Happy Hour at the Foo Bar</h1>
       </header>
       <section>
         <p>Come on Down!</p>
       </section>
     </body>
   </html>
   ```

Exercises

▶ Even if your main goal in reading this book is to create web content for your business, you might want to make a personal web page just for practice. Type a few paragraphs to introduce yourself to the world, and use the HTML tags you learned in this hour to make them into a web page.

▶ Throughout the book, you'll be following along with the code examples and making pages of your own. Take a moment now to set up a basic document template containing the document type declaration and tags for the core HTML document structure. That way, you can be ready to copy and paste that information whenever you need it.

HOUR 3
Understanding Cascading Style Sheets

In the previous hour, you learned the basics of HTML, including how to set up a skeletal HTML template for all your web content. In this hour, you learn how to fine-tune the display of your web content using *Cascading Style Sheets (CSS)*.

The concept behind stylesheets is simple: You create a stylesheet document that specifies the fonts, colors, spacing, and other characteristics that establish a unique look for a website. You then link every page that should have that look to the stylesheet instead of specifying all those styles repeatedly in each separate document. Therefore, when you decide to change your official corporate typeface or color scheme, you can modify all your web pages at once just by changing one or two entries in your stylesheet—you don't have to change them in all your static web files. So a *stylesheet* is a grouping of formatting instructions that control the appearance of several HTML pages at once.

Stylesheets enable you to set a great number of formatting characteristics, including exact typeface controls, letter and line spacing, and margins and page borders, just to name a few. Stylesheets also enable you to specify sizes and other measurements in familiar units, such as inches, millimeters, points, and picas. In addition, you can use stylesheets to precisely position graphics and text anywhere on a web page, either at specific coordinates or relative to other items on the page.

In short, stylesheets bring a sophisticated level of display to the web. And they do so, if you'll pardon the expression, with style.

WHAT YOU'LL LEARN IN THIS HOUR:

▶ How to create a basic stylesheet
▶ How to use style classes
▶ How to use style IDs
▶ How to construct internal stylesheets and inline styles

How CSS Works

The technology behind stylesheets is called CSS, or Cascading Style Sheets. CSS is a language that defines style constructs such as fonts, colors, and positioning, which describe how information on a web page is formatted and displayed. CSS styles can be stored directly in an HTML web page or in a separate stylesheet file. Either way, stylesheets contain style rules that apply styles to elements of a given type. When used externally, stylesheet rules are placed in an external stylesheet document with the file extension .css.

A *style rule* is a formatting instruction that can be applied to an element on a web page, such as a paragraph of text or a link. Style rules consist of one or more style properties and their associated values. An *internal stylesheet* is placed directly within a web page, whereas an *external stylesheet* exists in a separate document and is simply linked to a web page via a special tag—more on this tag in a moment.

The *cascading* part of the name CSS refers to the manner in which stylesheet rules are applied to elements in an HTML document. More specifically, styles in a CSS stylesheet form a hierarchy in which more specific styles override more general styles. It is the responsibility of CSS to determine the precedence of style rules according to this hierarchy, which establishes a cascading effect. If that sounds a bit confusing, just think of the cascading mechanism in CSS as being similar to genetic inheritance, in which general traits are passed from parents to a child, but more specific traits are entirely unique to the child. Base style rules are applied throughout a stylesheet but can be overridden by more specific style rules.

A quick example should clear things up. Take a look at the following code to see whether you can tell what's going on with the color of the text:

```
<div style="color:green">
  This text is green.
  <p style="color:blue">This text is blue.</p>
  <p>This text is still green.</p>
</div>
```

In the previous example, the color green is applied to the <div> tag via the color style property. Therefore, the text in the <div> tag is colored green. Because both <p> tags are children of the <div> tag, the green text style cascades down to them. However, the first <p> tag overrides the color style and changes it to blue. The end result is that the first line (not surrounded by a paragraph tag) is green, the first official paragraph is blue, and the second official paragraph retains the cascaded green color.

If you made it through that description on your own and came out on the other end unscathed, congratulations—that's half the battle. Understanding CSS isn't like understanding rocket science, and the more you practice, the more it will become clear. The real trick is developing the aesthetic design sense that you can then apply to your online presence through CSS.

Like many web technologies, CSS has evolved over the years. The original version of CSS, known as *Cascading Style Sheets Level 1* (*CSS1*), was created in 1996. The later CSS 2 standard was created in 1998, and CSS 2 is still in use today; all modern web browsers support CSS 2. The latest version of CSS is CSS3, which builds on the strong foundation laid by its predecessors but adds advanced functionality to enhance the online experience. Throughout this book, you learn core CSS, including new elements of CSS3 that are applicable to the basic design and functionality that this text covers. So when I talk about CSS throughout the book, I'm referring to CSS3.

You'll find a complete reference guide to CSS at http://www.w3.org/Style/CSS/. The rest of this hour explains the basics of putting CSS to good use.

A Basic Stylesheet

Despite their intimidating power, stylesheets can be simple to create. Consider the web pages shown in Figures 3.1 and 3.2. These pages share several visual properties that can be put into a common stylesheet:

- ▶ They use a large, bold Verdana font for the headings and a normal-size and -weight Verdana font for the body text.
- ▶ They use an image named `logo.gif` floating within the content and on the right side of the page.
- ▶ All text is black except for subheadings, which are purple.
- ▶ They have margins on the left side and at the top.
- ▶ They include vertical space between lines of text.
- ▶ They include a footer that is centered and in small print.

FIGURE 3.1
This page uses a stylesheet to fine-tune the appearance and spacing of the text and images.

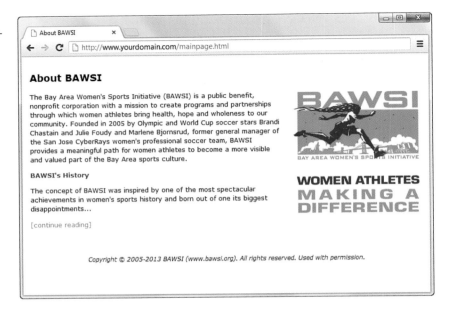

FIGURE 3.2
This page uses the same stylesheet as the one in Figure 3.1, thus maintaining a consistent look and feel.

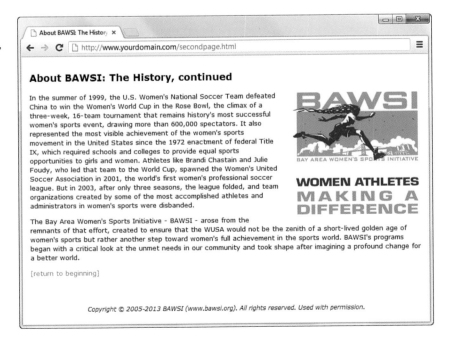

Listing 3.1 shows the CSS used in a stylesheet to specify these properties.

LISTING 3.1   A Single External Stylesheet

```
body {
  font-size: 10pt;
  font-family: Verdana, Geneva, Arial, Helvetica, sans-serif;
  color: black;
  line-height: 14pt;
  padding-left: 5pt;
  padding-right: 5pt;
  padding-top: 5pt;
}

h1 {
  font: 14pt Verdana, Geneva, Arial, Helvetica, sans-serif;
  font-weight: bold;
  line-height: 20pt;
}

p.subheader {
  font-weight: bold;
  color: #593d87;
}

img {
  padding: 3pt;
  float: right;
}

a {
  text-decoration: none;
}

a:link, a:visited {
  color: #8094d6;
}

a:hover, a:active {
  color: #FF9933;
}

footer {
  font-size: 9pt;
  font-style: italic;
  line-height: 12pt;
  text-align: center;
  padding-top: 30pt;
}
```

This might initially appear to be a lot of code, but if you look closely, you'll see that there isn't a lot of information on each line of code. It's fairly standard to place individual style rules on their own line, to help make style sheets more readable, but that is a personal preference; you could put all the rules on one line as long as you kept using the semicolon to separate each rule (more on that in a bit). Speaking of code readability, perhaps the first thing you noticed about this stylesheet code is that it doesn't look anything like normal HTML code. CSS uses a syntax all its own to specify stylesheets.

Of course, the listing includes some familiar HTML tags (although not all tags require an entry in the stylesheet). As you might guess, `body`, `h1`, `p`, `img`, `a`, and `footer` in the stylesheet refer to the corresponding tags in the HTML documents to which the stylesheet will be applied. The curly braces after each tag name describe how all content within that tag should appear.

In this case, the stylesheet says that all `body` text should be rendered at a size of 10 points, in the Verdana font (if possible), and with the color black, with 14 points between lines. If the user does not have the Verdana font installed, the list of fonts in the stylesheet represents the order in which the browser should search for fonts to use: Geneva, then Arial, and then Helvetica. If the user has none of those fonts, the browser will use whatever default sans serif font is available. Additionally, the page should have left, right, and top padding of 5 points each.

Any text within an `<h1>` tag should be rendered in boldface Verdana at a size of 14 points. Moving on, any paragraph that uses only the `<p>` tag will inherit all the styles indicated by the body element. However, if the `<p>` tag uses a special class named `subheader`, the text will appear bold and in the color #593d87 (a purple color).

The `pt` after each measurement in Listing 3.1 means *points* (there are 72 points in an inch). If you prefer, you can specify any stylesheet measurement in inches (`in`), centimeters (`cm`), pixels (`px`), or "widths of a letter *m*," which are called ems (`em`).

You might have noticed that each style rule in the listing ends with a semicolon (`;`). Semicolons are used to separate style rules from each other. It is therefore customary to end each style rule with a semicolon so that you can easily add another style rule after it. Review the remainder of the stylesheet in Listing 3.1 to see the presentation formatting applied to additional tags. Don't worry—you'll learn more about each of these types of entries throughout the lessons in this book.

To link this stylesheet to HTML documents, include a `<link />` tag in the `<head>` section of each document. Listing 3.2 shows the HTML code for the page shown in Figure 3.1. It contains the following `<link />` tag:

```
<link rel="stylesheet" type="text/css" href="styles.css" />
```

This assumes that the stylesheet is stored under the name `styles.css` in the same folder as the HTML document. As long as the web browser supports stylesheets—and all modern browsers do—the properties specified in the style sheet will apply to the content in the page without the need for any special HTML formatting code. This meets one of the goals of HTML, which is to provide a separation between the content in a web page and the specific formatting required to display that content.

LISTING 3.2   HTML Code for the Page Shown in Figure 3.1

```
<!DOCTYPE html>

<html lang="en">
  <head>
    <title>About BAWSI</title>
    <link rel="stylesheet" type="text/css" href="styles.css" />
  </head>
  <body>
    <section>

    <header>
    <h1>About BAWSI</h1>
    </header>

    <p><img src="logo.gif" alt="BAWSI logo"/>The Bay Area Women's
    Sports Initiative (BAWSI) is a public benefit, nonprofit
    corporation with a mission to create programs and partnerships
    through which women athletes bring health, hope and wholeness to
    our community. Founded in 2005 by Olympic and World Cup soccer
    stars Brandi Chastain and Julie Foudy and Marlene Bjornsrud,
    former general manager of the San Jose CyberRays women's
    professional soccer team, BAWSI provides a meaningful path for
    women athletes to become a more visible and valued part of the
    Bay Area sports culture.</p>

    <p class="subheader">BAWSI's History</p>
```

NOTE

You can specify font sizes as large as you like with stylesheets, although some display devices and printers will not correctly handle fonts larger than 200 points.

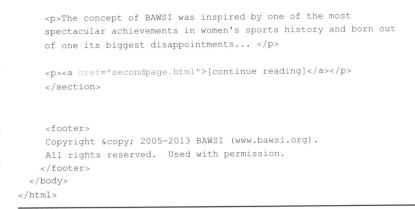

```
<p>The concept of BAWSI was inspired by one of the most
spectacular achievements in women's sports history and born out
of one its biggest disappointments... </p>

<p><a href="secondpage.html">[continue reading]</a></p>
</section>


<footer>
Copyright &copy; 2005-2013 BAWSI (www.bawsi.org).
All rights reserved.  Used with permission.
</footer>
</body>
</html>
```

The code in Listing 3.2 is interesting because it contains no formatting
of any kind. In other words, nothing in the HTML code dictates how
the text and images are to be displayed—no colors, no fonts, nothing.
Yet the page is carefully formatted and rendered to the screen, thanks
to the link to the external stylesheet, `styles.css`. The real benefit to
this approach is that you can easily create a site with multiple pages
that maintains a consistent look and feel. And you have the benefit
of isolating the visual style of the page to a single document (the
stylesheet) so that one change impacts all pages.

▼ TRY IT YOURSELF

**Create a Stylesheet
of Your Own**

Starting from scratch, create a new text document called `mystyles.css` and
add some style rules for the following basic HTML tags: `<body>`, `<p>`, `<h1>`,
and `<h2>`. After creating your stylesheet, make a new HTML file that contains
these basic tags. Play around with different style rules, and see for yourself
how simple it is to change entire blocks of text in paragraphs with one simple
change in a stylesheet file.

A CSS Style Primer

You now have a basic knowledge of CSS stylesheets and how they are
based on style rules that describe the appearance of information in
web pages. The next few sections of this hour provide a quick overview
of some of the most important style properties and allow you to get
started using CSS in your own stylesheets.

CSS includes various style properties that are used to control fonts, colors, alignment, and margins, to name just a few. The style properties in CSS can be generally grouped into two major categories:

▶ Layout properties, which consist of properties that affect the positioning of elements on a web page, such as margins, padding, and alignment.

▶ Formatting properties, which consist of properties that affect the visual display of elements within a website, such as the font type, size, and color.

Basic Layout Properties

CSS layout properties determine how content is placed on a web page. One of the most important layout properties is the `display` property, which describes how an element is displayed with respect to other elements. The `display` property has four basic values:

▶ `block`—The element is displayed on a new line, as in a new paragraph.

▶ `list-item`—The element is displayed on a new line with a list-item mark (bullet) next to it.

▶ `inline`—The element is displayed inline with the current paragraph.

▶ `none`—The element is not displayed; it is hidden.

Understanding the `display` property is easier if you visualize each element on a web page occupying a rectangular area when displayed—the `display` property controls the manner in which this rectangular area is displayed. For example, the `block` value results in the element being placed on a new line by itself, whereas the `inline` value places the element next to the content just before it. The `display` property is one of the few style properties that can be applied in most style rules. Following is an example of how to set the `display` property:

```
display:block;
```

You control the size of the rectangular area for an element with the `width` and `height` properties. As with many size-related CSS properties, `width` and `height` property values can be specified in several different units of measurement:

▶ `in`—Inches

▶ `cm`—Centimeters

NOTE

The `display` property relies on a concept known as *relative positioning*, which means that elements are positioned relative to the location of other elements on a page. CSS also supports *absolute positioning*, which enables you to place an element at an exact location on a page, independent of other elements. You'll learn more about both of these types of positioning in Hour 14, "Understanding the CSS Box Model and Positioning."

▶ mm—Millimeters

▶ %—Percentage

▶ px—Pixels

▶ pt—Points

You can mix and match units however you choose within a stylesheet, but it's generally a good idea to be consistent across a set of similar style properties. For example, you might want to stick with points for font properties and pixels for dimensions. Following is an example of setting the width of an element using pixel units:

```
width: 200px;
```

Basic Formatting Properties

CSS formatting properties to control the appearance of content on a web page, as opposed to controlling the physical positioning of the content. One of the most popular formatting properties is the border property, which establishes a visible boundary around an element with a box or partial box. Note that a border is always present in that space is always left for it, but the border does not appear in a way that you can see unless you give it properties that make it visible (like a color). The following border properties provide a means of describing the borders of an element:

▶ border-width—The width of the border edge

▶ border-color—The color of the border edge

▶ border-style—The style of the border edge

▶ border-left—The left side of the border

▶ border-right—The right side of the border

▶ border-top—The top of the border

▶ border-bottom—The bottom of the border

▶ border—All the border sides

The border-width property establishes the width of the border edge. It is often expressed in pixels, as the following code demonstrates:

```
border-width:5px;
```

Not surprisingly, the `border-color` and `border-style` properties set the border color and style. Following is an example of how these two properties are set:

```
border-color:blue;
border-style:dotted;
```

The `border-style` property can be set to any of the following basic values (you learn about some more advanced border tricks later in this book):

▶ `solid`—A single-line border

▶ `double`—A double-line border

▶ `dashed`—A dashed border

▶ `dotted`—A dotted border

▶ `groove`—A border with a groove appearance

▶ `ridge`—A border with a ridge appearance

▶ `inset`—A border with an inset appearance

▶ `outset`—A border with an outset appearance

▶ `none`—No border

▶ `hidden`—Effectively the same as `none`

The default value of the `border-style` property is `none`, which is why elements don't have a border *unless* you set the border property to a different style. Although `solid` is the most common border style, you will also see the other styles in use.

The `border-left`, `border-right`, `border-top`, and `border-bottom` properties enable you to set the border for each side of an element individually. If you want a border to appear the same on all four sides, you can use the single `border` property by itself, which expects the following styles separated by a space: `border-width`, `border-style`, and `border-color`. Following is an example of using the `border` property to set a border that consists of two (double) red lines that are a total of 10 pixels in width:

```
border:10px double red;
```

Whereas the color of an element's border is set with the `border-color` property, the color of the inner region of an element is set using the `color` and `background-color` properties. The `color` property sets the color of text in an element (foreground), and the `background-color` property sets the color of the background behind the text. Following is an example of setting both color properties to predefined colors:

```
color:black;
background-color:orange;
```

You can also assign custom colors to these properties by specifying the colors in hexadecimal (covered in more detail in Hour 7, "Working with Colors and Borders") or as RGB (Red Green Blue) decimal values:

```
background-color:#999999;
color:rgb(0,0,255);
```

You can also control the alignment and indentation of web page content without too much trouble. This is accomplished with the `text-align` and `text-indent` properties, as the following code demonstrates:

```
text-align:center;
text-indent:12px;
```

When you have an element properly aligned and indented, you might be interested in setting its font. The following basic font properties set the various parameters associated with fonts (you'll learn about some more advanced font usage in Hour 6, "Working with Fonts"):

▶ `font-family`—The family of the font

▶ `font-size`—The size of the font

▶ `font-style`—The style of the font (`normal` or `italic`)

▶ `font-weight`—The weight of the font (`normal`, `lighter`, `bold`, `bolder`, and so on)

The `font-family` property specifies a prioritized list of font family names. A prioritized list is used instead of a single value to provide alternatives in case a font isn't available on a given system. The `font-size` property specifies the size of the font using a unit of measurement, usually points. Finally, the `font-style` property sets the style of the font, and the `font-weight` property sets the weight of the font. Following is an example of setting these font properties:

```
font-family: Arial, sans-serif;
font-size: 36pt;
font-style: italic;
font-weight: normal;
```

Now that you know a whole lot more about style properties and how they work, refer back at Listing 3.1 and see whether it makes a bit more sense. Here's a recap of the style properties used in that style sheet, which you can use as a guide for understanding how it works:

▶ `font`—Lets you set many font properties at once. You can specify a list of font names separated by commas; if the first is not available, the next is tried, and so on. You can also include the words `bold` and/or `italic` and a font size. Alternatively, you can set each of these font properties separately with `font-family`, `font-size`, `font-weight`, and `font-style`.

▶ `line-height`—Also known in the publishing world as *leading*. This sets the height of each line of text, usually in points.

▶ `color`—Sets the text color using the standard color names or hexadecimal color codes (see Hour 7 for more details).

▶ `text-decoration`—Useful for turning off link underlining—simply set it to `none`. The values of `underline`, `italic`, and `line-through` are also supported. Hour 8, "Using External and Internal Links," covers applying styles to links in more detail.

▶ `text-align`—Aligns text to the `left`, `right`, or `center`, along with justifying the text with a value of `justify`.

▶ `padding`—Adds padding to the left, right, top, and bottom of an element; this padding can be in measurement units or a percentage of the page width. Use `padding-left` and `padding-right` if you want to add padding to the left and right of the element independently. Use `padding-top` or `padding-bottom` to add padding to the top or bottom of the element, as appropriate. You learn more about these style properties in Hour 13, "Working with Margins, Padding, Alignment, and Floating," and Hour 14, "Understanding the CSS Box Model and Positioning."

Using Style Classes

This is a "teach yourself" book, so you don't have to go to a single class to learn how to give your pages great style—although you *do* need to learn what a style class is. Whenever you want some of the text on your pages to look different from the other text, you can create what amounts to a custom-built HTML tag. Each type of specially formatted text you define is called a *style class*. A *style class* is a custom set of formatting specifications that can be applied to any element in a web page.

Before showing you a style class, I need to take a quick step back and clarify some CSS terminology. First off, a CSS *style property* is a specific style that you can assign a value, such as `color` or `font-size`. You associate a style property and its respective value with elements on a web page by using a selector. A *selector* is used to identify tags on a page to which you apply styles. Following is an example of a selector, a property, and a value all included in a basic style rule:

```
h1 { font: 36pt Courier; }
```

In this code, `h1` is the selector, `font` is the style property, and `36pt Courier` is the value. The selector is important because it means that the font setting will be applied to all `h1` elements in the web page. But maybe you want to differentiate between some of the `h1` elements—what then? The answer lies in style classes.

Suppose you want two different kinds of `<h1>` headings for use in your documents. You create a style class for each one by putting the following CSS code in a stylesheet:

```
h1.silly { font: 36pt Comic Sans; }
h1.serious { font: 36pt Arial; }
```

Notice that these selectors include a period (.) after `h1`, followed by a descriptive class name. To choose between the two style classes, use the `class` attribute, like this:

```
<h1 class="silly">Marvin's Munchies Inc. </h1>
<p>Text about Marvin's Munchies goes here. </p>
```

Or you could use this:

```
<h1 class="serious">MMI Investor Information</h1>
<p>Text for business investors goes here.</p>
```

When referencing a style class in HTML code, simply specify the class name in the `class` attribute of an element. In the previous example, the words `Marvin's Munchies Inc.` would appear in a 36-point Comic Sans font, assuming that you included a `<link />` to the stylesheet at the top of the web page and that the user has the Comic Sans font installed. The words `MMI Investor Information` would appear in the 36-point Arial font instead. You can see another example of classes in action in Listing 3.2: look for the `subheader <p>` class.

What if you want to create a style class that can be applied to any element instead of just headings or some other particular tag? In your

CSS, simply use a period (.) followed by any style class name you make up and any style specifications you choose. That class can specify any number of font, spacing, and margin settings all at once. Wherever you want to apply your custom tag in a page, just use an HTML tag plus the `class` attribute, followed by the class name you created.

For example, the stylesheet in Listing 3.1 includes the following style class specification:

```
p.subheader {
  font-weight: bold;
  color:#593d87;
}
```

This style class is applied in Listing 3.2 with the following tag:

```
<p class="subheader">
```

Everything between that tag and the closing `</p>` tag in Listing 3.2 appears in bold purple text.

What makes style classes so valuable is how they isolate style code from web pages, effectively allowing you to focus your HTML code on the actual content in a page, not how it is going to appear on the screen. Then you can focus on how the content is rendered to the screen by fine-tuning the stylesheet. You might be surprised by how a relatively small amount of code in a stylesheet can have significant effects across an entire website. This makes your pages much easier to maintain and manipulate.

Using Style IDs

When you create custom style classes, you can use those classes as many times as you like—they are not unique. However, in some instances, you want precise control over unique elements for layout or formatting purposes (or both). In such instances, look to IDs instead of classes.

A *style ID* is a custom set of formatting specifications that can be applied only to one element in a web page. You can use IDs across a set of pages, but only once per time within each page.

For example, suppose you have a title within the body of all your pages. Each page has only one title, but all the pages themselves

TIP

You might have noticed a change in the coding style when a style rule includes multiple properties. For style rules with a single style, you'll commonly see the property placed on the same line as the rule, like this:

```
p.subheader { font-weight:
bold; }
```

However, when a style rule contains multiple style properties, it's much easier to read and understand the code if you list the properties one per line, like this:

```
p.subheader {
  font-weight: bold;
  color:#593d87;
}
```

include one instance of that title. Following is an example of a selector with an ID indicated, plus a property and a value:

```
p#title {font: 24pt Verdana, Geneva, Arial, sans-serif}
```

Notice that this selector includes a hash mark, or pound sign (#), after `p`, followed by a descriptive ID name. When referencing a style ID in HTML code, simply specify the ID name in the `id` attribute of an element, like so:

```
<p id="title">Some Title Goes Here</p>
```

Everything between the opening and closing `<p>` tags will appear in 24-point Verdana text—but only once on any given page. You often see style IDs used to define specific parts of a page for layout purposes, such as a header area, footer area, main body area, and so on. These types of areas in a page appear only once per page, so using an ID rather than a class is the appropriate choice.

Internal Stylesheets and Inline Styles

In some situations, you want to specify styles that will be used in only one web page. You can enclose a stylesheet between `<style>` and `</style>` tags and include it directly in an HTML document. Stylesheets used in this manner must appear in the `<head>` of an HTML document. No `<link />` tag is needed, and you cannot refer to that stylesheet from any other page (unless you copy it into the beginning of that document, too). This kind of stylesheet is known as an internal stylesheet, as you learned earlier in the hour.

Listing 3.3 shows an example of how you might specify an internal stylesheet.

LISTING 3.3   A Web Page with an Internal Stylesheet

```
<!DOCTYPE html>

<html lang="en">
  <head>
    <title>Some Page</title>

    <style type="text/css">
      footer {
        font-size: 9pt;
```

```
        line-height: 12pt;
        text-align: center;
      }
    </style>
  </head>
  <body>
  ...
  <footer>
  Copyright 2013 Acme Products, Inc.
  </footer>
  </body>
</html>
```

In the listing code, the `footer` style class is specified in an internal stylesheet that appears in the head of the page. The style class is now available for use within the body of this page. In fact, it is used in the body of the page to style the copyright notice.

Internal stylesheets are handy if you want to create a style rule that is used multiple times within a single page. However, in some instances, you might need to apply a unique style to one particular element. This calls for an inline style rule, which allows you to specify a style for only a small part of a page, such as an individual element. For example, you can create and apply a style rule within a `<p>`, `<div>`, or `<span>` tag via the `style` attribute. This type of style is known as an *inline style* because it is specified right there in the middle of the HTML code.

Here's how a sample `style` attribute might look:

```
<p style="color:green">
  This text is green, but <span style="color:red">this text is
  red.</span>
  Back to green again, but...
</p>
<p>
  ...now the green is over, and we're back to the default color
  for this page.
</p>
```

This code makes use of the `<span>` tag to show how to apply the `color` style property in an inline style rule. In fact, both the `<p>` tag and the `<span>` tag in this example use the `color` property as an inline style. What's important to understand is that the `color:red` style property overrides the `color:green` style property for the text between the `<span>` and `</span>` tags. Then in the second paragraph, neither of the `color` styles applies because it is a completely new paragraph that adheres to the default color of the entire page.

NOTE

`<span>` and `</span>` are dummy tags that do nothing in and of themselves except specify a range of content to apply any `style` attributes that you add. The only difference between `<div>` and `<span>` is that `<div>` is a block element and, therefore, forces a line break, whereas `<span>` doesn't. Therefore, you should use `<span>` to modify the style of any portion of text that is to appear in the middle of a sentence or paragraph without any line break.

CAUTION

Using inline styles isn't considered a best practice when used beyond page-level debugging or the process of trying out new things in a controlled setting. The best practice of all is having your pages link to a centrally maintained stylesheet so that changes are immediately reflected in all pages that use it.

Validate Your Stylesheets

Just as it is important to validate your HTML or XHTML markup, it is important to validate your stylesheet. You can find a specific validation tool for CSS at http://jigsaw.w3.org/css-validator/. As with the validation tool discussed in Hour 2, "Structuring an HTML Document," you can point the tool to a web address, upload a file, or paste content into the form field provided. The ultimate goal is a result like the one in Figure 3.3: `valid`!

FIGURE 3.3
The W3C CSS Validator shows there are no errors in the stylesheet contents of Listing 3.1.

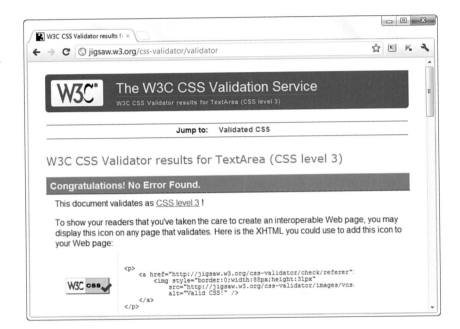

Summary

In this hour, you learned that a stylesheet can control the appearance of many HTML pages at once. It can also give you extremely precise control over the typography, spacing, and positioning of HTML elements. You also learned that, by adding a `style` attribute to almost any HTML tag, you can control the style of any part of an HTML page without referring to a separate stylesheet document.

You learned about three main approaches to including stylesheets in your website: a separate stylesheet file with the extension `.css` that is linked to in the `<head>` of your documents, a collection of style rules placed in the head of the document within the `<style>` tag, and rules placed directly in an HTML tag via the `style` attribute (although the latter is not a best practice for long-term use).

Table 3.1 summarizes the tags discussed in this hour. Refer to the CSS stylesheet standards at http://www.w3c.org for details on what options can be included after the `<style>` tag or the `style` attribute.

TABLE 3.1   HTML Tags and Attributes Covered in Hour 3

Tag/Attributes	Function
`<style>...</style>`	Allows an internal stylesheet to be included within a document. Used between `<head>` and `</head>`.
Attribute	
`type="contenttype"`	The Internet content type. (Always `"text/css"` for a CSS stylesheet.)
`<link />`	Links to an external stylesheet (or other document type). Used in the `<head>` section of the document.
Attribute	
`href="url"`	The address of the stylesheet.
`type="contenttype"`	The Internet content type. (Always `"text/css"` for a CSS stylesheet.)
`rel="stylesheet"`	The link type. (Always `"stylesheet"` for stylesheets.)
`<span>...</span>`	Does nothing but provide a place to put `style` or other attributes. (Similar to `<div>...</div>`, but does not cause a line break.)
Attribute	
`style="style"`	Includes inline style specifications. (Can be used in `<span>`, `<div>`, `<body>`, and most other HTML tags.)

Q&A

Q. Say I link a stylesheet to my page that says all text should be blue, but there's a `<span style="font-color:red">` **tag in the page somewhere. Will that text display as blue or red?**

A. Red. Local inline styles always take precedence over external stylesheets. Any style specifications you put between `<style>` and `</style>` tags at the top of a page also take precedence over external stylesheets (but not over inline styles later in the same page). This is the cascading effect of stylesheets that I mentioned earlier in the hour. You can think of cascading style effects as starting with an external stylesheet, which is overridden by an internal stylesheet, which is overridden by inline styles.

Q. Can I link more than one stylesheet to a single page?

A. Sure. For example, you might have a sheet for formatting (text, fonts, colors, and so on) and another one for layout (margins, padding, alignment, and so on)—just include a `<link />` for both. Technically, the CSS standard requires web browsers to give the user the option to choose between stylesheets when multiple sheets are presented via multiple `<link />` tags. However, in practice, all major web browsers simply include every stylesheet unless it has a `rel="alternate"` attribute. The preferred technique for linking in multiple stylesheets involves using the special `@import` command. The following is an example of importing multiple stylesheets with `@import`:

```
@import url(styles1.css);
@import url(styles2.css);
```

Similar to the `<link />` tag, the `@import` command must be placed in the head of a web page. You learn more about this handy little command in Hour 20, "Creating Print-Friendly Web Pages," when you learn how to create a stylesheet specifically for printing web pages.

Workshop

The Workshop contains quiz questions and exercises to help you solidify your understanding of the material covered. Try to answer all questions before looking at the "Answers" section that follows.

Quiz

1. What code would you use to create a stylesheet to specify 30-point blue Arial headings and all other text in 10-point blue Times Roman (or the default browser font)?

2. If you saved the stylesheet you made for Question 1 as `corporate.css`, how do you apply it to a web page named `intro.html`?

3. How many different ways are there to ensure that style rules can be applied to your content?

Answers

1. Your stylesheet would include the following:

```
h1 { font: 30pt blue Arial; }
body { font: 10pt blue "Times New Roman"; }
```

2. Put the following tag between the `<head>` and `</head>` tags of the `intro.html` document:

```
<link rel="stylesheet" type="text/css" href="corporate.css" />
```

3. Three: externally, internally, and inline.

Exercises

► Using the stylesheet you created earlier in this hour, add some style classes to your stylesheet. To see the fruits of your labor, apply those classes to the HTML page you created as well. Use classes with your `<h1>` and `<p>` tags to get the feel for things.

► Develop a standard stylesheet for your website, and link it into all your pages. (Use internal stylesheets and/or inline styles for pages that need to deviate from it.) If you work for a corporation, chances are, it has already developed font and style specifications for printed materials. Get a copy of those specifications, and follow them for company web pages, too.

▶ Be sure to explore the official stylesheet specs at http://www.w3.org/Style/CSS/, and try some of the more esoteric style properties not covered in this hour.

HOUR 4
A Closer Look at HTML5 Page Structure

As you learned in Hour 2, "Structuring an HTML Document," HTML5 includes tags that enable you to enhance the semantics—the meaning—of the information that you provide in your marked-up text. In this hour, you take a closer look at six elements that are fundamental to solid semantic structuring of your documents: `<header>`, `<section>`, `<article>`, `<nav>`, `<aside>`, and `<footer>`.

Throughout the remainder of this book, you will see these tags used appropriately in the code samples, so this lesson makes sure that you have a good grasp of their meaning before we continue.

Conceptualizing the Page

One of the best ways to understand the HTML5 semantic elements is to see them in action, but that can be a little difficult when the primary purpose of these elements is to provide *meaning* rather than design. That's not to say that you can't add design to these elements—you most certainly can, and you will in later lessons. But the "action" of the semantic elements is to hold content and provide meaning through doing so, as in Figure 4.1, which shows a common use of semantic elements for a basic web page.

WHAT YOU'LL LEARN IN THIS HOUR:

▶ How to use semantic tags to indicate header and footer content

▶ How to use semantic tags to indicate navigational and secondary content

▶ How to use semantic tags to better structure body content

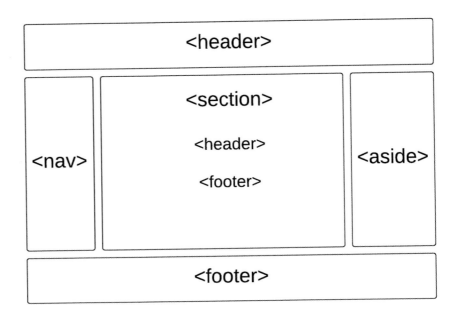

Initially, you might think, "Of *course*, that makes total sense, with the header at the top and the footer at the bottom," and feel quite good about yourself for understanding semantic elements at first glance—and you should! A second glance should then raise some questions: What if you want your navigation to be horizontal under your header? Does an aside have to be (literally) on the side? What if you don't want any asides? What's with the use of `<header>` and `<footer>` again within the main body section? And that's just to name a few! Another question you might ask is where the `<article>` element fits in; it isn't shown in this example but is part of this chapter.

This is the time when conceptualizing the page—and specifically the page *you* want to create—comes into play. If you understand the content you want to mark up and you understand that you can use any, all, or none of the semantic elements and still create a valid HTML document, then you can begin to organize the content of your page in the way that makes the most sense for it and for you (and, hopefully, for your readers).

Let's take a look at the elements used in Figure 4.1 before moving on to a second example and then a deeper exploration of the individual elements themselves. In Figure 4.1, you see a `<header>` at the top of the page and a `<footer>` at the bottom—straightforward, as already mentioned. The use of a `<nav>` element on the left side of the page matches a common display area for navigation, and the `<aside>` element on the right side of the page matches a common display area for secondary notes, pull quotes, helper text, and "for more information" links about the content. In Figure 4.2, you'll see some of these elements shifted around, so don't worry—Figure 4.1 is not some immutable example of semantic markup.

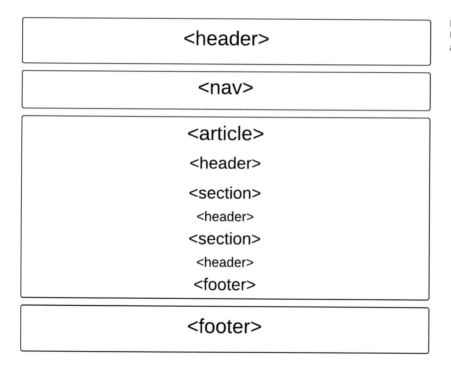

FIGURE 4.2
Using nested semantic elements to add more meaning to the content.

Something you might be surprised to see in Figure 4.1 is the `<header>` and `<footer>` inside the `<section>` element. As you'll learn shortly, the role of the `<header>` element is to introduce second example and then a deeper exploration of the individual elements themselves. In Figure 4.1, you see a `<header>` at the top of the page and a `<footer>` at the bottom—straightforward, as already mentioned. The use of a `<nav>` element on the left side of the page matches the content that comes after it, and the `<header>` element itself does not convey any level in a document outline. Therefore, you can use as many as you need to mark up your content appropriately; a `<header>` at the beginning of the page might contain introductory information about the page as a whole, and the `<header>` element within the `<section>` element might just as easily and appropriately contain introductory information about the content within it. The same is true for the multiple appearances of the `<footer>` element in this example.

Let's move on to Figure 4.2, which shifts around the `<nav>` element and also introduces use of the `<article>` element.

In Figure 4.2, the `<header>` and `<nav>` elements at the beginning of the page, and the `<footer>` element at the bottom of the page, should make perfect sense to you. And, although we haven't talked about the `<article>` element yet, if you think about it as a container element that has sections (`<section>`s, even!), and each of those sections has its own heading, then the chunk of semantic elements in the middle of the figure should make sense, too. As you can see, there's no single way to conceptualize page content—there's the conceptualization that you should do of each individual page's content.

If you marked up some content in the structure shown in Figure 4.2, it might look like Listing 4.1.

LISTING 4.1   Semantic Markup of Basic Content

```
<!DOCTYPE html>

<html lang="en">
  <head>
    <title>Semantic Example</title>
  </head>
  <body>
    <header>
        <h1>SITE OR PAGE LOGO GOES HERE</h1>
    </header>
    <nav>
        SITE OR PAGE NAV GOES HERE.
    </nav>
    <article>
      <header>
         <h2>Article Heading</h2>
      </header>
      <section>
        <header>
            <h3>Section 1 Heading</h3>
        </header>
        <p>Section 2 content here.</p>
      </section>
      <section>
        <header>
            <h3>Section 2 Heading</h3>
```

```
        </header>
        <p>Section 2 content here.</p>
      </section>
      <footer>
          <p>Article footer goes here.</p>
      </footer>
    </article>
    <footer>
      SITE OR PAGE FOOTER HERE
    </footer>
  </body>
</html>
```

If opened this HTML document in your web browser, you would see
something like Figure 4.3—a completely unstyled document, but one
that has semantic meaning (even if no one can "see" it).

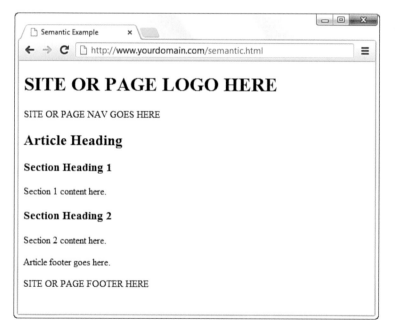

FIGURE 4.3
The output of Listing 4.1.

Just because there is no visible styling doesn't mean the meaning
is lost; as noted earlier in this section, machines can interpret the
structure of the document as provided for through the semantic
elements. You can see the outline of this basic document in Figure 4.4,
which shows the output of this file after examination by the HTML5
Outline tool at http://gsnedders.html5.org/outliner/.

FIGURE 4.4
The outline of this document
follows the semantic markup.

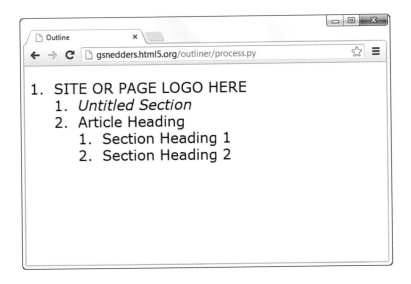

Now that you've seen some examples of conceptualizing the information represented in your documents, you're better prepared to start marking up those documents. The sections that follow take a look at the semantic elements individually.

Using `<header>` in Multiple Ways

At the most basic level, the `<header>` element contains introductory information. That information might take the form of an actual `<h1>` (or other level) element, or it might simply be a logo image or text contained within a `<p>` or `<div>` element. The *meaning* of the content should be introductory in nature, to warrant its inclusion within a `<header></header>` tag pair.

As you've seen in the examples so far in this lesson, a common placement of a `<header>` element is at the beginning of a page. When used in this way, containing a logo or an `<h1>`-level title makes sense, such as here:

```
<header>
    <img src="acmewidgets.jpg" alt="ACME Widgets LLC"/>
</header>
```

Or even:

```
<header>
    <img src="acmewidgets.jpg" alt="ACME Widgets LLC"/>
```

```
    <h1>The finest widgets are made here!</h1>
</header>
```

Both snippets are valid uses of <header> because the information contained within them is introductory to the page overall.

As you've also seen in this hour, you are not limited to only one <header>. You can go crazy with your <header> elements, as long as they are acting as containers for introductory information—Listing 4.1 showed the use of <header> elements for several <section> elements within an <article>, and this is a perfectly valid use of the element:

```
<section>
    <header>
       <h3>Section 1 Heading</h3>
    </header>
    <p>Section 2 content here.</p>
</section>
<section>
    <header>
       <h3>Section 2 Heading</h3>
    </header>
    <p>Section 2 content here.</p>
</section>
```

The <header> element can contain any other element in the flow content category, of which it is also a member. This means that a <header> *could* contain a <section> element, if you wanted, and be perfectly valid markup. However, when you are conceptualizing your content, think about whether that sort of nesting makes sense before you go off and do it.

The only exceptions to the permitted content within <header> are that the <header> element cannot contain *other* <header> elements, nor can it contain a <footer> element. Similarly, the <header> element cannot be contained within an <address> or <footer> element.

Understanding the <section> Element

The <section> element has a simple definition: It is "a generic section of a document" that is also "a thematic grouping of content, typically with a heading." That sounds pretty simple to me, and probably does to you as well. So you might be surprised to find that if you type "difference between section and article in HTML5" in your search

NOTE

In general, *flow content* elements are elements that contain text, images, or other multimedia embedded content; HTML elements fall into multiple categories.

If you want to learn more about the categorization of elements into content models, see www.w3.org/TR/2011/WD-html5-20110525/content-models.html.

engine of choice, you'll find tens of thousands of entries talking about the differences because the definitions trip people up all the time. We first discuss the `<section>` element and then cover the `<article>` element—and hopefully avoid any of the misunderstandings that seem to plague new web developers.

In Listing 4.1, you saw a straightforward example of using `<section>` within an `<article>` (repeated here); in this example, you can easily imagine that the `<section>`s contain a "thematic grouping of content," which is supported by the fact that they each have a heading.

```
<article>
    <header>
        <h2>Article Heading</h2>
    </header>
    <section>
        <header>
            <h3>Section 1 Heading</h3>
        </header>
        <p>Section 2 content here.</p>
    </section>
    <section>
        <header>
            <h3>Section 2 Heading</h3>
        </header>
        <p>Section 2 content here.</p>
    </section>
    <footer>
        <p>Article footer goes here.</p>
    </footer>
</article>
```

But here's an example of a perfectly valid use of `<section>` with no `<article>` element in sight:

```
<section>
    <header>
        <h1>Super Heading</h1>
    </header>
    <p>Super content!</p>
</section>
```

So, what's a developer to do? Let's say you have some generic content that you know you want to divide into sections with their own headings. In that case, use `<section>`. If you need to only *visually* delineate chunks of content (such as with paragraph breaks) that do not require additional headings, then `<section>` isn't for you—use `<p>` or `<div>` instead.

Because the `<section>` element can contain any other flow content element, and can be contained within any other flow content element (except the `<address>` element), it's easy to see why, without other limitations and with generic guidelines for use, the `<section>` element is sometimes misunderstood.

Using `<article>`

Personally, I believe that a lot of the misunderstanding regarding the use of `<section>` versus `<article>` has to do with the name of the `<article>` element. When I think of an article, I think specifically about an article in a newspaper or a magazine. I don't naturally think "any standalone body of work," which is how the `<article>` element is commonly defined. The HTML5 recommended specification defines it as "a complete, or self-contained, composition in a document, page, application, or site and that is, in principle, independently distributable or reusable," such as "a forum post, a magazine or newspaper article, a blog entry, a user-submitted comment, an interactive widget or gadget, or any other independent item of content."

In other words, an `<article>` element could be used to contain the entire page of a website (whether or not it is an article in a publication), an actual article in a publication, a blog post anywhere and everywhere, part of a threaded discussion in a forum, a comment on a blog post, and as a container that displays the current weather in your city. It's no wonder there are tens of thousands of results for a search on "difference between section and article in HTML5."

A good rule of thumb when trying to figure out when to use `<article>` and when to use `<section>` is simply to answer the following question: Does this content make sense on its own? If so, then no matter what the content seems to be to you (for example, a static web page, not an article in the *New York Times*), start by using the `<article>` element. If you find yourself breaking it up, do so in `<section>`s. And if you find yourself thinking that your "article" is, in fact, part of a greater whole, then change the `<article>` tags to `<section>` tags, and find the beginning of the document, and surround it from there with the more appropriately placed `<article>` tag at a higher level.

Implementing the `<nav>` Element

The `<nav>` element seems so simple (`<nav>` implies *navigation*), and it ultimately is—but it can also be used incorrectly. In this section, you learn some basic uses and also some incorrect uses to avoid. If your site has any navigational elements at all, either site-wide or within a long page of content, you have a valid use for the `<nav>` element.

For that site-wide navigation, you typically find a `<nav>` element within the primary `<header>` element; you are not required to do so, but if you want your navigational content to be introductory (and omnipresent in your template), you can easily make a case for your primary `<nav>` element to appear within the primary `<header>`. More important, that is valid HTML (as is `<nav>` outside a `<header>`)—a `<nav>` element can appear within any flow content, as well as contain any flow content.

The following code snippet shows the main navigational links of a website, placed within a `<header>` element:

```
<header>
    <img src="acmewidgets.jpg" alt="ACME Widgets LLC"/>
    <h1>The finest widgets are made here!</h1>
    <nav>
        <ul>
            <li><a href="#">About Us</a></li>
            <li><a href="#">Products</a></li>
            <li><a href="#">Support</a></li>
            <li><a href="#">Press</a></li>
        </ul>
    </nav>
</header>
```

You are not limited to a single `<nav>` element in your documents, which is good for site developers who create templates that include both primary *and* secondary navigation. For example, you might see horizontal primary navigation at the top of a page (often contained within a `<header>` element), and then vertical navigation in the left column of a page, representing the secondary pages within the main section. In that case, you simply use a second `<nav>` element, not contained within the `<header>`, placed and styled differently to delineate the two types visually in addition to semantically.

Remember, the `<nav>` element is used for *major* navigational content— primary and secondary navigation both count, as does the inclusion of tables of content within a page. For good and useful semantic use of the `<nav>` element, do not simply apply it to every link that allows a user to navigate anywhere. Note that I said "good and useful" semantic use, not necessarily "valid" use—it's true that you could apply `<nav>` to any list of links, and it would be valid according to the HTML specification because links are flow content. But it wouldn't be particularly *useful*—it wouldn't add meaning—to surround a list of links to social media sharing tools with the `<nav>` element.

When to Use `<aside>`

As you'll see by the number of tips and notes from me throughout this book, I'm a big fan of the type of content that is most appropriately marked up within the `<aside>` element. The `<aside>` element is meant to contain any content that is tangentially related to the content around it—additional explanation, links to related resources, pull quotes, helper text, and so on. You might think of the `<aside>` element as a sidebar, but be careful not to think of it only as a *visual* sidebar, or a column on the side of a page where you can stick anything and everything you want, whether or not it's related to the content or site at hand.

In Figure 4.5, you can see how content in an `<aside>` is used to create a *pull quote*, or a content excerpt that is specifically set aside to call attention to it. The `<aside>`, in this case, is used to highlight an important section of the text, but it could also have been used to define a term or link to related documents.

When determining whether to use the `<aside>` element, think about the content you want to add. Is it related directly to the content in which the `<aside>` would be contained, such as a definition of terms used in an article or a list of related links for the article? If your answer is an easy "yes," that's great! Use `<aside>` to your heart's content. If you're thinking of including an `<aside>` outside a containing element that is itself full of content, just make sure that the content of the `<aside>` is reasonably related to your site overall and that you're not just using the `<aside>` element for visual effect.

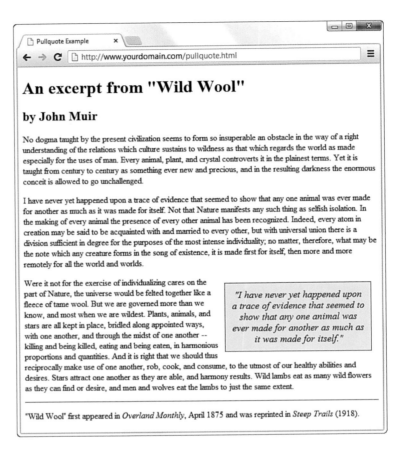

Using `<footer>` Effectively

The counterpart to the `<header>` element, the `<footer>` element, contains additional information about its containing element. The most common use of the `<footer>` element is to contain copyright information at the bottom of a page, such as here:

```
<footer>
   <p>&copy; 2013 Acme Widgets, LLC. All Rights Reserved.</p>
</footer>
```

Similar to the `<header>` element, the `<footer>` element can contain any other element in the flow content category, of which it is also a member, with the exception of *other* `<footer>` or `<header>` elements. Additionally, a `<footer>` element cannot be contained within an `<address>` element, but a `<footer>` element can contain an `<address>`

element—in fact, a `<footer>` element is a common location for an `<address>` element to live.

Placing useful `<address>` content within a `<footer>` element is one of the most effective uses of the `<footer>` element (not to mention the `<address>` element) because it provides specific contextual information about the page or section of the page to which it refers. The following snippet shows a use of `<address>` within `<footer>`:

```
<footer>
    <p>&copy; 2013 Acme Widgets, LLC. All Rights Reserved.</p>
    <p>Copyright Issues? Contact:</p>
        <address>
        Our Lawyer<br/>
        123 Main Street<br/>
        Somewhere, CA 95128<br/>
        <a href="mailto:lawyer@richperson.com">lawyer@richperson.com</a>
        </address>
</footer>
```

As with the `<header>` element, you are not limited to only one `<footer>`. You can use as many `<footer>` elements as you need, as long as they are containers for additional information about the containing element—Listing 4.1 showed the use of `<footer>` elements for both the page and an `<article>`, both of which are valid.

Summary

This hour introduced you to six semantic elements that help you better indicate header and footer content, navigational and secondary content, and generic body content in your documents. You also learned how to conceptualize your overall document structure before beginning to mark it up so that when you do, you are using the appropriate elements to help convey additional meaning to your readers.

Table 4.1 summarizes the HTML tags covered in this hour.

TABLE 4.1   HTML Tags Covered in Hour 4

Tag	Function
`<header>...</header>`	Contains introductory information
`<section>...</section>`	Contains thematically similar content, like a chapter of a book or a section of a page
`<article>...</article>`	Contains content that is a standalone body of work, such as a news article
`<nav>...</nav>`	Contains navigational elements
`<aside>...</aside>`	Contains secondary information for its containing element
`<footer>...</footer>`	Contains supplementary material for its containing element (commonly a copyright notice or author information)
`<address>...</address>`	Contains address information related to its nearest `<article>` or `<body>` element, often contained within a `<footer>` element

Q&A

Q. Do I have to use semantic markup at all? Didn't you say throughout this lesson that pages are valid with or without it?

A. True, none of these elements is required for a valid HTML document. You don't have to use any of them, but I urge you to think beyond the use of markup for visual display only and think about it for semantic meaning as well. Visual display is meaningless to screen readers, but semantic elements convey a ton of information through these machines.

Q. I'm still completely befuddled about when to use `<section>` and when to use `<aside>`. Can you make it more clear?

A. I don't blame you. There's a resource available at the HTML5 Doctor website that is one of the best I've seen to help eliminate the confusion. It's a flowchart for HTML5 sectioning, found at http://html5doctor.com/downloads/h5d-sectioning-flowchart.png. This flowchart asks the right questions about your content and helps you determine the correct container element to use.

Workshop

The Workshop contains quiz questions and exercises to help you solidify your understanding of the material covered. Try to answer all questions before looking at the "Answers" section that follows.

Quiz

1. Which of the semantic elements discussed in this hour is appropriate for containing the definition of a word used in an article?

2. Do you have to use an `<h1>`, `<h2>`, `<h3>`, `<h4>`, `<h5>`, or `<h6>` element within a `<header>` element?

3. How many different `<nav>` elements can you have in a single page?

Answers

1. The `<aside>` element is appropriate for this.

2. No. The `<header>` element can contain any other flow content besides another `<header>` element or a `<footer>` element. However, a heading element (`<h1>` through `<h6>`) is not required in a `<header>` element.

3. You can have as many `<nav>` elements as you need. The trick is to "need" only a few (perhaps for primary and secondary navigation only); otherwise, the meaning is lost.

Exercises

▶ In Hour 2, one of the exercises had you create a personal web page. Return to that document and add all the relevant semantic elements you learned about in this hour.

▶ Building off the single page, create a few more related pieces of content. Remember that some of your pages might contain `<article>` elements with no sections, but others might contain `<section>` elements with `<header>` and `<footer>` elements as well.

HOUR 5
Working with Text Blocks and Lists

In the early days of the web, text was displayed in only one font and one size. However, as you've learned in the first few hours of lessons, a combination of HTML and CSS now makes it possible to control the appearance of text and how it is aligned and displayed on a web page.

This hour shows you the basics of text alignment and guides you through the next steps: the use of lists. Because lists are so common, HTML provides tags that automatically indent text and add numbers, bullets, or other symbols in front of each listed item. You'll learn how to format different types of lists, which are part of the many ways to display content in your website.

WHAT YOU'LL LEARN IN THIS HOUR:

▶ How to align text on a page
▶ How to use the three types of HTML lists
▶ How to place lists within lists

Preparing Sample Text

You can make the most of learning how to style text throughout this hour if you have some sample text that you can indent, center, or otherwise manipulate:

▶ Any type of outline, bullet points from a presentation, numbered steps, a glossary, or a list of textual information from a database makes good material to work with.

▶ Any text will do, but try to find (or type) some text you want to put onto a web page. The text from a company brochure or from your résumé might be a good choice.

▶ If the text you'll be using is from a word processing or database program, be sure to save it to a new file in plain-text or ASCII format. You can then add the appropriate HTML tags and style attributes to format it as you go through this lesson.

▶ Before you use the code introduced in this hour to format the body text, add the set of skeleton HTML tags you've used in previous hours (the `<!DOCTYPE>` plus `<html>`, `<head>`, `<title>`, and `<body>` tag pairs).

Aligning Text on a Page

It's easy to take for granted the fact that most paragraphs are automatically aligned to the left when you're reading information on the web. However, there certainly are situations in which you might choose to align content to the right or even the center of a page. HTML gives you the option to align a single HTML block-level element, such as text contained within a `<p></p>` or `<div></div>` tag pair. Before we get into the details of aligning block elements, however, let's briefly note how attributes work.

Using Attributes

Attributes provide additional information related to an HTML tag. *Attributes* are special code words used inside an HTML tag to control exactly what the tag does. They are very important in even the simplest bit of web content, so it's important to be comfortable using them.

Attributes invoke the use of styles, classes, or IDs that are applied to particular tags. If you define a particular class or ID in a style sheet—as you learned in Hour 3, "Understanding Cascading Style

Sheets"—then you can invoke that class or ID using `class="someclass"` or `id="someid"` within the tag itself. When the browser renders the content for display, it looks to the style sheet to determine exactly how the content will appear according to the associated style definitions. Similarly, you can use the `style` attribute to include style information for a particular element without connecting the element to an actual style sheet—this is the inline style format you learned about in Hour 3.

For example, when you begin a paragraph with the `<p>` tag, you can specify whether the text in that particular paragraph should be aligned to the left margin, the right margin, or the center of the page by setting the `style` attribute. If you want to associate that particular paragraph with an existing class or ID, you set the `class` or `id` attribute.

In the following example, each paragraph can be left-aligned:

```
<p style="text-align: left;">Text goes here.</p>
<p class="leftAlignStyle">Text goes here.</p>
<p id="firstLeftAlign">Text goes here.</p>
```

In the first paragraph, the style appears directly in the `style` attribute—this is useful for debugging or for short-term formatting tests, but not so much for ongoing maintenance of your web content. In the second paragraph, the paragraph will be left-aligned if the style sheet entry for the `leftAlignStyle` class includes the `text-align` statement; remember, using a class means that other tags can reuse the class. Similarly, the third paragraph will be left-aligned if the style sheet entry for the `firstLeftAlign id` includes the text-align statement; remember, using an `id` means that these styles can be applied to only the one identified tag.

Aligning Text in Block-Level Elements

To align text in a block-level element such as `<p>` to the right margin without creating a separate class or ID in a style sheet, simply place `style="text-align:right"` inside the `<p>` tag at the beginning of the paragraph (or define it in a class or `id`). Similarly, to center the text in the element, use `<p style="text-align:center">`. To align text in a paragraph to the left, use `<p style="text-align:left">`.

The `text-align` part of the `style` attribute is referred to as a *style rule*, which means that it is setting a particular style aspect of an HTML element. You can use many style rules to carefully control the formatting of web content.

TIP

Every attribute and style rule in HTML has a default value that is assumed when you don't set the attribute yourself. In the case of the `text-align` style rule of the `<p>` tag, the default value is `left`, so using the bare-bones `<p>` tag has the same effect as using `<p style="text-align:left">`. Learning the default values for common style rules is an important part of becoming a good web page developer.

The `text-align` style rule is not reserved for just the `<p>` tag. In fact, you can use the `text-align` style rule with any block-level element, which includes semantic elements such as `<section>` and `<header>`, as well as `<h1>`, `<h2>`, the other heading-level tags, and the `<div>` tag, among others. The `<div>` tag is especially handy because it can encompass other block-level elements and thus allow you to control the alignment of large portions of your web content all at once. The *div* in the `<div>` tag is for *division*.

Listing 5.1 demonstrates the `style` attribute and `text-align` style rule with different block-level elements. Figure 5.1 displays the results.

LISTING 5.1   The `text-align` Style Rule Used with the `style` Attribute

```
<!DOCTYPE html>

<html lang="en">
  <head>
    <title>Bohemia</title>
  </head>

  <body>
    <section style="text-align:center">

    <header>
      <h1>Bohemia</h1>
      <h2>by Dorothy Parker</h2>
    </header>
    </section>
    <section>
      <p style="text-align:left">
      Authors and actors and artists and such<br />
      Never know nothing, and never know much.<br />
      Sculptors and singers and those of their kidney<br />
      Tell their affairs from Seattle to Sydney.
      </p>
      <p style="text-align:center">
      Playwrights and poets and such horses' necks<br />
      Start off from anywhere, end up at sex.<br />
      Diarists, critics, and similar roe<br />
      Never say nothing, and never say no.
      </p>
      <p style="text-align:right">
      People Who Do Things exceed my endurance;<br />
      God, for a man that solicits insurance!
      </p>
    </section>
  </body>
</html>
```

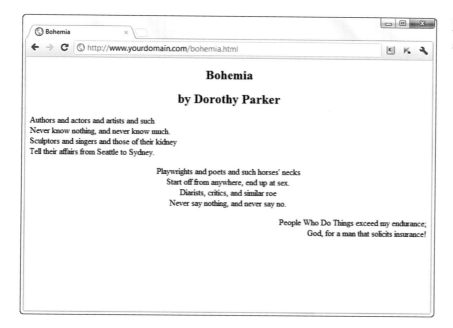

FIGURE 5.1
The results of using the text alignment in Listing 5.1.

The use of `<section style="text-align:center">` ensures that the content area, including the two headings, are centered. However, the inline styles applied to the individual paragraphs within the `<section>` override the setting and ensure that the text of the first paragraph is left-aligned, the second paragraph is centered, and the third paragraph is right-aligned.

The Three Types of HTML Lists

For clarity, it's often useful to present information on a web page as a list of items. Three basic types of HTML lists are offered. Figure 5.2 shows all three, and Listing 5.2 reveals the HTML used to construct them:

▶ **Ordered list**—An indented list that has numbers or letters before each list item. The ordered list begins with the `<ol>` tag and ends with a closing `</ol>` tag. List items are enclosed in the `<li></li>` tag pair, and line breaks appear automatically at each opening `<li>` tag. The entire list is indented.

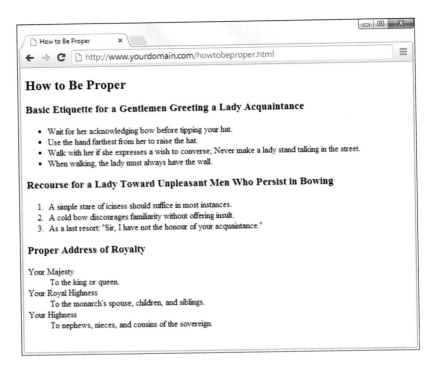

- ▶ **Unordered list**—An indented list that has a bullet or other symbol before each list item. The unordered list begins with the `<ul>` tag and closes with `</ul>`. As with the ordered list, its list items are enclosed in the `<li></li>` tag pair. A line break and symbol appear at each opening `<li>` tag, and the entire list is indented.

- ▶ **Definition list**—A list of terms and their meanings. This type of list, which has no special number, letter, or symbol before each item, begins with `<dl>` and ends with `</dl>`. The `<dt></dt>` tag pair encloses each term, and the `<dd></dd>` tag pair encloses each definition. Line breaks and indentations appear automatically.

LISTING 5.2   Unordered Lists, Ordered Lists, and Definition Lists

```
<!DOCTYPE html>

<html lang="en">
  <head>
    <title>How to Be Proper</title>
  </head>

  <body>
```

```
        <article>

        <header>
            <h1>How to Be Proper</h1>
        </header>
        <section>
            <header>
            <h1>Basic Etiquette for a Gentlemen Greeting a Lady
            Acquaintance</h1>
            </header>
            <ul>
            <li>Wait for her acknowledging bow before tipping your hat.</li>
            <li>Use the hand farthest from her to raise the hat.</li>
            <li>Walk with her if she expresses a wish to converse; Never
            make a lady stand talking in the street.</li>
            <li>When walking, the lady must always have the wall.</li>
            </ul>
        </section>

        <section>
            <header>
            <h1>Recourse for a Lady Toward Unpleasant Men Who Persist in
            Bowing</h1>
            </header>
            <ol>
            <li>A simple stare of iciness should suffice in most
            instances.</li>
            <li>A cold bow discourages familiarity without offering
            insult.</li>
            <li>As a last resort: "Sir, I have not the honour of your
            acquaintance."</li>
            </ol>
        </section>

        <section>
            <header>
            <h1>Proper Address of Royalty</h1>
            </header>

            <dl>
            <dt>Your Majesty</dt>
            <dd>To the king or queen.</dd>
            <dt>Your Royal Highness</dt>
            <dd>To the monarch's spouse, children, and siblings.</dd>
            <dt>Your Highness</dt>
            <dd>To nephews, nieces, and cousins of the sovereign.</dd>
            </dl>
        </section>
        </article>
    </body>
</html>
```

Note the use of semantic elements (`<article>`, `<section>`, and `<header>`)
in Listing 5.2 to provide a better sense of the content outline, including

NOTE

Remember that different web browsers can display web content quite differently. The HTML standard doesn't specify exactly how web browsers should format lists, so users with older web browsers might not see exactly the same indentation you see. You can use CSS to gain precise control over list items, which you learn about later in this hour.

TIP

Nesting refers to a tag that appears entirely within another tag. Nested tags are also referred to as child tags of the (parent) tag that contains them. It is a common (but not required) coding practice to indent nested tags so that you can easily see their relationship to the parent tag.

how the chunks of text relate to one another. Each of these elements could have their own styles applied to them, which would provide further visual separation of the elements.

Placing Lists Within Lists

Although definition lists are officially supposed to be used for defining terms, many web page authors use them anywhere they'd like to see some indentation. In practice, you can indent any text simply by putting <dl><dd> at the beginning of it and </dd></dl> at the end, and skipping over the <dt></dt> tag pair.

Because of the level of control over the display of your items that you have when using CSS, there is no need to use *nested* lists to achieve the visual appearance of indentation. Reserve your use of nested lists for when the content warrants it. In other words, use nested lists to show a hierarchy of information, such as in Listing 5.3.

Ordered and unordered lists can be nested inside one another, down to as many levels as you want. In Listing 5.3, a complex indented outline is constructed from several unordered lists. Notice in Figure 5.3 that the web browser automatically uses a different type of bullet for each of the first three levels of indentation, making the list very easy to read. This is common in modern browsers.

LISTING 5.3   Using Lists to Build Outlines

```
<!DOCTYPE html>

<html lang="en">
  <head>
    <title>Vertebrates</title>
  </head>

  <body>
    <section>

      <header>
      <h1>Vertebrates</h1>
      </header>

      <ul>
        <li><strong>Fish</strong>
          <ul>
            <li>Barramundi</li>
            <li>Kissing Gourami</li>
            <li>Mummichog</li>
          </ul>
```

```
      </li>
      <li><strong>Amphibians</strong>
        <ul>
          <li>Anura
            <ul>
              <li>Goliath Frog</li>
              <li>Poison Dart Frog</li>
              <li>Purple Frog</li>
            </ul>
          </li>
          <li>Caudata
            <ul>
              <li>Hellbender</li>
              <li>Mudpuppy</li>
            </ul>
          </li>
        </ul>
      </li>
      <li><strong>Reptiles</strong>
        <ul>
          <li>Nile Crocodile</li>
          <li>King Cobra</li>
          <li>Common Snapping Turtle</li>
        </ul>
      </li>
    </ul>
  </body>
</html>
```

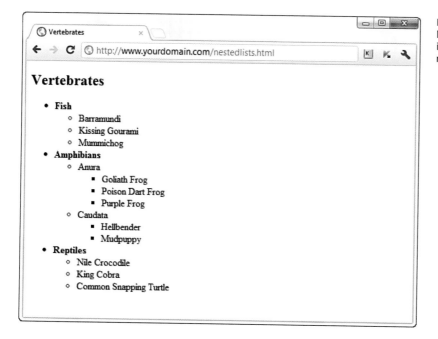

FIGURE 5.3
Multilevel unordered lists are neatly indented and bulleted for improved readability.

As Figure 5.3 shows, a web browser normally uses a solid disc for the first-level bullet, a hollow circle for the second-level bullet, and a solid square for all deeper levels. However, you can explicitly choose which type of bullet to use for any level by using `<ul style="list-style-type:disc">`, `<ul style="list-style-type:circle">`, or `<ul style="list-style-type:square">` instead of `<ul>`, either inline or in a specific style sheet.

You can even change the bullet for any single point within an unordered list by using the `list-style-type` style rule in the `<li>` tag. For example, the following codes displays a hollow circle in front of the words extra and super, and a solid square in front of the word special:

```
<ul style="list-style-type:circle">
  <li>extra</li>
  <li>super</li>
  <li style="list-style-type:square">special</li>
</ul>
```

The `list-style-type` style rule also works with ordered lists, but instead of choosing a type of bullet, you choose the type of numbers or letters to place in front of each item. Listing 5.4 shows how to use Roman numerals (`list-style-type:upper-roman`), capital letters (`list-style-type:upper-alpha`), lowercase letters (`list-style-type:lower-alpha`), and ordinary numbers in a multilevel list. Figure 5.4 shows the resulting outline, which is nicely formatted.

Although Listing 5.4 uses the `list-style-type` style rule only with the `<ol>` tag, you can also use it for specific `<li>` tags within a list (though it's hard to imagine a situation when you would want to do this). You can also explicitly specify ordinary numbering with `list-style-type:decimal`, and you can make lowercase Roman numerals with `list-style-type:lower-roman`.

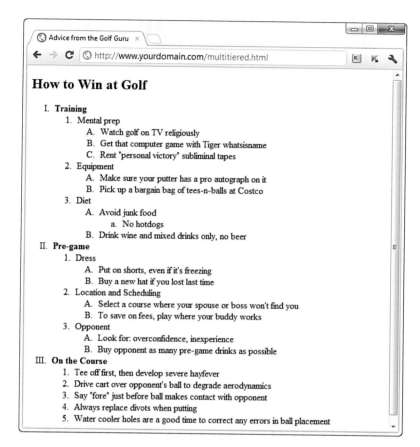

LISTING 5.4   Using the `list-style-type` Style Rule with the `style` Attribute in Multitiered Lists

```
<!DOCTYPE html>

<html lang="en">
  <head>
    <title>Advice from the Golf Guru</title>
  </head>

  <body>
    <article>

    <header>
    <h1>How to Win at Golf</h1>
    </header>

    <ol style="list-style-type:upper-roman">
      <li><strong>Training</strong>
        <ol>
```

```
    <li>Mental prep
      <ol style="list-style-type:upper-alpha">
        <li>Watch golf on TV religiously</li>
        <li>Get that computer game with Tiger whatsisname</li>
        <li>Rent "personal victory" subliminal tapes</li>
      </ol>
    </li>
    <li>Equipment
      <ol style="list-style-type:upper-alpha">
        <li>Make sure your putter has a pro autograph on it</li>
        <li>Pick up a bargain bag of tees-n-balls at Costco</li>
      </ol>
    </li>
    <li>Diet
      <ol style="list-style-type:upper-alpha">
        <li>Avoid junk food
          <ol style="list-style-type:lower-alpha">
            <li>No hotdogs</li>
          </ol>
        </li>
        <li>Drink  wine and mixed drinks only, no beer</li>
      </ol>
    </li>
  </ol>
</li>
<li><strong>Pre-game</strong>
  <ol>
    <li>Dress
      <ol style="list-style-type:upper-alpha">
        <li>Put on shorts, even if it's freezing</li>
        <li>Buy a new hat if you lost last time</li>
      </ol>
    </li>
    <li>Location and Scheduling
      <ol style="list-style-type:upper-alpha">
        <li>Select a course where your spouse or boss won't find
        you</li>
        <li>To save on fees, play where your buddy works</li>
      </ol>
    </li>
    <li>Opponent
      <ol style="list-style-type:upper-alpha">
        <li>Look for: overconfidence, inexperience</li>
        <li>Buy opponent as many pre-game drinks as possible</li>
      </ol>
    </li>
  </ol>
</li>
<li><strong>On the Course</strong>
  <ol>
    <li>Tee off first, then develop severe hayfever</li>
    <li>Drive cart over opponent's ball to degrade aerodynamics</li>
    <li>Say "fore" just before ball makes contact with opponent</li>
    <li>Always replace divots when putting</li>
```

```
      <li>Water cooler holes are a good time to correct any errors in
      ball placement</li>
    </ol>
  </li>
</ol>
</article>
</body>
</html>
```

Summary

In this hour, you learned that attributes are used to specify options and special behavior of many HTML tags. You learned to use the `style` attribute with CSS style rules to align text. You also learned how to create and combine three basic types of HTML lists: ordered lists, unordered lists, and definition lists. Lists can be placed within other lists to create outlines and other complex arrangements of text.

Table 5.1 summarizes the tags and attributes discussed in this hour. Don't feel like you have to memorize all these tags—great references are available for both HTML and CSS, such as the guides at the Mozilla Developer Network. See https://developer.mozilla.org/en-US/docs/Web/HTML/Element and https://developer.mozilla.org/en-US/docs/Web/CSS for guides to HTML and CSS, respectively.

TABLE 5.1   HTML Tags and Attributes Covered in Hour 5

Tag/Attribute	Function
`<div>...</div>`	A region of text to be formatted.
`<dl>...</dl>`	A definition list.
`<dt>...</dt>`	A definition term, as part of a definition list.
`<dd>...</dd>`	The corresponding definition to a definition term, as part of a definition list.
`<ol>...</ol>`	An ordered (numbered) list.
`<ul>...</ul>`	An unordered (bulleted) list.
`<li>...</li>`	A list item for use with `<ol>` or `<ul>`.

Attributes

`style="text-align:alignment"`	Align text to `center`, `left`, or `right`. (Can be used with `<section>`, `<article>`, `<p>`, `<h1>`, `<h2>`, `<h3>`, and so on.)
`style="list-style-type:numtype"`	The type of numerals used to label the list. Some common values are `decimal`, `lower-roman`, `upper-roman`, `lower-alpha`, `upper-alpha`, and `none`.
`style="list-style-type:bullettype"`	The bullet dingbat used to mark list items. Some possible values are `disc`, `circle`, `square`, and `none`.

Q&A

Q. I've seen web pages that use three-dimensional little balls or other special graphics for bullets. How do they do that?

A. That trick is a little bit beyond what this hour covers. You'll learn how to do it yourself in Hour 11, "Using Images in Your Website."

Q. How do I "full-justify" text so that both the left and right margins are flush?

A. You can use `text-align:justify` in your style declaration.

Workshop

The Workshop contains quiz questions and activities to help you solidify your understanding of the material covered. Try to answer all questions before looking at the "Answers" section that follows.

Quiz

1. How would you center all of the text on an entire page?

2. How would you indent a single word and put a square bullet in front of it?

3. What would you use to create a definition list to show that the word *glunch* means "a look of disdain, anger, or displeasure" and that the word *glumpy* means "sullen, morose, or sulky"?

Answers

1. If you thought about putting a `<div>` styled with `"text-align:center"` immediately after the `<body>` tag at the top of the page, and `</div>` just before the `</body>` tag at the end of the page, that is one correct answer. However, the `text-align` style is also supported directly by the `<body>` tag, which means you can forgo the `<div>` tag or other container elements, and apply `text-align:center` directly to the `<body>` tag either inline or in a style sheet. Presto, the entire page is centered!

2. You use this code:

```
<ul style="list-style-type:square">
  <li>supercalifragilisticexpealidocious</li>
</ul>
```

(Putting `style="list-style-type:square"` in the `<li>` tag, or defining either in the style sheet, gives the same result because there's only one item in this list.)

3. You use this code:

```
<dl>
<dt>glunch</dt><dd>a look of disdain, anger, or displeasure</dd>
<dt>glumpy</dt><dd>sullen, morose, or sulky</dd>
</dl>
```

Exercises

▶ Use the text alignment style attributes to place blocks of text in various places on your web page. Try nesting your paragraphs and divisions (`<p>` and `<div>`) to get a feel for how styles do or do not cascade through the content hierarchy.

▶ Try producing an ordered list outlining the information you want to put on your web pages. This gives you practice formatting HTML lists and also gives you a head start on thinking about the issues covered in later hours of this book.

HOUR 6
Working with Fonts

In the early days of the web, text was displayed in only one font and one size, but those days are long gone. A combination of HTML and CSS makes it possible to control all aspects of the appearance of text. In this hour, you learn how to change the visual display of the font—its font family, size, and weight—and how to incorporate boldface, italics, superscripts, subscripts, and strikethrough text into your pages. You also learn how to change typefaces and font sizes.

WHAT YOU'LL LEARN IN THIS HOUR:

▶ How to use special characters
▶ How to use boldface, italics, and special text formatting
▶ How to use text effects
▶ How to tweak the font
▶ How to use web fonts

▼ TRY IT YOURSELF

Preparing Sample Text

You can make the most of learning how to style text throughout this hour if you have some sample text that you can use to display different fonts and colors and that you can indent, center, or otherwise manipulate. It doesn't really matter what type of text you use because you have so many different stylistic possibilities to try that they would never appear all on the same web page anyway (unless you wanted to drive your visitors batty). Take this opportunity just to get a feel for how text-level changes can affect the appearance of your content.

- If the text you'll be using is from a word processing or database program, be sure to save it to a new file in plain-text or ASCII format. You can then add the appropriate HTML tags and style attributes to format it as you go through this lesson.

- Any text will do, but try to find (or type) some text you want to put onto a web page. The text from a company brochure or from your résumé might be a good choice.

- Any type of outline, bullet points from a presentation, numbered steps, a glossary, or a list of textual information from a database also makes good material to work with.

- Before you use the code introduced in this hour to format the body text, add the set of skeleton HTML tags you used in previous hours (at least the `<html>`, `<head>`, `<title>`, and `<body>` tags).

NOTE

When viewing other designers' web content, you might notice methods of marking up text that are different than those this book teaches. Some telltale signs of the old way of formatting text include the use of the `<b></b>` tag pair to indicate when a word should be bolded, the `<i></i>` tag pair to indicate when a word should be in italics, and the `<font></font>` tag pair to specify font family, size, and other attributes. However, this method is being phased out of HTML, and CSS is considerably more powerful.

Working with Special Characters

Before we rush headlong into font changes, let's talk for a minute about special characters within fonts. Most fonts include special characters for European languages, such as the accented é in *Café*. You'll also find a few mathematical symbols and special punctuation marks, such as the circular • bullet.

You can insert these special characters at any point in an HTML document using the appropriate codes in Table 6.1. You'll find an even more extensive list of codes for multiple character sets at http://www.webstandards.org/learn/reference/named_entities.html.

For example, you can produce the word *café* using either of the following methods:

```
caf&eacute;
caf&#233;
```

TABLE 6.1 Commonly Used English Language Special Characters

Character	Numeric Code	Code Name	Description
" "	&#34;	&quot;	Quotation mark
&	&#38;	&amp;	Ampersand
<	&#60;	&lt;	Less than
>	&#62;	&gt;	Greater than
¢	&#162;	&cent;	Cents sign
£	&#163;	&pound;	Pound sterling
¦	&#166;	¦ or &brkbar;	Broken vertical bar
§	&#167;	&sect;	Section sign
©	&#169;	&copy;	Copyright
®	&#174;	&reg;	Registered trademark
°	&#176;	&deg;	Degree sign
±	&#177;	&plusmn;	Plus or minus
²	&#178;	&sup2;	Superscript two
³	&#179;	&sup3;	Superscript three
·	&#183;	&middot;	Middle dot
¹	&#185;	&sup1;	Superscript one
¼	&#188;	&frac14;	Fraction one-fourth
½	&#189;	&frac12;	Fraction one-half
¾	&#190;	&frac34;	Fraction three-fourths
Æ	&#198;	&AElig;	Capital AE ligature
æ	&#230;	&aelig;	Small ae ligature
É	&#201;	&Eacute;	Accented capital E
é	&#233;	&eacute;	Accented lowercase e
×	&#215;	&times;	Multiplication sign
÷	&#247;	&divide;	Division sign

Although you can specify character entities by number, each symbol also has a mnemonic name that is often easier to remember.

HTML uses a special code known as a *character entity* to represent special characters such as © and ®. Character entities are always specified starting with & and ending with ;. Table 6.1 lists the most commonly used character entities, although HTML supports many more.

TIP

Looking for the copyright (©) and registered trademark (®) symbols? Those codes are © and ®, respectively.

To create an unregistered trademark (™) symbol, use ™.

Table 6.1 includes codes for the angle brackets, quotation, and ampersand. You must use those codes if you want these symbols to appear on your pages; otherwise, the web browser interprets them as HTML commands.

Listing 6.1 and Figure 6.1 show several of the symbols from Table 6.1 in use.

LISTING 6.1   Special Character Codes

```
<!DOCTYPE html>

<html lang="en">
  <head>
    <title>Punctuation Lines</title>

    <style type="text/css">
    section {
      margin-bottom: 20px;
      }
      </style>

  </head>

  <body>
    <section>
      Q: What should you do when a British banker picks a fight
      with you?<br />
      A: &pound; some &cent;&cent; into him.
    </section>
    <section>
      Q: What do you call it when a judge takes part of a law
      off the books?<br />
      A: &sect; violence.
    </section>
    <section>
      Q: What did the football coach get from the locker room
      vending machine in the middle of the game?<br />
      A: A &frac14; back at &frac12; time.
    </section>
    <section>
      Q: How hot did it get when the police detective interrogated
      the mathematician?<br />
      A: x&sup3;&deg;
    </section>
    <section>
      Q: What does a punctilious plagiarist do?<br />
      A: &copy;
    </section>
  </body>
</html>
```

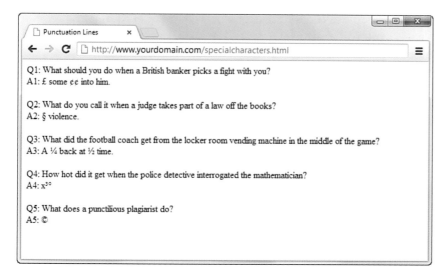

FIGURE 6.1
This is how the HTML page in Listing 6.1 looks in most web browsers.

Boldface, Italics, and Special Text Formatting

Way back in the age of the typewriter, we were content with a plain-text display and with using an occasional underline to show emphasis. Today **boldface** and *italic* text have become de rigueur in all paper communication. Naturally, you can add bold and italic text to your web content as well. Several tags and style rules make text formatting possible.

The old-school approach—discussed briefly here because invariably you will see it in the source code of many websites, if you choose to look—to adding bold and italic formatting to text involves the `<b></b>` and `<i></i>` tag pairs. For boldface text, you wrap the `<b>` and `</b>` tags around your text. Similarly, to make any text appear in italics, you enclose it in `<i>` and `</i>` tags. Although this approach still works fine in browsers, it isn't as flexible or powerful as the CSS style rules for text formatting and should be avoided.

Part III, "Advanced Web Page Design with CSS," covers CSS style rules in more depth, but a little foreshadowing is appropriate here just so that you understand some basic text formatting options. The `font-weight` style rule enables you to set the weight, or boldness, of a font using a style rule. Standard settings for `font-weight` include `normal`, `bold`, `bolder`, and `lighter` (with `normal` being the default). Italic text is

NOTE
Although you want to use styles wherever possible to affect presentation, an alternative to style rules when it comes to bold and italic text involves the `<strong></strong>` and `<em></em>` tag pairs. The `<strong>` tag does the same thing as the `<b>` tag in most browsers, whereas the `<em>` tag acts just like the tag `<i>` by formatting text as italics. Of course, you can style these tags however you'd like, but those are the defaults.

The `<strong>` and `<em>` tags are considered an improvement over `<b>` and `<i>` because they imply only that the text should receive special emphasis; they don't dictate exactly how that effect should be achieved. In other words, a browser doesn't necessarily have to interpret `<strong>` as meaning bold or `<em>` as meaning italic. This makes `<strong>` and `<em>` more fitting in HTML5 because they add meaning to text, along with affecting how the text should be displayed.

controlled via the `font-style` rule, which you can set to `normal`, `italic`, or `oblique`. You can specify style rules together as well if you want to apply more than one, as the following example demonstrates:

```
<p style="font-weight:bold; font-style:italic">This paragraph is bold and
italic!</p>
```

In this example, both style rules are specified in the `style` attribute of the `<p>` tag. The key to using multiple style rules is that they must be separated by a semicolon (`;`).

You aren't limited to using font styles in paragraphs, however. The following code shows how to italicize text in a bulleted list:

```
<ul>
  <li style="font-style:italic">Important Stuff</li>
  <li style="font-style:italic">Critical Information</li>
  <li style="font-style:italic">Highly Sensitive Material</li>
  <li>Nothing All That Useful</li>
</ul>
```

You can also use the `font-weight` style rule within headings, but a heavier font usually doesn't have an effect on headings because they are already bold by default.

Although using CSS enables you to apply rich formatting to text, a few other valid HTML5 tags are good for adding special formatting to text when you don't necessarily need to be as specific as CSS allows you to be. Following are some of these tags; all other text formatting should really be done with CSS. Listing 6.2 and Figure 6.2 demonstrate each tag in action.

- `<sup></sup>`—Superscript text

- `<sub></sub>`—Subscript text

- `<em></em>`—Emphasized (italic) text

- `<strong></strong>`—Strong (boldface) text

- `<pre></pre>`—Preformatted (typically monospaced) text, preserving spaces and line breaks

CAUTION

In the past, a `<u>` tag was useful in creating underlined text, but you don't want to use it now, for a couple reasons. First, users expect underlined text to be a link, so they might get confused if you underline text that isn't a link. Second, the `<u>` tag is *obsolete*, which means that it has been phased out of the HTML language (as has the `<strike>` tag). Both tags are still supported in web browsers and likely will be for quite a while, but using CSS is the preferred approach to creating underlined and strikethrough text.

LISTING 6.2   Special Formatting Tags

```html
<!DOCTYPE html>

<html lang="en">
  <head>
    <title>The Miracle Product</title>
  </head>

  <body>
    <p>
    New <sup>Super</sup><strong>Strength</strong> H<sub>2</sub>O
    <em>plus</em> will knock out any stain.<br/>Look for new
    <sup>Super</sup><strong>Strength</strong> H<sub>2</sub>O <em>plus</em>
    in a stream near you.
    </p>
    <pre>
NUTRITION INFORMATION (void where prohibited)

                Calories   Grams    USRDA
                /Serving   of Fat   Moisture
Regular            3         4        100%
Unleaded           3         2        100%
Organic            2         3         99%
Sugar Free         0         1        110%
    </pre>
  </body>
</html>
```

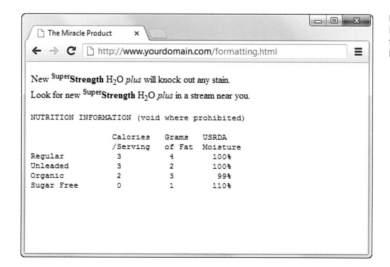

FIGURE 6.2
Here's what the character formatting from Listing 6.2 looks like.

The `<pre>` tag causes text to appear in the monospaced font—and does something else unique and useful. As you learned in Hour 2, "Structuring an HTML Document," multiple spaces and line breaks are normally ignored in HTML files, but `<pre>` causes exact spacing and line breaks to be preserved. For example, without `<pre>`, the text at the end of Figure 6.2 would look like the following:

```
calories grams usrda /serving of fat moisture regular
3 4 100% unleaded 3 2 100% organic 2 3 99% sugar free 0 1 110%
```

Even if you added `<br />` tags at the end of every line, the columns wouldn't line up properly. However, when you put `<pre>` at the beginning and `</pre>` at the end, the columns line up properly because the exact spaces are kept—no `<br />` tags are needed. The `<pre>` tag gives you a quick and easy way to preserve the alignment of any monospaced text files you might want to transfer to a web page, with minimum effort.

CSS provides you with more robust methods for lining up text (and doing anything with text, actually), and you'll learn more about them throughout Part III.

Tweaking the Font

Sometimes you want a bit more control over the size and appearance of your text than just some boldface or italics. Before I get into the appropriate way to tinker with the font using CSS, let's briefly look at how things were done *before* CSS—you might still find examples of this method when you look at the source code for other websites. Remember, just because these older methods are in use doesn't mean you should follow suit.

NOTE

I cannot stress enough that the `<font>` tag is not to be used! It is used here for illustrative and historical purposes only.

Before stylesheets entered the picture, the now-phased-out `<font>` tag was used to control the fonts in web page text.

For example, the following HTML was once used to change the size and color of some text on a page:

```
<font size="5" color="purple">This text will be big and purple.</font>
```

As you can see, the size and color attributes of the `<font>` tag made it possible to alter the font of the text without too much effort. Although this approach worked fine, it was replaced with a far superior approach to font formatting, thanks to CSS style rules. Following are a few of the main style rules used to control fonts:

- `font-family`—Sets the family (typeface) of the font
- `font-size`—Sets the size of the font
- `color`—Sets the color of the font

The `font-family` style rule enables you to set the typeface used to display text. You can (and usually should) specify more than one value for this style (separated by commas) so that if the first font isn't available on a user's system, the browser can try an alternative.

Providing alternative font families is important because each user potentially has a different set of fonts installed, at least beyond a core set of common basic fonts (Arial, Times New Roman, and so forth). By providing a list of alternative fonts, you have a better chance of your pages gracefully falling back on a known font when your ideal font isn't found. Following is an example of the `font-family` style used to set the typeface for a paragraph of text:

```
<p style="font-family:arial, sans-serif, 'times roman'">
```

This example has several interesting parts. First, `arial` is specified as the primary font. Capitalization does not affect the font family, so `arial` is no different than `Arial` or `ARIAL`. Another interesting point about this code is that single quotes are used around the `times roman` font name because it has a space in it. However, because `'times roman'` appears after the generic specification of `sans-serif`, it is unlikely that `'times roman'` would be used. Because `sans-serif` is in the second position, it says to the browser, "If Arial is not on this machine, use the default sans-serif font."

The `font-size` and `color` style rules are also commonly used to control the size and color of fonts. The `font-size` style can be set to a predefined size (such as `small`, `medium`, or `large`), or you can set it to a specific point size (such as `12pt` or `14pt`). The `color` style can be set to a predefined color (such as `white`, `black`, `blue`, `red`, or `green`), or you can set it to a specific hexadecimal color (such as `#ffb499`). Following is a better version of the previous paragraph example, and with the font size and color specified:

```
<p style="font-family:arial, 'times roman', sans-serif; font-size:14pt;
color:green">
```

NOTE

You learn more about controlling the color of the text on your pages in Hour 7, "Working with Colors and Borders." That lesson also shows you how to create your own custom colors and control the color of text links.

NOTE

You'll learn about hexadecimal colors in Hour 7. For now, just understand that the `color` style rule enables you to specify exact colors beyond just using `green`, `blue`, `orange`, and so forth.

The sample web content in Listing 6.3 and shown in Figure 6.3 uses some font style rules to create the beginning of a basic online résumé.

LISTING 6.3   Using Font Style Rules to Create a Basic Résumé

```
<!DOCTYPE html>

<html lang="en">
  <head>
    <title>R&eacute;sum&eacute; for Jane Doe</title>

    <style type="text/css">
      body {
        font-family: Verdana, sans-serif;
        font-size: 12px;
      }

      header {
        text-align: center;
      }

      h1 {
        font-family:Georgia, serif;
        font-size:28px;
        text-align:center;
      }

      p.contactinfo {
        font-size:14px;
      }

      p.categorylabel {
        font-size:12px;
        font-weight:bold;
        text-transform:uppercase;
      }

      div.indented {
        margin-left: 25px;
      }
    </style>
  </head>
  <body>
      <header>
      <h1>Jane Doe</h1>
      <p class="contactinfo">1234 Main Street, Sometown,
      CA 93829<br/>
      tel: 555-555-1212, e-mail: jane@doe.com</p>
      </header>
      <section>
      <p class="categorylabel">Summary of Qualifications</p>
      <ul>
      <li>Highly skilled and dedicated professional offering a
      solid background in whatever it is you need.</li>
```

```
<li>Provide comprehensive direction for whatever it is
that will get me a job.</li>
<li>Computer proficient in a wide range of industry-related
computer programs and equipment. Any industry.</li>
</ul>

</section>
<section>
<p class="categorylabel">Professional Experience</p>
<div class="indented">
        <p><strong>Operations Manager,
        Super Awesome Company, Some City, CA [Sept 2002 -
        present]</strong></p>
        <ul>
        <li>Direct all departmental operations</li>
        <li>Coordinate work with internal and external
        resources</li>
        <li>Generally in charge of everything</li>
        </ul>
        <p><strong>Project Manager,
        Less Awesome Company, Some City, CA [May 2000 - Sept
        2002]</strong></p>
        <ul>
        <li>Direct all departmental operations</li>
        <li>Coordinate work with internal and external
        resources</li>
        <li>Generally in charge of everything</li>
        </ul>
</div>
</section>
<section>
<p class="categorylabel">Education</p>
<ul>
<li>MBA, MyState University, May 2002</li>
<li>B.A, Business Administration, MyState University,
May 2000</li>
</ul>
</section>
<section>
<p class="categorylabel">References</p>
<ul>
<li>Available upon request.</li>
</ul>
</section>
</body>
</html>
```

FIGURE 6.3
Here's what the code used in
Listing 6.3 looks like.

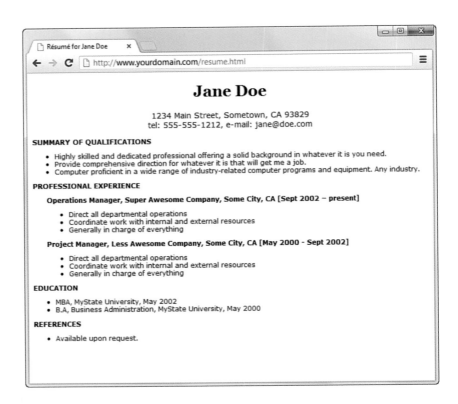

Using CSS, which organizes sets of styles into classes—as you learned in Hour 3, "Understanding Cascading Style Sheets"—you can see how text formatting is applied to different areas of this content. If you look closely at the definition of the `div.indented` class, you will see the use of the `margin-left` style. This style, which you learn more about in Part III, applies a certain amount of space (25 pixels, in this example) to the left of the element. That space accounts for the indentation shown in Figure 6.3.

Using Web Fonts

In the previous section, you saw uses of font families that we're pretty sure reside on everyone's computers. That is, you can be assured that most computers would render Arial or Times New Roman, or have a go-to default font for serif and sans-serif, if that's what your stylesheet calls for. But with the inclusion of the `@font-face` feature in CSS3, you can wield even greater design power over the content you place online.

In brief, the `@font-face` feature enables you to define fonts for use in your HTML5 markup so that they are displayed to users regardless of whether they have those fonts installed on their computer (and chances are incredibly great that users do not have your selected fancy font on their own computer). The definition of the font can be local (to your web server, if you care to include font files there) or remote (you can link to locations where many fonts are stored).

In your stylesheet, to define a new font for use throughout your page(s), you can simply use the following structure:

```
@font-face {
    font-family: 'some_name_goes_here';
    src: url('some_location_of_the_font_file');
}
```

After it's defined, you can refer to the `font-family` as you would anywhere else in your stylesheet, such as here:

```
h1 {
  font-family:some_name_goes_here;
  font-size:28px;
  text-align:center;
}
```

But where do you get fonts, you might ask? You can obtain fonts from many locations—some free, others not. A widely popular location is Google Web Fonts (http://www.google.com/fonts), not only because the fonts are free but because Google is widely recognized as providing a stable platform, which is important if your web typography relies on a font that's sitting on someone else's web server. Some other reliable pay sites for obtaining fonts are TypeKit (www.typekit.com/) and Fontspring (www.fontspring.com). Pay sites aren't necessarily bad—artists have to make money, too; I have a personal TypeKit subscription and am very happy with their service, but I also use Google Web Fonts for many projects.

Let's take a look at modifying the code in Listing 6.3 to include a Google Web Font for the `h1` element. If you go to http://www.google.com/fonts and select a font you like, Google gives you code to include in your HTML and CSS. I've selected a font called Cherry Swash, Google has advised me to include the following in my HTML template, in the `<head>` section:

```
<link href='http://fonts.googleapis.com/css?family=Cherry+Swash:400,700'
    rel='stylesheet' type='text/css' />
```

NOTE

If you look at the previous link location, you can see that it is Google's `@font-face` definition already done for us. Specifically, it says:

```
@font-face {
  font-family: 'Cherry Swash';
  font-style: normal;
  font-weight: 400;
  src: local('Cherry
Swash'), local('CherrySwash-
Regular'), url(http://themes.
googleusercontent.com/
static/fonts/cherryswash/
v1/HqOk7C7J1TZ5i3L-
ejF0vnhCUOGz7vYGh680lGh-uXM.
woff) format('woff');
}
@font-face {
  font-family: 'Cherry Swash';
  font-style: normal;
  font-weight: 700;
  src: local('Cherry Swash
Bold'), local('CherrySwash-
Bold'), url(http://themes.
googleusercontent.com/
static/fonts/cherryswash/v1/-
CfyMyQqfucZPQNB0nvYyH14twXkwp3_
u9ZoePkT564.woff)
format('woff');
}
```

Now that my code knows where to look for the font, we just refer to it:

```
h1 {
  font-family:'Cherry Swash';
  font-size:28px;
  text-align:center;
}
```

Figure 6.4 shows the new résumé with the web font in use.

FIGURE 6.4
The résumé, using Cherry Swash as the font in the heading.

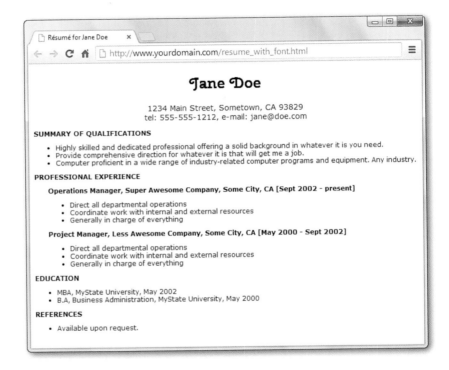

Summary

In this hour, you learned how to make text appear as boldface or italic and how to code superscripts, subscripts, special symbols, and accented letters. You saw how to make the text line up properly in preformatted passages of monospaced text and how to control the size, color, and typeface of any section of text on a web page. You also learned that attributes are used to specify options and special behavior of many HTML tags, and you learned to use the `style` attribute with CSS style rules to affect the appearance of text. Finally, you learned how to work with web fonts to enhance the presentation of your pages.

Table 6.2 summarizes the tags and attributes discussed in this hour.

TABLE 6.2   HTML Tags and Attributes Covered in Hour 6

Tag/Attribute	Function
`<em>...</em>`	Emphasis (usually italic).
`<strong>...</strong>`	Stronger emphasis (usually bold).
`<pre>...</pre>`	Preformatted text (exact line endings and spacing will be preserved—usually rendered in a monospaced font).
`<sub>...</sub>`	Subscript.
`<sup>...</sup>`	Superscript.
Attributes	
`style="font-family:typeface"`	The typeface (family) of the font, which is the name of a font, such as `Arial`. (Can also be used with `<p>`, `<h1>`, `<h2>`, `<h3>`, and so on.)
`style="font-size:size"`	The size of the font, which can be set to `small`, `medium`, `large`, `x-small`, `x-large`, and so on. Can also be set to a specific point size (such as `12pt`).
`style="color:color"`	Changes the color of the text.

Q&A

Q. **How do I find the exact name for a font I have on my computer?**

A. On a Windows computer, open the Control Panel and click the `Fonts` folder—the fonts on your system are listed (Vista users might have to switch to Classic View in the Control Panel). On a Mac, open Font Book in the Applications folder. When specifying fonts in the `font-family` style rule, use the exact spelling of font names. Font names are not case sensitive, however.

Q. **How do I put Kanji, Arabic, Chinese, and other non-European characters on my pages?**

A. First of all, users who need to read these characters on your pages must have the appropriate language fonts installed. They must also have selected that language character set and its associated font for their web browsers. You can use the Character Map program in Windows (or a similar program in other operating systems) to get the numerical codes for each character in any language font. To find Character Map, click Start, All Programs, Accessories, and then System Tools. (On a Mac, open Font Book in the Applications folder.) If the character you want has a code of `214`, use `&#214;` to place it on a web page. If you cannot find the Character Map program, use your operating system's built-in Help function to find the specific location.

The best way to include a short message in an Asian language (such as `We Speak Tamil-Call Us!`) is to include it as a graphics image. That way, every user will see it, even if they use English as their primary language for web browsing. But even to use a language font in a graphic, you will likely have to download a specific language pack for your operating system. Again, check your system's Help function for specific instructions.

Workshop

The Workshop contains quiz questions and activities to help you solidify your understanding of the material covered. Try to answer all questions before looking at the "Answers" section that follows.

Quiz

1. How can you create a paragraph in which the first three words are bold, using styles instead of the `<b>` or `<strong>` tags?

2. How do you represent the chemical formula for water?

3. How do you display © 2013, `Webwonks Inc.` on a web page?

4. How do you center all of the text on an entire page?

Answers

1. You can use this code:

```
<p><span style="font-weight: bold">First three words</span> are
bold.</p>
```

2. You use H`<sub>2</sub>`O.

3. You can use either of the following:

```
&copy; 2013, Webwonks Inc.
&#169; 2013, Webwonks Inc.
```

4. If you thought about putting a `<div style="text-align:center">` or another container element immediately after the `<body>` tag at the top of the page, and using `</div>` just before the `</body>` tag at the end of the page, then you're correct. However, the `text-align` style is also supported directly in the `<body>` tag, which means you can forgo the `<div>` tag and place the `style="text-align:center"` style directly in the `<body>` tag. Presto, the entire page is centered!

Exercises

▶ Apply the font-level style attributes you learned about in this chapter to various block-level elements, such as `<p>`, `<div>`, `<ul>`, and `<li>` items, as well as some of the semantic elements. Try nesting your elements to get a feel for how styles do or do not cascade through the content hierarchy.

▶ Use the text alignment style attributes to place blocks of text in various places on your web page. Try nesting your paragraphs and divisions (`<p>` and `<div>`) to get a feel for how styles do or do not cascade through the content hierarchy.

▶ Go crazy with web fonts—find some via Google Web Fonts and include them in your stylesheets and, ultimately, the layout of the page itself.

HOUR 7
Working with Colors and Borders

Each of these tasks is short and sweet, and will help you move your web development experience from the white background/black text examples so far in this book to more interesting (or at least colorful) examples. But that's not to say that dark text on a light background is bad—in fact, it's the most common color combination you'll find online.

Paying attention to color schemes and producing a visually appealing website is important, but you don't have to be an artist by trade to implement high-impact color schemes in your website, or to put a few appealing flourishes on what otherwise would be a drab, square world. This hour helps you understand the very basics of color theory and how to modify colors using CSS.

Best Practices for Choosing Colors

I can't tell you exactly which colors to use in your website, but I can help you understand certain considerations when selecting those colors on your own. The colors you use can greatly influence your visitors; for example, if you are running an e-commerce site, you want to use colors that entice your users to view your catalog and eventually purchase something. If you are creating a text-heavy site, you want to make sure the color scheme leads to easy-to-read text. Overall, you want to make sure you use colors judiciously and with respect.

You might wonder how respect enters into the mix when talking about colors, but remember that the World Wide Web is an international community and that people's interpretations differ. For instance, pink is very popular in Japan but very unpopular in Eastern European countries. Similarly, green is the color of money in the United States, but the vast majority of other countries have multicolored paper bills—"the color of money" thus isn't a single color at all, so the metaphor would be of no value to international visitors.

Besides using culturally sensitive colors, other best practices include the following:

▶ Use a natural palette of colors. This doesn't mean you should use earth tones, but use colors that you would naturally see on a casual stroll around town—avoid ultrabright colors that can cause eye strain.

▶ Use a small color palette. You don't need to use 15 different colors to achieve your goals. In fact, if your page includes text and images in 15 different colors, you might reevaluate the message you're attempting to send. Focus on three or four main colors, with a few complementary colors at most.

▶ Consider your demographics. You likely can't control your demographics, so you have to find a middle ground that accommodates everyone. The colors younger people enjoy are not necessarily the same ones older people appreciate, just as there are color biases between men and women and people from different geographic regions and cultures.

You might be thinking now that your color options are limited. Not so—you simply need to think about the decisions you're making before you make them. A search for "color theory" in the search engine of your choice should give you more food for thought, as will the use of the color wheel.

The *color wheel* is a chart that shows the organization of colors in a circular manner. Its method of display is an attempt to help you visualize the relationships among primary, secondary, and complementary colors. Color schemes are developed from working with the color wheel; understanding color schemes can help you determine the color palette to use consistently throughout your website. For example, knowing something about color relationships will hopefully enable you to avoid using orange text on a light blue background, or bright blue text on a brown background.

Some common color schemes in web design are as follows:

▶ **Analogous**—Using colors that are adjacent to each other on the color wheel, such as yellow and green. One color is the dominant color, and its analogous friend enriches the display.

▶ **Complementary**—Using colors that are opposite each other on the color wheel, such as a warm color (red) and a cool color (green).

▶ **Triadic**—Using three colors that are equally spaced around the color wheel. The triadic scheme provides balance while still allowing rich color use.

Entire books and courses are devoted to understanding color theory, so continuing the discussion in this book would indeed be a tangent. However, if you intend to work in web design and development, you will be served well with a solid understanding of the basics of color theory. Spend some time reading about it—an online search will provide a wealth of information.

Additionally, spend some hands-on time with the color wheel. The Color Scheme Designer at http://colorschemedesigner.com/ enables you to start with a base color and produce monochromatic, complementary, triadic, tetradic, analogic, and accented analogic color schemes.

Understanding Web Colors

Specifying a background color other than white for a web page is easier than you probably realize. For example, to specify blue as the background color for a page, put `style="background-color:blue"` inside the `<body>` tag or in the stylesheet rule for the body element. Of course, you can use many colors other than blue. In fact, the W3C standards list 17 colors: aqua, black, blue, fuchsia, gray, green, lime, maroon, navy, olive, orange, purple, red, silver, teal, white, and yellow.

Obviously many more than just those 17 colors are displayed on the web—in fact, you can use 140 color names with the assurance that all browsers will display these colors similarly. Here's a partial list of the 140 descriptive color names: azure, bisque, cornflowerblue, darksalmon, firebrick, honeydew, lemonchiffon, papayawhip, peachpuff, saddlebrown, thistle, tomato, wheat, and whitesmoke.

But names are subjective—for instance, if you look at the color chart of 140 cross-browser color names, you'll see that you can't distinguish between fuchsia and magenta. The associated hexadecimal color values for those two terms, fuchsia and magenta, are also exactly the same: `#ff00ff`. You learn about hexadecimal color values in the next

NOTE

For a complete list of the 140 descriptive color names, as well as their hexadecimal codes and an example of the color as displayed by your browser, visit http://www.w3.org/TR/SVG/types.html#ColorKeywords.

section, but for now, know that if you want to be standards compliant and use more than the 16 color names the W3C standards dictate, you need to use the hexadecimal color codes whenever possible.

Hexadecimal color codes make possible 16 million colors, and most modern computer displays can display all of them. However, be aware that not all computer monitors display colors in the same hues. What might appear as a beautiful light blue background color on your monitor might be more of a purple hue on another user's monitor. Neutral, earth-tone colors (such as medium gray, tan, and ivory) can produce even more unpredictable results on many computer monitors. These colors might even seem to change color on a single monitor, depending on lighting conditions in the room or time of day.

In addition to changing the background of your pages to a color other than white, you can change the color of text links, including various properties of links (such as the color for when a user hovers over a link versus when the user clicks a link—as you learned in previous hours). You can also set the background color of container elements (such as paragraphs, divs, blockquotes, and table cells), and you can use colors to specify the borders around those elements. You'll see some examples of colors and container elements later in this lesson.

There are plenty of very bad websites, some created by earnest people with no trace of irony whatsoever. However, The World's Worst Website, in Figure 7.1, was purposefully created to show some of the more egregious sins of website design, especially with its use of colors. A screenshot does not do it justice—visit and experience the site for yourself, at http://www.angelfire.com/super/badwebs/main.htm.

If you search for "bad website examples" in your search engine, you will find many sites that collect examples of bad design and explain just why such a site should be in a Hall of Shame rather than a Hall of Fame. Many sites are considered bad because of their visual displays, and that display begins with color selection. Therefore, understanding colors, as well as the nuances of their specification and use, is a crucial step to creating a good website.

FIGURE 7.1
A partial screenshot of The World's Worst Website.

Using Hexadecimal Values for Colors

To remain standards compliant, as well as to retain precise control over the colors in your website, you can reference colors by their hexadecimal value. The hexadecimal value of a color is an indication of how much red, green, and blue light should be mixed into each color. It works a little bit like Play-Doh—just mix in the amounts of red, blue, and green you want to get the appropriate color.

The hexadecimal color format is #rrggbb, in which rr, gg, and bb are two-digit hexadecimal values for the red (rr), green (gg), and blue (bb) components of the color. If you're not familiar with hexadecimal numbers, don't sweat it. Just remember that ff is the maximum and 00 is the minimum. Use one of the following codes for each component:

- ▶ ff means full brightness.
- ▶ cc means 80% brightness.

- ▶ 99 means 60% brightness.

- ▶ 66 means 40% brightness.

- ▶ 33 means 20% brightness.

- ▶ 00 means none of this color component.

For example, bright red is #ff0000, dark green is #003300, bluish-purple is #660099, and medium-gray is #999999. To make a page with a red background and dark green text, you could use the following HTML code within inline styles:

```
<body style="background-color:#ff0000; color:#003300">
```

Although only 6 examples of two-digit hexadecimal values are shown here, there are actually 225 combinations of two-digit hexadecimal values—0–9 and a–f, paired up. For example, f0 is a possible hex value (decimal value 240), 62 is a possible hex value (decimal value 98), and so on.

As previously discussed, the rr, gg, and bb in the #rrggbb hexadecimal color code format stand for the red, green, and blue components of the color. Each of those components has a decimal value ranging from 0 (no color) to 255 (full color).

So white (or #ffffff) translates to a red value of 255, a green value of 255, and a blue value of 255. Similarly, black (#000000) translates to a red value of 0, a green value of 0, and a blue value of 0. True red is #ff0000 (all red, no green, and no blue), true green is #00ff00 (no red, all green, no blue), and true blue is #0000ff (no red, no green, and all blue). All other hexadecimal notations translate to some variation of the 255 possible values for each of the three colors. The cross-browser compatible color name CornflowerBlue is associated with the hexadecimal notation #6495ed—a red value of 100, a green value of 149, and a blue value of 237 (almost all of the available blue values).

When picking colors, either through a graphics program or by finding something online that you like, you might see the color notion in hexadecimal or decimal. If you type "hexadecimal color converter" into your search engine, you will find numerous options to help you convert color values into something you can use in your stylesheets.

Using CSS to Set Background, Text, and Border Colors

When using CSS, you can use color values in three instances: when specifying the background color, the text color, or the border color of elements. In Hour 8, "Using External and Internal Links," you learn about using colors for various link states, so in this lesson, we focus on basic element display.

Figure 7.2 shows an example of color usage that could very easily go into a web design Hall of Shame. I can't imagine ever using these combinations of colors and styles in a serious website, but it serves here as an example of how color style *could* be applied to various elements. The image printed in this book will likely not do justice to the horrific colors used, so be sure to open the sample file or type up the code in Listing 7.1 and load it in your browser.

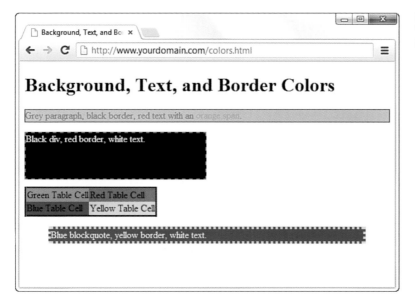

FIGURE 7.2
You can set background, text, and border colors using CSS.

Listing 7.1 shows the HTML and CSS styles used to produce Figure 7.2.

LISTING 7.1   Using Styles to Produce Background, Text, and Border
Colors

```html
<!DOCTYPE html>

<html lang="en">
  <head>
    <title>Background, Text, and Border Colors</title>

    <style type="text/css">
    #uglyparagraph {
       background-color:#cccccc;
       color:#ff0000;
       border:1px solid #000000;
    }
    .orange {
       color:#ffa500
    }
    #uglydiv {
       width:300px;
       height:75px;
       margin-bottom: 12px;
       background-color:#000000;
       border:2px dashed #ff0000;
       color: #ffffff;
    }
    table {
       border-width: 1px solid #000;
       border-spacing: 2px;
       border-style: outset;
       border-collapse: collapse;
    }
    .greencell {
       background-color: #00ff00;
    }
    .redcell {
       background-color: #ff0000;
    }
    .bluecell {
       background-color: #0000ff;
    }
    .yellowcell {
       background-color: #ffff00;
    }
    #uglybq {
       background-color:#0000ff;
       border:4px dotted #ffff00;
       color:#ffffff;
    }
    </style>
  </head>

  <body>
```

```
    <h1>Background, Text, and Border Colors</h1>

    <p id="uglyparagraph">Grey paragraph, black border, red text
    with an <span class="orange">orange span</span>.</p>

    <div id="uglydiv ">Black div, red border, white text. </div>

    <table>
    <tr>
    <td class="greencell">Green Table Cell</td>
    <td class="redcell">Red Table Cell</td>
    </tr>
    <tr>
    <td class="bluecell">Blue Table Cell</td>
    <td class="yellowcell">Yellow Table Cell</td>
    </tr>
    </table>

    <blockquote id="uglybq">
    Blue blockquote,  yellow border, white text.
    </blockquote>
  </body>
</html>
```

Looking at the styles in Listing 7.1, you should be able to figure out almost everything except some of the border styles. In CSS, you can't designate borders as a color without also having a width and type. In the first example in Listing 7.1, for `uglyparagraph`, the border width is `1px` and the border type is `solid`. In the example for `uglydiv`, the border width is `2px` and the border type is `dashed`. In the `uglybq` example, the border width is `4px` and the border type is `dotted`.

When picking colors for your website, remember that a little bit goes a long way—if you really like a bright and spectacular color, use it as an accent color, not throughout the primary design elements. For readability, remember that light backgrounds with dark text are much easier to read than dark backgrounds with light text.

Finally, consider the not-insignificant portion of your audience that might be colorblind. For accessibility, you might consider using the Colorblind Web Page Filter tool at http://colorfilter.wickline.org/ to see how your site looks to a person with colorblindness.

Creating Rounded Corners

The last color-related topic we cover in this hour is creating rounded corners on elements. You might question how making a square corner round is a color-related topic, but if you break it down into its components, making rounded corners is really just about modifying the border of the element and ensuring that the proper colors are showing in the proper areas.

At the most basic level, the CSS `border-radius` property controls rounded corners. Any element that can have a border applied to it can also have the `border-radius` property applied to it. All current versions of popular browsers (including most mobile browsers) support this property.

In brief, the creation of rounded corners is dependent upon the definition of ellipses that then take the place of the previously square corner. Now, if you're like me and you shy away from everything related to geometry, that sounds far too complicated to deal with. But if I show you that this bit of CSS defines the class used with the `<div>` element with rounded corners that you see in Figure 7.3, then things start to look a little brighter:

```
.rounded {
    background-color:#00ff00;
    border-radius: 20px;
    height: 150px;
    width: 150px;
}
```

FIGURE 7.3
Showing a `<div>` element with rounded corners, using `border-radius`.

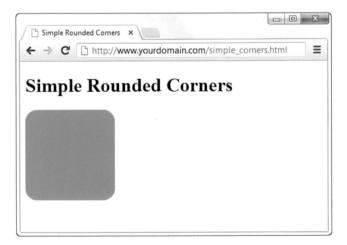

You already know what the `background-color`, `height`, and `width` properties do, so the only new item here is the `border-radius` property—in this case, it has a value of `20px`. The `border-radius` property is a shorthand property, meaning that it refers to several other properties. Much as the `border` property is shorthand for, or combines, the `border-top`, `border-right`, `border-bottom`, and `border-left` properties, so does `border-radius` combine the `border-top-left-radius`, `border-top-right-radius`, `border-bottom-right-radius`, and `border-bottom-left-radius` properties.

That is to say, just like this:

```
border: 5px;
```

is equivalent to:

```
border-top: 5px;
border-right: 5px;
border-bottom: 5px;
border-left: 5px;
```

Then so is this:

```
border-radius: 20px
```

equivalent to:

```
border-top-left-radius: 20px;
border-top-right-radius: 20px;
border-bottom-right-radius: 20px;
border-bottom-left-radius: 20px;
```

Now for the tricky part: What does "20px" actually refer to? In this case, it states that the both the horizontal and vertical radii of the ellipsis that makes up each rounded corner are 20 pixels in length and height, respectively. Figure 7.4 attempts to illustrate this point.

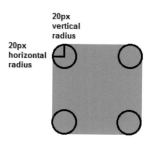

20px vertical radius

20px horizontal radius

FIGURE 7.4
Identifying the radii of the ellipses used to create the rounded corners.

There's a little more shorthand going on here. Because there are two radii for each ellipsis (horizontal and vertical), you can define both of them for each ellipsis. However, if you want them both to be the same, you can use the value once. If you want the radii to be different, use something like this:

```
border-top-left-radius: 20px 10px;
```

The previous example sets a horizontal radius of 20px and a vertical radius of 10px for the top-left corner of the element.

As you might have guessed, not only can the horizontal and vertical radii for a corner have different values, but each corner can have different values as well. In other words, you can go crazy with rounded corners. Figure 7.5 shows some additional examples of rounded corners, as well as the border-radius values that were used to create them.

FIGURE 7.5
Using border-radius to make shapes in CSS.

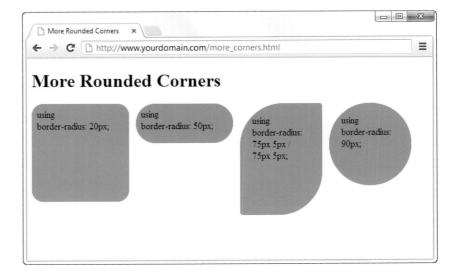

Summary

In this hour, you learned a few best practices for color use, and you learned how to use the color wheel to find colors that will complement your text. Additionally, you learned about hexadecimal notion for colors—all colors are expressed in notations related to the amount of red, green, and blue in them—and saw how hexadecimal notation enables you to apply nuanced colors to your elements. More important, you learned about the three color-related style properties that you can use to apply color to container backgrounds, borders, and text using CSS. Finally, you learned the method for creating rounded corners on elements using nothing but CSS and a little math.

Q&A

Q. Is black text on a white background really the best for reading text online? I find that color combination really hard on my eyes.

A. Black text on a white background is one of the most common color combinations for reading because it is the easiest way to achieve high contrast between the foreground and background colors—and high contrast means better legibility. But the bright glow of a pure white, bright monitor does bother some people, which is why most designers try to adhere to the spirit of the guideline, if not the letter of the law. That is, it is becoming more common to see a slightly off-white background color and a darker gray text color instead of pure white and pure black.

Workshop

The Workshop contains quiz questions and exercises to help you solidify your understanding of the material covered. Try to answer all questions before looking at the "Answers" section that follows.

Quiz

1. How would you give a web page a black background and make all text bright green? Based on what you've learned in this hour, would you even want to use that color combination?

2. What CSS properties and values would you use to ensure that a paragraph had a white background, orange text, and a 3-pixel-wide dashed green border?

3. What value would you use for `border-radius` if you wanted both the horizontal and vertical radii to be the same—say, 45 pixels—for all four corners?

Answers

1. Put the following at the beginning of the web page or use a style rule for the `body` element:

```
<body style="background-color:#000000; color:#00FF00">
```

2. The following properties and values would work:

```
background-color: #ffffff;
color: #ffa500;
border: 3px dashed #00ff00;
```

3. You can use this code:

```
border-radius: 45px;
```

Exercises

▶ Select a base color that you like—perhaps a lovely blue or an earthy tone—and use the Color Scheme Designer at http://colorschemedesigner.com/ to come up with a set of colors that you can use in a website. I recommend the tetrad or accented analogic scheme types.

▶ When you have a set of colors—or a few options for sets of colors—create a basic HTML page with an `<h1>` element, a paragraph of text, and perhaps some list items. Use the color-related styles you learned about in this hour to change the background color of the page and the text of the various block-level elements, to see how these sets of colors might work together. See how they interact, and determine which colors are best used for containers and which are best used for plain text, header text, and link text.

HOUR 8
Using External and Internal Links

So far, you have learned how to use HTML tags to create some basic web pages. However, at this point, those pieces of content are islands unto themselves, with no connection to anything else (although it is true that, in Hour 3, "Understanding Cascading Style Sheets," I sneaked a few page links into the examples). To turn your work into real web content, you need to connect it to the rest of the web—or at least to your other pages within your own personal or corporate sites.

This hour shows you how to create hypertext links to content within your own document and how to link to other external documents. Additionally, you will learn how to style hypertext links so that they display in the color and decoration you desire—not necessarily the default blue underlined display.

Using Web Addresses

The simplest way to store web content for an individual website is to place the files all in the same folder together. When files are stored together like this, you can link to them by simply providing the name of the file in the `href` attribute of the `<a>` tag.

An *attribute* is an extra piece of information associated with a tag that provides further details about the tag. For example, the `href` attribute of the `<a>` tag identifies the address of the page to which you are linking.

When you have more than a few pages, or when you start to have an organization structure to the content in your site, you should put your files into directories (or *folders*, if you will) whose names reflect the content within them. For example, all your images could be in an `images` directory, corporate information could be in an `about` directory,

WHAT YOU'LL LEARN IN THIS HOUR:

► How to use anchor links
► How to link between pages on your own site
► How to link to external content
► How to link to an email address
► How to use window targeting with your links
► How to style your links with CSS

Before we begin, you might want a refresher on the basics of where to put files on your server and how to manage files within a set of directories. This information is important to know when creating links in web content. Refer back to Hour 1, "Understanding How the Web Works," specifically the section titled "Understanding Where to Place Files on the Web Server."

The forward slash (/) is always used to separate directories in HTML. Don't use the backslash (\, which is normally used in Windows) to separate your directories. Remember, everything in the web moves forward, so use forward slashes.

and so on. Regardless of how you organize your documents within your own web server, you can use relative addresses, which include only enough information to find one page from another.

A *relative address* describes the path from one web page to another, instead of a full (or *absolute*) Internet address.

As you recall from Hour 1, the document root of your web server is the directory designated as the top-level directory for your web content. In web addresses, that document root is represented by the forward slash (/). All subsequent levels of directories are separated by the same type of forward slash. For example:

```
/directory/subdirectory/subsubdirectory/
```

Suppose you are creating a page named `zoo.html` in your document root, and you want to include a link to pages named `african.html` and `asian.html` in the `elephants` subdirectory. The links would look like the following:

```
<a href="/elephants/african.html">Learn about African elephants.</a>
<a href="/elephants/asian.html">Learn about Asian elephants.</a>
```

These specific addresses are actually called *relative-root addresses*, in that they are relative addresses that lack the entire domain name, but they are specifically relative to the document root specified by the forward slash.

Using a regular relative address, you can skip the initial forward slash. This type of address allow the links to become relative to whatever directory they are in—it could be the document root, or it could be another directory one or more levels down from the document root:

```
<a href="elephants/african.html">Learn about African elephants.</a>
<a href="elephants/asian.html">Learn about Asian elephants.</a>
```

Your `african.html` and `asian.html` documents in the `elephants` subdirectory could link back to the main `zoo.html` page in either of these ways:

```
<a href="http://www.yourdomain.com/zoo.html">Return to the zoo.</a>
<a href="/zoo.html">Return to the zoo.</a>
<a href="../zoo.html">Return to the zoo.</a>
```

The first link is an absolute link. With an absolute link, there is *absolutely* no doubt where the link should go because the full URL is provided—domain name included.

The second link is a relative-root link. It is relative to the domain you are currently browsing and, therefore, does not require the protocol type (for example, `http://`) or domain name (for example, `www.yourdomain.com`); the initial forward slash is provided to show that the address begins at the document root.

In the third link, the *double dot* (`..`) is a special command that indicates the folder that contains the current folder—in other words, the *parent folder.* Anytime you see the double dot, just think to yourself, "Go up a level" in the directory structure.

If you use relative addressing consistently throughout your web pages, you can move directories of pages to another folder, disk drive, or web server without changing the links.

Relative addresses can span quite complex directory structures, if necessary. Hour 23, "Organizing and Managing a Website," offers more detailed advice for organizing and linking large numbers of web pages.

TIP

The general rule surrounding relative addressing (`elephants/african.html`) versus absolute addressing (`http://www.takeme2thezoo.com/elephants/african.html`) is that you should use relative addressing when linking to files that are stored together, such as files that are all part of the same website. Use absolute addressing when you're linking to files somewhere else—another computer, another disk drive, or, more commonly, another website on the Internet.

TRY IT YOURSELF ▼

Creating a Simple Site Architecture

Hopefully by now you've created a page or two of your own while working through the lessons. Follow these steps to add a few more pages and link them together:

1. Use a home page as a main entrance and as a central hub to which all your other pages are connected. If you created a page about yourself or your business, use that page as your home page. You also might like to create a new page now for this purpose.

2. On the home page, put a list of links to the other HTML files you've created (or placeholders for the HTML files you plan to create soon). Be sure that the exact spelling of the filename, including any capitalization, is correct in every link.

3. On every other page besides the home page, include a link at the bottom (or top) leading back to your home page. That makes navigating around your site simple and easy.

4. You might also want to include a list of links to related or interesting sites, either on your home page or on a separate links page. People often include a list of their friends' personal pages on their own home page. However, businesses should be careful not to lead potential customers away to other sites too quickly—there's no guarantee they'll remember to use relative addressing for links between your own pages and absolute addressing for links to other sites.

Linking Within a Page Using Anchors

The `<a>` tag—the tag responsible for hyperlinks on the web—got its name from the word *anchor*, which means a link serves as a designation for a spot in a web page. In examples throughout this book so far, you've learned how to use the `<a>` tag to link to somewhere else, but that's only half its usefulness. Let's get started working with anchor links that link to content within the same page.

Identifying Locations in a Page with Anchors

The `<a>` tag can be used to mark a spot on a page as an anchor, enabling you to create a link that points to that exact spot. Listing 8.1, presented a bit later in this hour, demonstrates a link to an anchor within a page. To see how such links are made, let's take a quick peek ahead at the first `<a>` tag in the listing:

```
<a id="top"></a>
```

TIP

You can actually use an `id` attribute on many container elements in HTML5, and use the `</a>` tag to point to those elements as anchor links as well.

The `<a>` tag normally uses the `href` attribute to specify a hyperlinked target. The `<a href>` is what you click, and `<a id>` is where you go when you click there. In this example, the `<a>` tag is still specifying a target, but no actual link is created. Instead, the `<a>` tag gives a name to the specific point on the page where the tag occurs. The `</a>` tag must be included, and a unique name must be assigned to the `id` attribute, but no text between `<a>` and `</a>` is necessary.

Linking to Anchor Locations

Listing 8.1 shows a site with various anchor points placed throughout a single page. Take a look at the last `<a>` tag in Listing 8.1 to see an example:

```
<a href="#top">Return to Index.</a>
```

The # symbol means that the word `top` refers to a named anchor point within the current document rather than to a separate page. When a user clicks `Return to Index`, the web browser displays the part of the page starting with the `<a id="top">` tag.

LISTING 8.1   Setting Anchor Points by Using the `<a>` Tag with an `id`
Attribute

```
<!DOCTYPE html>

<html lang="en">
 <head>
  <title>Alphabetical Shakespeare</title>
 </head>

 <body>
   <article>

   <header>
     <h1><a id="top"></a>First Lines of Shakespearean Sonnets</h1>
   </header>

   <p>Don't you just hate when you go a-courting, and you're down
on one knee about to rattle off a totally romantic Shakespearean
sonnet, and zap! You space it. <em>"Um... It was, uh... I think it
started with a B..."</em></p>
   <p>Well, appearest thou no longer the dork. Simply refer to this page,
click on the first letter of the sonnet you want, and get an instant
reminder of the first line to get you started. <em>"Beshrew that
heart that makes my heart to groan..."</em></p>

   <p style="text-align:center"><strong>Alphabetical Index</strong></p>
   <div style="text-align:center">
   <a href="#A">A</a> <a href="#B">B</a> <a href="#C">C</a>
   <a href="#D">D</a> <a href="#E">E</a> <a href="#F">F</a>
   <a href="#G">G</a> <a href="#H">H</a> <a href="#I">I</a>
   <a href="#J">J</a> <a href="#K">K</a> <a href="#L">L</a>
   <a href="#M">M</a> <a href="#N">N</a> <a href="#O">O</a>
   <a href="#P">P</a> <a href="#Q">Q</a> <a href="#R">R</a>
   <a href="#S">S</a> <a href="#T">T</a> <a href="#U">U</a>
   <a href="#V">V</a> <a href="#W">W</a> <a href="#X">X</a>
   <a href="#Y">Y</a> <a href="#Z">Z</a>
   </div>
   <hr />

   <section>

   <header>
     <h1><a id="A"></a>A</h1>
   </header>
   <ul>
   <li>A woman's face with nature's own hand painted,</li>
   <li>Accuse me thus, that I have scanted all, </li>
   <li>Against my love shall be as I am now</li>
   <li>Against that time (if ever that time come) </li>
   <li>Ah wherefore with infection should he live, </li>
   <li>Alack what poverty my muse brings forth, </li>
   <li>Alas 'tis true, I have gone here and there, </li>
   <li>As a decrepit father takes delight, </li>
   <li>As an unperfect actor on the stage, </li>
   <li>As fast as thou shalt wane so fast thou grow'st, </li>
```

```
    </ul>
    <p><a href="#top">Return to Index.</a></p>
    </section>
    <hr />
    <!-- continue with the alphabet -->
    <section>

    <header>
        <h1><a id="Z"></a>Z</h1>
    </header>

    <p>(No sonnets start with Z.)</p>
    <p><a href="#top"><em>Return to Index.</em></a></p>
    </section>

  </article>
  </body>
</html>
```

Each of the `<a href>` links in Listing 8.1 makes an underlined link leading to a corresponding `<a id>` anchor—or it would if I had filled in all the text. Only A and Z will work in this example because only the A and Z links have corresponding text to link to, but feel free to fill in the rest on your own! Clicking the letter Z under Alphabetical Index in Figure 8.1, for example, takes you to the part of the page shown in Figure 8.2.

FIGURE 8.1
The `<a id>` tags in Listing 8.1 don't appear at all on the web page. The `<a href>` tags appear as underlined links.

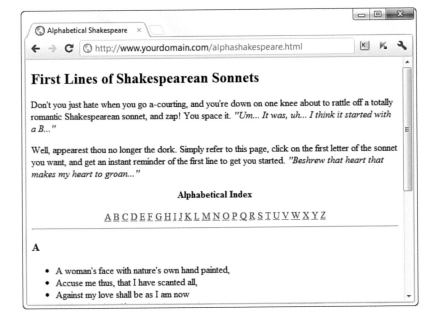

FIGURE 8.2
Clicking the letter Z on the page
shown in Figure 8.1 takes you
to the appropriate section of the
same page.

Having mastered the concept of linking to sections of text within a
single page, you can now learn to link other pieces of web content.

Linking Between Your Own Web Content

As you learned earlier in this hour, you do not need to include `http://`
before each address specified in the `href` attribute when linking to
content within your domain (or on the same computer, if you are
viewing your site locally). When you create a link from one file to
another file within the same domain or on the same computer, you
don't need to specify a complete Internet address. In fact, if the two
files are stored in the same folder, you can simply use the name of the
HTML file by itself:

```
<a href="pagetwo.html">Go to Page 2.</a>
```

As an example, Listing 8.2 and Figure 8.3 show a quiz page with a link
to the answers page shown in Listing 8.3 and Figure 8.4. The answers
page contains a link back to the quiz page. Because the page in Listing
8.2 links to another page in the same directory, the filename can be
used in place of a complete address.

FIGURE 8.3
This is the `historyquiz.html` file listed in Listing 8.2 and referred to by the link in Listing 8.3.

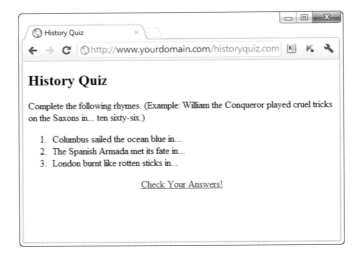

FIGURE 8.4
The `Check Your Answers!` link in Figure 8.3 takes you to this answers page. The `Return to the Questions` link takes you back to what's shown in Figure 8.3.

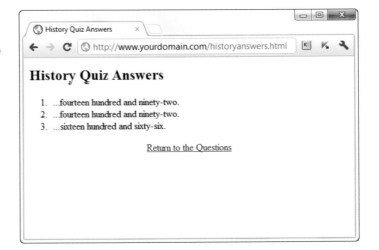

LISTING 8.2   The `historyanswers.html` File

```
<!DOCTYPE html>

<html lang="en">
 <head>
  <title>History Quiz</title>
 </head>

 <body>
  <section>

   <header>
```

```
<h1>History Quiz</h1>
</header>

<p>Complete the following rhymes. (Example: William the Conqueror
Played cruel tricks on the Saxons in... ten sixty-six.)</p>
<ol>
<li>Columbus sailed the ocean blue in...</li>
<li>The Spanish Armada met its fate in...</li>
<li>London burnt like rotten sticks in...</li>
</ol>
<p style="text-align: center;">
<a href="historyanswers.html">Check Your Answers!</a>
</p>

</section>
</body>
</html>
```

LISTING 8.3   The `historyanswers.html` File That `historyquiz.html` Links To

```
<!DOCTYPE html>

<html lang="en">
 <head>
  <title>History Quiz Answers</title>
 </head>

 <body>
  <section>

  <header>
  <h1>History Quiz Answers</h1>
  </header>

  <ol>
  <li>...fourteen hundred and ninety-two.</li>
  <li>...fifteen hundred and eighty eight.</li>
  <li>...sixteen hundred and sixty-six.</li>
  </ol>
  <p style="text-align: center;">
  <a href="historyquiz.html">Return to the Questions</a>
  </p>
  </section>
 </body>
</html>
```

Using filenames instead of complete Internet addresses saves you a lot of typing. More important, the links between your pages will work properly no matter where the group of pages is stored. You can test

NOTE

In both Listings 8.2 and 8.3, you'll see the use of the `<section></section>` tag pair around the bulk of the content. You might wonder whether that is entirely necessary—after all, it is the only content on the page. The answer is, no, it isn't entirely necessary. The HTML would validate just fine, and no one looking at this code would be confused by its organization if the `<section></section>` tags were not present. They are used here just to make sure you get used to seeing them throughout these code examples, and to allow me to write this note about how you *might* use the `<section></section>` tags at some point in the future.

For example, if you were to put both the questions section and the answers section on one page, and apply the use of styles and a little bit of JavaScript-based interactivity, you could hide one section (the questions) until the reader clicked a link that would then show the other section (the answers). This action is beyond the scope of the book, but it is an example of how the simplest bit of markup can set you up for bigger things later.

the links while the files are still on your computer's hard drive. You can then move them to a web server, a CD-ROM, a DVD, or a memory card, and all the links will still work correctly. There is nothing magic about this simplified approach to identifying web pages—it all has to do with web page addressing, as you've already learned.

Linking to External Web Content

The only difference between linking to pages within your own site and linking to external web content is that, when linking outside your site, you need to include the full address to that bit of content. The full address includes the `http://` before the domain name and then the full pathname to the file (for example, an HTML file, image file, multimedia file, and so on).

For example, to include a link to Google from within one of your own web pages, you would use this type of absolute addressing in your `<a>` link:

```
<a href="http://www.google.com/">Go to Google</a>
```

You can apply what you learned in previous sections to creating links to named anchors on other pages. Linked anchors are not limited to the same page. You can link to a named anchor on another page by including the address or filename followed by # and the anchor name. For example, the following link would take you to an anchor named `photos` within the african.html page inside the `elephants` directory on the (fictional) domain www.takeme2thezoo.com.

```
<a href="http://www.takeme2thezoo.com/elephants/african.html#photos">
Check out the African Elephant Photos!</a>
```

If you are linking from another page already on the www.takeme2thezoo.com domain (because you are, in fact, the site maintainer), your link might simply be as follows:

```
<a href="/elephants/african.html#photos">Check out the
African Elephant Photos!</a>
```

The `http://` and the domain name would not be necessary in that instance, as you have already learned.

CAUTION

As you might know, you can leave out the `http://` at the front of any address when typing it into most web browsers. However, you *cannot* leave that part out when you type an Internet address into an `<a href>` link on a web page.

CAUTION

Be sure to include the # symbol only in `<a href>` link tags. Don't put the # symbol in the `<a id>` tag; links to that name won't work in that case.

Linking to an Email Address

In addition to linking between pages and between parts of a single page, the `<a>` tag allows you to link to email addresses. This is the simplest way to enable your web page visitors to talk back to you. Of course, you could just provide visitors with your email address and trust them to type it into whatever email programs they use, but that increases the likelihood for errors. By providing a clickable link to your email address, you make it almost completely effortless for them to send you messages and eliminate the chance for typos.

An HTML link to an email address looks like the following:

```
<a href="mailto:yourusername@yourdomain.com">Send me an
email message.</a>
```

The words `Send me an email message` will appear just like any other `<a>` link.

If you want people to see your actual email address (so that they can make note of it or send a message using a different email program), include it both in the `href` attribute and as part of the message between the `<a>` and `</a>` tags, like this:

```
<a href="mailto:you@yourdomain.com">you@yourdomain.com</a>
```

In most web browsers, when a user clicks the link, that person gets a window into which he or she can type a message that is immediately sent to you—the email program the person uses to send and receive email will automatically be used. You can provide some additional information in the link so that the subject and body of the message also have default values. You do this by adding `subject` and `body` variables to the `mailto` link. You separate the variables from the email address with a question mark (?), separate the value from the variable with an equals sign (=), and then separate each of the variable and value pairs with an ampersand (&). You don't have to understand the variable/value terminology at this point. Here is an example of specifying a subject and body for the preceding email example:

```
<a href="mailto:author@somedomain.com?subject=Book Question&body=
When is the next edition coming out?">author@somedomain.com</a>
```

When a user clicks this link, an email message is created with `author@somedomain.com` as the recipient, `Book Question` as the subject of the message, and `When is the next edition coming out?` as the message body.

TIP

If you want to specify only an email message subject and not the body, you can just leave off the ampersand and the `body` variable, equals sign, and value text string, as follows:

```
<a href="mailto:author@
somedomain.com?subject=
Book Question">author@
somedomain.com</a>
```

Before you run off and start plastering your email address all over your web pages, I have to give you a little warning and then let you in on a handy trick. You're no doubt familiar with spammers that build up databases of email addresses and then bombard them with junk mail advertisements. One way spammers harvest email addresses is using programs that automatically search web pages for `mailto` links.

Fortunately, a little trick will thwart many (but not all) spammers. This trick involves using character entities to encode your email address, which confuses scraper programs that attempt to harvest your email address from your web pages. As an example, consider the email address `jcmeloni@gmail.com`. If you replace the letters in the address with their character entity equivalents, some email harvesting programs will be thrown off. Lowercase ASCII character entities begin at `&#97;` for the letter *a* and increase through the alphabet in order. For example, the letter *j* is `&#106`, *c* is `&#99`, and so on. Replacing all the characters with their ASCII attributes produces the following:

```
<a href="mailto:&#106;&#099;&#109;&#101;&#108;&#111;&#110;&#105;
&#064;&#103;&#109;&#097;&#105;&#108;&#046;&#099;&#111;&#109;">Send
me an email message.</a>
```

Because the browser interprets the character encoding as, well, characters, the end result is the same from the browser's perspective. However, automated email harvesting programs search the raw HTML code for pages, which, in this case, is showing a fairly jumbled-looking email address. If you don't want to figure out the character encoding for your own address, just type "email address encoder" into your search engine, and you will find some services online that will produce an encoded string for you.

Opening a Link in a New Browser Window

Now that you have a handle on how to create addresses for links—both internal (within your site) and external (to other sites)—there is one additional method of linking: forcing the user to open links in new windows.

You've no doubt heard of *pop-up windows*, which are browser windows—typically advertising products or services—that are intended to be opened and displayed automatically without the user's approval (many modern browsers disallow this behavior). However, the concept of opening another window or targeting another location serves a valid purpose in some instances. For example, you might want to present information in a smaller secondary browser window but still allow the user to see the information in the main window. This is often the case when clicking on a link to an animated demo, movie clip, or other multimedia element. You might also want to target a new browser window when you are linking to content off-site.

The word *target* is important because that is the name of the attribute used with the `<a>` tag. The `target` attribute points to a valid browsing context, or "new window to open."

A valid HTML link that opens in a new window is constructed like so:

```
<a href="/some/file.html" target="_blank">Open a Window!</a>
```

Remember, opening a new browser window on behalf of your user—especially when it's a full-size new window—goes against some principles of usability and accessibility, so be considerate if and when you do it.

Using CSS to Style Hyperlinks

The default display of a text-based hyperlink on a web page is underlined blue text. You might also have noticed that links you have previously visited appear as underlined purple text—that color is also a default. If you've spent any time at all on the web, you will also have noticed that not all links are blue or purple—and for that, I think, we are all thankful. Using a little CSS and knowledge of the various pseudoclasses for the `<a>` link, you can make your links look however you want.

A *pseudoclass* is a class that describes styles for elements that apply to certain circumstances, such as various states of user interaction with that element.

For example, the common pseudoclasses for the `<a>` tag are `link`, `visited`, `hover`, and `active`. You can remember them with the mnemonic "Love–Hate"—LV (love) HA (hate), if you choose.

▶ `a:link` describes the style of a hyperlink that has not been visited previously.

NOTE

You can use graphics as links (instead of using text as links) by putting an `<img />` tag between the opening `<a>` and closing `</a>` tags.

▶ `a:visited` describes the style of a hyperlink that has been visited previously and is present in the browser's memory.

▶ `a:hover` describes the style of a hyperlink as a user's mouse hovers over it (and before it has been clicked).

▶ `a:active` describes the style of a hyperlink that is in the act of being clicked but has not yet been released.

For example, let's say you want to produce a link with the following styles:

▶ A font that is bold and Verdana (and not underlined, meaning it has no text decoration)

▶ A base color that is light blue

▶ A color of red when users hover over it or when they are clicking it

▶ A color of gray after users have visited it

Your stylesheet entries might look like the following:

```
a {
    font-family: Verdana, sans-serif;
    font-weight: bold;
    text-decoration: none;
}
a:link {
    color: #6479A0;
}
a:visited {
    color: #CCCCCC;
}
a:hover {
    color: #E03A3E;
}
a:active {
    color: #E03A3E;
}
```

Because the sample link will be Verdana bold (and not underlined) regardless of the state it is in, those three property and value pairs can reside in the rule for the `a` selector. However, because each pseudoclass must have a specific color associated with it, we use a rule for each pseudoclass, as shown in the code example. The pseudoclass inherits the style of the parent rule, unless the rule for the pseudoclass specifically overrides that rule. In other words, all the pseudoclasses in the previous example will be Verdana bold (and not underlined). However, if we had used the following rule for the `hover` pseudoclass, the text would display in Comic Sans when users hovered over it (if, in fact, the user has the Comic Sans font installed):

```
a:hover {
   font-family: "Comic Sans MS";
   color: #E03A3E;
}
```

Additionally, because the `active` and `hover` pseudoclasses use the same font color, you can combine style rules for them:

```
a:hover, a:active {
   color: #E03A3E;
}
```

Listing 8.4 puts these code snippets together to produce a page using styled pseudoclasses; Figure 8.5 shows the results of this code.

FIGURE 8.5
A link can use particular styles to control the visual display.

LISTING 8.4   Using Styles to Display Link Pseudoclasses

```
<!DOCTYPE html>

<html lang="en">
 <head>
  <title>Sample Link Style</title>

  <style type="text/css">
   a {
    font-family: Verdana, sans-serif;
    font-weight: bold;
    text-decoration: none;
   }
   a:link {
    color: #6479A0;
```

```
    }
    a:visited {
     color: #CCCCCC;
    }
    a:hover, a:active {
     color: #FF0000;
    }
   </style>
  </head>
  <body>
     <h1>Sample Link Style</h1>
     <p><a href="simplelinkstyle.html">The first time you see me,
     I should be a light blue, bold, non-underlined link in
     the Verdana font</a>.</p>
  </body>
</html>
```

If you view the example in your web browser, indeed the link should be a light blue, bold, nonunderlined Verdana font. If you hover over the link, or click the link without releasing it, it should turn red. If you click and release the link, the page will simply reload because the link points to the file with the same name. However, at that point, the link will be in your browser's memory and thus will be displayed as a visited link—and it will appear gray instead of blue.

You can use CSS to apply a wide range of text-related changes to your links. You can change fonts, sizes, weights, decoration, and so on. Sometimes you might want several different sets of link styles in your stylesheet. In that case, you can create classes; you aren't limited to working with only one set of styles for the `<a>` tag. The following example is a set of stylesheet rules for a `footerlink` class for links I might want to place in the footer area of my website:

```
a.footerlink {
    font-family: Verdana, sans-serif;
    font-weight: bold;
    font-size: 75%;
    text-decoration: none;
}
a.footerlink:link, a.footerlink:visited {
    color: #6479A0;
}
a.footerlink:hover, a.footerlink:active {
    color: #E03A3E;
}
```

As you can see in the example that follows, the class name (`footerlink`) appears after the selector name (`a`), separated by a dot, and before the pseudoclass name (`hover`), separated by a colon:

```
selector.class:pseudoclass
a.footerlink:hover
```

Summary

The `<a>` tag is what makes hypertext "hyper." With it, you can create links between pages, as well as links to specific anchor points on any page. This hour focused on creating and styling simple links to other pages using either relative or absolute addressing to identify the pages.

You learned that when you're creating links to other people's pages, it's important to include the full Internet address of each page in an `<a href>` tag. For links between your own pages, include just the filenames and enough directory information to get from one page to another.

You also learned how to create named anchor points within a page and how to create links to a specific anchor. You learned how to link to your email address so that users can easily send you messages. You even learned how to protect your email address from spammers. Finally, you learned methods for controlling the display of your links using CSS.

Table 8.1 summarizes the `<a>` tag discussed in this hour.

TABLE 8.1   HTML Tags and Attributes Covered in Hour 8

Tag/Attribute	Function
`<a>...</a>`	With the `href` attribute, creates a link to another document or anchor. With the `id` attribute, creates an anchor that can be linked to.
Attributes	
`href="address"`	The address of the document or anchor point to link to.
`id="name"`	The name for this anchor point in the document.

Q&A

Q. What happens if I link to a page on the Internet, and then the person who owns that page deletes or moves it?

A. That depends on how the maintainer of that external page has set up his web server. Usually, you will see a `page not found` message or something to that effect when you click a link that has been moved or deleted. You can still click the Back button to return to your page. As a site maintainer, you can periodically run link-checking programs to ensure that your internal and external links are valid. An example of this is the Link Checker service, at http://validator.w3.org/checklink.

Q. One of the internal links on my website works fine on my computer, but when I put the pages on the Internet, the link doesn't work anymore. What's up?

A. These are the most likely culprits:

▶ **Capitalization problems.** On Windows computers, linking to a file named `MyFile.html` with `<a href="myfile.html">` works. On most web servers, the link must be `<a href="MyFile.html">` (or you must change the name of the file to `MyFile.html`). To make matters worse, some text editors and file transfer programs actually change the capitalization without telling you. The best solution is to stick with all-lowercase filenames for web pages.

▶ **Spaces in filenames.** Most web servers don't allow filenames with spaces. For example, you should never name a web page `my page.html`. Instead, name it `mypage.html` or even `my_page.html` or my-page.html (using an underscore or dash instead of a space).

▶ **Local absolute addresses.** If you link to a file using a local absolute address, such as `C:\mywebsite\news.html`, the link won't work when you place the file on the Internet. You should never use local absolute addresses; when this occurs, it is usually an accident caused by a temporary link that was created to test part of a page. So be careful to remove any test links before publishing a page on the Web.

Q. Can I put both `href` and `id` in the same `<a>` tag? Would I want to for any reason?

A. You can, and it might save you some typing if you have a named anchor point and a link right next to each other. It's generally better, however, to use `<a href>` and `<a id>` separately to avoid confusion because they play very different roles in an HTML document.

Q. What happens if I accidentally misspell the name of an anchor or forget to put the # in front of it?

A. If you link to an anchor name that doesn't exist within a page or you misspell the anchor name, the link goes to the top of that page.

Workshop

The Workshop contains quiz questions and exercises to help you solidify your understanding of the material covered. Try to answer all questions before looking at the "Answers" section that follows.

Quiz

1. Your best friend from elementary school finds you on the Internet and says he wants to trade home page links. How do you put a link to his site at http://www.supercheapsuits.com/~billybob/ on one of your pages?

2. What HTML would you use to make it possible for someone clicking the words "About the Authors" at the top of a page to skip down to a list of credits somewhere else on the page?

3. If your email address is bon@soir.com, how would you make the text "goodnight greeting" into a link that people can click to compose and send you an email message?

Answers

1. Put the following on your page:

```
<a href="http://www.supercheapsuits.com/~billybob/">Billy
   Bob's site</a>
```

2. Type this at the top of the page:

```
<a href="#credits">About the Authors</a>
```

   Type this at the beginning of the credits section:

```
<a id="credits"></a>
```

3. Type the following on your web page:

```
Send me a <a href="mailto:bon@soir.com">goodnight greeting</a>!
```

Exercises

▶ Create an HTML file consisting of a formatted list of your favorite websites. You might already have these sites bookmarked in your web browser, in which case you can visit them to find the exact URL in the browser's address bar.

▶ If you have created any pages for a website, look through them and consider whether there are any places in the text where you'd like to make it easy for people to contact you. Include a link to your email address there. You can never provide too many opportunities for people to contact you and tell you what they need or what they think about your products—especially if you're running a business.

HOUR 9
Using Tables and Columns

In this hour, you learn how to build HTML tables that you can use to control the spacing, layout, and appearance of tabular data in your web content. Although you can achieve similar results using CSS, there are definitely times when a table is the best way to present information in rows and columns. You also see in this hour how designers had to use tables for page layout in the past—and how to avoid ever doing that in the future. Finally, you'll learn the basics of using CSS to create columns for layout purposes.

Before we begin, remember that a table is simply an orderly arrangement of content into vertical columns and horizontal rows.

WHAT YOU'LL LEARN IN THIS HOUR:

▶ How to create simple tables

▶ How to control the size of tables

▶ How to align content and span rows and columns within tables

▶ How to use CSS columns

Creating a Simple Table

A table consists of rows of information with individual cells inside. To make tables, you have to start with a `<table>` tag. Of course, you end your tables with the `</table>` tag. CSS contains numerous properties that enable you to modify the table itself, such as the various border properties you learned about in previous chapters.

With the `<table>` tag in place, you next need the `<tr>` tag. The `<tr>` tag creates a table row, which contains one or more cells of information before the closing `</tr>`. To create these individual cells, use the `<td>` tag (`<td>` stands for *table data*). Place the table information between the `<td>` and `</td>` tags. A *cell* is a rectangular region that can contain any text, images, and HTML tags. Each row in a table consists of at least one cell. Multiple cells within a row form columns in a table.

One more basic tag is involved in building tables. The `<th>` tag works exactly like a `<td>` tag, except that `<th>` indicates that the cell is part of the heading of the table. Most web browsers automatically render the text in `<th>` cells as centered and boldface, as you can see with Chrome in Figure 9.1. However, if your browser does not automatically render this element with a built-in style, you have an element that you can style using CSS without using a class to differentiate among types of table data elements.

FIGURE 9.1
The code in Listing 9.1 creates a table with six rows and four columns.

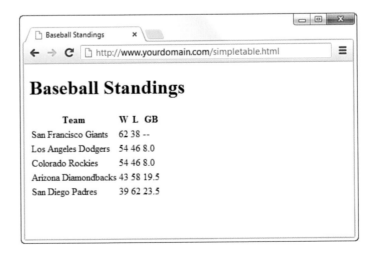

Baseball Standings

Team	W	L	GB
San Francisco Giants	62	38	--
Los Angeles Dodgers	54	46	8.0
Colorado Rockies	54	46	8.0
Arizona Diamondbacks	43	58	19.5
San Diego Padres	39	62	23.5

You can create as many cells as you want, but each row in a table should have the same number of columns as the other rows. The HTML code in Listing 9.1 creates a simple table using only the four table tags I've mentioned thus far. Figure 9.1 shows the resulting page as viewed in a web browser.

LISTING 9.1   Creating Tables with the `<table>`, `<tr>`, `<td>`, and `<th>` Tags

```
<!DOCTYPE html>

<html lang="en">
  <head>
    <title>Baseball Standings</title>
  </head>

  <body>
  <h1>Baseball Standings</h1>
    <table>
      <tr>
        <th>Team</th>
        <th>W</th>
        <th>L</th>
        <th>GB</th>
      </tr>
        <td>San Francisco Giants</td>
        <td>54</td>
        <td>46</td>
        <td>8.0</td>
      </tr>
      <tr>
        <td>Los Angeles Dodgers</td>
        <td>62</td>
        <td>38</td>
        <td>—</td>
      </tr>
      <tr>
      <tr>
        <td>Colorado Rockies</td>
        <td>54</td>
        <td>46</td>
        <td>8.0</td>
      </tr>
      <tr>
        <td>Arizona Diamondbacks</td>
        <td>43</td>
        <td>58</td>
        <td>19.5</td>
      </tr>
      <tr>
        <td>San Diego Padres</td>
        <td>39</td>
        <td>62</td>
```

```
      <td>23.5</td>
    </tr>
  </table>
 </body>
</html>
```

The table in the example contains baseball standings, which are perfect for arranging in rows and columns—but they're a little plain. For instance, this example doesn't even have any borders! You'll learn to jazz things up a bit in just a moment. The headings in the table show the Team, Wins (W), Losses (L), and Games Behind (GB) in the standings.

Adding the following stylesheet entries takes care of adding a basic border around the table and its cells:

```
table, tr, th, td {
    border: 1px solid black;
    border-collapse: collapse;
    padding: 3px;
}
```

You might wonder why you have to specify these styles for all four elements used to create the table instead of just the overall table element itself. Basically, this is because a table is made up of its elements, and each element can have these styles applied. The following figures demonstrate how the table would look with various elements styles or unstyled, to emphasize this point.

Figure 9.2 shows the output of the styles just listed. The `border-collapse` property, with a value of `collapse`, makes all the borders of the `<table>`, `<tr>`, and `<th>` or `<td>` elements collapse into one shared border. The padding adds a little breathing room to the content of the cells.

In Figure 9.3, you can see what the table would look like without the `border-collapse` property specified (the default value then takes effect, which is `separate`, for separate borders).

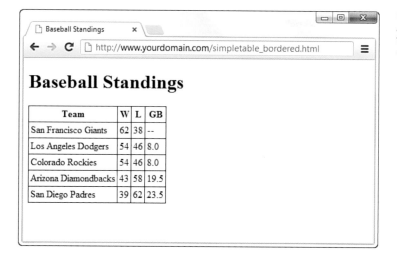

FIGURE 9.2
Adding some CSS styles to the table, including the use of `border-collapse`.

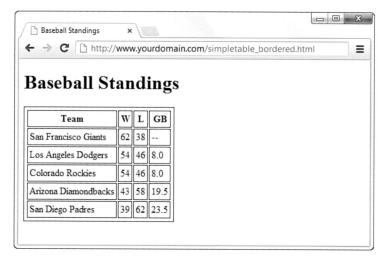

FIGURE 9.3
Removing the `border-collapse` property shows borders for all the elements.

In Figure 9.4, you can see what the table would look like without specifying any of the previous styles for the `<th>` and `<td>` elements—note the lack of border denoting the columns.

FIGURE 9.4
Removing the styles for the `<th>` and `<td>` elements.

Baseball Standings

Team	W L GB
San Francisco Giants	62 38 --
Los Angeles Dodgers	54 46 8.0
Colorado Rockies	54 46 8.0
Arizona Diamondbacks	43 58 19.5
San Diego Padres	39 62 23.5

TIP

You can employ three other useful but not required table-related tags when creating simple tables:

- `<thead></thead>`—Wrap your header rows in this element to add more meaning to the grouping and also allow these header rows to be printed across all pages (if your table is that long). You can then style the `<thead>` element instead of individual `<th>` cells.

- `<tbody></tbody>`—Wrap the rows that make up the "body" of this table (everything besides the header and the footer rows) in this element, to add more meaning to the grouping; you can then also style the `<tbody>` element as a whole instead of styling individual `<td>` cells.

- `<tfoot></tfoot>`—Much like the `<thead>` element, use this to wrap your footer rows (if you have any) in this element, to add more meaning to the grouping and style it as a whole. An example of a footer row might be a summation of the data presented in the columns, such as financial totals.

Controlling Table Sizes

When a table width is not specified, the size of a table and its individual cells automatically expand to fit the data you place into it. However, you can control the width of the entire table by defining the `width` CSS property for the `<table>` element; you can also define the width of each cell through the `width` CSS property assigned to the `<td>` elements. The `width` property can be specified as either pixels, ems, or percentages.

To make the first cell of a table 20 percent of the total table width and the second cell 80 percent of the table width, you use the following property definitions:

```
<table style="width:100%">
  <tr>
    <td style="width:20%">skinny cell</td>
    <td style="width:80%">fat cell</td>
  </tr>
</table>
```

Notice that the table is sized to 100 percent, which ensures that it fills the entire width of the browser window. When you use percentages instead of fixed pixel sizes, the table resizes automatically to fit any size browser window while maintaining the aesthetic balance you're seeking. In this case, the two cells within the table are automatically resized to 20 percent and 80 percent of the total table width, respectively.

In Listing 9.2, the simple table from Listing 9.1 (plus the border-related styles) is expanded to show very precise control over table cell widths (plus, the border-related styles have been added).

LISTING 9.2   Specifying Table Cell Widths

```
<!DOCTYPE html>

<html lang="en">
  <head>
    <title>Baseball Standings</title>

    <style type="text/css">
    table, tr, th, td {
       border: 1px solid black;
       border-collapse: collapse;
       padding: 3px;
    }
    </style>
  </head>

<body>
  <h1>Baseball Standings</h1>
    <table>
      <tr>
        <th style="width:200px;">Team</th>
        <th style="width:25px;">W</th>
        <th style="width:25px;">L</th>
        <th style="width:25px;">GB</th>
      </tr>
      <tr>
        <td>San Francisco Giants</td>
        <td>62</td>
        <td>38</td>
        <td>--</td>
      </tr>
      <tr>
        <td>Los Angeles Dodgers</td>
        <td>54</td>
        <td>46</td>
        <td>8.0</td>
      </tr>
      <tr>
        <td>Colorado Rockies</td>
        <td>54</td>
        <td>46</td>
        <td>8.0</td>
      </tr>
      <tr>
        <td>Arizona Diamondbacks</td>
        <td>43</td>
        <td>58</td>
        <td>19.5</td>
```

```
    </tr>
    <tr>
      <td>San Diego Padres</td>
      <td>39</td>
      <td>62</td>
      <td>23.5</td>
    </tr>
  </table>
 </body>
</html>
```

You can see the consistent column widths in Figure 9.5.

FIGURE 9.5
The code in Listing 9.2 creates a table with six rows and four columns, with specific widths used for each column.

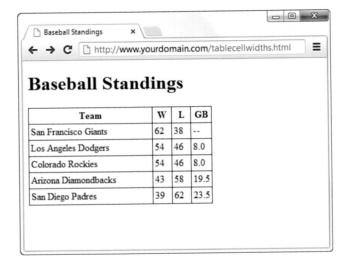

The addition of specific width style for each `<th>` element in the first row defines the widths of the columns. The first column is defined as 200px wide, and the second, third, and fourth columns are each 25px wide. In Figure 9.5, you can see whitespace after the text in the first column, indicating that the specified width is indeed greater than the column width would have been, had the table been allowed to render without explicit width indicators.

Also note that these widths are not repeated in the `<td>` elements in subsequent rows. Technically, you need to define the widths in only the first row; the remaining rows will follow suit because they are all part of the same table. However, if you'd used another formatting style (such as a style to change font size or color), you would've had to repeat that style for each element that should have those display properties.

Alignment and Spanning Within Tables

By default, anything you place inside a table cell is aligned to the left and vertically centered. All the figures so far in this lesson have shown this default alignment. However, you can align the contents of table cells both horizontally and vertically with the `text-align` and `vertical-align` style properties.

You can apply these alignment attributes to any `<tr>`, `<td>`, or `<th>` tag. Alignment attributes assigned to a `<tr>` tag apply to all cells in that row. Depending on the size of your table, you can save yourself some time and effort by applying these attributes at the `<tr>` level and not in each `<td>` or `<th>` tag.

The HTML code in Listing 9.3 uses a combination of text alignment styles to apply a default alignment to a row, but it is overridden in a few individual cells. Figure 9.6 shows the result of the code in Listing 9.3.

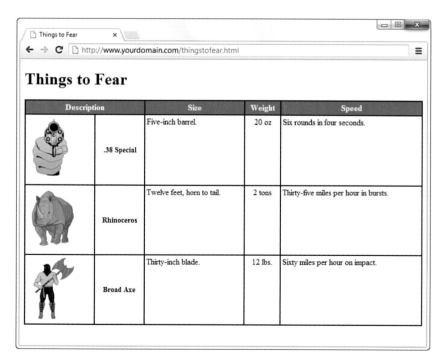

FIGURE 9.6
The code in Listing 9.3 shows the use of the `colspan` attribute and some alignment styles.

Following are some of the more commonly used `vertical-align` style property values: `top`, `middle`, `bottom`, `text-top`, `text-bottom`, and `baseline` (for text). These property values give you plenty of flexibility in aligning table data vertically.

LISTING 9.3   Alignment, Cell Spacing, Borders, and Background Colors in Tables

```html
<!DOCTYPE html>

<html lang="en">
  <head>
    <title>Things to Fear</title>
    <style type="text/css">
    table {
       border: 2px solid black;
       border-collapse: collapse;
       padding: 3px;
       width: 100%
    }

    tr, th, td {
       border: 2px solid black;
       border-collapse: collapse;
       padding: 3px;
    }

    thead {
       background-color: #ff0000;
       color: #ffffff;
    }

    .aligntop {
       vertical-align:top;
    }

    .description {
       font-size: 14px;
       font-weight:bold;
       vertical-align:middle;
       text-align:center;
    }

     .weight {
       text-align:center;
    }
    </style>

  </head>

  <body>
    <h1>Things to Fear</h1>
    <table>
      <thead>
```

```
    <tr>
      <th colspan="2">Description</th>
      <th>Size</th>
      <th>Weight</th>
      <th>Speed</th>
      </tr>
    </thead>
    <tr class="aligntop">
      <td><img src="handgun.gif" alt=".38 Special"/></td>
      <td class="description">.38 Special</td>
      <td>Five-inch barrel.</td>
      <td class="weight">20 oz.</td>
      <td>Six rounds in four seconds.</td>
    </tr>
    <tr class="aligntop">
      <td><img src="rhino.gif" alt="Rhinoceros" /></td>
      <td class="description">Rhinoceros</td>
      <td>Twelve feet, horn to tail.</td>
      <td class="weight">2 tons</td>
      <td>Thirty-five miles per hour in bursts.</td>
    </tr>
    <tr class="aligntop">
      <td><img src="axeman.gif" alt="Broad Axe" /></td>
      <td class="description">Broad Axe</td>
      <td>Thirty-inch blade.</td>
      <td class="weight">12 lbs.</td>
      <td>Sixty miles per hour on impact.</td>
    </tr>
  </table>
 </body>
</html>
```

At the top of Figure 9.6, a single cell (Description) spans two columns. This is accomplished with the colspan attribute in the <th> tag for that cell. As you might guess, you can also use the rowspan attribute to create a cell that spans more than one row.

Spanning is the process of forcing a cell to stretch across more than one row or column of a table. The colspan attribute causes a cell to span across multiple columns; rowspan has the same effect on rows.

Additionally, text styles are defined in the stylesheet and applied to the cells in the Description column to create bold text that is both vertically aligned to the middle and horizontally aligned to the center of the cell.

A few tricks in Listing 9.3 haven't been explained yet. You can give an entire table—and each individual row or cell in a table—its own background, distinct from any background you might use on the

TIP

Keeping the structure of rows and columns organized in your mind can be the most difficult part of creating tables with cells that span multiple columns or rows. The tiniest error can often throw the whole thing into disarray. You can save yourself time and frustration by sketching complicated tables on paper before you start writing the HTML to implement them.

web page itself. You can do this by placing the `background-color` or `background-image` style in the `<table>`, `<tr>`, `<td>`, `<th>`, `<thead>`, `<tbody>`, or `<tfooter>` tags (or assigning the value in the stylesheet for these elements), exactly as you would in the `<body>` tag. In Listing 9.3, only the top row has a background color; the stylesheet defines the `<thead>` element as one with a red background and white text in the cells in that row.

Similar to the `background-color` style property is the `background-image` property (not shown in this example), which is used to set an image for a table background. If you wanted to set the image `leaves.gif` as the background for a table, you would use `background-image:url(leaves.gif)"` in the stylesheet entry for the `<table>` element. Notice that the image file is placed within parentheses and preceded by the word `url`, which indicates that you are describing where the image file is located.

Tweaking tables goes beyond just using style properties. As Listing 9.3 shows, you can control the space around the content of the cell, within its borders by applying some padding to the cell. If you want to add some space between the borders of the cells themselves, you can use the `border-spacing` CSS property, which enables you to define the horizontal and vertical spacing like so:

```
border-spacing: 2px 4px;
```

In the example, spacing is defined as 2 pixels of space between the horizontal borders, and 4 pixels of space between the vertical borders. If you use only one value, the value is applied to all four borders.

Page Layout with Tables

At the beginning of this chapter, I indicated that designers have used tables for page layout, as well as to display tabular information. You will still find many examples of table-based layouts if you peek at another designer's source code. This method of design grew out of inconsistencies in browser support for CSS in the mid-1990s to early 2000s. Because all browsers supported tables and in generally the same way, web designers latched on to the table-based method of content layout to achieve the same visual page display across all browsers. However, now that support for CSS is relatively similar across all major browsers, designers can follow the long-standing standards-based recommendation *not* to use tables for page layout.

The World Wide Web Consortium (W3C), the standards body that oversees the future of the web, has long promoted stylesheets as the proper way to lay out pages (instead of using tables). Stylesheets are ultimately much more powerful than tables, which is why the bulk of this book teaches you how to use stylesheets for page layout.

The main reasons for avoiding using tables for layout include these:

▶ **Mixing presentation with content**—One goal of CSS and standards-compliant web design is to separate the presentation layer from the content layer.

▶ **Creating unnecessarily difficult redesigns**—To change a table-based layout, you have to change the table-based layout on every single page of your site (unless it is part of a complicated, dynamically driven site, in which case you have to undo all the dynamic pieces and remake them).

▶ **Addressing accessibility issues**—Screen reading software looks to tables for content and often tries to read layout tables as content tables.

▶ **Rendering on mobile devices**—Table layouts are often not flexible enough to scale downward to small screens (see Hour 15, "Creating Fixed or Liquid Layouts").

These are but a few of the issues in table-based web design. For a closer look at some of these issues, see the popular presentation "Why Tables for Layout is Stupid," at http://www.hotdesign.com/seybold/everything.html.

Using CSS Columns

If you have a large amount of text-only information, you might want to present it much like a physical newspaper does: in columns. Over a hundred years of research have shown a correlation between the length of a line and reading speed, and indicated a "sweet spot," or optimum length of a line that allows for both a quick and enjoyable reading experience. The continued presence of this sweet spot—lines that are around 4 inches long—is why physical newspapers still present information in columns.

If you have a lot of information to present to readers, or if you simply want to mimic the aesthetic of a newspaper layout, you can use CSS columns. True, you could also use a table, because tables are made of rows and columns, but the previous section explained some of the reasons to avoid a table-based layout. Also, columns aren't just for text; you can put anything you want into defined columns, such as advertisements or related text in a sidebar.

In Figure 9.7, you can see a basic use of CSS columns, to define a traditional newspaper-type layout.

FIGURE 9.7
The code in Listing 9.4 shows a three-column layout.

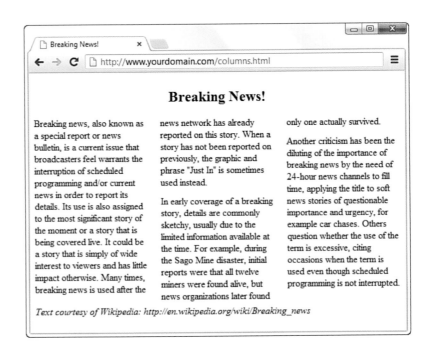

LISTING 9.4   Alignment, Cell Spacing, Borders, and Background Colors in Tables

```
<!DOCTYPE html>

<html lang="en">
  <head>
    <title>Breaking News!</title>
    <style type="text/css">
    article {
       -webkit-column-count: 3;
       -webkit-column-gap: 21px;

       -moz-column-count: 3;
       -moz-column-gap: 21px;
```

```
      column-count: 3;
      column-gap: 21px;
  }

  h1 {
      text-align: center;
      -webkit-column-span: all;
      -moz-column-span: all;
      column-span: all;
  }

  p {
      margin-top: 0px;
      margin-bottom: 12px;
  }

  footer {
      -webkit-column-span: all;
      -moz-column-span: all;
      column-span: all;
  }
  </style>
</head>

<body>
  <article>

    <header>
      <h1>Breaking News!</h1>
    </header>

      <p>Breaking news, also known as a special report or news bulletin,
      is a current issue that broadcasters feel warrants the interruption
      of scheduled programming and/or current news in order to report its
      details. Its use is also assigned to the most significant story of
      the moment or a story that is being covered live. It could be a
      story that is simply of wide interest to viewers and has little
      impact otherwise. Many times, breaking news is used after the news
      network has already reported on this story. When a story has not
      been reported on previously, the graphic and phrase "Just In" is
      sometimes used instead.</p>

      <p>In early coverage of a breaking story, details are commonly
      sketchy, usually due to the limited information available at the
      time. For example, during the Sago Mine disaster, initial reports
      were that all twelve miners were found alive, but news
      organizations later found only one actually survived.</p>

      <p>Another criticism has been the diluting of the importance of
      breaking news by the need of 24-hour news channels to fill time,
      applying the title to soft news stories of questionable importance
      and urgency, for example car chases. Others question whether the
      use of the term is excessive, citing occasions when the term is
      used even though scheduled programming is not interrupted.</p>
```

```
<footer>
  <em>Text courtesy of Wikipedia:
  http://en.wikipedia.org/wiki/Breaking_news</em>
</footer>

</article>
</body>
</html>
```

The code in Listing 9.4 is from a fake news article, so I've used the `<article>` element to hold all the content. Inside the `<article>` element is a `<header>` element that contains the "Breaking News!" heading (at the `<h1>` level), followed by three paragraphs of text and a `<footer>` element. All the styling is handled in the stylesheet at the beginning of the listing; styles are provided for four of the elements just named: `<article>`, `<h1>`, `<p>`, and `<footer>`.

In the stylesheet, I'm applying the primary definition of the columns within the `<article>` element. I've used `column-count` to define three columns, and I've used `column-gap` to define the space between the columns as 21 pixels wide. Next, I've added a definition for the `<h1>` element, first to make the text align in the center of the page, and second to ensure that the text spans across all the columns. I applied the same `column-span` property to the entry for the `<footer>` element, for the same reason.

After the entry for the `<h1>` element, I added some specific margins to the `<p>` element, namely a top margin of 0 pixels and a bottom margin of 12 pixels. I could have left well enough alone and just allowed the `<p>` elements to display as the default style, but that would have created a margin at the top of each paragraph. "What's the big deal?" you might ask, because it looks like I've manually added space between the paragraphs anyway—and that's true. However, I added the space *after* each paragraph and took away the space *before* each paragraph so that the first column doesn't begin with a space and thus misalign the tops of each of the three columns.

You can even add vertical lines between columns, as shown in Figure 9.8. The stylesheet entries I added to achieve this appearance are shown here; note that they look remarkably similar to how you define borders (as you learned in Hour 7).

```
-webkit-column-rule-width: 1px;
-moz-column-rule-width: 1px;
column-rule-width: 1px;
```

NOTE

In the stylesheet, note that, for each column-related property in the stylesheet, I've added two additional entries with `-webkit` and `-moz` prefixes. Because browser support for column-related CSS is still a bit inconsistent, using the properties with these prefixes ensures that the properties will work in all browsers.

```
-webkit-column-rule-style: solid;
-moz-column-rule-style: solid;
column-rule-style: solid;
-webkit-column-rule-color: #000;
-moz-column-rule-color: #000;
column-rule-color: #000;
```

FIGURE 9.8
The code in Listing 9.4, with the addition of vertical lines between the columns.

Summary

In this brief chapter, you learned to arrange text and images into organized rows and columns called tables. You learned the basic tags for creating tables and several CSS properties for controlling the alignment, spacing, and appearance of tables. You also learned that tables are never to be used for layout purposes, but that you can achieve a multicolumn layout using CSS columns.

Table 9.1 summarizes the tags covered in this hour.

TABLE 9.1   HTML Tags Covered in Hour 9

Tag	Function
`<table>...</table>`	Creates a table that can contain any number of rows and columns.
`<thead>...</thead>`	Defines the heading row of a table.
`<tbody>...</tbody>`	Defines the body rows of a table.
`<tfoot>...</tfoot>`	Defines the footer row of a table.
`<tr>...</tr>`	Defines a table row containing one or more cells (`<td>` tags).
`<th>...</th>`	Defines a table heading cell. (Accepts all the same styles as `<td>`.)
`<td>...</td>`	Defines a table data cell.

Q&A

Q. **I made a big table, and when I load the page, nothing appears on the page for a long time. Why the wait?**

A. Complex tables can take a while to appear on the screen. The web browser has to figure out the size of everything in the table before it can display any part of it. You can speed things up a bit by always including `width` and `height` attributes for every graphics image within a table. Defining specific widths for both the `<table>` and `<td>` elements also helps.

Q. **Can I use CSS columns for layout beyond the "newspaper" look?**

A. Yes, you can use CSS columns to create a column-based layout for your entire website, if you so desire. For example, a column for navigation next to a wider column for the body text, next to a third column for advertisements or other secondary content is a common template design.

Workshop

The Workshop contains quiz questions and exercises to help you solidify your understanding of the material covered. Try to answer all questions before looking at the "Answers" section that follows.

Quiz

1. How can you create a simple two-row, two-column table with a single-pixel black border to outline the table?

2. Expanding on Question 1, how can you add 9 pixels of space around the content within each cell?

3. How do you make the contents of an element span multiple columns?

Answers

1. Use the following HTML:

```
<table style="border: 1px solid #000000; border-collapse:
collapse;">
  <tr>
    <td>Top left...</td>
    <td>Top right...</td>
```

```
    </tr>
    <tr>
      <td>Bottom left...</td>
      <td>Bottom right...</td>
    </tr>
</table>
```

2. Add `padding: 9px` to the style declaration.

3. Apply the `column-span` property to the element, with a value of `all`.

Exercises

▶ Do you have any pages that have information visitors might be interested in viewing as lists or tables? Use a table to present some tabular information. Make sure each column has its own heading (or perhaps its own graphic). Play around with the various types of alignment and spacing that you learned in this chapter.

▶ You often see alternating row colors in a table, with one row having a gray background and the next a white background. The goal of alternating colors in table rows is so that the individual rows are easier to discern when looking quickly at the table full of data. Create a table with alternating row colors and text colors (if necessary).

HOUR 10
Creating Images for Use on the Web

Believe me, you don't have to be an artist by trade to put high-impact graphics on your web pages (although it does help). You don't need to spend hundreds or thousands of dollars on software packages, either, just to manipulate digital photographs or other source graphics you might want to use. The topics in this hour help you get started with creating images you can use in your website.

Although the sample figures in this hour use a popular and free graphics program for Windows, Mac, and Linux users (GNU Image Manipulation Program, or GIMP), you can apply the knowledge you learn in this hour to any major Windows or Macintosh graphics application—although the menus and options will look different, of course.

After you learn to create the graphics themselves, you'll be ready to include them in your website using HTML, CSS, or both.

Choosing Graphics Software

You can use almost any graphics program to create and edit images for your website, from the simple painting or drawing program that typically comes free with your computer's operating system, to an expensive professional program such as Adobe Photoshop. Similarly, if you have a digital camera or scanner attached to your computer, it probably came with some graphics software capable of creating images suitable for online use. Several free image editors also are available for download—or even online as a web application—and deal just with the manipulation of photographic elements.

WHAT YOU'LL LEARN IN THIS HOUR:

▶ How to select a software package to use
▶ How to prepare photographs for use online
▶ How to create banners and buttons
▶ How to reduce the number of colors in an image
▶ How to create transparent images
▶ How to prepare an image for a tiled background
▶ How to create animated web graphics

NOTE

Without a doubt, Adobe Photoshop is the cream of the crop when it comes to image-editing programs. However, it is expensive and quite complex if you don't have experience working with computer graphics. For more information on Adobe's products, visit the Adobe website at http://www.adobe.com/. If you are in the market for one of the company's products, you can download a free evaluation version from the site.

If you already have software you think might be good for creating web graphics, try using it to do everything described in these next sections. If your software can't handle some of the tasks covered here, it probably isn't a good tool for web graphics. In that case, download and install GIMP from www.gimp.org. This fully functional graphics program is completely free and can definitely perform the actions shown in this chapter.

Using Images Found Elsewhere

One of the best ways to save time creating the graphics and media files for web pages is, of course, to avoid creating them altogether. Grabbing a graphic from any web page is as simple as right-clicking it (or Option + Click an Apple mouse) and selecting Save Image As or Save Picture As (depending on your browser). Extracting a background image from a page is just as easy: Right-click it and select Save Background As.

However, you should *never* use images without the explicit permission of the owner, either by asking or by looking for a Creative Commons license. To take images without explicit permission is a copyright violation (and is also distasteful). To learn more about copyrights, I recommend the "Copyright Crash Course" online tutorial from the University of Texas, at http://copyright.lib.utexas.edu/.

You might also want to consider royalty-free clip art, which doesn't require you to get copyright permission. A good source of clip art online is Microsoft's Office Online Clip Art and Media website, at http://office.microsoft.com/clipart/. Clipart.com is another popular clip art destination; for a small fee, you have access to thousands of stock images.

If GIMP doesn't suit you, consider downloading the evaluation version of Adobe Photoshop or Corel DRAW. For photo manipulation only, you have many free options, all with helpful features. Google's Picasa, available free at http://picasa.google.com/, is one such option. Pixlr (pixlr.com) is another good option. Both of these programs are suited for editing images rather than creating them from scratch, and Picasa is also oriented toward organizing your digital photograph collection. These types of programs won't necessarily help you design a banner or button image for your site, but they can help you work with some supplementary images, and they are powerful enough that they're worth checking out.

The Least You Need to Know About Graphics

Two forces are always at odds when you post graphics and multimedia on the Internet. The users' eyes and ears want all your content to be as detailed and accurate as possible, and they also want that information displayed immediately. Intricate, colorful graphics mean big file sizes, which increase the transfer time even over a fast connection. How do you maximize the quality of your presentation while minimizing file size? To make these choices, you need to understand how color and resolution work together to create a subjective sense of quality.

The resolution of an image is the number of individual dots, or pixels, that make up an image (typically 72 dots per inch, or 72dpi). Large, high-resolution images generally take longer to transfer and display than small, low-resolution images. Image dimensions are usually specified as the width times the height of the image, expressed in pixels; a 300×200 image, for example, is 300 pixels wide and 200 pixels high.

You might be surprised to find that resolution isn't the most significant factor in determining an image file's storage size (and transfer time). This is because images used on web pages are always stored and transferred in compressed form. Image compression is the mathematical manipulation that images are put through to squeeze out repetitive patterns. The mathematics of image compression is complex, but the basic idea is that repeating patterns or large areas of the same color can be squeezed out when the image is stored on a disk. This makes the image file much smaller and allows it to be transferred faster over the Internet. The web browser then restores the original appearance of the image when the image is displayed.

In the sections that follow, you learn how to create graphics with big visual impact but small file sizes. The techniques you use to accomplish this depend on the contents and purpose of each image. There are as many uses for web graphics as there are web pages, but four types of graphics are by far the most common:

- ▶ Photos of people, products, and places

- ▶ Graphical banners and logos

- ▶ Buttons or icons to indicate actions and provide links

- ▶ Background textures for container elements

NOTE

Several types of image resolution are used, including pixel, spatial, spectral, temporal, and radiometric. You could spend hours just learning about each type—and if you were taking a graphics design class, you might do just that. For now, however, all you need to remember is that large images take longer to download and also use a lot of space in your display. Display size and storage or transfer size are factors to take into consideration when designing your website.

Preparing Photographic Images

To put photos on your web pages, you need to convert your print-based photos to digital images or create photos digitally by using a digital camera, which includes the ubiquitous camera in your smartphone. In the case of some older models of hardware, you might need to use the custom software that came with your device to transfer images to your hard drive, but in most cases, you should be able to connect your device and then drag and drop files to your hard drive. If you are using a scanner to create digital versions of your print photos, you can control just about any scanner directly from the graphics program of your choice—see your software documentation for details.

After you transfer the digital image files to your computer, you can use your graphics program to crop, resize, color-correct, and compress to get them ready for use in your website.

Cropping an Image

Because you want web page graphics to be as compact as possible, you usually need to crop your digital photos. When you *crop* a photo, you select the area you want to display and crop away the rest.

▼ TRY IT YOURSELF

Cropping in GIMP

The GIMP toolbox offers quick access to the crop tool and its possible attributes. Find an image file—either a digital image you have taken with your camera and stored on your hard drive, or an image you found online. After opening the image in GIMP, perform the following steps to crop it in GIMP:

1. In the GIMP toolbox, click the Crop tool (see Figure 10.1). Depending on the tool you select, you might have additional attributes you can select. For example, Figure 10.1 shows the attributes for the cropping tool (such as the aspect ratio, position, size, and so on).

TRY IT YOURSELF ▼

Cropping in GIMP
continued

FIGURE 10.1
Select the Crop tool from the toolbox.

2. In the image you want to crop, draw a box around the selection by clicking the upper-left corner of the portion of the image you want to keep and holding the left mouse button while you drag down to the lower-right corner. See Figure 10.2.

Cropping in GIMP
continued

FIGURE 10.2
Select the area of the image that
you want to display.

3. Click one of the corners of the selection to apply the cropping.

Your graphics program will likely have a different method than the one shown,
but the concept is the same: select the area to keep and then crop out the
rest.

TIP

Your graphics software will
likely have an omnipresent size
display somewhere in the image
window itself. In GIMP, you can
see the current image size in the
window title bar. Other programs
might show it in the lower-right
or lower-left corners. You might
also see the magnification ratio
in the window, and you might be
able to change it by zooming in
or out.

Even after your image has been cropped, it might be larger than it
needs to be for a web page. Depending on the design of a specific web
page, you might want to limit large images to no more than 800×600
pixels (if it is shown on a page by itself, such as an item catalog) or
even 640×480 pixels or smaller. When shown alongside text, images
tend to be in the range of 250 to 350 pixels for width, so there's just
enough room for the text as well. In some cases, you might want to
also provide a thumbnail version of the image that links to a larger
version; then you'll probably stick closer to 100 pixels in the larger
dimension for the thumbnail.

Resizing an Image

The exact tool necessary to change an image's size depends on the program you are using. In GIMP, go to the Image menu and click Scale Image to open the Scale Image dialog box (see Figure 10.3).

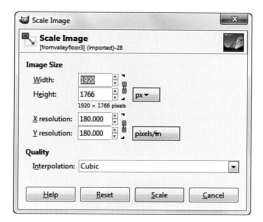

FIGURE 10.3
Use the Scale Image dialog box to change the size of an image.

You'll almost always want to resize using the existing aspect ratio, meaning that when you enter the width you'd like the image to be, the height is calculated automatically (and vice versa), to keep the image from squishing out of shape. In GIMP, the aspect ratio is locked by default, as indicated by the chain link displayed next to the Width and Height options shown in Figure 10.3. Clicking once on the chain unlocks it, enabling you to specify pixel widths and heights of your own choosing—squished or not.

In most, if not all, graphics programs, you can also resize the image based on percentages instead of providing specific pixel dimensions. For example, if my image started out as 1815×1721 and I didn't want to do the math to determine the values necessary to show it as half that width, I could simply select Percent (in this instance, from the drop-down next to the pixel display in Figure 10.3) and change the default setting (100) to 50. The image width would then become 908 pixels wide by 861 high—and no math was necessary on my part.

NOTE

As with many of the features in GIMP, the Scale Image dialog box appears in front of the window containing the image being resized. This placement enables you to make changes in the dialog box, apply them, and see the results immediately.

Tweaking Image Colors

If you are editing photographic images instead of creating your own graphics, you might need to use some color-correction tools to get the photo just right. As in many image-editing programs, GIMP offers several options for adjusting an image's brightness, contrast, and color balance, as well as a filter to reduce the dreaded red-eye. To remove red-eye using GIMP, go to Filters, click Enhance, and then click Red Eye Removal.

Most of these options are pretty intuitive. If you want the image to be brighter, adjust the brightness. If you want more red in your image, adjust the color balance. In GIMP, the Colors menu gives you access to numerous tools. As with the Scale Image dialog box described in the previous section, each tool displays a dialog box in the foreground of your workspace. As you adjust the colors, the image reflects those changes. This preview function is a feature included in most image-editing software.

Figure 10.4 shows the Adjust Hue/Lightness/Saturation tool, one of the many tools provided on the Colors menu. As shown in the figure, you can achieve many color-related changes by using various sliders in dialog boxes to adjust the values you are working with. The Preview feature enables you to see what you are doing as you are doing it. The Reset Color button returns the image to its original state without any changes applied.

Because of the numerous tools available to you, and the preview function available with each tool, a little playful experimentation is the best way to find out what each tool does.

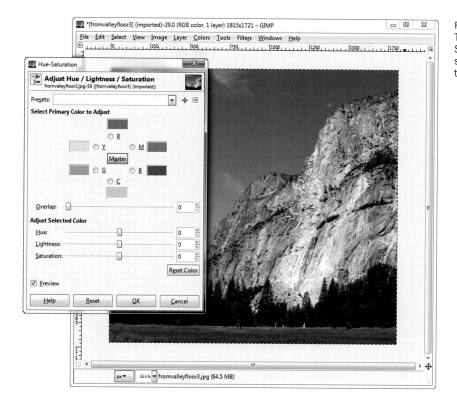

FIGURE 10.4
The Adjust Hue/Lightness/
Saturation tool is one of many
slider-based color-modification
tools available in GIMP.

Controlling JPEG Compression

Photographic images on the web work best when saved in the JPEG file format rather than GIF; JPG enables you to retain the number of colors in the file while still keeping the overall file size to a manageable level. When you're finished adjusting the size and appearance of your photo, select File, Export and choose JPEG as the file type. Your graphics program will likely provide you with another dialog box for controlling various JPEG options, such as compression.

Figure 10.5 shows the Export Image as JPEG dialog box you'll see when you export a JPEG in GIMP. You can see here that you can control the compression ratio for saving JPEG files by adjusting the Quality slider between 1 (low quality, small file size) and 100 (high quality, large file size).

FIGURE 10.5
GIMP enables you to reduce file size while still retaining image quality by saving in the JPEG format.

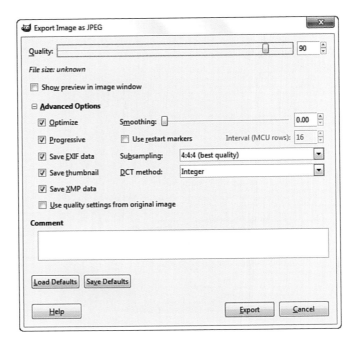

FIGURE 10.5
GIMP enables you to reduce file size while still retaining image quality by saving in the JPEG format.

You might want to experiment a bit to see how various JPEG compression levels affect the quality of your images, but 85 percent quality (or 15 percent compression) is generally a good compromise between file size (and, therefore, download speed) and quality for most photographic images.

Creating Banners and Buttons

Graphics that you create from scratch, such as banners and buttons, require you to make considerations uniquely different from those that apply to photographs.

The first decision you need to make when you produce a banner or button is how big it should be. Most people accessing the web now have a computer with a screen that is at least 1024×768 pixels in resolution, if not considerably larger. For example, my screen is currently set at 1440×900 pixels; 1366×768 is another popular resolution. It's a nice touch to plan your graphics so that they always fit within smaller screens (1024×768), with room to spare for scrollbars and margins. These days, though, you won't run into much trouble if you're designing for the desktop and nudge that minimal width up by a few pixels.

Assuming that you target a minimum resolution of 1024×768 pixels, full-size banners and title graphics should be no more than 900 pixels wide, which is the generally available viewable width of the page after you've accounted for scrollbars, toolbars, and other parts of the browser window. Within a page, normal photos and other images should be from 100 to 300 pixels in each dimension, and smaller buttons and icons should be 20 to 100 pixels tall and wide. Over the years, some generally acceptable sizes have been used for banner graphics and other advertisement-size images; you can see these sizes in use if you look at the banner ads available for affiliate and partner programs, such as the Amazon Affiliate program (see https://affiliate-program.amazon.com/). Common sizes include 120×600, 234×60, and 300×250, to name a new.

To create a new image in GIMP, go to File and choose New. The Create a New Image dialog box displays (see Figure 10.6). If you aren't sure how big the image needs to be, just accept the default size of a 640×480. Or you can choose one of the other predetermined sizes in the Template drop-down, such as Web Banner Common 468×60 or Web Banner Huge 728×90. Those two settings are conservative, yet perfectly acceptable, interpretations of "common" and "huge" for banners. From this dialog box, you can also enter your own width and height for the new image.

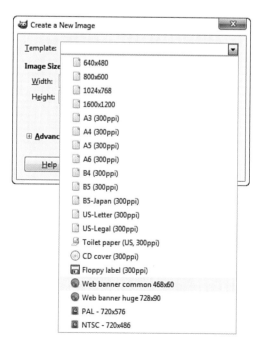

FIGURE 10.6
You must decide on the size of an image before you start working on it.

For the image's background color, you should usually choose white to match the background that most web browsers use for web pages (although as you learned in the previous hour, that color can be changed). When you know that you'll be creating a page with a background other than white, you can choose a different background color for your image. Or you might want to create an image with no background at all, in which case you select Transparency as the background color. When the final, web-ready image includes a transparent background, the web page (and its background color) behind the image is allowed to show through. In GIMP, select the background color for your new image by opening the Advanced Options in the Create a New Image dialog box.

After you enter the width and height of the image in pixels and click OK, you are faced with a blank canvas—an intimidating sight if you're as art-phobic as most of us! However, so many image-creation tutorials (not to mention entire books) are available to lead you through the process that I'm comfortable leaving you to your own creative devices. This section is all about introducing you to the things you want to keep in mind when creating graphics for use in your sites. This section does not necessarily teach you exactly how to do it, because being comfortable with the tool *you* choose is the first step to mastering them.

Reducing or Removing Colors in an Image

One of the most effective ways to reduce the size of an image—and, therefore, its download time—is to reduce the number of colors used in the image. This can drastically reduce the visual quality of some photographic images, but it works great for most banners, buttons, and other icons.

You'll be glad to know that there is a special file format for images with a limited number of colors, the Graphics Interchange Format (GIF). When you save or export an image as a GIF, you might be prompted to flatten layers or reduce the number of colors by converting to an indexed image because those are requirements for GIFs; check your software's help file regarding layers and indexed colors for a full understanding of what you might need to do.

Remember, the GIF image format is designed for images that contain areas of solid colors, such as web page titles and other illustrated graphics; the GIF format is not ideal for photographs (use JPG or PNG files instead).

PNG (pronounced "ping") is a useful file format that is supported in all major web browsers. Whereas the GIF image format enables you to specify a single transparent color, which means that the background of the web page will show through those areas of an image, the PNG format takes things a step further by enabling you to specify varying degrees of transparency.

You might have seen websites that use background colors or images in their container elements, but also have images present in the foreground that allow the background to show through parts of the foreground graphics. In these cases, the images in the foreground have portions that are transparent so that the images themselves—which are always on a rectangular canvas—do not show the areas of the canvas where the design does not occur. You often want to use these types of partially transparent images to make graphics look good over any background color or background image you have in place.

To make part of an image transparent, the image must be saved in the GIF or PNG file format. As mentioned previously in this lesson, most graphics programs that support the GIF format enable you to specify one color to be transparent, whereas PNG images allow for a range of transparency. Largely because of this transparency range, the PNG format is superior to GIF. All the latest web browsers already support PNG images.

The process of creating a transparent image depends on the type of image you are creating (GIF or PNG) and the graphics software you are using to create it. For instructions, look in your graphics program's help files or type "transparent images with [your program here]" into your search engine.

Creating Tiled Background Images

You can use any GIF, JPG, or PNG image as a background tile within a container element, but before you go off and create a tiled background, especially a highly patterned tiled background, ask yourself what that tiled background adds to the overall look and feel of your website. More important, ask yourself whether the text of the site can be read easily when placed over that pattern.

Think about the websites you frequent every day, and consider the fact that few use tiled, heavily patterned backgrounds on their entire pages. If you restrict your browsing to websites for companies, products, sports teams, or other sites in which information (primarily text) is privileged, the number of sites with tiled, heavily patterned backgrounds decreases even further. The web affords everyone the right of individuality in design, but if you are creating a site for your business, you might want to avoid using a highly patterned background with contrasting colored text.

If you do use a tiled background image for your entire site, remember that tiled images look best when you can't tell they're tiled images. In other words, you know you have a good image when the top edge of a background tile matches seamlessly with the bottom edge, and the left edge matches with the right.

Figures 10.7 and 10.8 show background tiles in use, both with seamless background, but with varying degrees of effectiveness.

FIGURE 10.7
This is an example of a seamless background image in which you can tell the background is tiled because you can see six identical shapes.

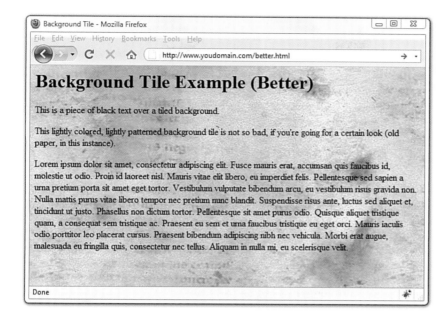

In Hour 11, "Using Images in Your Website," you learn how to place background images within your container elements. Despite my warnings so far in this section, background images can be powerful weapons in your design arsenal—just not when heavily patterned. You can find some great (and freely available) examples of background images—often referred to as *textures*—at the Subtle Patterns website, http://subtlepatterns.com/. I haven't shown an example of a good subtle tiled background because, for it to be an element of good design, it would likely be so subtle that it wouldn't be visible in a printed book.

Creating Animated Web Graphics

The GIF image format enables you to create animated images that add some motion to spice up any web page. Animated GIF images also transfer much faster than most of the video or multimedia files that are often used for similar effect. With the GIMP software package, you can create animated GIFs by creating multiple layers within an image and then modifying the Animated GIF options when saving the file. Additionally, if you have a series of images you want to animate, you can use the free, web-based GIF animation service at Gickr (www.gickr.com).

The first step in creating a GIF animation is to create a series of images to be displayed one after the other—or a series of layers, depending on your particular software program. Each of these images is called a *frame*. Just like how movies or cartoons are put together, the images that you see on the movie or television screen and the images in animated graphics are made up of many individual frames that have slight differences in their appearance. When you have your graphical frames in mind, the process of tying them together is relatively simple—the planning stage is the most difficult. Take some time to sketch out the frames in storyboard fashion, especially if you plan to have more than just a few frames. When you know how your frames are going to fit together, use the Gickr service mentioned earlier in this section, or read the documentation for your graphics software to learn its particular process for pulling it all together.

▼ TRY IT YOURSELF

Preparing Images for Use in Your Website

You should get two or three images ready now so that you can try putting them on your own pages as you follow along with the rest of this chapter. If you have some image files already saved in the GIF, PNG, or JPEG formats (the filenames end in .gif, .png, or .jpg), use those. It's also fine to use any graphics you created while reading the preceding section.

Search engines such as Google can become a gold mine of images by leading you to sites related to your own theme. Search engines can also help you discover the oodles of sites specifically dedicated to providing free and cheap access to reusable media collections. And don't forget Microsoft's massive clip art library at the Office Online Clip Art and Media website, http://office.microsoft.com/clipart/. Other valuable sources include Google Images (images.google.com) and Flickr (www.flickr.com)—look for images using Creative Commons licenses that allow free use with attribution.

Summary

In this hour, you learned the basics of preparing graphics for use on web pages. If nothing else, you learned that this is a complex topic, and you learned just enough in this chapter to whet your appetite. The examples in this chapter used the popular (and free!) GIMP software package, but feel free to use the graphics software that best suits your needs. Among the actions you learned were how to crop, resize, and tweak image colors, and you also learned about the different file formats. You must keep in mind many considerations when including graphics in your site, including graphic size and resolution, and how to use transparency, animated GIFs, and tiled backgrounds.

Q&A

Q. Instead of learning all this stuff myself, shouldn't I just hire a graphics artist to design my pages?

A. This is a difficult question to answer—and that's coming from someone who worked for a very long time for a web development and design agency. For individuals and small businesses, an agency isn't always the best solution. Hiring a graphic designer takes time and money. Additionally, many graphics artists do not produce work suitable for the web—they are specifically print-based artists, and the print world is quite different than the online world. Furthermore, hiring a graphics designer to create a website might not play to the strengths of that particular graphics designer. In other words, the designer might be good at designing the graphical elements of a website, but he or she might *not* be a good content architect or might not excel at working with HTML and CSS. If your site is simply a personal site, a completely outsourced professional design might not be where you want to spend your money. But if your site is intended to promote a business, a product, a school, or anything else in which your image is integral to your success, it's worth your while (and money) to consult with a web design professional at some point.

Q. I've produced graphics for printing on paper. Are web page graphics any different?

A. Yes. In fact, many of the rules for print graphics are reversed on the web. Web page graphics have to be low resolution, whereas print graphics should be as high resolution as possible. White washes out black on computer screens, whereas black bleeds into white on paper. Also, someone might stop a web page from loading when only half the graphics have been downloaded, which isn't a consideration when looking at images in print. Try to avoid falling into old habits if you've done a lot of print graphics design.

Workshop

The Workshop contains quiz questions and exercises to help you solidify your understanding of the material covered. Try to answer all questions before looking at the "Answers" section that follows.

Quiz

1. You have a scanned picture of a horse that you need to put on a web page. How big should you make it? In what file format should you save it?

2. What are some issues to watch out for when selecting a tiling background image?

3. If you have a square image of a blue flower on a transparent background, and the background color of the containing element is gray, will your flower image appear on the page as a square or some other shape?

Answers

1. Depending on how important the image is to your page, you should make it as small as 100×40 pixels or as large as 300×120 pixels. The JPEG format, with about 85 percent compression, would be best. Of course, you could also provide a thumbnail link to a larger image that is viewed by itself.

2. You need to make sure that the tile "seams" aren't visible when it repeats, that the pattern is not too overwhelming, and that the colors in the tile do not contrast with any other images or colors used on the page.

3. It will appear as the shape of the flower because the image has a transparent background. The gray background of the containing element will show through.

Exercises

▶ Before you start designing graphics for an important business site, sketch out on a piece of paper the general size and shape of the graphical elements that you might want to include. Refer to the beginning of this hour for information about typical graphic sizes and screen resolutions, to ensure the best fit.

▶ Using your graphics software program of choice, create a few simple animated graphics for placement on your website. Even if you put together only a few frames, you'll have the opportunity to practice putting frames together to achieve the best frame rate for display.

Using Images in Your Website

In the previous hour, you learned some of the basics for creating suitable images for your website; in this hour, you learn how to *use* these files in your website using HTML and CSS. Beyond just the basics of using the HTML `<img/>` tag to include images for display in a web browser, you'll learn how to provide descriptions of these images (and why). You'll also learn about image placement, including how to use images as backgrounds for different elements. Finally, you'll learn how to use imagemaps, which allow you to use a single image as a link to multiple locations.

Placing Images on a Web Page

To get started with image placement on your website, first move the image file into the same folder as the HTML file or into a directory named `images`—often used for easy organization.

In this first example, let's assume you have placed an image called `myimage.gif` in the same directory as the HTML file you want to use to display it. To display it, insert the following HTML tag at the point in the text where you want the image to appear, using the name of your image file instead of `myimage.gif`:

```
<img src="myimage.gif" alt="My Image" />
```

If your image file were in the `images` directory below the document root, you would use the following code, which you can see now contains the full path to `myimage.gif` in the `images` directory:

```
<img src="/images/myimage.gif" alt="My Image" />
```

NOTE

It doesn't matter to the web server, web browser, or end user just where you put your images, as long as you know where they are and you use the correct paths in your HTML code.

Personally, I prefer to put all my images in a separate `images` directory, or in a subdirectory of a generic `assets_directory` (such as `assets/images`) so that all my images or other assets, such as multimedia and JavaScript files, are neatly organized.

Both the `src` and the `alt` attributes of the `<img />` tag are required for valid HTML web pages. The `src` attribute identifies the image file, and the `alt` attribute enables you to specify descriptive text about the image. The `alt` attribute is intended to serve as an alternative to the image if a user is unable to view the image either because it is unavailable or because the user is using a text-only browser or screen reader. You'll read more on the `alt` attribute later, in the section "Describing Images with Text."

As an example of how to use the `<img />` tag, Listing 11.1 inserts an image at the top of the page, before a paragraph of text. Whenever a web browser displays the HTML file in Listing 8.2, it automatically retrieves and displays the image file as shown in Figure 11.1.

FIGURE 11.1
When a web browser displays the HTML code shown in Listing 11.1, it renders the `hd.jpg` image.

NOTE

The `<img />` tag is one of the HTML tags that also supports a `title` attribute; you can also use this attribute to describe an image, much like the `alt` attribute. However, the `title` attribute is problematic, in that it is displayed inconsistently across different user agents and thus cannot be relied upon. You might see the `title` attribute being used, and your HTML will be valid if you use it, but please do not use it in place of an `alt` attribute; doing so will limit your site's usefulness on many types of devices.

Listing 11.1   Using the `<img />` Tag to Place Images on a Web Page

```
<!DOCTYPE html>
<html lang="en">
 <head>
  <title>A Spectacular Yosemite View</title>
 </head>

 <body>
  <section>
    <header>
      <h1>A Spectacular Yosemite View</h1>
    </header>
    <img src="hd.jpg" alt="Half Dome" />
    <p><strong>Half Dome</strong> is a granite dome in Yosemite National
    Park, located in northeastern Mariposa County, California, at the
    eastern end of Yosemite Valley. The granite crest rises more than
    4,737 ft (1,444 m) above the valley floor.</p>
    <p>This particular view is of Half Dome as seen from Washburn
    Point.</p>
  </section>
 </body>
</html>
```

If you guessed that `img` refers to "image," you're right. Likewise, `src` refers to "source," or a reference to the location of the image file. As discussed at the beginning of this book, an image is always stored in a file separate from the text of your web page (your HTML file), even though it appears to be part of the same page when viewed in a browser.

As with the `<a>` tag used for hyperlinks, you can specify any complete Internet address as the location of an image file in the `src` attribute of the `<img />` tag. You can also use relative addresses, such as `/images/birdy.jpg` or `../smiley.gif`.

Describing Images with Text

The `<img />` tag in Listing 11.1 includes a short text message—in this case, `alt="Half Dome"`. The `alt` stands for *alternate text*, which is the message that appears in place of the image itself if it does not load. An image might not load if its address is incorrect, if the Internet connection is very slow and the data has not yet transferred, or if the user is using a text-only browser or screen reader. Figure 11.2 shows one example of `alt` text used in place of an image. Each web browser renders `alt` text differently, but the information is still provided when it is part of your HTML document.

NOTE

You can include an image from any website within your own pages. In those cases, the image is retrieved from the other page's web server whenever your page is displayed. You could do this, but you shouldn't! Not only is it bad manners (and probably a copyright violation) because you are using the other person's bandwidth for your own personal gain, but it also can make your pages display more slowly. Additionally, you have no way of controlling when the image might be changed or deleted.

If you are granted permission to republish an image from another web page, always transfer a copy of that image to your computer and use a local file reference, such as `<img src="myimage.jpg" />` instead of `<img src="http://www.otherserver.com/theirimage.jpg" />`. This advice is not applicable, however, when you host your images—such as photographs—at a service specifically meant as an image repository, such as Flickr (www.flickr.com). Services such as Flickr provide you with a URL for each image, and each URL includes Flickr's domain in the address. The same is true if you want to link to images you have taken with mobile applications such as Instagram or Streamzoo (to name but a couple)—these services also provide you with a full URL to an image that you can then link to in your own website.

FIGURE 11.2
Users will see alt messages when
images do not appear.

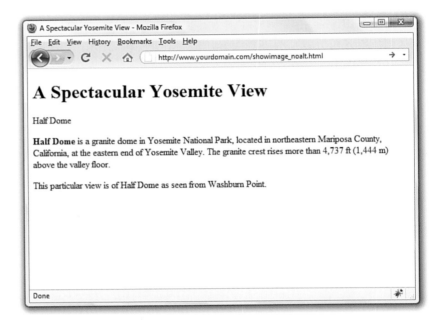

FIGURE 11.2
Users will see alt messages when images do not appear.

Even when graphics have fully loaded and are visible in the web browser, the alt message might appear in a little box (known as a *ToolTip*) whenever the mouse pointer passes over an image. The alt message also helps any user who is visually impaired (or is using a voice-based interface to read the web page).

You must include a suitable alt attribute in every <img /> tag on your web pages, keeping in mind the variety of situations in which people might see that message. A very brief description of the image is usually best, but web page authors sometimes put short advertising messages or subtle humor in their alt messages; too much humor and not enough information is frowned upon, because it is not all that useful. For small or unimportant images, it's tempting to omit the alt message altogether, but the alt attribute is a required attribute of the <img /> tag. This doesn't mean your page won't display properly, but it does mean you'll be in violation of HTML standards. I recommend assigning an empty text message to alt if you absolutely don't need it (alt=""), which is sometimes the case with small or decorative images.

Specifying Image Height and Width

Because text moves over the Internet much faster than graphics, most web browsers end up displaying the text on a page before they display images. This gives users something to read while they're waiting to see the pictures, which makes the whole page seem to load faster.

You can make sure that everything on your page appears as quickly as possible and in the right places by explicitly stating each image's height and width. That way, a web browser can immediately and accurately make room for each image as it lays out the page and while it waits for the images to finish transferring.

For each image you want to include in your site, you can use your graphics program to determine its exact height and width in pixels. You might also be able to find these image properties by using system tools. For example, in Windows, you can see an image's height and width by right-clicking the image, selecting Properties, and then selecting Details. When you know the height and width of an image, you can include its dimensions in the `<img />` tag, like this:

```
<img src="myimage.gif" alt="Fancy Picture" width="200" height="100" />
```

Aligning Images

Just as you can align text on a page, you can align images on the page using special attributes. You can align images both horizontally and vertically with respect to text and other images that surround them.

Horizontal Image Alignment

As discussed in Hour 5, "Working with Text Blocks and Lists," you can use the `text-align` CSS property to align content within an element as centered, aligned with the right margin, or aligned with the left margin. These style settings affect both text and images, and they can be used within any block element, such as `<p>`.

Like text, images are normally lined up with the left margin unless another alignment setting indicates that they should be centered or right-justified. In other words, `left` is the default value of the `text-align` CSS property.

TIP

The height and width specified for an image don't have to match the image's actual height and width. A web browser tries to squish or stretch the image to display whatever size you specify. However, this is generally a bad idea because browsers aren't particularly good at resizing images. If you know you want an image to display smaller, you're definitely better off just resizing it in an image editor.

NOTE

At the time of this writing, web developers and designers are discussing the creation and implementation of what are known as responsive images, or images that are displayed at different sizes and resolutions depending on the browser and media type. A new HTML5 element called `<picture>` has been introduced but is not yet part of the standard, nor is it implemented by many web browsers. If you plan to do any work with images on the web in the future, file away this information and check up on the status of this new element from time to time at http://picture.responsiveimages.org/.

You can also wrap text around images by using the `float` CSS property directly within the `<img />` tag.

In Listing 11.2, `<img style="float:left" />` aligns the first image to the left and wraps text around the right side of it, as you might expect. Similarly, `<img style="float:right" />` aligns the second image to the right and wraps text around the left side of it. Figure 11.3 shows how these images align on a web page. There is no concept of floating an image to the center because there would be no way to determine how to wrap text on each side of it.

FIGURE 11.3
Showing the image alignment from Listing 11.2.

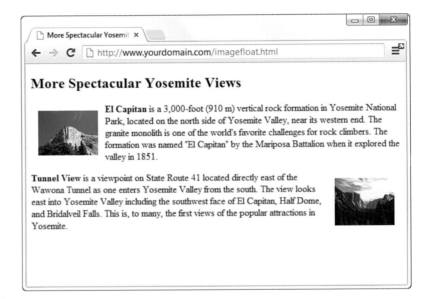

LISTING 11.2 Using `float` Style Properties to Align Images on a Web Page

```
<!DOCTYPE html>

<html lang="en">
 <head>
  <title>More Spectacular Yosemite Views</title>
 </head>

 <body>
  <section>
    <header>
    <h1>More Spectacular Yosemite Views</h1>
    </header>
    <p><img src="elcap_sm.jpg" alt="El Capitan" width="100"
```

```
height="75" style="float:left; padding: 12px;"/><strong>El
Capitan</strong> is a 3,000-foot (910 m) vertical rock formation
in Yosemite National Park, located on the north side of Yosemite
Valley, near its western end. The granite monolith is one of the
world's favorite challenges for rock climbers. The formation was
named "El Capitan" by the Mariposa Battalion when it explored the
valley in 1851.</p>
<p><img src="tunnelview_sm.jpg" alt="Tunnel View" width="100"
height="80" style="float:right; padding: 12px;"/><strong>Tunnel
View</strong> is a viewpoint on State Route 41 located directly east
of the Wawona Tunnel as one enters Yosemite Valley from the south.
The view looks east into Yosemite Valley including the southwest face
of El Capitan, Half Dome, and Bridalveil Falls. This is, to many, the
first views of the popular attractions in Yosemite.</p>
</section>
</body>
</html>
```

NOTE

Notice the addition of padding in the style attribute for both `<img/>` tags used in Listing 11.2. This padding provides some breathing room between the image and the text—12 pixels on all four sides of the image. You learn more about padding in Hour 13, "Working with Margins, Padding, Alignment, and Floating."

Vertical Image Alignment

Sometimes you want to insert a small image in the middle of a line of text, or you want to put a single line of text next to an image as a caption. In either case, having some control over how the text and images line up vertically would be handy. Should the bottom of the image line up with the bottom of the letters, or should the text and images all be arranged so that their middles line up? You can choose between these and several other options:

▶ To line up the top of an image with the top of the tallest image or letter on the same line, use `<img style="vertical-align:text-top" />`.

▶ To line up the bottom of an image with the bottom of the text, use `<img style="vertical-align:text-bottom" />`.

▶ To line up the middle of an image with the overall vertical center of everything on the line, use `<img style="vertical-align:middle" />`.

▶ To line up the bottom of an image with the baseline of the text, use `<img style="vertical-align:baseline" />`.

NOTE

The `vertical-align` CSS property also supports values of `top` and `bottom`, which can align images with the overall top or bottom of a line of elements, regardless of any text on the line.

All four of these options are used in Listing 11.3 and displayed in Figure 11.4. Four thumbnail images are now listed vertically down the page, along with descriptive text next to each image. Various settings for the `vertical-align` CSS property are used to align each image and its relevant text. This is certainly not the most beautiful page, but the various alignments should be clear to you.

TIP

If you don't assign any
vertical-align CSS property in
an <img /> tag or class used
with an <img /> tag, the bottom
of the image will line up with
the baseline of any text next
to it. That means you never
actually have to use vertical-
align:baseline because it is
assumed by default. However,
if you specify a margin for
an image and intend for the
alignment to be a bit more
exacting with the text, you
might want to explicitly set the
vertical-align attribute to
text-bottom.

LISTING 11.3 Using vertical-align Styles to Align Text with Images

```
<!DOCTYPE html>

<html lang="en">
 <head>
  <title>Small But Mighty Spectacular Yosemite Views</title>
 </head>

 <body>
  <section>
    <header>
      <h1>Small But Mighty Yosemite Views</h1>
    </header>
    <p><img src="elcap_sm.jpg" alt="El Capitan" width="100"
    height="75" style="vertical-align:text-top;"/><strong>El
    Capitan</strong> is a 3,000-foot (910 m) vertical rock formation
    in Yosemite National Park.</p>
    <p><img src="tunnelview_sm.jpg" alt="Tunnel View" width="100"
    height="80" style="vertical-align:text-bottom;"/><strong>Tunnel
    View</strong> looks east into Yosemite Valley.</p>
    <p><img src="upperyosefalls_sm.jpg" alt="Upper Yosemite Falls"
    width="87" height="100" style="vertical-align:middle;"/><strong>Upper
    Yosemite Falls</strong> are 1,430 ft and are among the twenty highest
    waterfalls in the world. </p>
    <p><img src="hangingrock_sm.jpg" alt="Hanging Rock" width="100"
    height="75" style="vertical-align:baseline;"/><strong>Hanging
    Rock</strong>, off Glacier Point, used to be a popular spot for people
    to, well, hang from. Crazy people.</p>
  </section>
 </body>
</html>
```

FIGURE 11.4
Showing the vertical image alignment options used in Listing 11.3.

Turning Images into Links

You probably noticed in Figure 11.1 that the image on the page is quite large. This is fine in this particular example, but it isn't ideal when you're trying to present multiple images. It makes more sense to create smaller image thumbnails that link to larger versions of each image. Then you can arrange the thumbnails on the page so that visitors can easily see all the written content, even if they see only a smaller version of the actual (larger) image. Thumbnails are one of the many ways you can use image links to spice up your pages.

To turn any image into a clickable link to another page or image, you can use the `<a>` tag that you learned about in Hour 8, "Using External and Internal Links," to make text links. Listing 11.4 contains the code to display thumbnails of images within text, with those thumbnails linking to larger versions of the images. To ensure that the user knows to click the thumbnails, the image and some helper text are enclosed in a `<div>`, as shown in Figure 11.5.

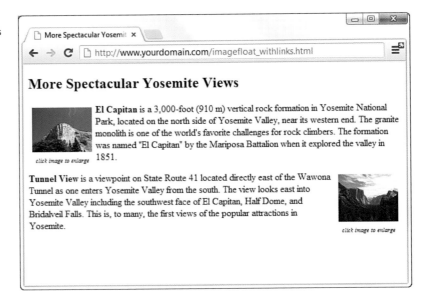

LISTING 11.4   Using Thumbnails for Effective Image Links

```
<!DOCTYPE html>

<html lang="en">
 <head>
  <title>More Spectacular Yosemite Views</title>
   <style type="text/css">
   div.imageleft {
    float:left;
    clear: all;
    text-align:center;
    font-size:10px;
    font-style:italic;
    }
   div.imageright {
    float:right;
    clear: all;
    text-align:center;
    font-size:10px;
    font-style:italic;
    }
   img {
    padding: 6px;
    border: none;
    }
```

```
    </style>
  </head>
  <body>
   <section>
     <header>
     <h1>More Spectacular Yosemite Views</h1>
     </header>
     <div class="imageleft">
     <a href="http://www.flickr.com/photos/nofancyname/614253439/"><img
     src="elcap_sm.jpg" alt="El Capitan" width="100" height="75"/></a>
     <br/>click image to enlarge</div>
     <p><strong>El Capitan</strong> is a 3,000-foot (910 m) vertical rock
     formation in Yosemite National Park, located on the north side of
     Yosemite Valley, near its western end. The granite monolith is one
     of the world's favorite challenges for rock climbers. The formation
     was named "El Capitan" by the Mariposa Battalion when it explored
     the valley in 1851.</p>
     <div class="imageright">
     <a href="http://www.flickr.com/photos/nofancyname/614287355/"><img
     src="tunnelview_sm.jpg" alt="Tunnel View" width="100" height="80"/></a>
     <br/>click image to enlarge</div>
     <p><strong>Tunnel View</strong> is a viewpoint on State Route 41
     located directly east of the Wawona Tunnel as one enters Yosemite
     Valley from the south. The view looks east into Yosemite Valley
     including the southwest face of El Capitan, Half Dome, and
     Bridalveil Falls. This is, to many, the first views of the
     Popular attractions in Yosemite.</p>
     </section>
  </body>
</html>
```

The code in Listing 11.4 uses additional styles that are explained in more detail in later chapters, but you should be able to figure out the basics:

▶ The `<a>` tags link these particular images to larger versions, which, in this case, are stored on an external server (at Flickr).

▶ The `<div>` tags, and their styles, are used to align those sets of graphics and caption text (and also include some padding).

Unless instructed otherwise, web browsers display a colored rectangle around the edge of each image link. As with text links, the rectangle usually appears blue for links that haven't been visited recently and purple for links that have been visited recently—unless you specify different-colored links in your stylesheet. Because you seldom, if ever, want this unsightly line around your linked images, you should usually include `style="border:none"` in any `<img />` tag within a link. In this instance, the `border:none` style is made part of the stylesheet entry for the `<img/>` element because we use the same styles twice.

When you click one of the thumbnail images on the sample page shown, the link opens in the browser, as shown in Figure 11.6.

Using Background Images

As you learned in Hour 10, "Creating Images for Use on the Web," you can use background images to act as a sort of wallpaper in a container element so that the text or other images appear on top of this underlying design.

The basic CSS properties that work together to create a background are as follows:

▶ `background-color`: Specifies the background color of the element. Although it is not image related, it is part of the set of background-related properties. If an image is transparent or does not load, the user will see the background color instead.

▶ `background-image`: Specifies the image to use as the background of the element using the following syntax: `url('imagename.gif')`.

- ▶ `background-repeat`: Specifies how the image should repeat, both horizontally and vertically. By default (without specifying anything), background images repeat both horizontally and vertically. Other options are `repeat` (same as default), `repeat-x` (horizontal), `repeat-y` (vertical), and `no-repeat` (only one appearance of the graphic).

- ▶ `background-position`: Specifies where the image should be initially placed, relative to its container. Options include `top-left`, `top-center`, `top-right`, `center-left`, `center-center`, `center-right`, `bottom-left`, `bottom-center`, `bottom-right`, and specific pixel and percentage placements.

When specifying a background image, you can put all these specifications together into one property, like so:

```
body {
   background: #ffffff url('imagename.gif') no-repeat top right;
}
```

In the previous stylesheet entry, the body element of the web page will be white and will include a graphic named `imagename.gif` at the top right. Another use for the `background` property is the creation of custom bullets for your unordered lists. To use images as bullets, first define the style for the `<ul>` tag, as follows:

```
ul {
  list-style-type: none;
  padding-left: 0;
  margin-left: 0;
}
```

Next, change the declaration for the `<li>` tag to this:

```
li {
  background: url(mybullet.gif) left center no-repeat
}
```

Make sure that `mybullet.gif` (or whatever you name your graphic) is on the web server and accessible; in this case, all unordered list items will show your custom image instead of the standard filled disc bullet.

We return to the specific use of background properties in Part III, "Advanced Web Page Design with CSS," when using CSS for overall page layouts.

Using Imagemaps

Sometimes you want to use an image as navigation, but beyond the simple button-based or link-based navigation that you often see in websites. For example, perhaps you have a website with medical information, and you want to show an image of the human body that links to pages that provide information about various body parts. Or you have a website that provides a world map that users can click to access information about countries. You can divide an image into regions that link to different documents, depending on where users click within that image. This is called an *imagemap*, and any image can be made into an imagemap.

Why Imagemaps Aren't Always Necessary

The first point to know about imagemaps is that you probably won't need to use them except in very special cases. It's almost always easier and more efficient to use several ordinary images that are placed directly next to one another and provide a separate link for each image.

For example, see Figure 11.7. This is a web page that shows 12 different corporate logos; this example is a common type of web page in the business world, in which you give a little free advertisement to your partners. You *could* present these logos as one large image and create an imagemap that provides links to each of the 12 companies. Users could click each logo in the image to visit each company's site. But every time you wanted to add a new logo to the imagemap, you would have to modify the entire image and remap the hotspots—not a good use of anyone's time. Instead, in this case when an imagemap is not warranted, you simply display the images on the page as in this example, by using 12 separate images (one for each company) and having each image include a link to that particular company.

An imagemap is the best choice for an image that has numerous parts, is oddly arranged, or has a design that is itself too complicated to divide into separate images. Figure 11.8 shows an image that is best suited as an imagemap—a public domain image provided by the United States CIA of the standard time zones of the world.

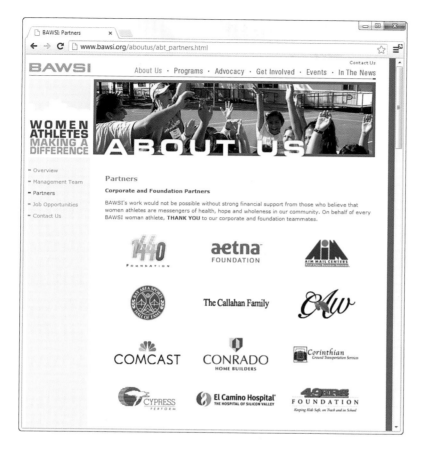

FIGURE 11.7
Web page with 12 different logos; this could be presented as a single imagemap or divided into 12 separate pieces.

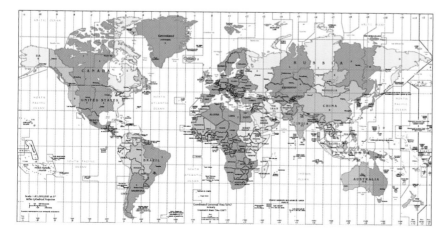

FIGURE 11.8
This image wouldn't respond well to being sliced up into perfectly equal parts—better make it an imagemap.

Mapping Regions Within an Image

To create any type of imagemap, you need to figure out the numerical pixel coordinates of each region within the image that you want to turn into a clickable link. These clickable links are also known as *areas*. Your graphics program might provide you with an easy way to find these coordinates. Or you might want to use a standalone imagemapping tool such as Mapedit (http://www.boutell.com/mapedit/) or an online imagemap maker such as the one at http://www.image-maps.com/. In addition to helping you map the coordinates, these tools provide the HTML code necessary to make the maps work.

Using an imagemapping tool is often as simple as using your mouse to draw a rectangle (or a custom shape) around the area you want to be a link. Figure 11.9 shows the result of one of these rectangular selections, as well as the interface for adding the URL and the title or alternate text for this link. Several pieces of information are necessary to creating the HTML for your imagemap: coordinates, target URL, and alternate text for the link.

FIGURE 11.9
Using an imagemapping tool to create linked areas of a single graphic.

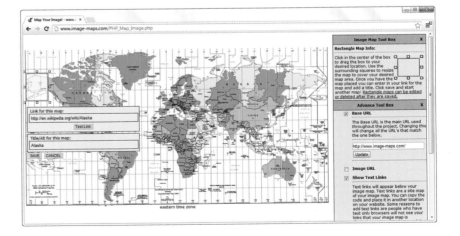

You're more likely to remember how to make imagemaps if you get an image of your own and turn it into an imagemap as you continue with this chapter:

▶ For starters, it's easiest to choose a fairly large image that is visually divided into roughly rectangular regions.

▶ If you don't have a suitable image handy, use your favorite graphics program to make one. Perhaps use a single photograph showing several people, and use each person as an area of the imagemap.

▶ Try a few different imagemapping tools to determine which you like best. Start with standalone software such as MapEdit (http://www.boutell.com/mapedit/), and move to the online imagemap maker at http://www.image-maps.com/. There are others; use the search engine of your choice to find variations on the imagemap software theme.

Creating the HTML for an Imagemap

If you use an imagemap generator, it will provide the necessary HTML for creating the imagemap. However, it is a good idea to understand the parts of the code so that you can check it for accuracy. The following HTML code is required to start any imagemap:

```
<map name="mapname">
```

Keep in mind that you can use whatever name you want for the `name` of the `<map>` tag, although it helps to make it as descriptive as possible. Next, you need an `<area />` tag for each region of the image. Following is an example of a single `<area />` tag that was produced by the actions shown in Figure 11.9:

```
<area shape="rect" coords="1,73,74,163"
    href="http://en.wikipedia.org/wiki/Alaska"
    alt="Alaska"   title="Alaska" />
```

This `<area />` tag has five attributes, which you use with every area you describe in an imagemap:

▶ `shape` indicates whether the region is a rectangle (`shape="rect"`), a circle (`shape="circle"`), or an irregular polygon (`shape="poly"`).

▶ `coords` gives the exact pixel coordinates for the region. For rectangles, give the x,y coordinates of the upper-left corner followed by the x,y coordinates of the lower-right corner. For circles, give the x,y center point followed by the radius in pixels.

For polygons, list the x,y coordinates of all the corners in a connect-the-dots order.

Here is an example of a mapped polygon—they can get a little crazy looking:

```
<area shape="poly"
coords="233,0,233,20,225,22,225,101,216,121,212,154,212,167,212,
181,222,195,220,209,226,214,226,234,232,252,224,253,223,261,231,
264,232,495,254,497,274,495,275,482,258,463,275,381,270,348,257,
338,266,329,272,313,271,301,258,292,264,284,262,262,272,263,272,
178,290,172,289,162,274,156,274,149,285,151,281,134,272,137,274,3"
href="http://en.wikipedia.org/wiki/Eastern_Time_Zone"
alt="Eastern Time Zone" title="Eastern Time Zone"/>
```

▶ href specifies the location to which the region links. You can use any address or filename that you would use in an ordinary <a> link tag.

▶ alt enables you to provide a piece of text that is associated with the shape; as you learned previously, providing this text is important to users browsing with text-only browsers or screen readers. The use of title ensures that ToolTips containing the information are also visible when the user accesses the designated area.

Each distinct clickable region in an imagemap must be described as a single area, which means that a typical imagemap consists of a list of areas. After you've coded the <area /> tags, you are done defining the imagemap, so wrap things up with a closing </map> tag.

The last step in creating an imagemap is wiring it up to the actual map image. The map image is placed on the page using an ordinary <img /> tag. However, an extra usemap attribute is coded like this:

```
<img src="timezonemap.png" usemap="#timezonemap"
  style="border:none; width:977px;height:498px"
  alt="World Timezone Map" />
```

When specifying the value of the usemap attribute, use the name you put in the id of the <map> tag (and don't forget the # symbol). Also include the style attribute to specify the height and width of the image and to turn off the border around the imagemap, which you might or might not elect to keep in imagemaps of your own.

Listing 11.5 shows the complete code for a sample web page containing the map graphic, its imagemap, and a few mapped areas.

LISTING 11.5   Defining the Regions of an Imagemap with `<map>` and
`<area />` Tags

```
<!DOCTYPE html>

<html lang="en">
 <head>
  <title>Testing an Imagemap</title>
 </head>

 <body>
  <section>
    <header>
      <h1>Testing an Imagemap</h1>
    </header>
    <div style="text-align:center"> Click on an area to learn more about
    that location or time zone.<br/>
    <img src="timezonemap.png" usemap="#timezonemap"
    style="border:none; width:977px;height:498px "
    alt="World Timezone Map" /></div>

    <map name="timezonemap" id="timezonemap">
    <area shape="poly" coords=" 233,0,233,20,225,22,225,101,216,121,212,
     154,212,167,212,181,222,195,220,209,226,214,226,234,232,252,224,253,
     223,261,231,264,232,495,254, 497,274,495,275,482,258,463,275,381,270,
     348,257,338,266,329,272,313,271,301,258,292,264,284,262, 262,272,263,
     272,178,290, 172,289,162,274,156,274,149,285,151,281,134,272,137,
     274,3 "
    href="http://en.wikipedia.org/wiki/eastern_time_zone"
    alt="Eastern Time Zone" title="Eastern Time Zone" />
    <area shape="rect" coords="1,73,74,163 "
    href="http://en.wikipedia.org/wiki/Alaska"
    alt="Alaska" title="Alaska" />
    </map>
  </section>
 </body>
</html>
```

Figure 11.10 shows the imagemap in action. When you hover the
mouse over an area, the `alt` or `title` text for that area—in this
example, `Eastern Time Zone`—is displayed on the imagemap.

NOTE

One method of producing
mapped images relies solely on
CSS, not the HTML `<map>` tag.
You will learn more about this
in Hour 16, "Using CSS to Do
More with Lists."

FIGURE 11.10
The imagemap defined in Listing
11.5 as it displays on the web
page.

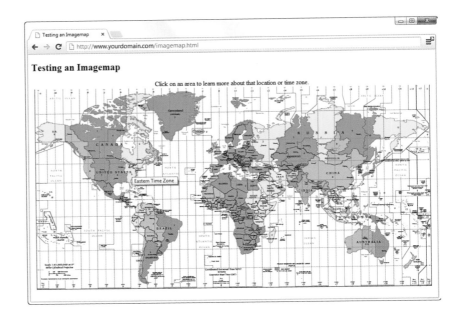

Summary

In this hour, you learned how to use images in your web pages. After creating, editing, or otherwise finding some images to use, you learned how to place them in your pages using the `<img />` tag. You learned how to include a short text message that appears in place of the image as it loads and that also appears whenever users move the mouse pointer over the image. You also learned how to control the horizontal and vertical alignment of each image, and how to wrap text around the left or right of an image.

You learned how to use images as links—either by using the `<a>` tag around the images or by creating imagemaps. You also learned a little about how to use images in the background of container elements.

Table 11.1 summarizes the tags and attributes covered in this hour.

TABLE 11.1   Tags and Attributes Covered in Hour 11

Tag	Function
`<img />`	Places an image file within the page.
`<map>...</map>`	A client-side imagemap referenced by `<img usemap="..." />`. Includes one or more `<area />` tags.
`<area />`	Defines a clickable link within a client-side imagemap.

Attribute/Style	Function
`style="background-color:color"`	Sets the background color of an element (such as `<body>`, `<p>`, `<div>`, `<blockquote>`, and other containers).
`style="color:color"`	Sets the color of text within an element.
`style="border:size type color"`	Sets the color of the four borders around an element. Border colors cannot be used without also specifying the width and type of the border.
`src="address"`	Gives the address or filename of the image.
`alt="altdescription"`	Gives an alternative description of the image that is displayed in place of the image, primarily for users who can't view the image itself.
`title="title"`	A text message that is displayed as an image title, typically in a small pop-up box (ToolTip) over the image.
`width="width"`	Specifies the width of the image (in pixels).
`height="height"`	Specifies the height of the image (in pixels).
`style="border:attributes"`	Gets rid of the border around the image if the image is serving as a link.
`style="vertical-align:alignment"`	Aligns the image vertically to `text-top`, `top`, `text-bottom`, `bottom`, `middle`, or `baseline`.
`style="float:float"`	Floats the image to one side so that text can wrap around it. Possible values are `left`, `right`, and `none` (default).
`usemap="name"`	The name of an imagemap specification for client-side image mapping. Used with `<map>` and `<area />`.
`shape="value"`	Within the `<area />` tag, specifies the shape of the clickable area. Valid options for this attribute are `rect`, `poly`, and `circle`.
`coords="values"`	Within the `<area />` tag, specifies the coordinates of the clickable region within an image. Its meaning and setting vary according to the type of area.
`href="linkurl"`	Within the `<area />` tag, specifies the URL that should be loaded when the area is clicked.

Q&A

Q. I used the `<img />` **tag just as you advised, but when I view the page, all I see is a little box with some shapes in it. What's wrong?**

A. The broken image icon you're seeing can mean one of two things: Either the web browser couldn't find the image file or the image isn't saved in a format the browser recognizes. To solve these problems, first check to make sure that the image is where it is supposed to be. If it is, then open the image in your graphics editor and save it again as a GIF, JPG, or PNG.

Q. What happens if I overlap areas on an imagemap?

A. You are allowed to overlap areas on an imagemap. Just keep in mind that, when determining which link to follow, one area will has precedence over the other area. Precedence is assigned according to which areas are listed first in the imagemap. For example, the first area in the map has precedence over the second area, which means that a click in the overlapping portion of the areas will link to the first area. If you have an area within an imagemap that doesn't link to anything (known as a *dead area*), you can use this overlap trick to deliberately prevent this area from linking to anything. To do this, just place the dead area before other areas so that the dead area overlaps them, and then set its `href` attribute to `""`.

Workshop

The Workshop contains quiz questions and exercises to help you solidify your understanding of the material covered. Try to answer all questions before looking at the "Answers" section that follows.

Quiz

1. How can you insert an `elephant.jpg` image file at the very top of a web page?

2. How would you make the word `Elephant` available to users when a web browser can't display the actual `elephant.jpg` image or if a screen reader were in use?

3. If you had an image called `myimage.png` and you wanted to align it so that a line of text lined up at the middle of the image, what style property would you use?

Answers

1. Copy the image file into the same directory folder as the HTML text file. Immediately after the `<body>` tag in the HTML text file, type `<p><img src="elephant.jpg" alt="" /></p>`.

2. Use the following HTML:

```
<img src="elephant.jpg" alt="elephant" />
```

3. You would use `vertical-align:middle` to ensure that the text lined up at the middle of the image.

Exercises

▶ Practicing any of the image placement methods in this chapter will go a long way toward helping you determine the role that images can, and will, play in the websites you design. Using a few sample images, practice using the `float` style to place images and text in relation to one another. Remember, the possible values for `float` are `left`, `right`, and `none` (default).

▶ Much like the previous exercise, use the various types of vertical alignment to lay out images and text on a web page of your choice.

HOUR 12
Using Multimedia in Your Website

The term *multimedia* encompasses everything we see and hear on a web page: audio, video, and animation, as well as static images and text. In previous hours, you learned how to use images and text; in this hour, you learn about including the other types of multimedia in your websites. You don't learn how to create any particular audio or video, but you do learn how to include such files in your site, through either linking or embedding the content.

Before even thinking about including multimedia in your site, remember that not every user has devices that will play your media type, nor do all users have broadband Internet connections that allow these large files to transfer quickly. Always warn your visitors that the links they click will take them to multimedia files, and offer them the choice to view or listen to the content—don't force the files upon them.

WHAT YOU'LL LEARN IN THIS HOUR:

▶ How to link to multimedia files

▶ How to embed multimedia files

▶ How to use HTML5 audio and video elements

▶ Additional tips for using multimedia

Create or Find Some Multimedia to Use in Your Website

Before you learn how to place multimedia on your web pages, you need to have some multimedia content.

Creating multimedia of any kind can be a challenging and complicated task. If you're planning to create your own content from scratch, you need far more than this book to become the next crackerjack multimedia developer. When you have some content, however, you can use the tips in this lesson to show you how to place your new creations into your web pages.

If you're artistically challenged, you can obtain useful multimedia assets in several alternative ways. Aside from the obvious (such as hiring an artist), here are a few suggestions:

▶ Much of the material on the Internet is free. Of course, it's still a good idea to double-check with the author or current owner of the content; you don't want to be sued for copyright infringement. In addition, various offices of the U.S. government generate content that, by law, belongs to all Americans. (For example, any NASA footage found online is free for your use.)

▶ Many search engines have specific search capabilities for finding multimedia files. As long as you are careful about copyright issues, this can be an easy way to find multimedia related to a specific topic. A simple search for "sample Flash animations," "sample QuickTime movie," or "sample audio files" will produce more results than you can handle.

▶ If you are creatively inclined, determine the medium you like most—video production, audio production, or animation, for example. When you have a starting point, look into the various types of software that will enable you to create such artistic masterpieces. Many companies, including Adobe (www.adobe.com) and Apple (www.apple.com), provide multimedia software.

Linking to Multimedia Files

The simplest and most reliable option for incorporating a video or audio file into your website is to simply link it in with an `<a>` tag, exactly as you would link to another HTML file.

For example, you could use the following line to offer an MOV video of an adorable kitten:

```
<a href="cute_kitten.mov">View an adorable kitten!</a>
```

When the user clicks the words `View an adorable kitten!`, the `cute_kitten.mov` QuickTime video file is transferred to his or her computer from your web server. Whichever helper application or plug-in the user has installed automatically starts as soon as the file has finished downloading. If no compatible helper or plug-in can be found, the web browser offers the user a chance to download the appropriate plug-in or save the video on the hard drive for later viewing.

Listing 12.1 contains the code for a web page that uses a simple image link to play a video in Windows Media file format. In addition to the image link, a link is placed within the text to provide context for the user.

Listing 12.1   Linking an Image to a Windows Media Video

```
<!DOCTYPE html>

<html lang="en">
  <head>
    <title>Fun in the Pond</title>
  </head>

  <body>
    <h1>This Kitten Loves to Play!</h1>
    <div style="border-style:none; float:left; padding:12px"><a
    href="kitten.wmv"><img src="projector.gif" alt="Kitten Video" /></a>
    </div>
    <p>All kittens love to play, but this one is particularly fond of her
    yellow stuffed banana toy!</p>
    <p>Click <a href="kitten.wmv">here</a> or on the projector graphic to
    see a movie clip of this kitten in action.</p>
  </body>
</html>
```

This code simply uses the `projector.gif` GIF image as a link to the `kitten.wmv` video clip. Figure 12.1 shows the pond sample page with the projector image in view. When the image is clicked, the Windows Media Player is invoked and begins to play the movie.

To view the video, you need only click the animated projector (or the text link in the paragraph). This action results in the browser either playing the video with the help of a plug-in (if one is found that can play the clip) or deferring to a suitable helper application.

NOTE

In case you're unfamiliar with *helper applications* (*helper apps*, for short), they are the external programs that a web browser calls on to display any type of file it can't handle on its own. Generally, the helper application associated with a file type is called on whenever a web browser can't display that type of file on its own.

Plug-ins are a special sort of helper application installed directly into a web browser. They enable you to view multimedia content directly in the browser window.

FIGURE 12.1
The `projector.gif` GIF image
is used as an image link to a
Windows Media file that launches
an external helper application.

If you change the link from `kitten.wmv` (Windows Media) to
`kitten.mov` (QuickTime), your browser handles the link differently.
Instead of launching another program, the QuickTime plug-in
enables you to view the movie clip directly in the browser window (see
Figure 12.2).

FIGURE 12.2
When you follow the image link,
the `kitten.mov` QuickTime movie
is played using the QuickTime
browser plug-in.

As you might have guessed, this approach of using a simple link to play multimedia files offers the best backward compatibility because the browser bears all the responsibility of figuring out how to play a multimedia clip. The downside to this is that you don't have much control over how a clip is played, and you definitely can't play a clip directly in the context of a page.

Embedding Multimedia Files

HTML has long contained a standard `<object>` element for embedding multimedia files in a web page. This element is widely supported in both desktop and mobile browsers and is used to represent a type of resource to be viewed or played in the browser but using an external plug-in.

Embedding a multimedia file into a web page produces a set of software controls that allow the file to be played directly—no secondary window is necessary, and there's no need to navigate away from the page you are on. Following is code to embed the kitten video, which you saw earlier, using the `<object>` tag:

```
<object
   width="320"
   height="240"
   type="video/x-ms-wmv"
   data="pond.wmv"
</object>
```

You can see the result of this code in Figure 12.3. This code isn't much more complicated than adding an image to your web page; the only real difference is that here you specify the file type (in this case, `video/x-ms-wmv`).

The `width` and `height` attributes of the `<object>` element determine the size of the embedded player (Windows Media Player, in this example). Some browsers automatically size the embedded player to fit the content if you leave these attributes off, whereas others don't show anything. Play it safe by setting them to a size that suits the multimedia content being played.

FIGURE 12.3
The `<object>` tag enables you to embed a video clip on a web page.

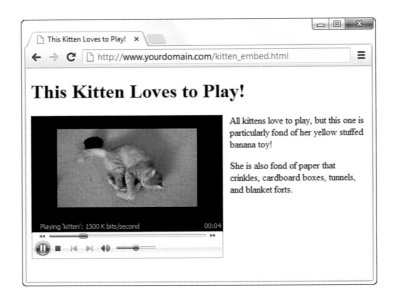

Only two other attributes are necessary to display the appropriate video file: the `data` attribute, which has a value of the filename (or URL to the file) you want to play, and the `type` attribute, which identifies the type of media being displayed. In this case, the file is a Windows Media Video (WMV) file, specified by the MIME types. A *MIME type* is an identifier for uniquely identifying different types of media objects on the Internet. MIME stands for Multipurpose Internet Mail Extensions, and this name comes from the fact that MIME types were originally used to identify email attachments. These MIME types should be used in the `type` attribute of the `<object>` element to identify what kind of multimedia object the `data` attribute is referencing.

Following are the MIME types for several popular sound and video formats you might want to use in your web pages:

▶ WAV Audio—`audio/vnd.wave`

▶ MP3 Audio—`audio/mpeg`

▶ MP4 Audio—`audio/mp4`

▶ WMV—`video/x-ms-wmv`

▶ MPEG Video—`video/mpeg`

▶ MPEG4 Video—`video/mp4`

▶ QuickTime—`video/quicktime`

Listing 12.2 shows the relevant code for the pond web page, where you can see the `<object>` element as it appears in context.

LISTING 12.2 Using an `<object>` Element to Directly Embed a WMV Video Clip

```
<!DOCTYPE html>

<html lang="en">
  <head>
    <title>This Kitten Loves to Play!</title>
  </head>

  <body>
    <h1>This Kitten Loves to Play!</h1>
    <div style="float:left; padding:12px">
    <object
       width="320"
       height="240"
       data="kitten.wmv"
       type="video/x-ms-wmv">
    </object>
    </div>
    <p>All kittens love to play, but this one is particularly fond
    of her yellow stuffed banana toy!</p>
    <p>She is also fond of paper that crinkles, cardboard boxes, tunnels,
    and blanket forts.</p>
  </body>
</html>
```

Although this section has discussed "embedding" a multimedia object using the `<object>` element, you can use another element to achieve the same goal: the appropriately named `<embed />` element. There's a good reason I didn't talk about the `<embed />` element first—it has a negative and confusing history. In the days before HTML5, multimedia objects could be embedded in web pages in two ways: using `<object>` (part of the official specification) or using `<embed />` (not part of the official specification, but implemented by the old Netscape browser). During this time, if you wanted to ensure that your embedded multimedia object was visible in all browsers, you used a little trickery and wrapped your `<embed />` element inside an `<object>` element, like so:

```
<object
        width="320"
        height="240"
        data="kitten.wmv"
        type="video/x-ms-wmv">
```

```
<embed
      width="320"
      height="240"
      type="video/x-ms-wmv"
      src="kitten.wmv" />
</object>
```

Browsers that knew what to do with `<object>` elements did so and ignored the `<embed />` element. But browsers that ignored the `<object>` element and knew what to do with the `<embed />` element did just that. This was as annoying to web developers then as it is confusing to explain now.

Now, in the era of HTML5, both the `<object>` and `<embed />` elements are valid, and you can use either one without having to use both. The only difference between the general usage of the two is that the `<object>` element uses the `data` attribute to refer to the multimedia resource, whereas the `<embed />` element uses the `src` attribute (much like the `<img />` tag).

Using Pure HTML5 for Audio and Video Playback

In the previous section, you learned more about the confusing history of the `<object>` and `<embed />` elements than you probably imagined existed. The end result of this confusing history is that although you most certainly can continue to use `<object>` or `<embed />` elements to embed audio or video in your web pages, and rely on external plug-ins to play those files, HTML5 contains native elements for playing audio and video. In this instance, *native* refers to the browser's capability to play multimedia files without external plug-ins, and all major browsers on all platforms (including mobile) support these elements. This will be the preferred method of playing back audio and video moving forward.

Listing 12.3 shows how to use the `<audio>` element to embed an audio file that will be played natively by the browser. The `<audio>` element is quite simple and requires only one attribute—`src`, or the location of the resource you want to play. However, as you see in Listing 12.3, you'll probably want to use a few other handy attributes.

LISTING 12.3   Using the `<audio>` Element to Embed and Play an Audio File

```
<!DOCTYPE html>

<html lang="en">
  <head>
    <title>Let's Hear Some Music</title>
  </head>

  <body>
    <h1>Let's Hear Some Music</h1>
    <p>Better yet, let's use the HTML5 &lt;audio&gt; element to do so!</p>
    <audio
        src="manhattan_beach.mp3"
        preload="auto"
        controls
        autoplay
        loop>

        <!-- Message to display in case the audio element isn't
        supported. -->
        <p>Your browser does not support the audio element.</p>
    </audio>
  </body>
</html>
```

In addition to the `src` attribute, which, in this case, has a value of `manhattan_beach.mp3` because that is the name of the audio file I want to play, I'm using four other attributes in this `<audio>` element:

- `preload`—Has three possible values: `none`, `auto`, and `metadata`. Use `none` if you do not want to buffer the file, use `auto` to buffer the file, and use `metadata` if you want to buffer only the metadata for the file.

- `controls`—If present, shows the controls for the audio player.

- `autoplay`—If present, plays the file as soon as it loads.

- `loop`—If present, continues to play the file repeatedly until it is manually stopped.

Figure 12.4 shows the page in Listing 12.3 as rendered by the Chrome web browser.

TIP

Notice the inclusion of a message to users inside the `<audio>` element. Although current versions of all major browsers support the `<audio>` element, if a user's browser does not, that user will instead see the message within the `<p></p>` tags.

FIGURE 12.4
Using the `<audio>` element to play a sound file.

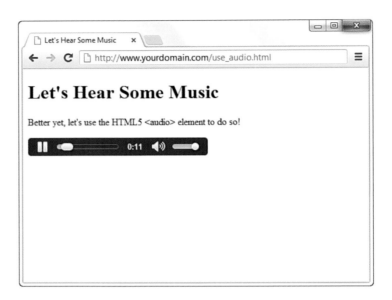

In practice, you probably wouldn't want to automatically play and loop a sound file in your website—doing so is typically considered a particularly negative user experience. However, if you *do* automatically play a sound file (please don't!), be sure to include the player controls so that users can immediately turn off the sound.

Using the HTML5 `<video>` element is quite similar to using the `<audio>` element. Listing 12.4 shows an example of this, in which the only real changes besides some text changes are the use of `height` and `width` attributes to define the space taken up by the video player and the video clip.

LISTING 12.4   Using the `<video>` Element to Embed and Play a Video File

```
<!DOCTYPE html>

<html lang="en">
  <head>
    <title>Let's Watch a Video</title>
  </head>

  <body>
    <h1>Let's Watch a Video</h1>
    <p>Better yet, let's use the HTML5 &lt;video&gt; element to do so!</p>
    <video
         src="kitten.mov"
         preload="auto"
         width="320"
```

```
        height="240"
        controls
        autoplay
        loop>

        <!-- Message to display in case the video element isn't
        supported. -->
        <p>Your browser does not support the video element.</p>
    </video>
    </body>
</html>
```

The `preload`, `controls`, `autoplay`, and `loop` attributes do exactly the same for the `<video>` element as they do for the `<audio>` element. Figure 12.5 shows the page in Listing 12.4 as rendered by the Chrome web browser.

FIGURE 12.5
Using the `<video>` element to play a video file.

Additional Tips for Using Multimedia

Before you add video, audio, or animations to your website, ask yourself whether you really should do so. When you use these types of multimedia, be sure to do so for a reason. Gratuitous sound and video, just like gratuitous images, can detract from your overall message. Then again, if your message is "Look at the videos I've made" or

"Listen to my music and download some songs," then multimedia absolutely must play a role in your website.

Keep a few additional tips in mind:

▶ Don't include multimedia in a page and set it to automatically play when the page loads. Always give users the option to start (and stop) your sound or video.

▶ When providing files for direct download, give users a choice of file type. Don't limit yourself to providing multimedia content playable by only one type of player on only one operating system.

▶ Multimedia files are larger than the typical graphics and text files, which means you need to have the space on your web server to store them, as well as the bandwidth allotment to transfer them to whomever requests them via your website.

▶ If your site is entirely audio or video and offers very little by way of text or graphics, understand that a certain segment of your audience won't see or hear what you want to present because of the limitations of their system or bandwidth. Provide these users with additional options to get your information.

▶ Leverage free online video hosting services, such as YouTube (www.youtube.com). Not only does YouTube provide storage for your video clips, but it also gives you the code necessary to embed the video in your own web page.

Summary

In this hour, you learned how to embed video and sound in a web page. You learned how to use a simple link to a multimedia file, which is the most broadly supported but least flexible option for playing media content. You then learned how to use the `<object>` or `<embed />` elements to embed a media player directly in a web page, which can be used to include a vast array of media types, including WAV, MP3, AVI, WMV, and QuickTime videos, to name just a few. Finally, you learned about the `<audio>` and `<video>` elements in HTML5, which enable the browser to render audio or video files natively, or without external plug-in support.

Table 12.1 summarizes the tags discussed in this hour.

TABLE 12.1   HTML Tags and Attributes Covered in Hour 12

Tag/Attribute	Function
`<object>...</object>`	Embeds images, videos, Java applets, ActiveX controls, or other objects into a document.
Attributes	
`width="width"`	Specifies the width of the embedded object in pixels.
`height="height"`	Specifies the height of the embedded object in pixels.
`data="mediaurl"`	Gives the URL of the resource you want to embed.
`type="mimetype"`	Specifies the MIME type of the multimedia content.
`<embed />`	Embeds a multimedia file to be read or displayed by a plug-in application.
Attributes	
`width="width"`	Specifies the width of the embedded object in pixels.
`height="height"`	Specifies the height of the embedded object in pixels.
`src="mediaurl"`	Gives the URL of the file to embed.
`type="mimetype"`	Specifies the MIME type of the multimedia content.
`<audio>...</ audio >`	Plays an audio file natively in the browser.
Attributes	
`src="mediaurl"`	Gives the URL of the file to embed.
`preload="preloadtype"`	Tells whether to preload the media file. Options are `none`, `auto`, and `metadata`.
`controls`	Instructs the browser to show the audio player controls.
`autoplay`	Instructs the browser to play the file when it has finished loading.
`loop`	Instructs the browser to play the file until it is explicitly stopped.
`<video>...</ video >`	Plays a video file natively in the browser.
Attributes	
`src="mediaurl"`	Gives the URL of the file to embed.
`preload="preloadtype"`	Tells whether to preload the media file. Options are `none`, `auto`, and `metadata`.

width="width"	Specifies the width of the embedded object in pixels.
height="height"	Specifies the height of the embedded object in pixels.
controls	Instructs the browser to show the video player controls.
autoplay	Instructs the browser to play the file when it has finished loading.
loop	Instructs the browser to play the file until it is explicitly stopped.

Q&A

Q. **I hear a lot about streaming video and audio. What does that mean?**

A. In the past, video and audio files took minutes and sometimes hours to retrieve through most modems, which severely limited the inclusion of video and audio on web pages. The goal everyone is moving toward is streaming video or audio, which plays while the data is being received. In other words, you don't have to completely download the clip before you can start to watch it or listen to it.

Streaming playback is now widely supported through most media players, in both standalone versions and plug-ins. When you embed a media object using the `<object>` or `<embed />` elements, the underlying media player automatically streams the media clip if the player supports streaming. When using the `<video>` element, you have more fine-grained control over the buffering and playback of your multimedia resource.

Q. **How do I choose an audiovisual file format among QuickTime, Windows AVI/WAV, MPEG, and others? Is there any significant difference among them?**

A. QuickTime is the most popular video format among Macintosh users, although QuickTime players are available for Windows as well. Similarly, AVI/WMV and WAV/WMA are the video and audio formats for Windows users, but you can get players for the Macintosh that support these formats. MPEG is another popular audio and video standard. MPEG-3 (MP3) is already extremely popular as the high-fidelity audio standard of choice. One other audio format that is based on MPEG is Apple's AAC format, which might be more familiar to you because this is the native iTunes music format.

If most of your audience uses Windows, use AVI/WMV for video and WAV/WMA or MP3 for audio. If your audience includes a significant number of Macintosh users, use QuickTime or at least offer some alternative. MP3 is also an option for Mac audio.

Workshop

The Workshop contains quiz questions and activities to help you solidify your understanding of the material covered. Try to answer all questions before looking at the "Answers" section that follows.

Quiz

1. What's the simplest method to provide access to a video on your website for the widest possible audience?

2. What basic HTML5 code would you use to embed a video file named `myvideo.mov` into a web page? The video requires an area on the page that is 320×305 pixels in size, and you want to show the video controls but do not want to automatically play or loop the file.

3. How would you code the `<audio>` element so that a media clip plays repeatedly? Assume that the audio file is called `myaudio.mp3`.

Answers

1. Just link to it:

```
<a href="myvideo.mov">my video</a>
```

2. The code follows:

```
<video width="320" height="305" src="myvideo.mov" controls></video>
```

3. Use the following:

```
<audio src="myaudio.mp3" autoplay></audio>
```

Exercises

▶ Find some freely available audio and video clips on the web, and practice placement within your text using the HTML5 `<audio>` and `<video>` elements.

▶ The techniques and tags covered in this hour for embedding media with the `<object>` and `<embed/>` elements also work with Flash files. To find out how you can use Flash to add interactive animations to your web pages, check out the Flash home page at http://www.adobe.com/products/flash.html.

HOUR 13
Working with Margins, Padding, Alignment, and Floating

Now that you've learned some of the basics of creating web content, in this hour, you learn the nitty-gritty of using CSS to enhance that content. In the hours that follow, you dive into using CSS to control aspects of your entire web page, not just individual pieces of text or graphics.

Before tackling page layout, however, it is important to understand four particular CSS properties individually before putting them all together:

- **The** `margin` **and** `padding` **properties**—For adding space around elements
- **The** `align` **and** `float` **properties**—To place your elements in relation to others

The examples provided in this hour are not the most stylish examples of web content ever created, but they are not intended to be. Instead, the examples clearly show just how HTML and CSS are working together. When you master CSS through this and other sections of the book, and through ongoing practice of what you've learned, you'll be able to use your own design skills to enhance what can be (and often is) the relatively basic underlying scaffolding.

Using Margins

Stylesheet *margins* enable you to add empty space around the *outside* of the rectangular area for an element on a web page. It is important to remember that the `margin` property works with space outside the element.

WHAT YOU'LL LEARN IN THIS HOUR:

▶ How to add margins around elements

▶ How to add padding within elements

▶ How to keep everything aligned

▶ How to use the `float` property

Following are the style properties for setting margins:

- ▶ `margin-top`—Sets the top margin

- ▶ `margin-right`—Sets the right margin

- ▶ `margin-bottom`—Sets the bottom margin

- ▶ `margin-left`—Sets the left margin

- ▶ `margin`—Sets the top, right, bottom, and left margins as a single property

You can specify margins using any of the individual margin properties or using the single `margin` property. Margins can be specified as auto, meaning that the browser itself sets the margin in specific lengths (pixels, points, or ems) or in percentages. If you decide to set a margin as a percentage, keep in mind that the percentage is calculated based on the size of the containing element. So if you set the `margin-left` property an element within the body to 25%, the left margin of the element will end up being 25% of the width of the entire page. However, if you set the `margin-left` property an element within *that* element to 25%, it will be 25% of whatever that original 25% was calculated to be.

The code in Listing 13.1 produces four rectangles on the page, each 250 pixels wide and 100 pixels high, with a 5-pixel solid black border (see Figure 9.2). Each rectangle—or `<div>`, in this case—has a different background color. We want the margin around each `<div>` to be 15 pixels on all sides, so we can use the following:

```
margin-top:15px;
margin-right:15px;
margin-bottom:15px;
margin-left:15px;
```

You can also write that in shorthand, using the `margin` property:

```
margin:15px 15px 15px 15px;
```

When you use the `margin` property (or `padding` or `border`) and you want all four values to be the same, you can simplify this even further and use this:

```
margin:15px;
```

When using shorthand for setting margins, padding, or borders, three approaches apply, which vary based on how many values you use when setting the property:

▶ **One value**—The size of all the margins

▶ **Two values**—The size of the top/bottom margins and the left/right margins (in that order)

▶ **Three values**—The size of the top margin, the left and right margins (they are given the same value), and the bottom margin (in that order)

▶ **Four values**—The size of the top, right, bottom, and left margins (in that order)

You might find it easier to stick to either using one value or using all four values, but that's certainly not a requirement.

LISTING 13.1   Simple Code to Produce Four Colored `<div>`s with Borders and Margins

```
<!DOCTYPE html>

<html lang="en">
  <head>
  <title>Color Blocks</title>
    <style type="text/css">
        div {
            width:250px;
            height:100px;
            border:5px solid #000000;
            color:black;
            font-weight:bold;
            text-align:center;
        }

        div#d1 {
           background-color:red;
           margin:15px;
        }

        div#d2 {
           background-color:green;
           margin:15px;
        }

        div#d3 {
           background-color:blue;
           margin:15px;
        }

        div#d4 {
           background-color:yellow;
           margin:15px;
        }
    </style>
  </head>
```

```
<body>
  <div id="d1">DIV #1</div>
  <div id="d2">DIV #2</div>
  <div id="d3">DIV #3</div>
  <div id="d4">DIV #4</div>
</body>
</html>
```

You can see the output of Listing 13.1 in Figure 13.1.

FIGURE 13.1
The basic color blocks sample page shows four color blocks, each with equal margins.

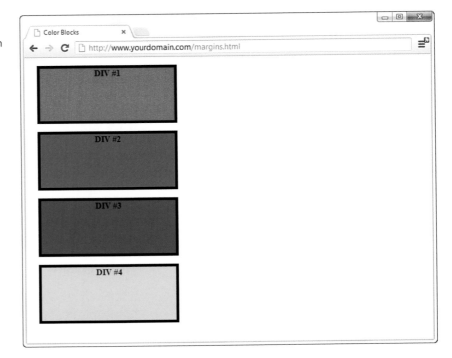

Next, working with just the `margin` property in the style sheet entries in Listing 13.1, let's shift the margins. In this example, you can't really see the right-side margin on any of these `<div>` elements because there's nothing to the right of them and they're not aligned to the right. With that in mind, let's set `margin-right` to `0px` in all of these. Beyond that, the next set of goals is to produce the following:

- No margin around the first color block
- A left-side margin of 15 pixels, a top margin of 5 pixels, and no bottom margin around the second color block

▶ A left-side margin of 75 pixels and no top margin or bottom margin around the third color block

▶ A left-side margin of 250 pixels and a top margin of 25 pixels around the fourth color block

This seems like it would be straightforward—no margin is being set around the first block. But we want a margin at the top of the second block, so really there *will* be a visible margin between the first and second blocks, even if we are not specifying a margin for the first block.

The new stylesheet entries for the four named `<div>`s now look like this:

```
div#d1 {
  background-color:red;
  margin:0px;
}

div#d2 {
  background-color:green;
  margin:5px 0px 0px 15px;
}

div#d3 {
  background-color:blue;
  margin:0px 0px 0px 75px;
}

div#d4 {
  background-color:yellow;
  margin:25px 0px 0px 250px;
}
```

The result of the code changes (see Figure 13.2) seems random but is actually quite useful for pointing out a few other important points. For example, when you recall that one of the goals was to produce no margin around the first color block, you might expect the border of the color block to be flush with the browser window. But as Figure 13.2 shows, there is a clear space between the content of the page and the frame of the browser window.

If we were working on element placement—which we get to in the next hour—this would cause a problem in the layout. To ensure that your placements and margins are counted from a position flush with the browser, you need to address the margin of the `<body>` element itself. In this case, you add the following to your stylesheet:

```
body {
  margin:0px;
}
```

FIGURE 13.2
Modifications to the color blocks
sample page display some different
margins.

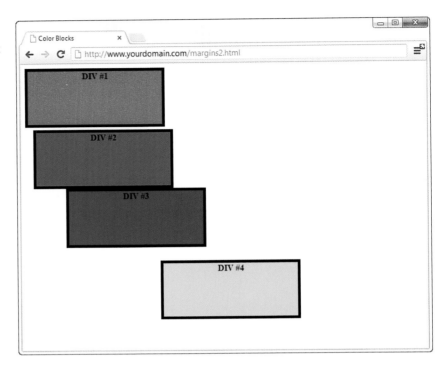

Another "gotcha" to remember is that if you have two bordered elements stacked on top of each other, but with no margin between them, the point at which they touch appears to have a double border. You might then consider making the top element's `border-bottom` half the width and then also make the bottom element's `border-top` half the width. If you do this, the borders appear to be the same width as the other sides when stacked on top of each other.

In addition, you might have thought that using a left-side margin of 250 pixels—the width of the `<div>`s—would begin the fourth color block where the third color block ended. That is not the case, however, because the third color block has a `margin-left` of 75 pixels. For them to even be close to lining up, the `margin-left` value for the fourth `div` would have to be 325 pixels.

Changing the styles to those shown in the following code produces the spacing shown in Figure 13.3:

```
body {
    margin:0px;
}
div {
```

```
  width:250px;
  height:100px;
  color:black;
  font-weight:bold;
  text-align:center;
}
div#d1 {
  border:5px solid #000000;
  background-color:red;
  margin:0px;
}
div#d2 {
  border-width:6px 6px 3px 6px;
  border-style:solid;
  border-color:#000000;
  background-color:green;
  margin:10px 0px 0px 15px;
}
div#d3 {
  border-width:3px 6px 6px 6px;
  border-style:solid;
  border-color:#000000;
  background-color:blue;
  margin:0px 0px 0px 15px;
}
div#d4 {
  border:5px solid #000000;
  background-color:yellow;
  margin:0px 0px 0px 265px;
}
```

These changes give the `<body>` element a zero margin, thus ensuring
that a `margin-left` value of 25 pixels truly is 25 pixels from the edge
of the browser frame. It also shows the second and third color blocks
stacked on top of each other, but with modifications to the `border`
element so that a double border does not appear. Additionally, the
fourth color block begins where the third color block ends.

As you can see in Figure 13.3, some overlap occurs between the right
edge of the third color block and the left edge of the fourth color
block. Why is that the case, if the color blocks are 250 pixels wide, the
third color block has a `margin-left` value of 15 pixels, and the fourth
color block is supposed to have a 265 pixel margin to its left? Well, it
does have that 265 pixel margin, but that margin size is not enough
because you also have to factor in the 6 pixels of border. Changing
the `margin` property for the fourth color block to reflect the following
code makes the third and fourth blocks line up according to plan (see
Figure 13.4):

```
margin:0px 0px 0px 276px;
```

FIGURE 13.3
A third modification to the color blocks pulls items into closer relation with each other.

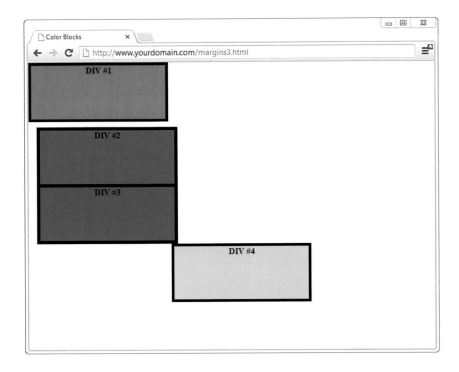

FIGURE 13.4
Changing the margin to allow for 11 pixels of border width.

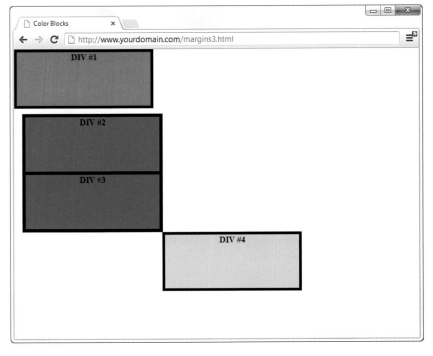

As shown in these examples, margin specifications are incredibly useful for element placement, but you must use caution when setting these specifications.

Padding Elements

Padding is similar to margins, in that it adds extra space to elements. The big difference is where that space is located. Recall that margins are added to the outside of elements. On the other hand, padding adds space *inside* the rectangular area of an element. As an example, if you create a style rule for an element that establishes a width of 50 pixels and a height of 30 pixels, and then sets the padding of the rule to 5 pixels, the remaining content area will be 40 pixels by 20 pixels. Also, because the padding of an element appears within the element's content area, it assumes the same style as the content of the element, including the background color.

You specify the padding of a style rule using one of the `padding` properties, which work much like the `margin` properties. The following padding properties are available for use in setting the padding of style rules:

- `padding-top`—Sets the top padding
- `padding-right`—Sets the right padding
- `padding-bottom`—Sets the bottom padding
- `padding-left`—Sets the left padding
- `padding`—Sets the top, right, bottom, and left padding as a single property

As with margins, you can set the padding of style rules using individual padding properties or the single `padding` property. You can also express padding using either a unit of measurement or a percentage.

Following is an example of how you might set the left and right padding for a style rule so that there are 10 pixels of padding on each side of an element's content:

```
padding-left:10px;
padding-right:10px;
```

As with margins, you can set all the padding for an element with a single property (the `padding` property). To set the `padding` property, you can use the same three approaches available for the `margin` property.

Following is an example of how you would set the vertical padding (top/bottom) to 12 pixels and the horizontal padding (left/right) to 8 pixels for a style rule:

```
padding:12px 8px;
```

Following is more explicit code that performs the same task by specifying all the padding values:

```
padding:12px 8px 12px 8px;
```

In all the previous figures, note that the text DIV #1, DIV #2, and so on appears at the top of the colored block, with just a little space between the border and the text. That amount of space hasn't been specified by any padding value, but it appears as a sort of default within the element. If you want specific control over your element padding, Listing 13.2 shows some examples. All the color blocks are 250 pixels wide and 100 pixels high, have a 5-pixel solid black border, and have 25 pixels of margin (see Figure 13.5). The fun stuff happens within the padding values for each individual <div>.

FIGURE 13.5
The basic color blocks sample page shows four color blocks with variable padding.

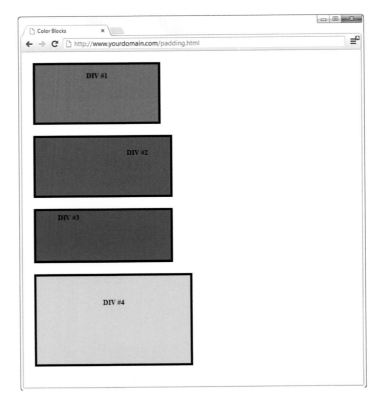

LISTING 13.2   Simple Code to Produce Four Colored `<div>`s with Borders, Margins, and Padding

```
<!DOCTYPE html>

<html lang="en">
  <head>
    <title>Color Blocks</title>
    <style type="text/css">
      body {
          margin:0px;
      }
      div {
          width:250px;
          height:100px;
          border:5px solid #000000;
          color:black;
          font-weight:bold;
          margin:25px;
      }

      div#d1 {
          background-color:red;
          text-align:center;
          padding:15px;
      }

      div#d2 {
          background-color:green;
          text-align:right;
          padding:25px 50px 6px 6px;
      }

      div#d3 {
          background-color:blue;
          text-align:left;
          padding:6px 6px 6px 50px;
      }

      div#d4 {
          background-color:yellow;
          text-align:center;
          padding:50px;
      }
    </style>
  </head>

  <body>
    <div id="d1">DIV #1</div>
    <div id="d2">DIV #2</div>
    <div id="d3">DIV #3</div>
    <div id="d4">DIV #4</div>
  </body>
</html>
```

You should immediately recognize that something is amiss in this example. The color blocks are all supposed to be 250 pixels wide and 100 pixels high. The color blocks in Figure 13.5 are not uniform because, despite our efforts to control the size of the `<div>`, the padding applied later overrides that initial size declaration.

If you place the text in a `<p>` element and give that element a white background (see Figure 13.6), you can see where the padding is in relation to the text. When there just isn't room to use all the padding that is defined, the surrounding element has to make adjustments. You will learn about this effect in detail in Hour 14, "Understanding the CSS Box Model and Positioning."

FIGURE 13.6
Showing the padding in relation to the text.

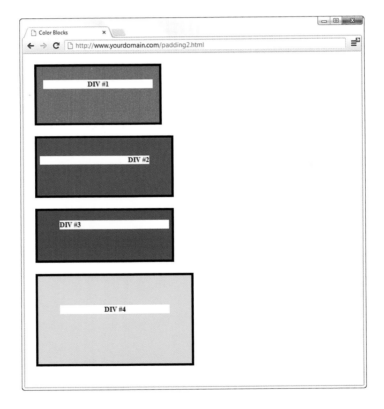

The greatest number of tweaks or nudges you make in your web design with CSS will have to do with margins and padding. Just remember: Margins are outside the element; padding is inside it.

Keeping Everything Aligned

Knowing that content on a web page doesn't always fill the entire width of the rectangular area in which it is displayed, it is often helpful to control the alignment of the content. Even if text within a rectangular area extends to multiple lines, alignment enters the picture because you might want the text left-justified, right-justified, or centered. Two style properties enable you to control the alignment of elements: `text-align` and `vertical-align`.

You saw examples of these style properties in action (when aligning images) in Hour 11, but it doesn't hurt to mention these properties again here because alignment plays a role in overall page design as well.

As a refresher, using `text-align` aligns an element horizontally within its bounding area, and it can be set to `left`, `right`, `center`, or `justify`.

The `vertical-align` property is similar to `text-align` except that it is used to align elements vertically. The `vertical-align` property specifies how an element is aligned with its parent or, in some cases, the current line of elements on the page. "Current line" refers to the vertical placement of elements that appear within the same parent element—in other words, inline elements. If several inline elements appear on the same line, you can set their vertical alignments the same to align them vertically. A good example is a row of images that appear one after the next—the `vertical-align` property enables you to align them vertically.

Following are common values for use with the `vertical-align` property:

- `top`—Aligns the top of an element with the current line
- `middle`—Aligns the middle of an element with the middle of its parent
- `bottom`—Aligns the bottom of an element with the current line
- `text-top`—Aligns the top of an element with the top of its parent
- `baseline`—Aligns the baseline of an element with the baseline of its parent
- `text-bottom`—Aligns the bottom of an element with the bottom of its parent

Alignment works in conjunction with margins, padding, and (as you learn in the next section) the `float` property to enable you to maintain control over your design.

Understanding the `Float` Property

Understanding the `float` property is fundamental to understanding CSS-based layout and design; it is one of the last pieces in the puzzle of how all these elements fit together. Briefly stated, the `float` property allows elements to be moved around in the design so that other elements can wrap around them. You often find `float` used in conjunction with images (as you saw in Hour 11), but you can—and many designers do—float all sorts of elements in their layout.

Elements float horizontally, not vertically, so all you have to concern yourself with are two possible values: `right` and `left`. When used, an element that floats will float as far right or as far left (depending on the value of `float`) as the containing element will allow it. For example, if you have three `<div>`s float values of `left`, they will all line up to the left of the containing body element. If you have your `<div>`s within another `<div>`, they will line up to the left of *that* element, even if that element itself is floated to the right.

Floating is best understood by seeing a few examples, so let's move on to Listing 13.3. This listing simply defines three rectangular `<div>`s and floats them next to each other (floating to the left).

LISTING 13.3   Using `float` to Place `<div>`s

```
<!DOCTYPE html>

<html lang="en">
  <head>
    <title>Color Blocks</title>
    <style type="text/css">
      body {
         margin:0px;
      }
      div {
         width:250px;
         height:100px;
         border:5px solid #000000;
         color:black;
         font-weight:bold;
         margin:25px;
      }

      div#d1 {
         background-color:red;
         float:left;
      }

      div#d2 {
```

```
            background-color:green;
            float:left;
        }

        div#d3 {
            background-color:blue;
            float:left;
        }
    </style>
  </head>

  <body>
    <div id="d1">DIV #1</div>
    <div id="d2">DIV #2</div>
    <div id="d3">DIV #3</div>
  </body>
</html>
```

Figure 13.7 shows the resulting page. Already you can see a problem—
these three color blocks were supposed to be floated next to each other.
Well, actually they *are* floated next to each other, but the browser
window is not wide enough to display these three 250-pixel-wide blocks
with 25 pixels of margin between them. Because they are floating, the
third one simply floats to the next line.

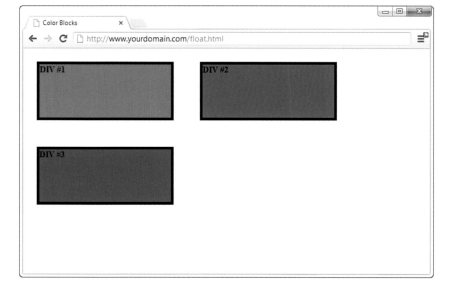

FIGURE 13.7
Using `float` to place the color
blocks.

You can imagine that this could be a problem in a specifically designed visual layout, so pay attention to your margins, padding, alignment, and floating while also testing within a target browser window size. Granted, the browser window in Figure 13.7 is a small one to make this point about floating elements moving to the next line when there is no room for them to fit where they should. In other words, if you open the same HTML file with a larger browser window, you might not see the issue—this is why you should also check your sites at different resolutions to see if a fix is needed. The fix here is to adjust the margins and other size-related properties of your <div>s.

Figure 13.8 shows another interesting possibility when using the float property. The only changes made to the code from Listing 13.3 involved making the color blocks only 100-pixels wide, reducing the margins to 10px, and changing the float alignment of the second color block to right (instead of left).

FIGURE 13.8
Using float to place the color blocks.

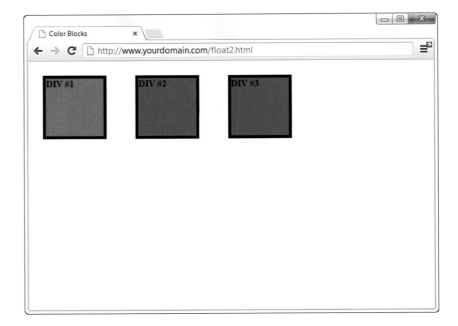

However, something interesting happened. The second color block now appears visually as the third color block because it is flush right. The second color block has a float value of right, so it has floated all the way to the right. The first and third color blocks are floating as left as possible, regardless of the way in which the `<div>` code appears in the HTML, which is as follows:

```
<div id="d1">DIV #1</div>
<div id="d2">DIV #2</div>
<div id="d3">DIV #3</div>
```

Floating takes a lot of practice to get used to, especially when your page has additional elements in your page, not just a few colored blocks. For example, what happens when you add a basic paragraph to the mix? All elements placed after the floating element then float around that element. To avoid that, use the `clear` property.

The `clear` property has five possible values: `left`, `right`, `both`, `none`, and `inherit`. The most common values are `left`, `right`, and `both`. Specifying `clear:left` ensures that no other floating elements are allowed to the left, `clear:right` ensures that no other floating elements are allowed to the right, and so on. Floating and clearing is a learn-by-doing process, so look for more situations in the Workshop at the end of this hour.

Summary

This hour introduced you to some of the most fundamental style properties in CSS-based design: `margin`, `padding`, and `float`. You learned how the `margin` property controls space around the outside of elements and how the `padding` property works with space within the elements.

After a refresher on the `text-align` and `vertical-align` properties you learned about in a previous hour, you learned about the `float` property. The `float` property allows for specific placement of elements and additional content around those elements.

Q&A

Q. **The examples of margins and padding all had to do with boxes and text. Can I apply margins and padding to images as well?**

A. Yes, you can apply margins and padding to any block-level element, such as a `<p>`, a `<div>`, an `<img/>`, and lists such as `<ul>` and `<ol>`, as well as list items (`<li>`)—just to name a few.

Workshop

The Workshop contains quiz questions and exercises to help you solidify your understanding of the material covered. Try to answer all questions before looking at the "Answers" section that follows.

Quiz

1. To place two `<div>` elements next to each other, but with a 30-pixel margin between them, what entry or entries can you use in the stylesheet?

2. Which CSS style property and value is used to ensure that content does not appear to the left of a floating element?

3. What stylesheet entry is used to place text within a `<div>` to appear 12 pixels from the top of the element?

Answers

1. You can use several entries. The first `<div>` uses a style property of `margin-right:15px`. The second `<div>` uses a style property of `margin-left:15px`. Or you can assign the full 30 pixels to either `<div>` using `margin-right` or `margin-left`, as appropriate. Additionally, at least the first `<div>` needs to have `float:left` assigned to it.

2. In this instance, use `clear:left`.

3. `padding-top:12px`

Exercises

▶ Fully understanding margins, padding, alignment, and floating takes practice. Using the color blocks code or `<div>`s of your own, practice all manner and sorts of spacing and floating before moving on to the next hour. The next hour discusses the CSS box model as a whole, which encompasses the individual items discussed in this hour.

▶ While you're at it, practice applying margins and padding to every block-level element you've learned so far. Get used to putting images within blocks of text and putting margins around the images so that the text does not run right up to the edge of the graphic.

Understanding the CSS Box Model and Positioning

In the previous hour, I mentioned the CSS box model a few times. This hour begins with a discussion of the box model and explains how the information you learned in the previous hour helps you understand this model. If you know how the box model works, you won't tear your hair out when you create a design and then realize that the elements don't line up or that they seem a little "off." You'll know that, in almost all cases, something—the margin, the padding, the border— just needs a little tweaking.

You'll also learn more about CSS positioning, including stacking elements on top of each other in a three-dimensional way (instead of a vertical way). Finally, you'll learn about controlling the flow of text around elements using the `float` property.

The CSS Box Model

Every element in HTML is considered a "box," whether it is a paragraph, a `<div>`, an image, and so on. Boxes have consistent properties, whether we see them or not, and whether the stylesheet specifies them or not. They're always present, and as designers, we have to keep their presence in mind when creating a layout.

Figure 14.1 is a diagram of the box model. The box model describes the way in which every HTML block-level element has the potential for a border, padding, and margin and, specifically, how the border, padding, and margin are applied. In other words, all elements have some padding between the content and the border of the element. Additionally, the border might or might not be visible, but space for it is here, just as there is a margin between the border of the element and any other content outside the element.

- ▶ How to conceptualize the CSS box model
- ▶ How to position your elements
- ▶ How to control the way elements stack up
- ▶ How to manage the flow of text

FIGURE 14.1
Every element in HTML is
represented by the CSS box model.

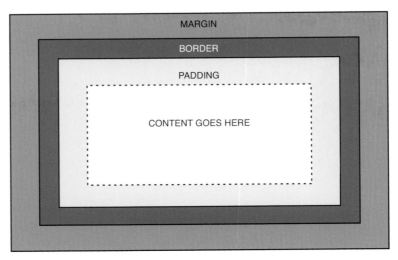

Here's yet another explanation of the box model, going from the
outside inward:

▶ The *margin* is the area outside the element. It never has color; it is
always transparent.

▶ The *border* extends around the element, on the outer edge of any
padding. The border can be of several types, widths, and colors.

▶ The *padding* exists around the content and inherits the
background color of the content area.

▶ The *content* is surrounded by padding.

Here's where the tricky part comes in: To know the true height and
width of an element, you have to take all the elements of the box
model into account. Think back to the example from the previous
hour: Despite specifically indicating that a `<div>` should be 250
pixels wide and 100 pixels high, that `<div>` had to grow larger to
accommodate the padding in use.

You already know how to set the width and height of an element using
the width and height properties. The following example shows how to
define a `<div>` that is 250 pixels wide and 100 pixels high, with a red
background and a black single-pixel border:

```
div {
  width: 250px;
  height: 100px;
  background-color: #ff0000;
  border: 1px solid #000000;
}
```

Figure 14.2 shows this simple `<div>`.

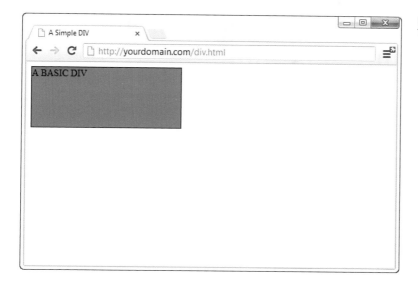

FIGURE 14.2
This is a simple `<div>`.

If we define a second element with these same properties, but also add
`margin` and `padding` properties of a certain size, we begin to see how the
size of the element changes. This is because of the box model.

The second `<div>` will be defined as follows, just adding 10 pixels of
margin and 10 pixels of padding to the element:

```
div#d2 {
  width: 250px;
  height: 100px;
  background-color: #ff0000;
  border: 5px solid #000000;
  margin: 10px;
  padding: 10px;
}
```

The second `<div>`, in Figure 14.3, is defined as the same height and
width as the first one, but the overall height and width of the entire
box surrounding the element itself is much larger when margins and
padding are put in play.

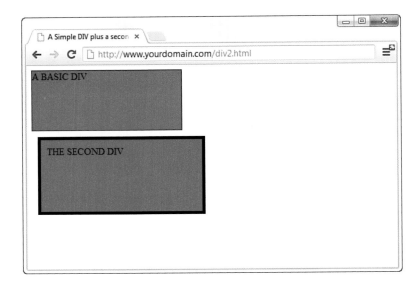

The total *width* of an element is the sum of the following:

```
width + padding-left + padding-right + border-left + border-right +
margin-left + margin-right
```

The total *height* of an element is the sum of the following:

```
height + padding-top + padding-bottom + border-top + border-bottom +
margin-top + margin-bottom
```

Therefore, the second `<div>` has an actual width of 300 (250 + 10 + 10 + 5 + 5 + 10 + 10) and an actual height of 150 (100 + 10 + 10 + 5 + 5 + 10 + 10).

By now, you can begin to see how the box model affects your design. Let's say that you have only 250 pixels of horizontal space, but you like 10 pixels of margin, 10 pixels of padding, and 5 pixels of border on all sides. To accommodate what you like with what you have room to display, you must specify the `width` of your `<div>` as only 200 pixels so that 200 + 10 + 10 + 5 + 5 + 10 + 10 adds up to that 250 pixels of available horizontal space.

The mathematics of the model are important as well. In dynamically driven sites or sites in which user interactions drive the client-side display (such as through JavaScript events), your server-side or client-side code could draw and redraw container elements on the fly. In other words, your code will produce the numbers, but you have to provide the boundaries.

Now that you've been schooled in the way of the box model, keep it in mind throughout the rest of the work you do in this book and in your web design. Among other things, it will affect element positioning and content flow, which are the two topics we tackle next.

The Whole Scoop on Positioning

Relative positioning is the default type of positioning HTML uses. You can think of relative positioning as being akin to laying out checkers on a checkerboard: The checkers are arranged from left to right, and when you get to the edge of the board, you move on to the next row. Elements that are styled with the `block` value for the `display` style property are automatically placed on a new row, whereas `inline` elements are placed on the same row immediately next to the element preceding them. As an example, `<p>` and `<div>` tags are considered block elements, whereas the `<span>` tag is considered an inline element.

The other type of positioning CSS supports is known as *absolute positioning* because it enables you to set the exact position of HTML content on a page. Although absolute positioning gives you the freedom to spell out exactly where an element is to appear, the position is still relative to any parent elements that appear on the page. In other words, absolute positioning enables you to specify the exact location of an element's rectangular area with respect to its parent's area, which is very different from relative positioning.

With the freedom of placing elements anywhere you want on a page, you can run into the problem of overlap, when an element takes up space another element is using. Nothing is stopping you from specifying the absolute locations of elements so that they overlap. In this case, CSS relies on the z-index of each element to determine which element is on the top and which is on the bottom. You'll learn more about the z-index of elements later in this lesson. For now, let's look at exactly how you control whether a style rule uses relative or absolute positioning.

The type of positioning (relative or absolute) a particular style rule uses is determined by the `position` property, which is capable of having one of the following two values: `relative` or `absolute`. After specifying the type of positioning, you provide the specific position using the following properties:

- ▶ `left`—The left position offset
- ▶ `right`—The right position offset

- ▶ `top`—The top position offset

- ▶ `bottom`—The bottom position offset

You might think that these position properties make sense only for absolute positioning, but they actually apply to both types of positioning. Under relative positioning, the position of an element is specified as an offset relative to the original position of the element. So if you set the `left` property of an element to `25px`, the left side of the element shifts over 25 pixels from its original (relative) position. An absolute position, on the other hand, is specified relative to the parent of the element to which the style is applied. So if you set the `left` property of an element to `25px` under absolute positioning, the left side of the element appears 25 pixels to the right of the parent element's left edge. On the other hand, using the `right` property with the same value positions the element so that its *right* side is 25 pixels to the right of the parent's *right* edge.

Let's return to the color blocks example to show how positioning works. In Listing 14.1, the four color blocks have relative positioning specified. As you can see in Figure 14.4, the blocks are positioned vertically.

FIGURE 14.4
The color blocks are positioned vertically, with one on top of the other.

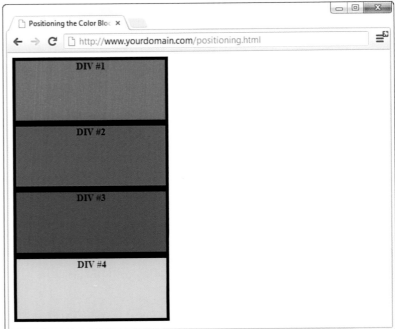

LISTING 14.1   Showing Relative Positioning with Four Color Blocks

```html
<!DOCTYPE html>

<html lang="en">
 <head>
  <title>Positioning the Color Blocks</title>
   <style type="text/css">
   div {
      position:relative;
      width:250px;
      height:100px;
      border:5px solid #000;
      color:black;
      font-weight:bold;
      text-align:center;
      }
      div#d1 {
      background-color:red;
      }

      div#d2 {
       background-color:green;
      }

      div#d3 {
       background-color:blue;
      }

      div#d4 {
       background-color:yellow;
      }
   </style>

 </head>
 <body>
  <div id="d1">DIV #1</div>
  <div id="d2">DIV #2</div>
  <div id="d3">DIV #3</div>
  <div id="d4">DIV #4</div>
 </body>
</html>
```

The style sheet entry for the <div> element itself sets the position style
property for the <div> element to relative. Because the remaining style
rules are inherited from the <div> style rule, they inherit its relative
positioning. In fact, the only difference between the other style rules is
that they have different background colors.

Notice in Figure 14.4 that the <div> elements are displayed one after
the next, which is what you would expect with relative positioning.
But to make things more interesting, which is what we're here to do,

you can change the positioning to absolute and explicitly specify the placement of the colors. In Listing 14.2, the style sheet entries are changed to use absolute positioning to arrange the color blocks.

Listing 14.2   Using Absolute Positioning of the Color Blocks

```html
<!DOCTYPE html>

<html lang="en">
 <head>
  <title>Positioning the Color Blocks</title>
    <style type="text/css">
    div {
     position:absolute;
     width:250px;
     height:100px;
     border:5px solid #000;
     color:black;
     font-weight:bold;
     text-align:center;
    }
    div#d1 {
     background-color:red;
     left:0px;
     top: 0px;
    }
    div#d2 {
     background-color:green;
     left:75px;
     top:25px;
    }
    div#d3 {
     background-color:blue;
     left:150px;
     top:50px;
    }
    div#d4 {
     background-color:yellow;
     left:225px;
     top:75px;
    }
    </style>
 </head>
 <body>
  <div id="d1">DIV #1</div>
  <div id="d2">DIV #2</div>
  <div id="d3">DIV #3</div>
  <div id="d4">DIV #4</div>
 </body>
</html>
```

This style sheet sets the `position` property to `absolute`, which is necessary for the stylesheet to use absolute positioning. Additionally, the `left` and `top` properties are set for each of the inherited `<div>` style rules. However, the position of each of these rules is set so that the elements are displayed overlapping each other, as Figure 14.5 shows.

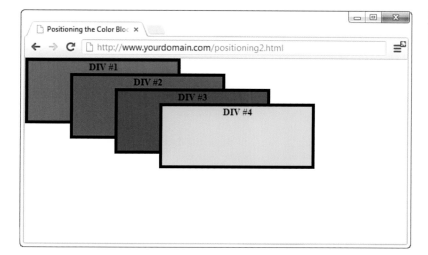

FIGURE 14.5
The color blocks are displayed using absolute positioning.

Now we're talking layout! Figure 14.5 shows how absolute positioning enables you to place elements exactly where you want them. It also reveals how easy it is to arrange elements so that they overlap. You might be curious about how a web browser knows which elements to draw on top when they overlap. The next section covers how you can control stacking order.

Controlling the Way Things Stack Up

In certain situations, you want to carefully control the manner in which elements overlap each other on a web page. The `z-index` style property enables you to set the order of elements with respect to how they stack on top of each other. The name *z-index* might sound a little strange, but it refers to the notion of a third dimension (Z) that points into the computer screen, in addition to the two dimensions that go across (X) and down (Y) the screen. Another way to think of the z-index is to consider the relative position of a single magazine within a stack of magazines. A magazine nearer the top of the stack has a higher z-index than a magazine lower in the stack. Similarly, an overlapped element with a higher z-index is displayed on top of an element with a lower z-index.

The `z-index` property is used to set a numeric value that indicates the relative z-index of a style rule. The number assigned to `z-index` has meaning only with respect to other style rules in a style sheet, which means that setting the `z-index` property for a single rule doesn't mean much. On the other hand, if you set `z-index` for several style rules that apply to overlapped elements, the elements with higher `z-index` values appear on top of elements with lower `z-index` values.

Listing 14.3 contains another version of the color blocks style sheet and HTML that uses `z-index` settings to alter the natural overlap of elements.

LISTING 14.3   Using `z-index` to Alter the Display of Elements in the Color Blocks Sample

```
<!DOCTYPE html>

<html lang="en">
 <head>
  <title>Positioning the Color Blocks</title>
   <style type="text/css">
   div {
     position:absolute;
     width:250px;
     height:100px;
     border:5px solid #000;
     color:black;
     font-weight:bold;
     text-align:center;
   }
   div#d1 {
     background-color:red;
     left:0px;
     top:0px;
     z-index:0;
   }
   div#d2 {
     background-color:green;
     left:75px;
     top:25px;
     z-index:3;
   }
   div#d3 {
     background-color:blue;
     left:150px;
     top:50px;
     z-index:2;
   }
```

NOTE

Regardless of the `z-index` value you set for a style rule, an element displayed with the rule will always appear on top of its parent.

```
  div#d4 {
    background-color:yellow;
    left:225px;
    top:75px;
    z-index:1;
    }
  </style>
</head>
<body>
  <div id="d1">DIV #1</div>
  <div id="d2">DIV #2</div>
  <div id="d3">DIV #3</div>
  <div id="d4">DIV #4</div>
</body>
</html>
```

The only change in this code from what you saw in Listing 14.2 is
the addition of the z-index property in each of the numbered div style
classes. Notice that the first numbered div has a z-index setting of
0, which should make it the lowest element in terms of the z-index,
whereas the second div has the highest z-index. Figure 14.6 shows
the color blocks page as displayed with this style sheet, which clearly
shows how the z-index affects the displayed content and makes it
possible to carefully control the overlap of elements.

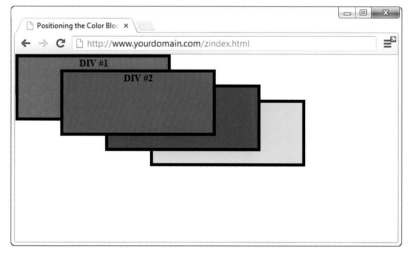

FIGURE 14.6
Using z-index to alter the display
of the color blocks.

Although the examples show color blocks that are simple <div>
elements, the z-index style property can affect any HTML content,
including images.

Managing the Flow of Text

Now that you've seen some examples of placing elements relative to other elements or placing them absolutely, it's time to revisit the flow of content around elements. The conceptual *current line* is an invisible line used to place elements on a page. This line has to do with the flow of elements on a page; it comes into play as elements are arranged next to each other across and down the page. Part of the flow of elements is the flow of text on a page. When you mix text with other elements (such as images), it's important to control how the text flows around those other elements.

You've already seen two of these style properties in Hour 13, "Working with Margins, Padding, Alignment, and Floating." Following are some style properties that give you control over text flow:

► `float`—Determines how text flows around an element

► `clear`—Stops the flow of text around an element

► `overflow`—Controls the overflow of text when an element is too small to contain all the text

The `float` property controls how text flows around an element. It can be set to either `left` or `right`. These values determine where to position an element with respect to flowing text. So setting an image's `float` property to `left` positions the image to the left of flowing text.

As you learned in the previous hour, you can prevent text from flowing next to an element by using the `clear` property, which you can set to `none`, `left`, `right`, or `both`. The default value for the clear property is `none`, indicating that text is to flow with no special considerations for the element. The `left` value causes text to stop flowing around an element until the left side of the page is free of the element. Likewise, the `right` value means that text is not to flow around the right side of the element. The `both` value indicates that text isn't to flow around either side of the element.

The `overflow` property handles overflow text, which is text that doesn't fit within its rectangular area; this can happen if you set the `width` and `height` of an element too small. The `overflow` property can be set to `visible`, `hidden`, or `scroll`. The `visible` setting automatically enlarges the element so that the overflow text fits within it; this is the default setting for the property. The `hidden` value leaves the element the same size, allowing the overflow text to remain hidden from view. Perhaps the most interesting value is `scroll`, which adds scrollbars to the element so that you can move around and see the text.

Summary

This hour began with an important discussion about the CSS box model and how to calculate the width and height of elements when taking margins, padding, and borders into consideration. The lesson continued by tackling absolute positioning of elements, and you learned about positioning using `z-index`. You then learned about a few nifty style properties that enable you to control the flow of text on a page.

This lesson was brief but chock full of fundamental information about controlling the design of your site. It is worth rereading and working through the examples so that you have a good foundation for your work.

Q&A

Q. **How would I determine when to use relative positioning and when to use absolute positioning?**

A. Although there are no set guidelines regarding the usage of relative versus absolute positioning, the general idea is that absolute positioning is required only when you want to exert a finer degree of control over how content is positioned. This has to do with the fact that absolute positioning enables you to position content down to the exact pixel, whereas relative positioning is much less predictable in terms of how it positions content. This isn't to say that relative positioning can't do a good job of positioning elements on a page; it just means that absolute positioning is more exact. Of course, this also makes absolute positioning potentially more susceptible to changes in screen size, which you can't really control.

Q. **If I don't specify the z-index of two elements that overlap each other, how do I know which element will appear on top?**

A. If the `z-index` property isn't set for overlapping elements, the element that appears later in the web page will appear on top. The easy way to remember this is to think of a web browser drawing each element on a page as it reads it from the HTML document; elements read later in the document are drawn on top of those that were read earlier.

Workshop

The Workshop contains quiz questions and exercises to help you solidify your understanding of the material covered. Try to answer all questions before looking at the "Answers" section that follows.

Quiz

1. What's the difference between relative positioning and absolute positioning?

2. Which CSS style property controls the manner in which elements overlap each other?

3. What HTML code could you use to display the words `Where would you like to` starting exactly at the upper-left corner of the browser window, and display the words GO TODAY? in large type exactly 80 pixels down and 20 pixels to the left of the corner?

Answers

1. In relative positioning, content is displayed according to the flow of a page, with each element physically appearing after the element preceding it in the HTML code. Absolute positioning, on the other hand, allows you to set the exact position of content on a page.

2. The `z-index` style property controls the manner in which elements overlap each other.

3. You can use this code:

```
<span style="position:absolute;left:0px;top:0px">
Where would you like to</span>
<h1 style="position:absolute;left:80px;top:20px">GO TODAY?</h1>
```

Exercises

▶ Practice working with the intricacies of the CSS box model by creating a series of elements with different margins, padding, and borders, and see how these properties affect their height and width.

▶ Find a group of images that you like, and use absolute positioning and maybe even some `z-index` values to arrange them in a sort of gallery. Try to place your images so that they form a design (such as a square, triangle, or circle).

HOUR 15
Creating Fixed or Liquid Layouts

So far, you've learned a lot about styling web content, from font sizes and colors to images, block elements, lists, and more. But what we haven't yet discussed is a high-level overview of page layout. In general, there are two types of layouts—fixed and liquid. But it's also possible to use a combination of the two, with some elements fixed and others liquid.

In this hour, you first learn about the characteristics of these two types of layouts and see a few examples of websites that use them. At the end of the chapter, you see a basic template that combines elements of both types of layouts. Ultimately, the type of layout you choose is up to you—it's hard to go wrong as long as your sites follow HTML and CSS standards.

WHAT YOU'LL LEARN IN THIS HOUR:

▶ How fixed layouts work

▶ How liquid layouts work

▶ How to create a fixed/liquid hybrid layout

▶ How to think about and begin to implement a responsive design

A good place for examples of liquid layouts is the WordPress Theme Gallery, at http://wordpress.org/themes/. WordPress began as a blogging platform but in recent years has seen an increase in use as a nonblog content or site-management tool. The WordPress Theme Gallery shows hundreds of examples of both fixed-width and liquid layouts that give you an idea, if not all the code, for what you can create. Even though you are not working with a WordPress blog or site as part of the exercises in this book, the template gallery is a place where you can see and interact with many variations on designs.

Spend some time looking at the WordPress examples and perhaps the CSS Zen Garden as well, at http://www.csszengarden.com/. This will help you get a feel for the types of layouts you like without being swayed by the content within the layout.

Understanding Fixed Layouts

A fixed layout, or fixed-width layout, is just that: a layout in which the body of the page is set to a specific width. That width is typically controlled by a master "wrapper" element that contains all the content. The `width` property of a wrapper element, such as a `<div>`, is set in the stylesheet entry if the `<div>` was given an ID value such as `main` or `wrapper` (although the name is up to you).

When creating a fixed-width layout, the most important decision is determining the minimum screen resolution you want to accommodate. For many years, 800×600 has been the "lowest common denominator" for web designers, resulting in a typical fixed width of approximately 760 pixels. However, the number of people using 800×600 screen resolution for nonmobile browsers is now less than 4%. Given that, many web designers consider 1,024×768 the current minimum screen resolution, so if they create fixed-width layouts, the fixed width typically is somewhere between 800 and 1,000 pixels wide.

A main reason for creating a fixed-width layout is so that you can have precise control over the appearance of the content area. However, if users visit your fixed-width site with smaller or much larger screen resolutions than the resolution you had in mind while you designed it, they will encounter scrollbars (if their resolution is smaller) or a large amount of empty space (if their resolution is greater). Finding fixed-width layouts is difficult among the most popular websites these days because site designers know they need to cater to the largest possible audience (and therefore make no assumptions about browser size). However, fixed-width layouts still have wide adoption, especially by site administrators using a content management system with a strict template.

The following figures show one such site, for San Jose State University (university websites commonly use a strict template and content management system, so this was an easy example to find); it has a wrapper element fixed at 960 pixels wide. In Figure 15.1, the browser window is a shade under 900 pixels wide. On the right side of the image, important content is cut off (and at the bottom of the figure, a horizontal scrollbar displays in the browser).

FIGURE 15.1
A fixed-width example with a smaller screen size.

However, Figure 15.2 shows how this site looks when the browser window is more than 1,400 pixels wide: You see a lot of empty space (or "real estate") on both sides of the main body content, which some consider aesthetically displeasing.

FIGURE 15.2
A fixed-width example with a larger screen size.

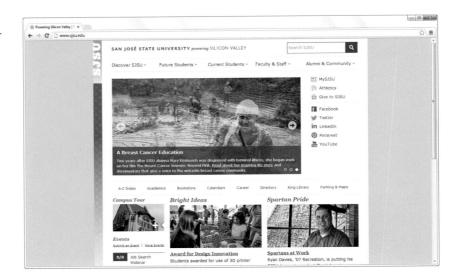

Besides the decision to create a fixed-width layout in the first place is determining whether to place the fixed-width content flush left or whether to center it. Placing the content flush left produces extra space on the right side only; centering the content area creates extra space on both sides. However, centering at least provides balance, whereas a flush-left design could end up looking like a small rectangle shoved in the corner of the browser, depending on the size and resolution of a user's monitor.

Understanding Liquid Layouts

A liquid layout—also called a *fluid* layout—is one in which the body of the page does not use a specified width in pixels, although it might be enclosed in a master "wrapper" element that uses a percentage width. The idea behind the liquid layout is that it can be perfectly usable and still retain the overall design aesthetic even if the user has a very small or very wide screen.

Figures 15.3, 15.4, and 15.5 show three examples of a liquid layout in action.

FIGURE 15.3
A liquid layout as viewed in a relatively small screen.

In Figure 15.3, the browser window is approximately 770 pixels wide. This example shows a reasonable minimum screen width before a horizontal scrollbar appears. In fact, the scrollbar does not appear until the browser is 735 pixels wide. On the other hand, Figure 15.4 shows a very small browser window (less than 600 pixels wide).

In Figure 15.4, you can see a horizontal scrollbar; in the header area of the page content, the logo graphic is beginning to take over the text and appear on top of it. But the bulk of the page is still quite usable. The informational content on the left side of the page is still legible and is sharing the available space with the input form on the right side.

Figure 15.5 shows how this same page looks in a very wide screen. In Figure 15.5, the browser window is approximately 1,330 pixels wide. There is plenty of room for all the content on the page to spread out. This liquid layout is achieved because all the design elements have a percentage width specified (instead of a fixed width). In doing so, the layout makes use of all the available browser real estate.

FIGURE 15.4
A liquid layout as viewed in a very small screen.

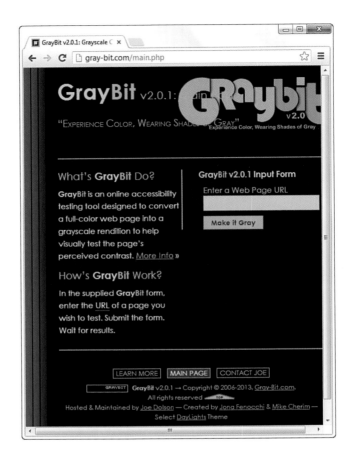

FIGURE 15.5
A liquid layout as viewed in a wide screen.

The liquid layout approach might seem like the best approach at first glance—after all, who wouldn't want to take advantage of all the screen real estate available? But there's a fine line between taking advantage of space and not allowing the content to breathe. Too much content is overwhelming; not enough content in an open space is underwhelming.

The pure liquid layout can be quite impressive, but it requires a significant amount of testing to ensure that it is usable in a wide range of browsers at varying screen resolutions. You might not have the time and effort to produce such a design; in that case, a reasonable compromise is the fixed/liquid hybrid layout, or a fully responsive design, as you learn about later in this hour.

Creating a Fixed/Liquid Hybrid Layout

A fixed/liquid hybrid layout is one that contains elements of both types of layouts. For example, you could have a fluid layout that includes fixed-width content areas either within the body area or as anchor elements (such as a left-side column or as a top navigation strip). You can even create a fixed content area that acts like a frame, in which a content area remains fixed even as users scroll through the content.

Starting with a Basic Layout Structure

In this example, you learn to create a template that is liquid but with two fixed-width columns on either side of the main body area (which is a third column, if you think about it, only much wider than the others). The template also has a delineated header and footer area. Listing 15.1 shows the basic HTML structure for this layout.

LISTING 15.1   Basic Fixed/Liquid Hybrid Layout Structure

```
<!DOCTYPE html>

<html lang="en">
  <head>
    <title>Sample Layout</title>
    <link href="layout.css" rel="stylesheet" type="text/css" />
  </head>

  <body>
```

```
<header>HEADER</header>
<div id="wrapper">
  <div id="content_area">CONTENT</div>
  <div id="left_side">LEFT SIDE</div>
  <div id="right_side">RIGHT SIDE</div>
</div>
<footer>FOOTER</footer>
</body>
</html>
```

First, note that the stylesheet for this layout is linked to with the `<link>` tag instead of included in the template. Because a template is used for more than one page, you want to be able to control the display elements of the template in the most organized way possible. This means you need to change the definitions of those elements in only one place—the stylesheet.

Next, notice that the basic HTML is just that: extremely basic. Truth be told, this basic HTML structure can be used for a fixed layout, a liquid layout, or the fixed/liquid hybrid you see here because all the actual styling that makes a layout fixed, liquid, or hybrid happens in the stylesheet.

With the HTML structure in Listing 15.1, you actually have an identification of the content areas you want to include in your site. This planning is crucial to any development; you have to know what you want to include before you even think about the type of layout you are going to use, let alone the specific styles that will be applied to that layout.

At this stage, the `layout.css` file includes only this entry:

```
body {
    margin:0;
    padding:0;
}
```

If you look at the HTML in Listing 15.1 and say to yourself, "But those `<div>` elements will just stack on top of each other without any styles," you are correct. As shown in Figure 15.6, there is no layout to speak of.

NOTE

I am using elements with named identifiers in this example instead of the semantic elements such as `<section>` or `<nav>` because I'm illustrating the point in the simplest way possible without being prescriptive to the content itself. However, if you know that the `<div>` on the left side is going to hold navigation, you should use the `<nav>` tag instead of a `<div>` element with an `id` of `left_side`.

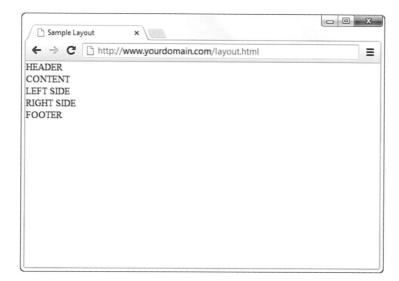

FIGURE 15.6
A basic HTML template with no styles applied to the container elements.

Defining Two Columns in a Fixed/Liquid Hybrid Layout

We can start with the easy things. Because this layout is supposed to be liquid, we know that whatever we put in the header and footer areas will extend the width of the browser window, regardless of how narrow or wide the window might be.

Adding the following code to the stylesheet gives the header and footer area each a width of 100% as well as the same background color and text color:

```
header, footer {
  float: left;
  width: 100%;
  background-color: #7152f4;
  color: #ffffff;
}
```

Now things get a little trickier. We have to define the two fixed columns on either side of the page, plus the column in the middle. In the HTML we're using here, note that a `<div>` element, called `wrapper`, surrounds both. This element is defined in the stylesheet as follows:

```
#wrapper {
  float: left;
  padding-left: 200px;
  padding-right: 125px;
}
```

The two padding definitions essentially reserve space for the two fixed-width columns on the left and right of the page. The column on the left will be 200 pixels wide, the column on the right will be 125 pixels wide, and each will have a different background color. But we also have to position the items relative to where they would be placed if the HTML remained unstyled (see Figure 15.6). This means adding `position: relative` to the stylesheet entries for each of these columns. Additionally, we indicate that the `<div>` elements should float to the left.

But in the case of the `left_side` `<div>`, we also indicate that we want the rightmost margin edge to be 200 pixels in from the edge (this is in addition to the column being defined as 200 pixels wide). We also want the margin on the left side to be a full negative margin; this will pull it into place (as you will soon see). The `right_side` `<div>` does not include a value for `right`, but it does include a negative margin on the right side:

```
#left_side {
  position: relative;
  float: left;
  width: 200px;
  background-color: #52f471;
  right: 200px;
  margin-left: -100%;
}

#right_side {
  position: relative;
  float: left;
  width: 125px;
  background-color: #f452d5;
  margin-right: -125px;
}
```

At this point, let's also define the content area so that it has a white background, takes up 100% of the available area, and floats to the left relative to its position:

```
#content_area {
  position: relative;
  float: left;
  background-color: #ffffff;
  width: 100%;
}
```

At this point, the basic layout should look something like Figure 15.7, with the areas clearly delineated.

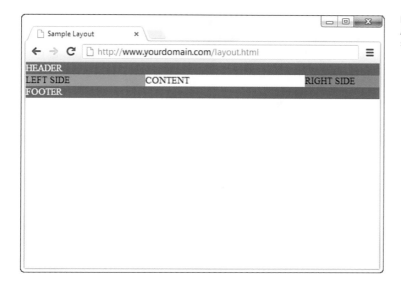

FIGURE 15.7
A basic HTML template after some
styles have been put in place.

However, there's a problem with this template if the window is resized below a certain width. Because the left column is 200 pixels wide and the right column is 125 pixels wide, and you want at least *some* text in the content area, you can imagine that this page will break if the window is only 350 to 400 pixels wide. We address this issue in the next section.

Setting the Minimum Width of a Layout

Although users won't likely visit your site with a desktop browser that displays less than 400 pixels wide, the example serves its purpose within the confines of this lesson. You can extrapolate and apply this information broadly: Even in fixed/liquid hybrid sites, at some point, your layout will break down unless you do something about it.

One of those "somethings" is to use the `min-width` CSS property. The `min-width` property sets the minimum width of an element, not including padding, borders, or margins. Figure 15.8 shows what happens when `min-width` is applied to the `<body>` element.

Figure 15.8 shows a small portion of the right column after scrolling to the right, but the point is that the layout does not break apart when resized below a minimum width. In this case, the minimum width is 525 pixels:

```
body {
    margin: 0;
    padding: 0;
    min-width: 525px;
}
```

The horizontal scrollbar appears in this example because the browser window itself is less than 500 pixels wide. The scrollbar disappears when the window is slightly larger than 525 pixels wide.

Handling Column Height in a Fixed/Liquid Hybrid Layout

This example is all well and good except for one problem: It has no content. When content is added to the various elements, more problems arise. As Figure 15.9 shows, the columns become as tall as necessary for the content they contain.

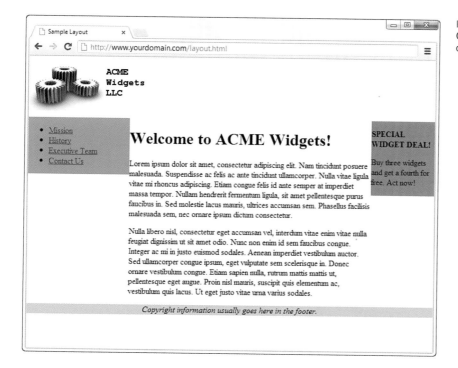

FIGURE 15.9
Columns are only as tall as their contents.

Because you cannot count on a user's browser being a specific height, or the content always being the same length, you might think this poses a problem with the fixed/liquid hybrid layout. Not so. If you think a little outside the box, you can apply a few more styles to bring all the pieces together.

First, add the following declarations in the stylesheet entries for the `left_side`, `right_side`, and `content_area` ids:

```
margin-bottom: -2000px;
padding-bottom: 2000px;
```

These declarations add a ridiculous amount of padding and assign a too-large margin to the bottom of all three elements. You must also add `position:relative` to the footer element definitions in the stylesheet so that the footer is visible despite this padding.

At this point, the page looks like Figure 15.10—still not what we want, but closer.

NOTE

Because we have moved beyond the basic layout example, I also took the liberty to remove the background and text color properties for the header and footer, which is why the example no longer shows white text on a very dark background. Additionally, I've centered the text in the `<footer>` element, which now has a light gray background.

FIGURE 15.10
Color fields are now visible, despite
the amount of content in the
columns.

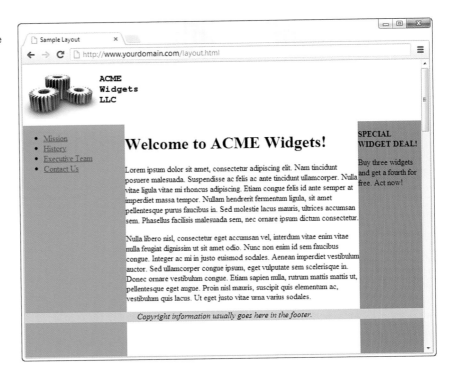

To clip off all that extra color, add the following to the stylesheet for
the wrapper ID:

```
overflow: hidden;
```

Figure 15.11 shows the final result: a fixed-width/liquid hybrid layout
with the necessary column spacing. I also took the liberty of styling
the navigational links and adjusting the margin around the welcome
message; you can see the complete stylesheet in Listing 15.3.

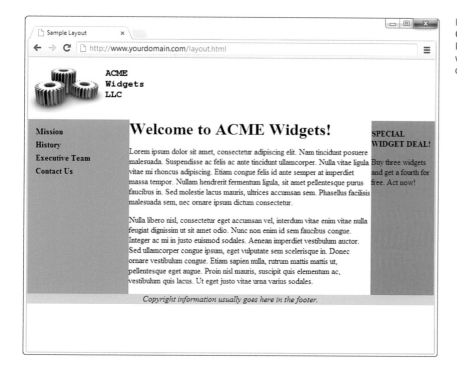

FIGURE 15.11
Congratulations! It's a fixed-width/
liquid hybrid layout (although you'll
want to do something about those
colors!).

The full HTML code appears in Listing 15.2, and Listing 15.3 shows the
final stylesheet.

LISTING 15.2   Basic Fixed/Liquid Hybrid Layout Structure (with Content)

```
<!DOCTYPE html>

<html lang="en">
  <head>
      <title>Sample Layout</title>
      <link href="layout.css" rel="stylesheet" type="text/css" />
  </head>

  <body>
    <header><img src="acmewidgets.jpg" alt="ACME Widgets
      LLC"/></header>
    <div id="wrapper">
      <div id="content_area">
      <h1>Welcome to ACME Widgets!</h1>
      <p>Lorem ipsum dolor sit amet, consectetur adipiscing elit.
      Nam tincidunt posuere malesuada. Suspendisse ac felis ac ante
      tincidunt ullamcorper. Nulla vitae ligula vitae mi rhoncus
      adipiscing. Etiam congue felis id ante semper at imperdiet
      massa tempor. Nullam hendrerit fermentum ligula, sit amet
```

```
          pellentesque purus faucibus in. Sed molestie lacus mauris,
          ultrices accumsan sem. Phasellus facilisis malesuada sem, nec
          ornare ipsum dictum consectetur.</p>
          <p>Nulla libero nisl, consectetur eget accumsan vel, interdum
          vitae enim vitae nulla feugiat dignissim ut sit amet odio.
          Nunc non enim id sem faucibus congue. Integer ac mi in justo
          euismod sodales. Aenean imperdiet vestibulum auctor. Sed
          ullamcorper congue ipsum, eget vulputate sem scelerisque in.
          Donec ornare vestibulum congue. Etiam sapien nulla, rutrum
          mattis mattis ut, pellentesque eget augue. Proin nisl mauris,
          suscipit quis elementum ac, vestibulum quis lacus. Ut eget
          justo vitae urna varius sodales. </p>
        </div>
        <div id="left_side">
          <ul>
          <li><a href="#">Mission</a></li>
          <li><a href="#">History</a></li>
          <li><a href="#">Executive Team</a></li>
          <li><a href="#">Contact Us</a></li>
          </ul>
        </div>
        <div id="right_side">
          <p><strong>SPECIAL WIDGET DEAL!</strong></p>
          <p>Buy three widgets and get a fourth for free. Act now!</p>
        </div>
      </div>
      <footer>
      Copyright information usually goes here in the footer.
      </footer>
    </body>
</html>
```

LISTING 15.3   Full Stylesheet for Fixed/Liquid Hybrid Layout

```
body {
  margin:0;
  padding:0;
  min-width: 525px;
}

header {
  float: left;
  width: 100%;
}

footer {
  position:relative;
  float: left;
  width: 100%;
  background-color: #cccccc;
  text-align:center;
  font-style: italic;
}
```

```
#wrapper {
  float: left;
  padding-left: 200px;
  padding-right: 125px;
  overflow: hidden;
}

#left_side {
  position: relative;
  float: left;
  width: 200px;
  background-color: #52f471;
  right: 200px;
  margin-left: -100%;
  margin-bottom: -2000px;
  padding-bottom: 2000px;

}

#right_side {
  position: relative;
  float: left;
  width: 125px;
  background-color: #f452d5;
  margin-right: -125px;
  margin-bottom: -2000px;
  padding-bottom: 2000px;

}

#content_area {
  position: relative;
  float: left;
  background-color: #ffffff;
  width: 100%;
  margin-bottom: -2000px;
  padding-bottom: 2000px;

}

h1 {
  margin: 0;
}

#left_side ul {
  list-style: none;
  margin: 12px 0px 0px 12px;
  padding: 0px;
}

#left_side li a:link, #nav li a:visited {
  font-size: 12pt;
  font-weight: bold;
  padding: 3px 0px 3px 3px;
  color: #000000;
  text-decoration: none;
```

```
    display: block;
}

#left_side li a:hover, #nav li a:active {
    font-size: 12pt;
    font-weight: bold;
    padding: 3px 0px 3px 3px;
    color: #ffffff;
    text-decoration: none;
    display: block;
}
```

Considering a Responsive Web Design

In 2010, web designer Ethan Marcotte coined the term *responsive web design* to refer to a web design approach that builds on the basics of fluid design you just learned a bit about. The goal of a responsive web design is that content is easy to view, read, and navigate, regardless of the device type and size on which you are viewing it. In other words, a designer who sets out to create a responsive website is doing so to ensure that the site is similarly enjoyable to and usable by audience members viewing on a large desktop display, a small smartphone, or a medium-size tablet.

Responsive design is based on fluid (liquid) grid layouts, much like you learned about earlier in this hour, but with a few modifications and additions. First, those grid layouts should always be in relative units rather than absolute ones. In other words, designers should use percentages rather than pixels to define container elements.

Second—and this is something we have not discussed in previous lessons—all images should be flexible. By this, I mean that instead of using a specific height and width for each image, relative percentages are used so that the images always display within the (relatively sized) element that contains them.

Finally, spend some time developing specific stylesheets for each media type, and use media queries to employ these different rules based on the type. You learn more about media-specific stylesheets in Hour 20, "Creating Print-Friendly Web Pages," but in general, know that you can specify a link to a stylesheet like the following:

```
<link rel="stylesheet" type="text/css"
   media="screen and (max-device-width: 480px)"
   href="wee.css" />
```

In this example, the `media` attribute contains a type and a query: The type is `screen` and the query portion is `(max-device-width: 480px)`. This means that if the device attempting to render the display is one with a screen (as opposed to, say, a printer, which you see in Hour 20) and the horizontal resolution (device width) is less than 480 pixels wide—as with a smartphone—then load the stylesheet called `wee.css` and render the display using the rules found within it.

Of course, a few short paragraphs in this book cannot do justice to the entirety of responsive web design. I highly recommend reading Marcotte's book *Responsive Web Design* (http://www.abookapart.com/products/responsive-web-design) after you have firmly grounded yourself in the basics of HTML5 and CSS3 that this book is teaching you. Additionally, several of the HTML and CSS frameworks discussed in Hour 23, "Organizing and Managing a Website," take advantage of principles of responsive design, and that makes a great starting point for building up a responsive site and tinkering with the fluid grid, image resizing, and media queries that make it so.

Summary

In this hour, you saw some practical examples of the three main types of layouts: fixed, liquid, and a fixed/liquid hybrid. In the third section of the lesson, you saw an extended example that walked you through the process of creating a fixed/liquid hybrid layout in which the HTML and CSS all validate properly. Remember, the most important part of creating a layout is figuring out the sections of content you think you might need to account for in the design.

Finally, you were introduced to the concept of responsive web design, which itself is a book-length topic. Given the brief information you learned here, such as using a fluid grid layout, responsive images, and media queries, you have some basic concepts to begin testing on your own.

Q&A

Q. I've heard about something called an *elastic layout*. How does that differ from the liquid layout?

A. An *elastic layout* is a layout whose content areas resize when the user resizes the text. Elastic layouts use ems, which are inherently proportional to text and font size. An em is a typographical unit of measurement equal to the point size of the current font. When ems are used in an elastic layout, if a user forces the text size to increase or decrease in size using Ctrl and the mouse scroll wheel, the areas containing the text increase or decrease proportionally. Elastic layouts are often quite difficult to achieve.

Q. You've spent a lot of time talking about liquid layouts and hybrid layouts—are they better than a purely fixed layout?

A. *Better* is a subjective term; in this book, the concern is with standards-compliant code. Most designers will tell you that liquid layouts take longer to create (and perfect), but the usability enhancements are worth it, especially when it leads to a responsive design. When might the time not be worth it? If your client does not have an opinion and is paying you a flat rate instead of an hourly rate. In that case, you are working only to showcase your own skills (that might be worth it to you, however).

Workshop

The Workshop contains quiz questions and activities to help you solidify your understanding of the material covered. Try to answer all questions before looking at the "Answers" section that follows.

Quiz

1. Which is the best layout to use, in general: fixed, liquid, or a hybrid?

2. Can you position a fixed layout anywhere on the page?

3. What does `min-width` do?

Answers

1. This was a trick question; there is no "best" layout. It depends on your content and the needs of your audience. (Note that the

author ultimately leans toward liquid and then responsive layouts as the "best," however, if you have the time and resources to do so.)

2. Sure. Although most fixed layouts are flush left or centered, you can assign a fixed position on an xy-axis where you could place a `<div>` that contains all the other layout `<div>`s.

3. The `min-width` property sets the minimum width of an element, not including padding, borders, or margins.

Exercises

▶ Figure 15.11 shows the finished fixed/liquid hybrid layout, but notice a few areas for improvement: There isn't any space around the text in the right-side column, there aren't any margins between the body text and either column; in addition, the footer strip is a little sparse, and so on. Take some time to fix these design elements.

▶ Using the code you fixed in the previous exercise, try to make it responsive, using only the brief information you learned in this hour. Just converting container elements to relative sizes should go a long way toward making the template viewable on your smartphone or other small device, but a media query and alternate stylesheet certainly wouldn't hurt, either.

HOUR 16
Using CSS to Do More with Lists

Hour 5, "Working with Text Blocks and Lists," introduced you to three types of HTML lists. Hour 13, "Working with Margins, Padding, Alignment, and Floating," covered margins, padding, and alignment of elements. In this hour, you learn how to apply margins, padding, and alignment styles to different types of HTML lists, helping you produce some powerful design elements purely in HTML and CSS.

Specifically, you learn how to modify the appearance of list elements—beyond the use of the `list-style-type` property that you learned in Hour 5. You will put into practice many of the CSS styles you've learned thus far, and the knowledge you gain in this hour enable you to use lists for more than just simply presenting a bulleted or numbered set of items.

HTML List Refresher

As you learned in Hour 5, HTML lists come in three basic types. Each presents content in a slightly different way, based on its type and the context:

▶ The *ordered list* is an indented list that displays numbers or letters before each list item. The ordered list is surrounded by `<ol>` and `</ol>` tags, and list items are enclosed in the `<li></li>` tag pair. This list type is often used to display numbered steps or levels of content.

▶ The *unordered list* is an indented list that displays a bullet or other symbol before each list item. The unordered list is surrounded by `<ul>` and `</ul>` tags, and list items are enclosed in the `<li></li>` tag pair. This list type is often used to provide a visual cue that brief yet specific bits of information will follow.

WHAT YOU'LL LEARN IN
THIS HOUR:

▶ How the CSS box model affects lists

▶ How to customize the list item indicator

▶ How to use list items and CSS to create an image map

▶ A *definition list* is often used to display terms and their meanings, thereby providing information hierarchy within the context of the list itself—much like the ordered list, but without the numbering. The definition list is surrounded by `<dl>` and `</dl>` tags, with `<dt>` and `</dt>` tags enclosing the term and `<dd>` and `</dd>` tags enclosing the definitions.

When the content warrants it, you can nest your ordered and unordered lists—or place lists within other lists. Nested lists produce a content hierarchy, so reserve their use for when your content actually has a hierarchy you want to display (such as content outlines or tables of content). Or as you will learn later on, you can use nested lists when your site navigation contains subnavigational elements.

How the CSS Box Model Affects Lists

Specific list-related styles include `list-style-image` (for placement of an image as a list item marker), `list-style-position` (indicating where to place the list item marker), and `list-style-type` (the type of list item marker itself). But although these styles control the structure of the list and list items, you can use `margin`, `padding`, `color`, and `background-color` styles to achieve even more specific displays with your lists.

In Hour 13, you learned that every element has some padding between the content and the border of the element; you also learned that there is a margin between the border of the element and any other content. This is true for lists, and when you are styling lists, you must remember that a "list" is actually made up of two elements: the parent list element type (`<ul>` or `<ol>`) and the individual list items themselves. Each of these elements has margins and padding that can be affected by a style sheet.

The examples in this hour show you how different CSS styles affect the visual display of HTML lists and list items. Keep these basic differences in mind as you practice working with lists in this hour, and you will be able to use lists to achieve advanced visual effects within site navigation.

Listing 16.1 creates a basic list containing three items. In this listing, the unordered list itself (the `<ul>`) is given a blue background, a black border, and a specific width of 100 pixels, as Figure 16.1 shows. The list items (the individual `<li>`) have a gray background and a yellow border. The list item text and indicators (the bullet) are black.

NOTE

Some older browsers handle margins and padding differently, especially around lists and list items. However, at the time of writing, the HTML and CSS in this hour and other lessons in this book are displayed identically in current versions of the major web browsers (Apple Safari, Google Chrome, Microsoft Internet Explorer, Mozilla Firefox, and Opera). Of course, you should still review your web content in all browsers before you publish it online, but the need for "hacking" style sheets to accommodate the rendering idiosyncrasies of browsers is fading.

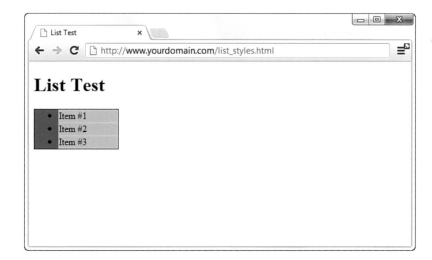

FIGURE 16.1
Styling the list and list items with colors and borders.

LISTING 16.1   Creating a Basic List with Color and Border Styles

```html
<!DOCTYPE html>

<html lang="en">
  <head>
    <title>List Test</title>
    <style type="text/css">
      ul {
        background-color: #6666ff;
        border: 1px solid #000000;
        width:100px;
      }
      li {
        background-color: #cccccc;
        border: 1px solid #ffff00;
      }
    </style>
  </head>

  <body>
    <h1>List Test</h1>
    <ul>
      <li>Item #1</li>
      <li>Item #2</li>
      <li>Item #3</li>
    </ul>
  </body>
</html>
```

As Figure 16.1 shows, the `<ul>` creates a box in which the individual
list items are placed. In this example, the entirety of the box has a
blue background. But also note that the individual list items—in this
example, they use a gray background and a yellow border—do not
extend to the left edge of the box created by the `<ul>`.

This is because browsers automatically add a certain amount of
padding to the left side of the `<ul>`. Browsers don't add padding to the
margin because that would appear around the outside of the box; they
add padding inside the box and only on the left side. That padding
value is approximately 40 pixels.

The default left-side padding value remains the same, regardless of the
type of list. If you add the following line to the style sheet, creating a
list with no item indicators, you will see that the padding remains the
same (see Figure 16.2):

```
list-style-type: none;
```

FIGURE 16.2
The default left-side padding
remains the same with or without
list item indicators.

When you are creating a page layout that includes lists of any type,
play around with padding to place the items "just so" on the page.
Similarly, just because no default margin is associated with lists doesn't
mean you can't assign some to the display; adding margin values to the
declaration for the ul selector provides additional layout control.

But remember, so far we've worked with only the list definition itself;
we haven't worked with the application of styles to the individual

list items. In Figures 16.1 and 16.2, the gray background and yellow border of the list item show no default padding or margin. Figure 16.3 shows the different effects created by applying padding or margin values to list items instead of the overall list "box" itself.

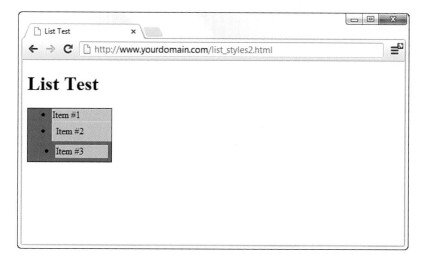

FIGURE 16.3
Different values affect the padding and margins on list items.

The first list item is the base item, with no padding or margin applied to it. However, the second list item uses a class called padded, defined in the stylesheet as padding: 6px; you can see the 6 pixels of padding on all sides (between the content and the yellow border surrounding the element). Note that the placement of the bullet remains the same as the placement of the first list item. The third list item uses a class called margined, defined in the stylesheet as margin: 6px, to apply 6 pixels of margin around the list item; this margin allows the blue background of the <ul> to show through.

Placing List Item Indicators

All this talk of margins and padding raises another issue: the control of list item indicators (when used) and how text should wrap around them (or not). The default value of the list-style-position property is outside—this placement means that the bullets, numbers, and other indicators are kept to the left of the text, outside the box created by the <li></li> tag pair. When text wraps within the list item, it wraps within that box and remains flush left with the left border of element.

But when the value of `list-style-position` is `inside`, the indicators are inside the box created by the `<li></li>` tag pair. Not only are the list item indicators then indented further (they essentially become part of the text), but the text wraps beneath each item indicator.

Figure 16.4 shows an example of both outside and inside list style positions. The only changes between Listing 16.1 and the code used to produce the example in Figure 16.4 (not including the filler text added to Item #2 and Item #3) is that the second list item uses a class called `outside`, defined in the stylesheet as `list-style-position: outside`, and the third list item uses a class called `inside`, defined in the stylesheet as `list-style-position: inside`.

FIGURE 16.4
The difference between `outside` and `inside` values for `list-style-position`.

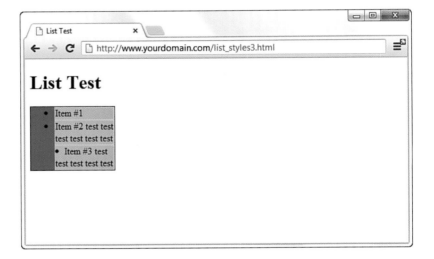

The additional filler text used for the second list item shows how the text wraps when the width of the list is defined as a value that is too narrow to display all on one line. You could have achieved the same result without using `list-style-position: outside` because that is the default value of `list-style-position` without any explicit statement in the code.

However, you can clearly see the difference when the `inside` position is used. In the third list item, the bullet and the text are both within the gray area bordered by yellow—the list item itself. Margins and padding affect list items differently when the value of `list-style-position` is `inside` (see Figure 16.5).

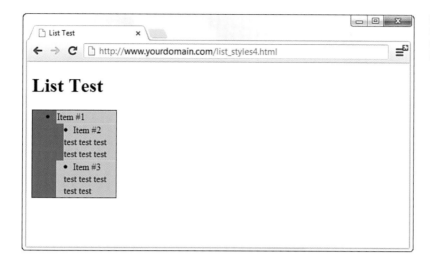

FIGURE 16.5
Margin and padding changes the display of items using the `inside` `list-style-position`.

In Figure 16.5, both the second and third list items have a `list-style-position` value of `inside`. However, the second list item has a `margin-left` value of 12 pixels, and the third list item has a `padding-left` value of 12 pixels. Although both content blocks (list indicator plus the text) show text wrapped around the bullet, and the placement of these blocks within the gray area defining the list item is the same, the affected area is the list item within the list itself.

As you would expect, the list item with the `margin-left` value of 12 pixels displays 12 pixels of red showing through the transparent margin surrounding the list item. Similarly, the list item with the `padding-left` value of 12 pixels displays 12 pixels of gray background (of the list item) before the content begins. Padding is within the element; margin is outside the element.

By understanding the way margins and padding affect both list items and the list in which they appear, you can create navigation elements in your website that are pure CSS and do not rely on external images. Later in this hour, you learn how to create both vertical and horizontal navigation menus, as well as menu drop-downs.

Creating Image Maps with List Items and CSS

In Hour 11, "Using Images in Your Website," you learned how to create client-side image maps using the `<map>` tag in HTML. Image maps enable you to define an area of an image and assign a link to that area (instead of having to slice an image into pieces, apply links to individual pieces, and stitch the image back together in HTML). However, you can also create an image map purely out of valid HTML and CSS.

The code in Listing 16.2 produces the image map that Figure 16.6 shows. When the code is rendered in a web browser, it simply looks like a web page with an image placed in it. The actions happen when your mouse hovers over a "hot" area, as you can see in Figure 16.6: The thicker white border and image `alt` text shows the area the mouse hovered over, and in the lower left of the browser window, you can see the URL assigned to that hot spot.

FIGURE 16.6
CSS enables you to define hot spots in an image map.

LISTING 16.2   Creating an Image Map Using CSS

```
<!DOCTYPE html>

<html lang="en">
  <head>
    <title>CSS Image Map Example</title>
    <style type="text/css">
    #theImg {
       width:500px;
       height:375px;
       background:url(tea_shipment.jpg) no-repeat;
       position:relative;
       border: 1px solid #000000;
    }
    #theImg ul {
       margin:0px;
       padding:0px;
       list-style:none;
    }
    #theImg a {
       position:absolute;
       text-indent: -1000em;
    }
    #theImg a:hover {
       border: 4px solid #ffffff;
    }
    #ss a {
       top:0px;
       left:5px;
       width:80px;
       height:225px;
    }
    #gn a {
       top:226px;
       left:15px;
       width:70px;
       height:110px;
    }
    #ib a {
       top:225px;
       left:85px;
       width:60px;
       height:90px;
    }
    #iTEA1 a {
       top:100px;
       left:320px;
       width:178px;
       height:125px;
    }
    #iTEA2 a {
       top:225px;
       left:375px;
       width:123px;
       height:115px;
```

```
      }
    </style>
  </head>
  <body>
    <div id="theImg">
    <ul>
    <li id="ss"><a href="[some URL]"
        title="Sugarshots">Sugarshots</a></li>
    <li id="gn"><a href="[some URL]"
        title="Golden Needle">Golden Needle</a></li>
    <li id="ib"><a href="[some URL]"
        title="Irish Breakfast">Irish Breakfast</a></li>
    <li id="iTEA1"><a href="[some URL]"
        title="IngenuiTEA">IngenuiTEA</a></li>
    <li id="iTEA2"><a href="[some URL]"
        title="IngenuiTEA">IngenuiTEA</a></li>
    </ul>
  </div>
  </body>
</html>
```

As Listing 16.2 shows, the style sheet has quite a few entries, but the actual HTML is quite short. List items are used to create five distinct clickable areas; those "areas" are list items that are assigned a specific height and width and then placed over an image that sits in the background. If the image is removed from the background of the `<div>` that surrounds the list, the list items still exist and are still clickable.

Let's walk through the style sheet so that you understand the pieces that make up this HTML and CSS image map, which is—at its most basic level—just a list of links.

The list of links is enclosed in a `<div>` named `theImg`. In the style sheet, this `<div>` is defined as block element that is 500 pixels wide and 375 pixels high, with a 1-pixel solid black border. The background of this element is an image named `tea_shipment.jpg` that is placed in one position and does not repeat. The next bit of HTML that you see is the beginning of the unordered list (`<ul>`). In the style sheet, this unordered list is given margin and padding values of 0 pixels all around and a `list-style` of `none`—list items will not be preceded by any icon.

The list item text itself never appears to the user because of this trick in the style sheet entry for all `<a>` tags within the `<div>`:

```
text-indent: -1000em;
```

By indenting the text *negative* 1,000 ems, you can be assured that the text will never appear. It does exist, but it exists in a nonviewable area 1,000 ems to the left of the browser window. In other words, if you raise your left hand and place it to the side of your computer monitor, `text-indent:-1000em` places the text somewhere to the left of your pinky finger. But that's what we want because we don't need to see the text link. We just need an area to be defined as a link so that the user's cursor changes as it does when rolling over any link in a website.

When the user's cursor hovers over a list item containing a link, that list item shows a 4-pixel border that is solid white, thanks to this entry in the style sheet:

```
#theImg a:hover {
   border: 4px solid #ffffff;
}
```

The list items themselves are then defined and placed in specific positions based on the areas of the image that are supposed to be the clickable areas. For example, the list item with the `ss` ID, for `Sugarshots`—the name of the item shown in the figure—has its top-left corner placed 0 pixels from the top of the `<div>` and 5 pixels in from the left edge of the `<div>`. This list item is 80 pixels wide and 225 pixels high. Similar style declarations are made for the `#gn`, `#ib`, `#iTEA1`, and `#iTEA2` list items so that the linked areas associated with those IDs appear in certain positions relative to the image.

Summary

This hour began with examples of how lists and list elements are affected by padding and margin styles. You learned about the default padding associated with lists and how to control that padding. Next, you learned how to modify padding and margin values, and how to place the list item indicator either inside the list item or outside it—you began to think about how styles and lists can affect your overall site design. Finally, you learned how to leverage lists and list elements to create a pure HTML and CSS image map, thus reducing the need for slicing up linked images or using the `<map>` tag.

After learning to "think outside the (list) box," if you will, you learned how to use unordered lists to produce horizontal or vertical navigation within your website. By using CSS instead of graphics, you have more flexibility in both the display and maintenance of your site. Throughout this hour, you learned that, with a few entries in your style sheet, you can turn plain underlined text links into areas with borders and background colors and other text styles. Additionally, you learned how to present nested lists within menus.

Q&A

Q. **An awful lot of web pages talk about the "box model hack" regarding margins and padding, especially for lists and list elements. Are you sure I don't have to use a hack?**

A. At the beginning of this hour, you learned that the HTML and CSS in this hour (and others) all look the same in the current versions of the major web browsers. This is the product of several years of web developers having to do code hacks and other tricks before modern browsers began handling things according to CSS specifications, not their own idiosyncrasies. Additionally, there is a growing movement to rid Internet users of the *very* old web browsers that necessitated most of these hacks in the first place. So although I wouldn't necessarily advise you to design *only* for the current versions of the major web browsers, I also wouldn't recommend that you spend a ton of time implementing hacks for the older versions of browsers—which less than 5% of the Internet population uses, by the way. You should continue to write solid code that validates and adheres to design principles, test your pages in a suite of browsers that best reflects your audience, and release your site to the world.

Q. **The CSS image map seems like a lot of work. Is the** `<map>` **tag so bad?**

A. The `<map>` tag isn't at all bad and is indeed valid HTML5. Determining coordinates used in client-side image maps can be difficult, however, especially without graphics software or software intended for the creation of client-side image maps. The CSS version gives you more options for defining and displaying clickable areas, only one of which you've seen here.

Workshop

The Workshop contains quiz questions and activities to help you solidify your understanding of the material covered. Try to answer all questions before looking at the "Answers" section that follows.

Quiz

1. What is the difference between the `inside` and `outside list-style-position` values? Which is the default value?

2. Does a `list-style` with a value of `none` still produce a structured list, either ordered or unordered?

3. When using an unordered list to create image hot spots, how do you draw the hot spot area?

Answers

1. The `list-style-position` value of `inside` places the list item indicator inside the block created by the list item. A value of `outside` places the list item indicator outside the block. When `inside`, content wraps beneath the list item indicator. The default value is `outside`.

2. Yes. The only difference is that no list item indicator is present before the content within the list item.

3. The hot spot area is drawn by giving the list item a specific `height` and `width`, along with a starting point indicated by a value for `right` and `left`.

Exercises

▶ Be sure you really understand the different effects of padding and margins, and `inside` and `outside` list item placement, by creating lists and list items and then adjusting these values much as we did in the beginning of this hour.

▶ Find an image, and try your hand at mapping areas using the technique shown in this hour. Select an image that has areas where you can use hot spots or clickable areas leading either to other web pages on your site or to someone else's site. Then create the HTML and CSS to define the clickable areas and the URLs where they should lead.

HOUR 17
Using CSS to Design Navigation

In the previous lesson, you learned how margins, padding, and alignment styles can be applied to different types of HTML lists, helping you produce some powerful design elements purely in HTML and CSS. In this hour, you learn a few of the many ways to use lists as vertical or horizontal navigation, including how to use lists to create drop-down menus.

The methods explained in this chapter represent a very small subset of the numerous and varied navigation methods you can create using lists. However, the concepts are all similar; different results come from your own creativity and application of these basic concepts. To help you get your creative juices flowing, I provide pointers to other examples of CSS-based navigation at the end of this chapter.

WHAT YOU'LL LEARN IN THIS HOUR:

► How navigation lists differ from regular lists

► How to create vertical navigation with CSS

► How to create horizontal navigation with CSS

How Navigation Lists Differ from Regular Lists

When we talk about using lists to create navigation elements, we really mean using CSS to display content in the way website visitors expect navigation to look—in short, *different* from simple bulleted or numbered lists. Although it is true that a set of navigation elements is essentially a list of links, those links are typically displayed in a way that makes it clear that users should interact with the content:

► The user's mouse cursor changes to indicate that the element is clickable.

► The area around the element changes appearance when the mouse hovers over it.

► The content area is visually set apart from regular text.

Older methods of creating navigation tended to rely on images—such as graphics with beveled edges and the use of contrasting colors for backgrounds and text—plus client-side programming with JavaScript to handle image swapping based on mouse actions. But using pure CSS to create navigation from list elements produces a more usable, flexible, and search engine-friendly display that is accessible by users using all manner and sorts of devices.

Regardless of the layout of your navigational elements—horizontal or vertical—this hour discusses two levels of navigation: primary and secondary. *Primary navigation* takes users to the introductory pages of main sections of your site; *secondary navigation* reflects those pages within a certain section.

Creating Vertical Navigation with CSS

Depending on your site architecture—both the display template you have created and the manner in which you have categorized the information in the site—you might find yourself using vertical navigation for either primary navigation or secondary navigation.

For example, suppose you have created a website for your company with the primary sections About Us, Products, Support, and Press. Within the primary About Us section, you might have several other pages, such as Mission, History, Executive Team, and Contact Us—these other pages are the secondary navigation within the primary About Us section.

Listing 17.1 sets up a basic secondary page with vertical navigation in the side of the page and content in the middle of the page. The links in the side and the links in the content area of the page are basic HTML list elements.

This listing and the example in Figure 17.1 provides a starting point for showing you how CSS enables you to transform two similar HTML structures into two different visual displays (and thus two different contexts).

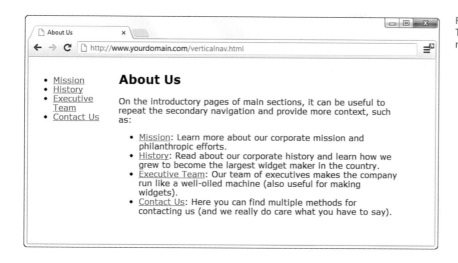

FIGURE 17.1
The starting point: unstyled list
navigation.

LISTING 17.1 Basic Page with Vertical Navigation in a List

```
<!DOCTYPE html>

<html lang="en">
  <head>
    <title>About Us</title>
    <style type="text/css">
      body {
         font: 12pt Verdana, Arial, Georgia, sans-serif;
      }
      nav {
         width:150px;
         float:left;
         margin-top:12px;
         margin-right:18px;
      }
      section {
         width:550px;
         float:left;
      }
    </style>
  </head>

  <body>
    <nav>
    <ul>
      <li><a href="#">Mission</a></li>
      <li><a href="#">History</a></li>
      <li><a href="#">Executive Team</a></li>
      <li><a href="#">Contact Us</a></li>
    </ul>
    </nav>
    <section>
```

```
    <header>
    <h1>About Us</h1>
    </header>
    <p>On the introductory pages of main sections, it can be useful
    to repeat the secondary navigation and provide more context,
    such as:</p>
    <ul>
    <li><a href="#">Mission</a>: Learn more about our corporate
    mission and philanthropic efforts.</li>
    <li><a href="#">History</a>: Read about our corporate history
    and learn how we grew to become the largest widget maker
    in the country.</li>
    <li><a href="#">Executive Team</a>: Our team of executives makes
    the company run like a well-oiled machine (also useful for
    making widgets).</li>
    <li><a href="#">Contact Us</a>: Here you can find multiple
    methods for contacting us (and we really do care what you
    have to say).</li>
    </ul>
  </section>
  </body>
</html>
```

The contents of this page are set up in two sections: a `<nav>` element containing navigation, and a single `<section>` element containing the primary text of the page. The only styles assigned to anything in this basic page are the width, margin, and float values associated with each element. No styles have been applied to the list elements.

To differentiate between the links present in the list in the content area and the links present in the list in the side navigation, add the following styles to the stylesheet:

```
nav a {
   text-decoration: none;
}
section a {
   text-decoration: none;
   font-weight: bold;
}
```

These styles simply say that all `<a>` links in the `<nav>` have no underline, and all `<a>` links in the `<section>` have no underline and are bold. Figure 17.2 shows the difference.

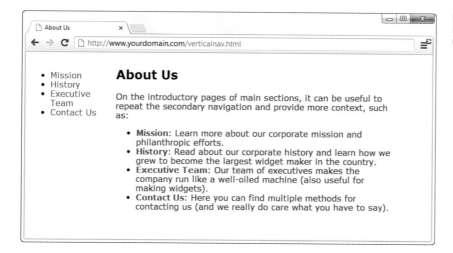

FIGURE 17.2
Differentiating the list elements using CSS.

But to really make the side navigation list look like something special, you have to dig deeper into the stylesheet.

Styling the Single-Level Vertical Navigation

The goal with this particular set of navigation elements is simply to present them as a block of links without bullets and with background and text colors that change depending on their link state (regular link, visited link, hovering over the link, or activated link). The first step in the process is already complete: separating the navigation from the content. We've done that by putting the navigation in a `<nav>` element.

Next, you need to modify the `<ul>` that defines the link within the `<nav>` element. Let's take away the list indicator and ensure that there is no extra margin or padding besides the top margin. That top margin is used to line up the top of the navigation with the top of the "About Us" header text in the content area of the page:

```
nav ul {
   list-style: none;
   margin: 12px 0px 0px 0px;;
   padding: 0px;
}
```

Because the navigation list items themselves will appear as colored areas, give each list item a bottom border so that some visual separation of the content can occur:

```
nav li {
    border-bottom: 1px solid #ffffff;
}
```

Now on to building the rest of the list items. The idea is that when the list items simply sit there acting as links, they are a special shade of blue with bold white text (although they are a smaller font size than the body text itself). To achieve that, add the following:

```
nav li a:link, nav li a:visited {
    font-size: 10pt;
    font-weight: bold;
    display: block;
    padding: 3px 0px 3px 3px;
    background-color: #628794;
    color: #ffffff;
}
```

All the styles used previously should be familiar to you, except perhaps the use of `display: block;` in the stylesheet entry. Setting the `display` property to `block` ensures that the entire `<li>` element is in play when a user hovers the mouse over it. Figure 17.3 shows the vertical list menu with these new styles applied to it.

FIGURE 17.3
The vertical list is starting to look like a navigation menu.

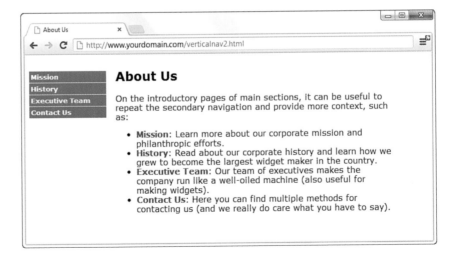

When the user's mouse hovers over a navigational list element, the idea is for some visual change to takes place so that the user knows the element is clickable. This is akin to how most software menus change color when a user's cursor hovers over the menu items. In this case, we'll change the background color of the list item and change the text color of the list item; they'll be different from the blue and white shown previously.

```
nav li a:hover, nav li a:active {
   font-size: 10pt;
   font-weight: bold;
   display: block;
   padding: 3px 0px 3px 3px;
   background-color: #6cac46;
   color: #000000;
}
```

Figure 17.4 shows the results of all the stylistic work so far. A few entries in a stylesheet have transformed the simple list into a visually differentiated menu.

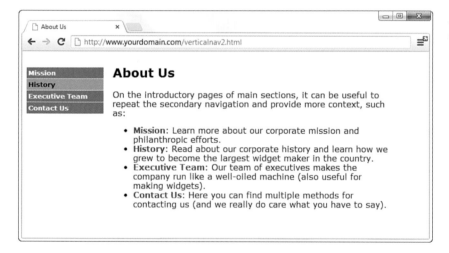

FIGURE 17.4
The list items now change color when the mouse hovers over them.

Styling the Multilevel Vertical Navigation

What if your site architecture calls for another level of navigation that you want your users to see at all times? That is represented by nested lists (which you learned about in previous hours) and more stylesheet entries. In this case, assume that there are four navigation elements under the Executive Team link. In the HTML, modify the list as follows:

```
<ul>
  <li><a href="#">Mission</a></li>
  <li><a href="#">History</a></li>
```

```
<li><a href="#">Executive Team</a>
    <ul>
    <li><a href="#">&raquo; CEO</a>
    <li><a href="#">&raquo; CFO</a>
    <li><a href="#">&raquo; COO</a>
    <li><a href="#">&raquo; Other Minions</a>
    </ul>
</li>
<li><a href="#">Contact Us</a></li>
</ul>
```

This code produces a nested list under the Executive Team link (see Figure 17.5). The `&raquo;` HTML entity produces the right-pointing arrows that are displayed before the text in the new links.

FIGURE 17.5
Creating a nested navigation list
(but one that is not yet styled well).

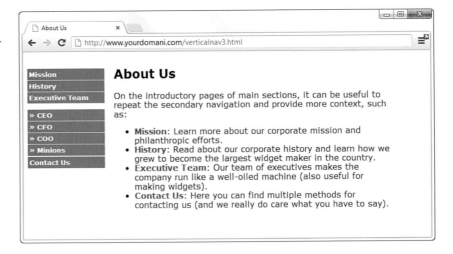

The new items appear as block elements within the list, but the hierarchy of information is not visually represented. To add some sort of visual element that identifies these items as subnavigational elements attached to the Executive Team link, modify the stylesheet again to add some indentation.

But before doing that, you want to modify some of the other stylesheet entries as well. In the previous section, we added selectors such as `nav ul` and `nav li`, which indicate "all `<ul>` in the `<nav>` element" and "all `<li>` in the `<nav>` element," respectively. However, we now have two instances of `<ul>` and another set of `<li>` elements with the `<nav>` element, all of which we want to appear different from the original set.

To ensure that both sets of list items are styled appropriately, make sure that the stylesheet selectors clearly indicate the hierarchy of the lists. To do that, use entries such as `nav ul` and `nav ul li` for the first level of lists, and use `nav ul ul` and `nav ul ul li` for the second level of lists. Listing 17.2 shows the new version of stylesheet entries and HTML that produces the menu shown in Figure 17.6.

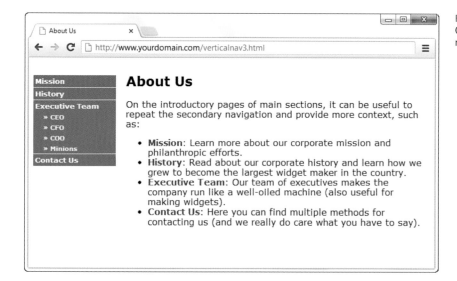

FIGURE 17.6
Creating two levels of vertical navigation using CSS.

LISTING 17.2   Multilevel Vertical Navigation in a List

```
<!DOCTYPE html>

<html lang="en">
  <head>
    <title>About Us</title>
    <style type="text/css">
      body {
          font: 12pt Verdana, Arial, Georgia, sans-serif;
      }
      nav {
          width:150px;
          float:left;
          margin-top:12px;
          margin-right:18px;
      }
      section {
          width:550px;
          float:left;
      }
      nav a {
```

```
      text-decoration: none;
    }
    section a {
      text-decoration: none;
      font-weight: bold;
    }
    nav ul {
      list-style: none;
      margin: 12px 0px 0px 0px;
      padding: 0px;
    }
    nav ul li {
      border-bottom: 1px solid #ffffff;
    }
    nav ul li a:link, nav ul li a:visited {
      font-size: 10pt;
      font-weight: bold;
      display: block;
      padding: 3px 0px 3px 3px;
      background-color: #628794;
      color: #ffffff;
    }
    nav ul li a:hover, nav ul li a:active {
      font-size: 10pt;
      font-weight: bold;
      display: block;
      padding: 3px 0px 3px 3px;
      background-color: #c6a648;
      color: #000000;
    }
    nav ul ul {
      margin: 0px;
      padding: 0px;
    }
    nav ul ul li {
      border-bottom: none;
    }
    nav ul ul li a:link, nav ul ul li a:visited {
      font-size: 8pt;
      font-weight: bold;
      display: block;
      padding: 3px 0px 3px 18px;
      background-color: #628794;
      color: #ffffff;
    }
    nav ul ul li a:hover, nav ul ul li a:active {
      font-size: 8pt;
      font-weight: bold;
      display: block;
      padding: 3px 0px 3px 18px;
      background-color: #c6a648;
      color: #000000;
    }
  </style>
</head>
```

```
<body>
  <nav>
  <ul>
    <li><a href="#">Mission</a></li>
    <li><a href="#">History</a></li>
    <li><a href="#">Executive Team</a>
      <ul>
      <li><a href="#">&raquo; CEO</a></li>
      <li><a href="#">&raquo; CFO</a></li>
      <li><a href="#">&raquo; COO</a></li>
      <li><a href="#">&raquo; Other Minions</a></li>
      </ul>
    </li>
    <li><a href="#">Contact Us</a></li>
  </ul>
  </nav>
  <section>
    <header>
    <h1>About Us</h1>
    </header>
    <p>On the introductory pages of main sections, it can be useful
    to repeat the secondary navigation and provide more context,
    such as:</p>
    <ul>
    <li><a href="#">Mission</a>: Learn more about our corporate
    mission and philanthropic efforts.</li>
    <li><a href="#">History</a>: Read about our corporate history
    and learn how we grew to become the largest widget maker
    in the country.</li>
    <li><a href="#">Executive Team</a>: Our team of executives makes
    the company run like a well-oiled machine (also useful for
    making widgets).</li>
    <li><a href="#">Contact Us</a>: Here you can find multiple
    methods for contacting us (and we really do care what you
    have to say.</li>
    </ul>
  </section>
</body>
</html>
```

The different ways of styling vertical navigation are limited only by your own creativity. You can use colors, margins, padding, background images, and any other valid CSS to produce vertical navigation that is quite flexible and easily modified. If you type "CSS vertical navigation" into your search engine, you will find millions of examples—and they are all based on the simple principles you've learned in this hour.

Creating Horizontal Navigation with CSS

The lessons on navigation began with vertical navigation because the concept of converting a list into navigation is easier to grasp when the navigation still looks like a list of items that you might write vertically on a piece of paper, such as with a grocery list. When creating horizontal navigation, you still use HTML list elements, but instead of achieving a vertical display by using the `inline` value of the `display` property for both the `<ul>` and the `<li>`, use the `block` value of the `display` property instead. It really is as simple as that.

Listing 17.3 shows a starting point for a page featuring horizontal navigation. The page contains a `<header>` element for a logo and navigation and a `<section>` element for content. Within the `<header>` element, a `<div>` containing a logo is floated next to a `<nav>` element containing the navigational links. The list that appears in the `<nav>` element has a `display` property value of `inline` for both the list and the list items. You can see these elements and their placement in Figure 17.7.

FIGURE 17.7
Creating functional—but not necessarily beautiful—horizontal navigation using inline list elements.

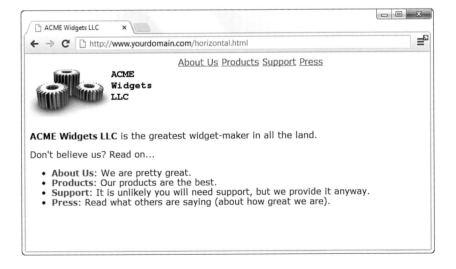

LISTING 17.3   Basic Horizontal Navigation from a List

```
<!DOCTYPE html>

<html lang="en">
  <head>
    <title>ACME Widgets LLC</title>
    <style type="text/css">
      body {
        font: 12pt Verdana, Arial, Georgia, sans-serif;
      }
      header {
        width: auto;
      }
      #logo {
        float:left;
      }
      nav {
        float:left;
      }
      nav ul {
        list-style: none;
        display: inline;
      }
      nav li {
        display: inline;
      }
      section {
        width: auto;
        float: left;
        clear: left;
      }
      section a {
        text-decoration: none;
        font-weight: bold;
      }
    </style>
  </head>
  <body>
    <header>
      <div id="logo">
        <img src="acmewidgets.jpg" alt="ACME Widgets LLC" />
      </div>
      <nav>
        <ul>
        <li><a href="#">About Us</a></li>
        <li><a href="#">Products</a></li>
        <li><a href="#">Support</a></li>
        <li><a href="#">Press</a></li>
        </ul>
      </nav>
    </header>
    <section>
      <p><strong>ACME Widgets LLC</strong> is the greatest widget-maker
```

```
        in all the land.</p>
        <p>Don't believe us? Read on...</p>
        <ul>
        <li><a href="#">About Us</a>: We are pretty great.</li>
        <li><a href="#">Products</a>: Our products are the best.</li>
        <li><a href="#">Support</a>: It is unlikely you will need support,
        but we provide it anyway.</li>
        <li><a href="#">Press</a>: Read what others are saying (about how
        great we are).</li>
        </ul>
    </section>
  </body>
</html>
```

Modifying the display of this list occurs purely through CSS; the structure of the content within the HTML itself is already set. To achieve the desired display, use the following CSS. First, the `<nav>` element is modified to be a particular width, to display a background color and border, and to use a top margin of 85 pixels (so that it displays near the bottom of the logo).

```
nav {
    float:left;
    margin: 85px 0px 0px 0px;
    width: 400px;
    background-color: #628794;
    border: 1px solid black;
}
```

The definition for the `<ul>` remains the same as in Listing 17.3, except for the changes in margin and padding:

```
nav ul {
    margin: 0px;
    padding: 0px;
    list-style: none;
    display: inline;
}
```

The definition for the `<li>` remains the same as in Listing 17.3, except that it has been given a line-height value of 1.8em:

```
nav li {
    display: inline;
    line-height: 1.8em;
}
```

The link styles are similar to those used in the vertical navigation; these entries have different padding values, but the colors and font sizes remain the same:

```
nav ul li a:link, nav ul li a:visited {
    font-size: 10pt;
    font-weight: bold;
    text-decoration: none;
    padding: 7px 10px 7px 10px;
    background-color: #628794;
    color: #ffffff;
}
nav ul li a:hover, nav ul li a:active {
    font-size: 10pt;
    font-weight: bold;
    text-decoration: none;
    padding: px 10px 7px 10px;
    background-color: #c6a648;
    color: #000000;
}
```

Putting these styles together, you produce the display shown in
Figure 17.8.

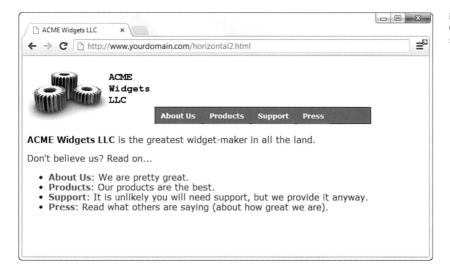

FIGURE 17.8
Creating horizontal navigation with
some style.

When the user rolls over the navigation elements, the background and
text colors change in the same way they did when the user hovered
the mouse over the vertical navigation menu. Also, just as you did
with the vertical navigation menu, you can use nested lists to produce
drop-down functionality in your horizontal menu. Try it yourself!

Summary

The entire point of this lesson was for you to learn how to use unordered lists to produce horizontal or vertical navigation within your website. By using CSS instead of graphics, you gain more flexibility in both the display and maintenance of your site. Throughout this hour, you learned that, with a few entries in your stylesheet, you can turn plain underlined text links into areas with borders and background colors and other text styles. Additionally, you learned how to present nested lists within menus.

Q&A

Q. Can I use graphics in the navigation menus as a custom list indicator?

A. Yes. You can use graphics within the HTML text of the list item or as background images within the `<li>` element. You can style your navigation elements just as you style any other list element. The only differences between an HTML unordered list and a CSS-based horizontal or vertical navigation list is that you are calling it that, and you are using the unordered list for a specific purpose outside the body of the text. Along with that, you then style the list to show the user that it is indeed something different—and you can do that with small graphics to accentuate your lists.

Q. Where can I find more examples of what I can do with lists?

A. The last time I checked, typing "CSS navigation" into a search engine returned approximately 44 million results. Here are a few starting places:

▶ A List Apart's CSS articles, at http://alistapart.com/topic/css

▶ Maxdesign's CSS Listamatic, at http://css.maxdesign.com.au/listamatic/

▶ Vitaly Friedman's CSS Showcase, at www.alvit.de/css-showcase/

Workshop

The Workshop contains quiz questions and activities to help you solidify your understanding of the material covered. Try to answer all questions before looking at the "Answers" section that follows.

Quiz

1. To create a horizontal list, do you use the `inline` or `block_display` property?

2. When creating list-based navigation, how many levels of nested lists can you use?

3. When creating a navigation list of any type, can the four pseudoclasses for the `a` selector have the same values?

Answers

1. Horizontal lists use the `inline` value of `display`; vertical lists use `block`.

2. Technically, you can nest your lists as deep as you want to. But from a usability standpoint, there is a limit to the number of levels you *want* to use to nest your lists. Three levels is typically the limit—more than that, and you run the risk of creating a poorly organized site or simply giving users more options than they need to see at all times.

3. Sure, but then you run the risk of users not realizing that your beautiful menus are indeed menus (because no visual display would occur for a mouse action).

Exercises

▶ Using the techniques shown for a multilevel vertical list, add subnavigation items to the vertical list created at the end of the chapter.

▶ Look at the numerous examples of CSS-based navigation used in websites, and find some tricky-looking actions. Using the View Source function of your web browser, look at the CSS these sites use, and try to implement something similar for yourself.

Using Mouse Actions to Modify Text Display

Throughout this book, you have seen examples of how mouse actions can affect the display of text. The simplest example is when the hover pseudoclass of the <a> link is defined in the stylesheet to display text in a different color when a user's mouse hovers over it. In the previous hour, you learned how the hover pseudoclass changed both the text color and the background color of an <li> element.

In this hour, you learn how to achieve two specific actions that combine CSS and mouse actions—displaying additional text when a user rolls over an item with the mouse, and using a mouse click to change the color of a container element. These two actions are useful in some circumstances, to be sure—but more important, they provide an entry point into more advanced work you might want to tackle later in your web development.

Creating a ToolTip with CSS

A *ToolTip* is an element within a graphical user interface—this could be a software program or a website—that provides additional information when a cursor hovers over a specific item. Figure 18.1 shows a ToolTip in action: the mouse rolls over the linked text "markup language," and the ToolTip displays "Markup language" in a small box. In this case, the text displayed in the ToolTip comes from the title attribute of the <a> tag.

WHAT YOU'LL LEARN IN THIS HOUR:

▶ How to display tooltips when users move their mouse

▶ How to use mouse events to change something about the page

FIGURE 18.1
A standard ToolTip in action.

The display of the ToolTip in Figure 18.1 is controlled by the software itself. That is, its display and appearance is not something you, the web developer, can control. However, you can create your own ToolTips with a little CSS by applying concepts you've already practiced in previous hours.

Listing 18.1 contains the stylesheet entries and HTML for a page that contains images and links, but with one link that also displays a custom ToolTip.

LISTING 18.1   Creating a Simple ToolTip with CSS

```
<!DOCTYPE html>

<html lang="en">
  <head>
    <title>Steptoe Butte</title>
    <style type="text/css">
    a {
       text-decoration: none;
       font-weight: bold;
    }
    a.tip {
```

```
      position:relative;
      z-index:24;
  }
  a.tip:hover {
      z-index:25;
  }
  a.tip span {
      display: none;
  }
  a.tip:hover span {
      font-weight: normal;
      font-style: italic;
      display: block;
      position: absolute;
      top: 20px;
      left: 25px;
      width: 150px;
      padding: 3px;
      border:1px solid #000;
      background-color:#ddd;
      color:#000;
  }
  img {
      float:left;
      margin-right: 12px;
      margin-bottom: 6px;
      border: 1px solid #000;
  }
  </style>
</head>
<body>
  <header>
      <h1>Steptoe Butte</h1>
  </header>
  <p><img src="steptoebutte.jpg" alt="View from Steptoe Butte" />
  Steptoe Butte is a quartzite island jutting out of the silty loess of
  the <a class="tip" href="http://en.wikipedia.org/wiki/Palouse">Palouse
  <span>Learn more about the Palouse!</span></a> hills in Whitman
  County, Washington. The rock that forms the butte is over 400 million
  years old, in contrast with the 15-7 million year old
  <a href="http://en.wikipedia.org/wiki/Columbia_River">
  Columbia River</a> basalts that underlie the rest of the Palouse (such
  "islands" of ancient rock have come to be called buttes, a butte being
  defined as a small hill with a flat top, whose width at top does not
  exceed its height).</p>
  <p>A hotel built by Cashup Davis stood atop Steptoe Butte from 1888 to
  1908, burning down several years after it closed. In 1946, Virgil
  McCroskey donated 120 acres (0.49 km2) of land to form Steptoe Butte
  State Park, which was later increased to over 150 acres (0.61 km2).
  Steptoe Butte is currently recognized as a National Natural Landmark
  because of its unique geological value. It is named in honor of
  <a href="http://en.wikipedia.org/wiki/Colonel_Edward_Steptoe">Colonel
  Edward Steptoe</a>.</p>
  <p>Elevation: 3,612 feet (1,101 m), approximately 1,000 feet (300 m)
  above the surrounding countryside.</p>
```

```
  <footer>
     <em>Text from
     <a href="http://en.wikipedia.org/wiki/Steptoe_Butte">Wikipedia</a>,
     photo by the author.</em>
  </footer>
 </body>
</html>
```

Note that the first link in the text has a class associated with it. That class is called `tip`—the name differentiates it from other links that do not contain ToolTips. However, because this is a class and not an `id`, it can be used for all the other links in the page as well.

Note that the `tip` class itself has a defined `position` and `z-index`. The `position` value (`relative`) ensures that it remains presented as it naturally occurs in the text; the `z-index`, when compared to the `z-index` used by other related styles, ensures that the text of the link remains below other text with higher `z-index` values. The hover state of links using the `tip` class has a higher `z-index` value, for example.

The next two styles relate to the `<span>` tag in use. Text within the `<span>` tag within the `<a>` tag is not displayed unless the user invokes the ToolTip by hovering the mouse over the visible link. For example, the link text looks like this:

```
<a class="tip" href="http://en.wikipedia.org/wiki/Palouse">Palouse
<span>Learn more about the Palouse!</span></a>
```

When you look at this bit of HTML, it looks like the words `Palouse Learn more about the Palouse!` should all be a link. However, because `Learn more about the Palouse!` is enclosed in the `<span>` tag, and a specific style is applied to that `<span>` in the stylesheet, the words do not appear until the user's mouse hovers over the actual link (the word `Palouse`). Figure 18.2 displays this result.

The text `Learn more about the Palouse!` is placed in a `<span>` tag in the HTML but is styled within the stylesheet. Namely, the `a.tip:hover span` selector creates a box that is 150 pixels wide with a gray background and black border. This box appears 20 pixels from the top of the element and 25 pixels in from the left of the parent element. This creates the ToolTip, which you can customize as you wish.

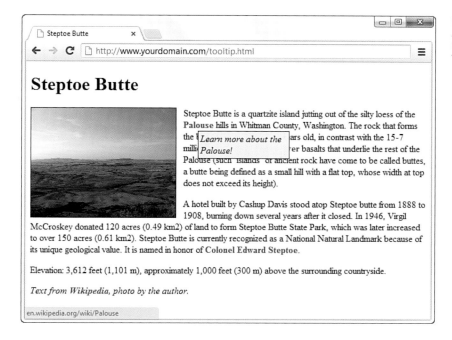

FIGURE 18.2
A custom ToolTip appears when the mouse hovers over the first link in the page.

Displaying Additional Rollover Text with CSS

A ToolTip serves a specific purpose: to show a textual "tip" attached to a link. But you can use the same concept to show hidden text somewhere else in your layout, based on a mouse action. Take, for example, the ACME Widgets LLC main page from Hour 17, "Using CSS to Design Navigation"—the version with horizontal navigation. By using the same concepts as those in Listing 17.1, you can show additional text above the menu when users roll over one of the main section links. Figure 18.3 shows one of these in action; I recaptured some of that white space above the navigation and to the right of the logo.

The only change made to the CSS from Listing 17.3 and the modifications that follow it in Hour 17 is the addition of the following four styles. These four styles perform the same tasks as the `tip` class styles used in Listing 18.1, but the display is slightly different than the display in Listing 18.1.

FIGURE 18.3
Custom text above another
element, visible only on rollover.

```
nav a.more {
    position:relative;
    z-index:24;
}
nav a.more:hover {
    z-index:25;
}
nav a.more span {
    display: none;
}
nav a.more:hover span {
    font-weight: bold;
    display: block;
    position: absolute;
    top: -35px;
    width: 300px;
    color:#ff0000;
    line-height: 1em;
}
```

The value of `-25px` for the `top` property places the text enclosed in the `<span>` tag 25 pixels above the top-left corner of the parent tag, as opposed to the previous example, which placed it 20 pixels below the top-left corner of the parent tag. The changes to the HTML are similar to the changes in the previous section, in that the text that is hidden until rollover appears in a `<span>` tag within an `<a>` link:

```
<ul>
  <li><a class="more" href="#">About Us <span>We are pretty
  great.</span></a></li>
  <li><a class="more" href="#">Products <span>Our products are
  the best!</span></a></li>
  <li><a class="more" href="#">Support <span>It is unlikely you
  will need support, but we provide it anyway.</span></a></li>
  <li><a class="more" href="#">Press <span>Read what others are
  saying (about how great we are).</span></a></li>
</ul>
```

Using these basic concepts, you can make any text appear anywhere you want based on the user's mouse actions when hovering over an `<a>` link. In the next section, you learn how to use event attributes plus a little JavaScript to do even more with mouse actions and CSS.

Accessing Events

A user interaction such as a mouse click or key press is known as an *event*. The process of a script taking action based on an event is known as *event handling*. You can use special attributes to associate event-handling script code with elements on a web page. The use of JavaScript, or JavaScript libraries such as jQuery (http://jquery.org/), is beyond the scope of this book, but it is useful to address this common question and start you on the path toward thinking about the next step in your learning process.

Following are some of the commonly used event attributes that come in handy in JavaScript, along with a description of when they occur with respect to a web page element:

▶ `onload`—Browser loads the element

▶ `onkeydown`—User presses a key

▶ `onkeyup`—User releases a key

▶ `onclick`—User clicks the element with the left mouse button

▶ `ondblclick`—User double-clicks the element with the left mouse button

▶ `onmousedown`—User presses either mouse button while the mouse pointer is over the element

▶ `onmouseup`—User releases either mouse button while the mouse pointer is over the element

- ▶ onmouseover—User moves the mouse pointer into the boundaries of the element

- ▶ onmousemove—User moves the mouse pointer while the pointer is over the element

- ▶ onmouseout—User moves the mouse pointer out of the boundaries of the element

As you can see, event attributes are used to respond to common user input events such as mouse clicks and key presses. You can associate JavaScript with an event by assigning the code to the event attribute, like this:

```
<h1 onclick="this.style.color = 'red';">I turn red when clicked.</h1>
```

In the previous code snippet, a bit of JavaScript is assigned to the onclick event attribute of an <h1> tag, which means that the code runs in response to a user clicking the left mouse button on the text. The script code responds by setting the color of the text to red. In this way, interactivity is added to normally bland text by changing the color of the text in response to a mouse click. This is the basis for how client-side scripts work in conjunction with your web browser.

In the next section, you see an example of how to use event handling to change the appearance of a <div>. Specifically, the contents of a <div> appear or disappear based on a mouse click.

Using onclick to Change <div> Appearance

You can use the onclick event to invoke all sorts of action. You might think of a mouse click as a way to submit a form by clicking a button, but you can capture this event and use it to provide interactivity within your pages as well. In this example, you see how you can use the onclick event to show or hide information contained in a <div>. Using text and images that look quite similar to those in Listing 18.1, you will see how to add interactivity to your page by allowing the user to show previously hidden information when clicking a piece of text. I've referred to this text as a "piece of text" because, strictly speaking, the text is not a link—that is, it looks and acts like a link, but it is not marked up within an <a> tag.

Listing 18.2 provides the complete code for this example, shown initially in Figure 18.4.

LISTING 18.2   Using `onclick` to Show or Hide Content

```html
<!DOCTYPE html>

<html lang="en">
  <head>
    <title>Steptoe Butte</title>
    <style type="text/css">
    a {
        text-decoration: none;
        font-weight: bold;
    }
    img {
        margin-right: 12px;
        margin-bottom: 6px;
        border: 1px solid #000;
    }
    .mainimg {
        float: left;
    }
    #hide_e {
        display: none;
    }
    #elevation {
        display: none;
    }
    #hide_p {
        display: none;
    }
    #photos {
        display: none;
    }
    #show_e {
        display: block;
    }
    #show_p {
        display: block;
    }
    .fakelink {
        cursor:pointer;
        text-decoration: none;
        font-weight: bold;
        color: #E03A3E;
    }
    section {
        margin-bottom: 6px;
    }
    </style>
  </head>
```

```
<body>
    <header>
        <h1>Steptoe Butte</h1>
    </header>

    <section>
        <p><img src="steptoebutte.jpg" alt="View from Steptoe Butte"
        class="mainimg" />Steptoe Butte is a quartzite island jutting out of the
        silty loess of the <a
        href="http://en.wikipedia.org/wiki/Palouse">Palouse </a> hills in Whitman
        County, Washington. The rock that forms the butte is over 400 million
        years old, in contrast with the 15-7 million year old
        <a href="http://en.wikipedia.org/wiki/Columbia_River">Columbia River</a>
        basalts that underlie the rest of the Palouse (such "islands" of ancient
        rock have come to be called buttes, a butte being defined as a small hill
        with a flat top, whose width at top does not exceed its height).</p>
        <p>A hotel built by Cashup Davis stood atop Steptoe Butte from 1888 to
        1908, burning down several years after it closed. In 1946, Virgil McCroskey
        donated 120 acres (0.49 km2) of land to form Steptoe Butte State Park,
        which was later increased to over 150 acres (0.61 km2). Steptoe Butte is
        currently recognized as a National Natural Landmark because of its unique
        geological value. It is named in honor of
        <a href="http://en.wikipedia.org/wiki/Colonel_Edward_Steptoe">Colonel
        Edward Steptoe</a>.</p>
    </section>

    <section>
        <div class="fakelink"
            id="show_e"
            onclick="this.style.display='none';
            document.getElementById('hide_e').style.display='block';
            document.getElementById('elevation').style.display='inline';
        ">&raquo; Show Elevation</div>
        <div class="fakelink"
            id="hide_e"
            onclick="this.style.display='none';
            document.getElementById('show_e').style.display='block';
            document.getElementById('elevation').style.display='none';
        ">&raquo; Hide Elevation</div>

        <div id="elevation">3,612 feet (1,101 m), approximately 1,000 feet (300 m)
        above the surrounding countryside.</div>
    </section>

    <section>
        <div class="fakelink"
            id="show_p"
            onclick="this.style.display='none';
            document.getElementById('hide_p').style.display='block';
            document.getElementById('photos').style.display='inline';
        ">&raquo; Show Photos from the Top of Steptoe Butte</div>
```

```
    <div class="fakelink"
      id="hide_p"
      onclick="this.style.display='none';
      document.getElementById('show_p').style.display='block';
      document.getElementById('photos').style.display='none';
      ">&raquo; Hide Photos from the Top of Steptoe Butte</div>

      <div id="photos"><img src="steptoe_sm1.jpg" alt="View from Steptoe
      Butte" /><img  src="steptoe_sm2.jpg" alt="View from Steptoe
      Butte" /><img  src="steptoe_sm3.jpg" alt="View from Steptoe
      Butte" /></div>
  </section>

  <footer>
    <em>Text from
    <a href="http://en.wikipedia.org/wiki/Steptoe_Butte">Wikipedia</a>,
    photos by the author.</em>
  </footer>
  </body>
</html>
```

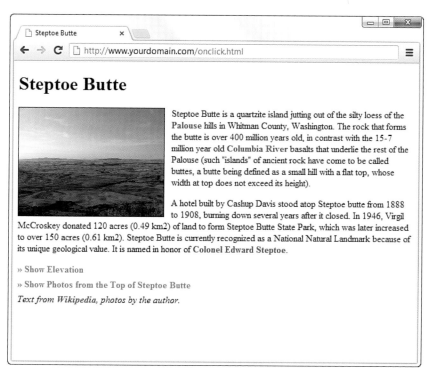

FIGURE 18.4
The initial display of Listing 18.2. Note that the mouse pointer changes to a hand when hovering over the red text, despite the fact it is not an `<a>` link.

To begin, look at the 11 entries in the style sheet. The first entry simply styles links that are surrounded by the `<a></a>` tag pair; these links display as nonunderlined, bold, blue links. You can see these regular links in the two paragraphs of text in Figure 18.4 (and in the line at the bottom of the page). The next two entries make sure that the images used in the page have appropriate margins; the entry for `<img />` element sets some margins and a border, and the `.mainimg` class enables you to apply a style to the main image on the page, but not the set of three images at the bottom of the page.

The next four entries are for specific IDs, and those IDs are all set to be invisible (`display: none`) when the page initially loads. In contrast, the two IDs that follow are set to display as block elements when the page initially loads. Again, strictly speaking, these two IDs do not have to be defined as block elements because that is the default display. However, this stylesheet includes these entries to illustrate the differences between the two sets of elements. If you count the number of `<div>` elements in Listing 18.2, you will find six in the code: four invisible and two that are visible upon page load.

The goal in this example is to change the display value of two IDs when another ID is clicked. But first you have to make sure users realize that a piece of text is clickable, and that typically happens when users see their mouse pointers change to reflect a present link. Although you can't see it in Figure 18.4, if you load the example code on your machine and view it in your browser, the mouse pointer changes to a hand with a finger pointing at a particular link.

This functionality is achieved by defining a class for this particular text; the class is called `fakelink`, as you can see in this snippet of code:

```
<div class="fakelink"
    id="show_e"
    onclick="this.style.display='none';
    document.getElementById('hide_e').style.display='block';
    document.getElementById('elevation').style.display='inline';
">&raquo; Show Elevation</div>
```

The `fakelink` class ensures that the text is rendered as nonunderlined, bold, and red; `cursor: pointer` causes the mouse pointer to change in such a way that users think the text is a link of the type that would normally be enclosed in an `<a>` element. But the really interesting stuff happens when we associate an `onclick` attribute with a `<div>`. In the example snippet just shown, the value of the `onclick` attribute is a series of commands that change the current value of CSS elements.

Let's look at them separately:

```
this.style.display='none';
document.getElementById('hide_e').style.display='block';
document.getElementById('elevation').style.display='inline';
```

Here you are looking at different JavaScript methods meant to change particular elements. In general, JavaScript is well beyond the scope of this book, but I think you can follow along what is happening here (and you'll learn a bit more about JavaScript in Hour 21, "Understanding Dynamic Websites and HTML5 Applications").

In the first line of the snippet, the `this` keyword refers to the element itself. In other words, `this` refers to the `<div>` ID called `show_e`. The keyword `style` refers to the `style` object; the `style` object contains all the CSS styles that you assign to the element. In this case, we are most interested in the `display` style. Therefore, `this.style.display` means "the display style of the `show_e` ID," and we are setting the value of the `display` style to `none` when the text itself is clicked.

But three actions also occur within the `onclick` attribute. The other two actions begin with `document.getElementByID()` and include a specific ID name within the parentheses. We use `document.getElementByID()` instead of `this` because the second and third actions set CSS style properties for elements that are not the parent element. As you can see in the snippet, in the second and third actions, we are setting the display property values for the element IDs `hide_e` and `elevation`. When users click the currently visible `<div>` called `show_e`, the following happens:

- The `show_e` `<div>` becomes invisible.
- The `hide_e` `<div>` becomes visible and is displayed as a block.
- The `elevation` `<div>` becomes visible and is displayed inline.

Figure 18.5 shows the result of these actions.

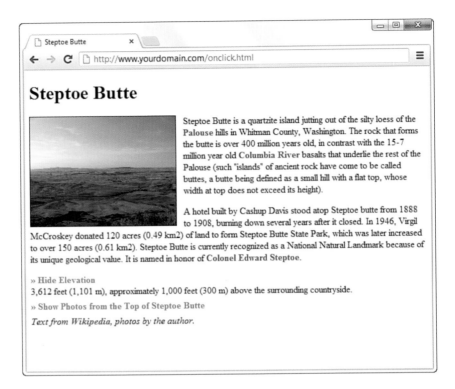

Another set of `<div>` elements exists in the code in Listing 18.2, the ones that control the visibility of the additional photos. These elements are not affected by the `onclick` actions in the elevation-related elements. That is, when you click either Show Elevation or Hide Elevation the photos-related `<div>` elements do not change. You can show the elevation and not the photos (as seen in Figure 18.5), the photos and not the elevation, or both the elevation and photos at the same time (see Figure 18.6).

This brief example has shown you the very beginning of the layout and interaction possibilities that await you when you master CSS in conjunction with events. For example, you can code your pages so that your users can change elements of the stylesheet or change to an entirely different stylesheet, move blocks of text to other places in the layout, take quizzes or submit forms, and much, much more.

FIGURE 18.6
The page after clicking both Show Elevation and Show Photos from the Top of Steptoe Butte.

Summary

In this hour, you learned how mouse actions can affect the display of text. In the first two sections, these actions were based on styles associated with the `hover` pseudoclass of the `<a>` tag. Later in the hour, you became acquainted with the actions associated with specific user interaction events. The specific event in the example was the `onclick` event, but you also saw a list of other possible events, such as `onload` and `onmouseover`, just to name a few.

The only new code introduced in the code itself was the use of the `cursor` property. Assigning a `cursor` property of `pointer` enabled you to indicate to users that particular text was acting as a link even though it was not enclosed in `<a></a>` tags as users might be accustomed to seeing.

Q&A

Q. Some of the events covered in this hour sound a lot like the pseudoclasses for the `<a>` tag. What's the difference?

A. True, the `onmousedown` event is like the active state, and `onmouseup` and `onmouseover` are much like the hover state. No specific rule covers when to use events instead of pseudoclasses, but it stands to reason that if you have no other reason to use an `<a>` tag, you shouldn't just use the `<a>` tag only to use the pseudoclasses.

Q. Can you capture mouse or keyboard events on elements other than text, such as images?

A. Yes, you can apply these types of events to actions related to clicking on or rolling over images as well as text. However, users do not interact with other multimedia objects, such as embedded YouTube videos or Flash files, in the same way; those objects are played via additional software for which other mouse or keyboard actions are applicable. For instance, if you click on a YouTube video embedded in your web page, you are interacting with the YouTube player and no longer your actual web page—that action cannot be captured in the same way.

Workshop

The Workshop contains quiz questions and activities to help you solidify your understanding of the material covered. Try to answer all questions before looking at the "Answers" section that follows.

Quiz

1. What happens when you use a negative value for the `top` property?

2. Which event is used to change something about the page when the user moves the mouse out of the boundaries of a particular element?

3. If you saw the `cursor: crosshair` style in a style sheet, what would you assume it did?

Answers

1. Using a negative value for `top` places content above the top-left corner of the parent element (not below it).

2. The `onmouseout` event is used.

3. You would likely assume that it turns the user's mouse pointer into a large plus sign (or crosshair). It is unclear why you would do that, though, because this is an atypical presentation of the cursor. In other words, users will wonder why you did that to their interfaces; they won't appreciate it as a design decision on your part.

Exercises

▶ Create your own page with rollover ToolTip texts, using colors and other styles that work with your own display template.

▶ Add commands to the `onclick` attributes in Listing 18.2 so that only one of the `<div>` elements (the elevation or photos) is visible at a time.

HOUR 19
Implementing CSS3 Transformations, Transitions, and Animations

Combining HTML5 and CSS3 makes for an incredibly powerful design medium, and this book barely scratches the surface—after all, HTML5 and CSS3 form the basis of many mobile applications and are beginning to gain traction in video game development as well. (All of that is well beyond the scope of this little book.) But I firmly believe that beginners should be exposed to the foundations of these advanced topics, and this hour is a prime example. Advanced interactivity using CSS3 is (at the time of writing) still experimental, but designers have been fiddling with it for a few years—and so can you!

Accounting for Browser Differences

Before we begin our foray into the experimental world of CSS3 transformations, transitions, and animations, it's important to understand what "experimental" means in this situation and how to account for it. These particular elements of CSS3 have been in use for several years, but are still considered experimental because the CSS3 specifications for transformations, transitions, and animations have not yet stabilized. The developers of the various web browsers approach the implementation of the specification through vendor-specific prefixes.

Vendor prefixes, such as `-webkit` (for WebKit-based browsers such as Chrome and Safari), `-moz` (for Mozilla Firefox), `-ms` (for Microsoft Internet Explorer), and `-o` (for Opera), are used by browser developers to add support for experimental features, but in a sort of temporary (and sometimes browser-specific) way. After a specification has settled down and stabilized, and when rules have been created around the

WHAT YOU'LL LEARN IN THIS HOUR:

▶ How to move, rotate, scale, and skew 2D elements

▶ How to apply perspective and move and rotate 3D elements

▶ How to animate objects created in HTML and CSS

NOTE
You first encountered vendor-specific prefixes in Hour 9, "Using Tables and Columns," when learning about CSS3 columns.

implementation of specific features, browser vendors implement those rules in a standardized way and without the necessary vendor prefix.

In the examples that follow in this hour, vendor prefixes are used along with the standard property so that the examples will be usable both now and in the future. Writing out the vendor-prefixed properties is a bit tiresome, writing this:

```
-webkit-transform: translate(100px) rotate(20deg);
-webkit-transform-origin: 60% 100%;
-moz-transform: translate(100px) rotate(20deg);
-moz-transform-origin: 60% 100%;
-ms-transform: translate(100px) rotate(20deg);
-ms-transform-origin: 60% 100%;
-o-transform:translate(100px) rotate(20deg);
-o-transform-origin:60% 100%;
```

instead of just the standard properties:

```
transform: translate(100px) rotate(20deg);
transform-origin: 60% 100%;
```

At least you can be sure of as much coverage as possible. In time, the specifications will stabilize and the vendor prefixes can be dropped; you can check the handy website at http://caniuse.com to see how support changes over time.

Using 2D Transformations

When we look at content on web pages, we're looking at two-dimensional (2D) objects that exist on the same plane and have a length and a width. Showing off a photo of your kitten? That image has a height and a width; it's a 2D image. The same is true for HTML container elements—a `<div>` and `<p>` and `<section>` all have lengths and widths that can be specified and also manipulated.

NOTE
For all the figures in this hour, start with static placements of elements that then *do something*. When used, the figures show the initial placement of elements, but you should open the sample HTML files in your browser to see the full effect of the code and the movement of the elements.

Performing 2D transformations using CSS3 allows you to change the position, length, and width of these elements by translating, rotating, and scaling the elements using the CSS3 `transform` property. We take a look at each of these use cases in the following sections.

Translating Elements

Translating an element in a 2D space sounds much more intriguing than it actually is; *translating* just means "moving." Using the `translate()` function of the `transform` CSS3 property enables you to place your elements along the x-axis (horizontally) or y-axis (vertically). This method seemed the easiest to understand, so let's get started and build on it.

Figure 19.1 shows one 2D box, the result of the code in Listing 19.1.

FIGURE 19.1
Showing a basic 2D element.

LISTING 19.1   Transforming a 2D Element

```html
<!DOCTYPE html>

<html lang="en">
  <head>
    <title>Translating a 2D Element</title>
    <style type="text/css">
    #theBox {
        height: 250px;
        width: 250px;
        background-color: #ddd;
        border: 1px solid #000;
        text-align: center;
        display:table-cell;
        vertical-align:middle;
        font-size: 150%;
        font-weight: bold;
      }
    #theBox:hover {
        -moz-transform: translate(75px,100px);
        -ms-transform: translate(75px,100px);
        -o-transform: translate(75px,100px);
```

```
      -webkit-transform: translate(75px,100px);
      transform: translate(75px,100px);
    }
  </style>
</head>

<body>
  <div id="theBox">
      I am a box!<br/>Watch me move!
  </div>
</body>
</html>
```

The code in Listing 19.1 uses some stylesheet entries to style a `<div>` with an ID of `theBox` that is 250 pixels wide and 250 pixels high, has a black border and a gray background, and contains some aligned text. But the second stylesheet entry, for the `hover` state of the `<div>` with an ID of `theBox`, contains the functions used to `translate` (move) the box by using the CSS3 `transform` property. Specifically, these functions (one for each vendor prefix, plus the "standard") tell the browser to translate (move) the element 75 pixels along the x-axis and 100 pixels along the y-axis when hovering over the element. Go ahead and try it.

You might notice that the movement is quick and not terribly smooth. If you imagined a smooth, easily flowing transition from one position to another, don't despair—we cover how to achieve that using CSS3 transitions later in this hour. For now, let's just get a solid foundation with 2D and 3D transformation basics.

Rotating Elements

Rotating an element in a 2D space means that it turns from an origin point and continues clockwise from 0° to 360° (you can also indicate counterclockwise movement using negative degrees). To achieve rotation, use the `rotate()` function of the `transform` CSS3 property and specify the degrees as an argument. For example, the following rotates an element 45° clockwise:

```
transform: rotate(45deg);
```

Figure 19.2 shows one 2D box that begins already rotated 45° counterclockwise. The code in Listing 19.2 goes on to set it right side up.

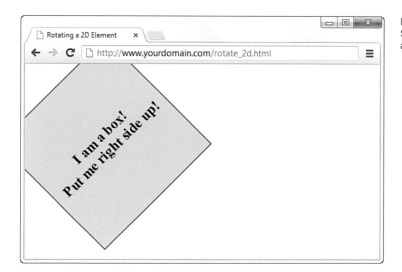

FIGURE 19.2
Showing a basic 2D element,
already rotated.

LISTING 19.2   Rotating a 2D Element

```
<!DOCTYPE html>

<html lang="en">
  <head>
    <title>Rotating a 2D Element</title>
    <style type="text/css">
    #theBox {
        height: 250px;
        width: 250px;
        background-color: #ddd;
        border: 1px solid #000;
        text-align: center;
        display:table-cell;
        vertical-align:middle;
        font-size: 150%;
        font-weight: bold;
        -moz-transform: rotate(-45deg);
        -ms-transform: rotate(-45deg);
        -o-transform: rotate(-45deg);
        -webkit-transform: rotate(-45deg);
        transform: rotate(-45deg);
     }
    #theBox:hover {
        -moz-transform: rotate(0deg);
        -ms-transform: rotate(0deg);
        -o-transform: rotate(0deg);
        -webkit-transform: rotate(0deg);
        transform: rotate(0deg);
    }
    </style>
  </head>
```

```
<body>
  <div id="theBox">
      I am a box!<br/>Put me right side up!
  </div>
</body>
</html>
```

NOTE

All rotations (and skewing and other transformations) begin at a point of origin, which you can set using the `transform-origin` property. If you do not specify a value for `transform-origin`, the default is used; the default is as if you specified the following in your stylesheet:

`transform-origin: 50% 50%;`

This default value means that the origin of the transformation should be 50 percent along the x-axis and 50 percent along the y-axis, or smack in the middle of the element.

As with Listing 19.1, the code in Listing 19.2 uses some stylesheet entries to style a `<div>` with an ID of `theBox` that is 250 pixels wide and 250 pixels high, has a black border and a gray background, and contains some aligned text. Also note that we use the `rotate()` function of the `transform` property to set the initial display of the `<div>` at –45° (45° counterclockwise).

The second stylesheet entry is used for the `hover` state of the `<div>` with an ID of `theBox`, and it contains the functions used to rotate the box back to an upright position (0°). If you hover over the box with your mouse, the box rotates 45° clockwise from its position at –45° (or 315°, if you prefer to think of it that way) to a position of 0°.

Scaling Elements

Scaling an element in a 2D space means that it appears to change in size along both the x-axis and the y-axis. To achieve rotation, use the `scale()` function of the `transform` CSS3 property and specify a value less than or greater than 1, depending on how you would like it to scale—use a value from `.01` to `.99` to scale the element smaller than the original, and use a value greater than 1 to scale the element larger than the original. For example, the following scales an element to half the original size:

`transform: scale(.5);`

You can scale an element along the x-axis or y-axis, using the following syntax:

`transform: scale(value_for_x_axis, value_for_y_axis);`

If you do not specify separate values, then it will be assumed that you mean to scale the element similarly along both the x-axis and the y-axis, which is typical. So `scale(.5)` in the previous example scales an element equally along both the x-axis and the y-axis.

The code in Listing 19.3 scales the basic box we've used in examples so far to half its size. Give it a try!

LISTING 19.3   Scaling a 2D Element

```html
<!DOCTYPE html>

<html lang="en">
  <head>
    <title>Scaling a 2D Element</title>
    <style type="text/css">
    #theBox {
        height: 250px;
        width: 250px;
        background-color: #ddd;
        border: 1px solid #000;
        text-align: center;
        display:table-cell;
        vertical-align:middle;
        font-size: 150%;
        font-weight: bold;
      }
    #theBox:hover {
        -moz-transform: scale(.5);
        -ms-transform: scale(.5);
        -o-transform: scale(.5);
        -webkit-transform: scale(.5);
        transform: scale(.5);
      }
    </style>
  </head>

  <body>
    <div id="theBox">
        I am a box!<br/>Watch me shrink!
    </div>
  </body>
</html>
```

As with the previous listings in this hour, the code in Listing 19.3 uses some stylesheet entries to style a <div> with an ID of theBox that is 250 pixels wide and 250 pixels high, has a black border and a gray background, and contains some aligned text. The second stylesheet entry is used for the hover state of the <div> with an ID of theBox; it contains the functions used to scale the box to half its size. If you wanted to scale the box to three times its original size, you would use this line:

```
transform: scale(3);
```

If you wanted to scale just the height of the box to three times its original size, you would use the following, and you would see something like Figure 19.3:

```
transform: scale(1, 3);
```

FIGURE 19.3
Showing a basic 2D element with
its height scaled to three times its
original size.

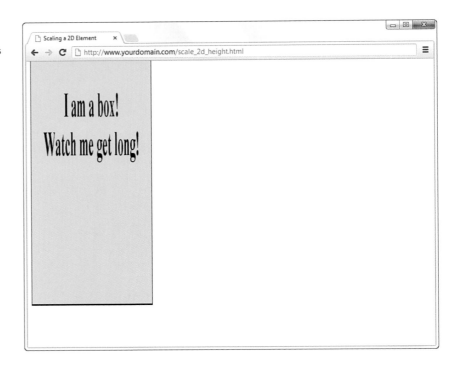

Note that not just the box is scaled—everything inside the container
element is scaled as well, as with the text in this example.

Skewing Elements

To skew an element in a 2D space is to distort it along the x-axis
or y-axis by a certain number of degrees. To skew an element, use
either the `skewX()` or `skewY()` function of the `transform` CSS3 property
(depending on how you'd like to skew it) and specify the value of an
angle in degrees, from –90° to 90°. For example, the following skews an
element 45° along the x-axis:

```
transform: skewX(45deg);
```

Figures 19.4 and 19.5 show the basic gray box we've been using in this
hour, skewed to a 45° angle along the x-axis and then the y-axis (for
example, using `skewX(45deg)` and `skewY(45deg)`, as appropriate).

NOTE

Although you can specify the
value of an angle from -90°
to 90°, values of -90, 90, or
0 result in an imperceptible
element. The angle will be
there, and skewed appropriately,
but your browser won't be able
to render it. If you use an angle
value of 1 or 89, you'll begin to
see why.

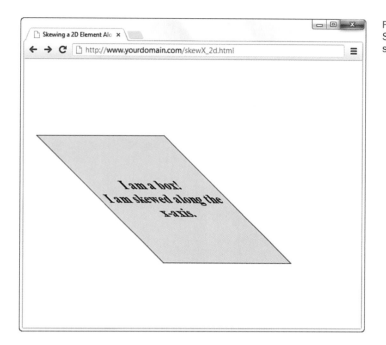

FIGURE 19.4
Showing a basic 2D element skewed along the x-axis.

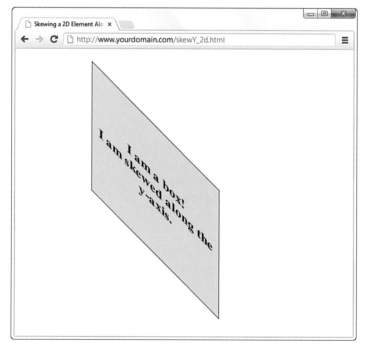

FIGURE 19.5
Showing a basic 2D element skewed along the y-axis.

Using 3D Transformations

As mentioned previously, when we view content on web pages, we do so in 2D. So how do we make the leap from 2D to 3D spaces in what is essentially still a 2D interface? Using CSS, we can create a space that appears to display objects in three dimensions by adding depth to the height and width that makes up two-dimensional space. In the sections that follow, you'll see how to perform some of the same types of transformations that you did earlier in this lesson in the 2D space, but in a 3D space.

Applying Perspective

In general, *perspective* is the process of drawing 2D objects in a particular fashion, to give the proper representation of their height, width, and depth all in relation to one another when viewed from a specific point (the *vanishing point*).

While working with 2D objects, you used the x-axis and y-axis; now the z-axis comes into play. The syntax of the `perspective` CSS property is simply this:

```
perspective: length;
```

Length can be in pixels or ems and must be greater than *0*.

You can also use functional notation to add the `perspective()` function to a list of functions of the `transform` property, like so:

```
transform: perspective(length) property(value);
```

Applying perspective to an element does not itself make a difference in the display; it has to happen in conjunction with using one of the 3D transformations, as you'll see in a moment. But to better understand perspective before moving on, glance back at Figure 19.2, which is a 2D element that has been rotated –45°. Compare that image with Figure 19.6.

NOTE

By default, the vanishing point of an element is placed at the center of the element, but it can be modified using the `perspective-origin` CSS property in the same way that `transform-origin` has a default but can also be set manually.

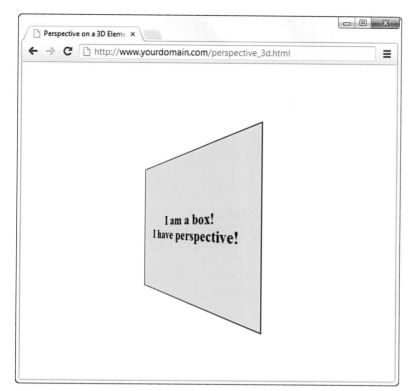

FIGURE 19.6
An element with a perspective
value of 300 pixels, rotated –45°
on the y-axis.

You should be able to see the depth that has been added to the object.
In this case, the `perspective` value is 300 pixels, which provides for a
visible effect. However, in Figure 19.7, the `perspective` value is 3000px,
which results in a barely perceptible 3D effect because the greater the
value, the greater the distance there is between the viewer and the
object, resulting in a much more subtle appearance of perspective.

FIGURE 19.7
An element with a perspective
value of 3,000 pixels, rotated −45°
on the y-axis.

Finally, contrast this object with the one in Figure 19.8, which has a perspective value of 100 pixels—the effect is dramatic!

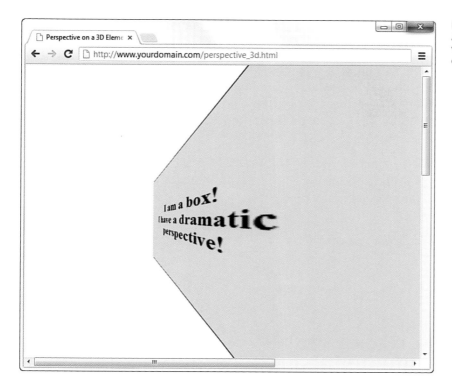

FIGURE 19.8
An element with a perspective value of 100 pixels, rotated –45 degrees on the y-axis.

Moving and Rotating in 3D Space

Moving (or *translating*) and rotating objects in a 3D space is quite similar to performing the same operations in a 2D space. In 2D space, as you've seen previously, you can use the `translate()` and `rotate()` functions of the `transform` property to perform these actions; in a 3D space, the functions are as follows:

▶ `rotateX(angle)`, `rotateY(angle)`, and `rotateY(angle)_rotateX(angle)`—Rotates an object *around* the appropriate axis, in contrast to the 2D `rotate(angle)` transformation function, which just shifts an object along the x- or y-axis. This difference is seen when comparing Figure 19.2 and Figure 19.6.

▶ `translateZ(value)`—Positions an object closer to or farther from the viewer.

Creating and Manipulating a Cube

The best way to get a handle on 3D objects is to make one that can be easily visualized as a 3D object—a six-sided cube, perhaps. Creating a 3D cube out of HTML and CSS might seem daunting, but I have faith that you'll be able to understand it and put together all the pieces. (There are, in fact, six pieces, for the six sides of the cube, to put together.)

I've gone ahead and created a 3D cube; see Listing 19.4. The result of this listing appears in Figure 19.9. After the listing, I explain each step of the creation of the cube.

LISTING 19.4   Creating a 3D Cube

```
<!DOCTYPE html>
<html lang="en">
  <head>
    <title>Creating a 3D Cube</title>

    <style type="text/css">
    body {
       margin: 75px 0px 0px 75px ;
    }

    #wrapper {
       -moz-perspective: 500px;
       -webkit-perspective: 500px;
       perspective: 500px;
    }

    #the_cube {
      -moz-transform-style: preserve-3d
      -webkit-transform-style: preserve-3d
      transform-style: preserve-3d
    }

    #the_cube div {
      width: 150px;
      height: 150px;
      position: absolute;

      border: 1px solid black;
      background: rgba(200,200,200,0.5);

      font-size: 125%;
      font-weight: bold;
      line-height: 125px;
      text-align: center;
    }

    .front {
```

```css
    -moz-transform: translateZ(75px);
    -ms-transform: translateZ(75px);
    -o-transform: translateZ(75px);
    -webkit-transform: translateZ(75px);
    transform: translateZ(75px);
  }

  .back {
    -moz-transform: rotateY(180deg) translateZ(75px);
    -ms-transform: rotateY(180deg) translateZ(75px);
    -o-transform: rotateY(180deg) translateZ(75px);
    -webkit-transform: rotateY(180deg) translateZ(75px);
    transform: rotateY(180deg) translateZ(75px);
  }

  .right {
    -moz-transform: rotateY(90deg) translateZ(75px);
    -ms-transform: rotateY(90deg) translateZ(75px);
    -o-transform: rotateY(90deg) translateZ(75px);
    -webkit-transform: rotateY(90deg) translateZ(75px);
    transform: rotateY(90deg) translateZ(75px);
  }

  .left {
    -moz-transform: rotateY(-90deg) translateZ(75px);
    -ms-transform: rotateY(-90deg) translateZ(75px);
    -o-transform: rotateY(-90deg) translateZ(75px);
    -webkit-transform: rotateY(-90deg) translateZ(75px);
    transform: rotateY(-90deg) translateZ(75px);
  }

  .top {
    -moz-transform: rotateX(90deg) translateZ(75px);
    -ms-transform: rotateX(90deg) translateZ(75px);
    -o-transform: rotateX(90deg) translateZ(75px);
    -webkit-transform: rotateX(90deg) translateZ(75px);
    transform: rotateX(90deg) translateZ(75px);
  }

  .bottom {
    -moz-transform: rotateX(-90deg) translateZ(75px);
    -ms-transform: rotateX(-90deg) translateZ(75px);
    -o-transform: rotateX(-90deg) translateZ(75px);
    -webkit-transform: rotateX(-90deg) translateZ(75px);
    transform: rotateX(-90deg) translateZ(75px);
  }
  </style>
</head>

<body>

  <div id="wrapper">
    <div id="the_cube">
      <div class="front">FRONT</div>
      <div class="back">BACK</div>
```

```
        <div class="left">LEFT</div>
        <div class="right">RIGHT</div>
        <div class="top">TOP</div>
        <div class="bottom">BOTTOM</div>
      </div>
    </div>
  </body>
</html>
```

FIGURE 19.9
A basic 3D cube created in HTML and CSS.

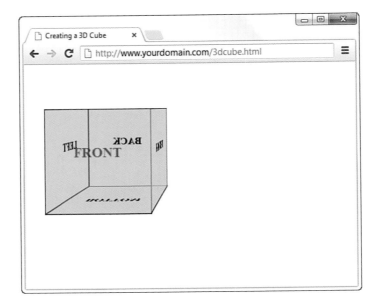

NOTE

Even with the vendor prefixes in use, working with transforms is a tricky business and can change as different versions of browsers are released. Don't be alarmed if your results look slightly different than mine, especially if you are using a browser other than Chrome. Consider it a good opportunity to make small changes to your code to try to make it work—fiddling around with code just to see what happens is what professionals do, too, and don't let anyone tell you otherwise!

The bulk of this code is all the stylesheet entries, which themselves are lengthy because of the need to use vendor-specific prefixes for several CSS properties. For a moment, skip over all that and look closely at the set of `<div>`s:

▶ `<div id="wrapper">` wraps itself around all the others and acts as the 3D space, with a perspective set for it (500px, in this case).

▶ `<div id="the_cube">` sets the stage for something we intend to remain three-dimensional, through the use of the `transform-style` property with a value of `preserve-3d`.

▶ `<div class="front">` (and all the other `<div>`s with class names corresponding to sides of the cube) acts as a side of the cube.

Now go back and take a closer look at the stylesheet, beginning with the entry for all `<div>`s that are children of the `<div>` with an ID of `#the_cube`—in other words, each face of the cube:

```
#the_cube div  {
    width: 150px;
    height: 150px;
    position: absolute;

    border: 1px solid black;
    background: rgba(200,200,200,0.5);

    font-size: 125%;
    font-weight: bold;
    line-height: 125px;
    text-align: center;
}
```

This entry ensures that each face of the cube has the same height, width, border, background color, and font attributes. You can see in Figure 19.9 that all the sides do indeed look the same (except for the specific text printed on each one).

Now comes the tricky part: walking through the transformations for each of the faces. To avoid clutter, in the following reference to the stylesheet entries, I'm using only the basic property (for example, transform), not all the vendor-specific versions, which you can see in Listing 19.3. Let's get started, with the front face:

```
.front {
    transform: translateZ(75px);
}
```

The front face is the face of the cube we want to see first; as such, we do not rotate it or apply any transformations whatsoever except to move it forward on the z-axis by half its length, or 75 pixels. Seems simple enough. If you want to see what happens if you change the value of translateZ() to something else, go for it—you'll note a gap between the faces of your cube.

Next we begin to rotate the remaining faces of the cube so that their edges line up with all the other faces. Take a look at the entry for the left face:

```
.left {
    transform: rotateY(-90deg) translateZ(75px);
}
```

Here, the 150×150 square face maintains the 500-pixel perspective that is set for the 3D field and is rotated on its y-axis by –90°. Moving the face forward on the z-axis by 75 pixels makes the edges line up, as you can see in Figure 19.10.

FIGURE 19.10
Lining up the front and left faces of the 3D cube.

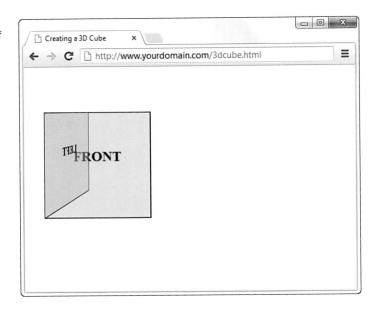

The remaining faces are defined similarly: First they are rotated into position along either the x- or y-axis, and then they are moved along the z-axis:

```
.back {
    transform: rotateY(180deg) translateZ(75px);
}
.right {
    transform: rotateY(90deg) translateZ(75px);
}
.top {
    transform: rotateX(90deg) translateZ(75px);
}
.bottom {
    transform: rotateX(-90deg) translateZ(75px);
}
```

The result is the 3D cube that you see in Figure 19.9. To get a better feel for how rotating the faces of the cube along the x- or y-axis works, I urge you to change the values of rotateX() and rotateY() to see how the faces do or do not line up. Later in this lesson, we build on the 3D cube example and learn to spin it around with CSS3 animation.

Implementing CSS3 Transitions

Early in this lesson, you saw some examples of moving, rotating, and scaling 2D elements when the user hovered over it with the mouse. At that time, you probably noticed that the movement was quick and not all that smooth, and I promised a fix for that in a later part of the lesson. It's now time for that fix, which happens by using CSS3 transitions.

Transitions occur when moving between CSS properties, such as moving from the initial state of an object to one that is scaled down in size. If you do not control the transition (the initial examples in this lesson did not), the user will see the first state and then immediately see the other, thus making the "transition" barely perceptible.

To control the transition, use the `transition` CSS property (don't forget the appropriate vendor prefixes for WebKit, Mozilla, and Opera; Internet Explorer does not require a vendor prefix), which uses the following syntax:

```
transition: property duration timing-function delay;
```

Although `property` refers to the name of the property you will be transitioning—for example, using `transform` to scale an object—the `duration`, `timing-function`, and `delay` values are new to you. The `duration` value is the time in seconds between the two states, `timing-function` is one of several functions that help you define the acceleration of the transition (for example, is it fast at the beginning or the end of the transition?), and `delay` is the time in seconds before the transition begins.

Refer to Listing 19.3, which scales a 2D element to half its original size. To control the transition between the element and the shrunken version, you add these lines to the stylesheet entry for `#theBox`:

```
-moz-transition: -moz-transform 5s ease-in 1s;
-o-transition: -o-transform 5s ease-in 1s;
-webkit-transition: -webkit-transform 5s ease-in 1s;
transition: transform 5s ease-in 1s;
```

These entries tell the browser to transition to the new value of the `transform` property (in this case, it is `scale(.5)`) by waiting 1 second and then easing into the new value over 5 seconds. If you loaded the modified code in your browser, you would see that, indeed, when you hover over the 2D box, it pauses for a moment and then slowly begins

NOTE

You can also specify the properties individually, instead of putting them all in the `transition` property, by using the `transition-property`, `transition-duration`, `transition-timing-function`, and `transition-delay` properties on separate lines in your stylesheet.

to shrink, finishing 5 seconds later. It's impossible to show you that process in a static image, so you'll have to try it yourself.

For more information on CSS3 transitions, especially the options for `transition-timing-function`, see https://developer.mozilla.org/en-US/docs/Web/Guide/CSS/Using_CSS_transitions.

Getting Started with CSS3 Animation

You can think of CSS3 animation as a souped-up set of transition controls. The process happening onscreen is indeed a transition (or several) between properties, but there are more considerations—and, therefore, subproperties—in the `animation` CSS property than in the `transition` CSS property.

In Hour 10, "Creating Images for Use on the Web," you might recall a brief discussion about creating animated web graphics. Specifically, the first step in creating an animated web graphic is to create a series of images that then are displayed one after the other, just as movies and cartoons put individual frames together to create the moving picture. In CSS3 animation, the animation is built by defining *keyframes*, which themselves define how the browser should display a particular element during an animation sequence.

Keyframes are defined in a stylesheet using the following syntax (don't forget the appropriate vendor prefixes for all four vendors):

```
@keyframes name_of_keyframe {
   from {
      property: value;
   }
   to {
      property: value;
   }
}
```

To use a practical example, let's return to the 3D cube created in Listing 19.3. Suppose you wanted to spin that cube so that it appeared to be tumbling through space—that would require rotating it around both the x- and the y-axis, from 0° to 360°:

```
@keyframes spin {
    from { transform: rotateY(0deg) rotateX(0deg); }
    to   { transform: rotateY(360deg) rotateX(360deg);}
}
```

Having thus created a keyframe called spin, we need to refer to it in the animation property; in this example, the animation property is applied to the definition of #the_cube. Take a look at the full example:

```
#the_cube {
    -moz-transform-style: preserve-3d;
    -webkit-transform-style: preserve-3d;
    transform-style: preserve-3d;

    -webkit-animation: spin 5s infinite linear;
    -moz-animation: spin 5s infinite linear;
    -ms-animation: spin 5s infinite linear;
    -o-animation: spin 5s infinite linear;
    animation: spin 5s infinite linear;
}
```

The syntax for the animation property in this example is:

```
animation: keyframe_name time iteration_count timing_function
```

In this example, I defined the animation to spin infinitely but complete its linear rotation in 5 seconds. If I changed linear to ease, you would notice a slight pause before each iteration. As with the previous example in the section on transitions, it's impossible to show you this process in a static image—you'll have to try it yourself.

To learn more about the numerous subproperties of the animation property, I recommend visiting https://developer.mozilla.org/en-US/docs/Web/CSS/animation.

Summary

This hour introduced you to the basics of moving, rotating, scaling, and skewing 2D and 3D elements (as well as the content within them). You learned that creating 3D elements from 2D elements begins with the application of perspective, and you saw how to control that perspective to achieve the look you want. Finally, you took the first steps toward controlling the transitions between CSS properties, using two different sets of transition and animation controls.

Q&A

Q. **If all this CSS is experimental, is it really safe to use?**

A. Much of the HTML5 and CSS3 specifications are still labeled as experimental (in fact, HTML5 is still just a recommendation and does not yet have an official specification), yet designers have been using such elements for years because browsers include rendering support for the experimental elements. If you use vendor-specific prefixes when implementing experimental features and provide fallback options for even older browsers, there's no need to wait until specifications are final to dream up designs and interactivity that take advantage of experimental functionality if you determine that they provide better experiences for your users. As always, continue to review and test your site in the browsers that are most popular with the users of your site, to ensure they are having the viewing experience you intend.

Workshop

The Workshop contains quiz questions and exercises to help you solidify your understanding of the material covered. Try to answer all questions before looking at the "Answers" section that follows.

Quiz

1. How do you rotate a 2D element 90° counter-clockwise? Be sure to use vendor prefixes in your answer.

2. What is the difference between `scale(3)` and `scale(1,3)`?

3. What does the z-axis represent?

Answers

1. You use this:

   ```
   -moz-transform: rotate(-90deg);
   -ms-transform: rotate(-90deg);
   -o-transform: rotate(-90deg);
   -webkit-transform: rotate(-90deg);
   transform: rotate(-90deg);
   ```

2. The first example scales an element equally in width and height to three times the original size of each. The second example keeps the width the same as the original but scales the height to three times the original size.

3. The z-axis represents depth.

Exercises

▶ Spend some time with the 3D cube example and modify the size, color, and placement of the six sides, to get a better feel for how the parts of the whole come together.

▶ Look into the numerous options available for the `transition` and `animation` properties (see https://developer.mozilla.org/en-US/docs/Web/CSS/transition and https://developer.mozilla.org/en-US/docs/Web/CSS/animation, respectively), and modify the 2D scale and rotation and 3D spinning cube examples to take advantage of different aspects of these properties.

HOUR 20
Creating Print-Friendly Web Pages

If you've ever used an online map application such as MapQuest or Google Maps before taking a trip into an area with no connectivity for your smartphone, you've no doubt experienced the need to print a web page. Similarly, the proliferation of coupons offered only online, purchase receipts for items from online resellers, and web-based flight check-in and the capability to print boarding passes from your home computer have increased the need for print-friendly pages. It's true, not all web pages are designed entirely for viewing on the screen!

You might not realize this, but it's possible to specifically design and offer print-friendly versions of your pages for users who want to print a copy for offline reading—something that Google Maps offers after showing you the onscreen version of content. I'm a big fan of all things paperless, but some people just prefer to have hard-copy backups of some documents (and directions). Using CSS, it is easy to create web pages that change appearance based on how they are viewed. In this hour, you learn how to create such pages.

WHAT YOU'LL LEARN IN THIS HOUR:

▶ What makes a print-friendly page

▶ How to apply a media-specific stylesheet

▶ How to create a stylesheet for print pages

▶ How to view your web page in Print Preview mode

▼ TRY IT YOURSELF

Reviewing Your Content for Print Friendliness

As you work your way through this chapter, consider any of your own web pages that might look good in print. Then think about what you would want to change about them to make them look even better on the printed page. Here are some ideas to consider:

▶ Even against warnings in previous lessons in this book, do you have pages that use a patterned background image or an unusual background color with contrasting text? This kind of page can be difficult to print because of the background, so consider offering a print version of the page that doesn't use a custom background image or color and simply uses black text. When preparing a page for printing, stick to black text on a white background, if possible.

▶ Do your pages include a lot of links? If so, consider changing the appearance of links for printing so that they don't stand out—remove any underlining, for example. Remember, you can't click a piece of paper!

▶ Finally, is every image on your pages absolutely essential? Colorful images cost valuable ink to print on most printers, so consider leaving some, if not all, images out of your print-friendly pages.

What Makes a Page Print-Friendly?

It's important to point out that some web pages are print-friendly already. If your pages use white backgrounds with dark contrasting text and few images, you might not even need to concern yourself with a special print-friendly version. On the other hand, pages with dark backgrounds, dynamic links, and several images might prove to be unwieldy for the average printer (or just annoying for readers).

The main things to keep in mind as you consider what it takes to make your pages more print-friendly are the limitations imposed by the medium. In other words, what is it about a printed page that makes it uniquely different from a computer screen? The obvious difference is size—a printed page is at a fixed size, typically 8 1/2 by 11 inches in the United States, whereas the size of screens can vary greatly. Printed pages also have color limitations (even on color printers). Very few users want to waste the ink required to print a full-color background when they really just want to print the text on the page.

Most users also aren't interested in printing more than the text that serves as the focus on the page. For example, Figure 20.1 shows a travel route mapped out from Independence, Missouri, to Oregon City, Oregon (an approximation of the historic Oregon Trail).

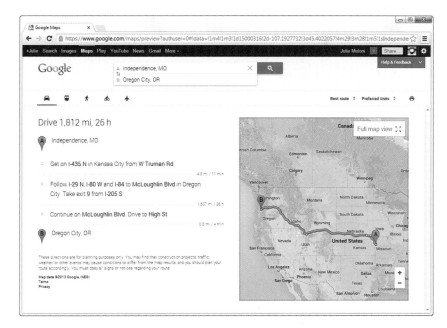

FIGURE 20.1
This page isn't very print-friendly because of the form inputs and the large image with its own display controls.

The page in Figure 20.1 contains form input fields, a large image that can itself be controlled (moved, zoomed), and other ancillary items that you come to expect in web content. Google has done a little magic (which you'll learn how to do as well) to ensure that when this page is printed, some of those ancillary items go away, and more information currently hidden in the online display is actually shown. Without that little bit of magic—the inclusion of a print-friendly stylesheet—you would be left thinking that there are only two turns on that 1,800-mile trip instead of the multitude of directions you see when the page is printed. If you click the Print link in the body of the page, or use the print function of your web browser, your web browser displays a page (see Figure 20.2) that Google has formatted specifically to be printed.

FIGURE 20.2
The preview of the print-friendly
version of the page includes all the
driving instructions, even if they're
not showing on your screen, and
removes other page elements.

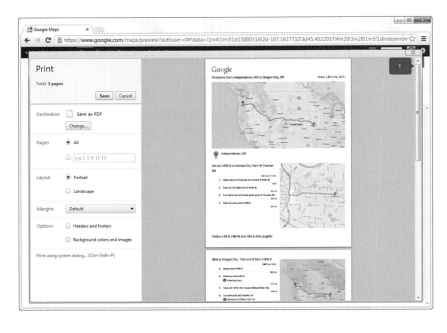

FIGURE 20.2
The preview of the print-friendly version of the page includes all the driving instructions, even if they're not showing on your screen, and removes other page elements.

As the figure shows, the print-friendly version of this page represents an improvement over the original, at least from the perspective of a printer. All the form inputs were removed, the navigational elements of the website itself were removed, and all directions were made visible. One could argue that an even *more* print-friendly version would have all the images removed.

In the spirit of giving you a better grasp on what, specifically, to consider as you move toward creating print-friendly pages, the following is a list of changes you want to at least consider:

NOTE

If the font of printer-specific pages is sans serif, some web designers recommend changing the font to serif, which is considered easier to read in print. If you use a sans-serif font on your pages, it's up to you to decide whether you want to maintain the core look of a page when it's printed—which means you don't change the font to serif.

▶ Remove the background of the page, if you have one, to give the printed page a white background. Some browsers will take care of this automatically, but there's no reason you can't be explicit about it to accommodate older browsers that don't remove backgrounds automatically.

▶ Change text colors to black; it's okay to have some color in the text, but black is preferred.

▶ Make sure that the font size is large enough that the page can be easily read when printed. You might have to test some different sizes.

▶ Remove link formatting, or simply revert to a basic underlined link. Some designers like to retain an underline just so that a visitor knows that a link exists in the original page.

▶ Remove any and all nonessential images. This typically includes any images that aren't critical to conveying the content in the page, such as navigation buttons, advertisements, and animated images (which certainly won't animate on a printed page).

In addition to these suggestions, you might find it useful to add a byline with information about the author of the page, along with a URL for the page and copyright information. This is information that could potentially get lost when the user leaves your website and has only the printed version of the page in hand.

You probably don't need to make these changes to your pages just yet. The idea here is to plant the seed of what constitutes a print-friendly page so that you can do a better job of creating a printer-specific stylesheet. That's right: It's possible to create a stylesheet that is applied to pages only when they are printed—you learn about that in the next section.

Applying a Media-Specific Stylesheet

Figure 20.1 showed how one company (although Google is not alone in this practice) uses a small printer icon linked to a print-friendly page to enable users to preview and then print a page better suited for printing than online reading. This feature is helpful for users because they might not want to hassle with printing a page and wasting paper and ink on the graphics and ads that accompany the content they want to read. Although the printer icon and link approach is intuitive and works great, there is an option that does not require creating separate print-friendly content.

This second option involves using a print-specific stylesheet that is *automatically* applied to a page when the user elects to print the page. As you learned briefly in Hour 15, "Creating Fixed or Liquid Layouts," CSS supports the concept of *media-specific style sheets*, which are stylesheets or stylesheet entries that target a particular medium, such as the screen or printer. CSS doesn't stop with those two forms of media, however. Check out the following list of specific media types that CSS enables you to support with a unique stylesheet:

- `all`—For all devices
- `aural`—For speech synthesizers
- `braille`—For Braille tactile feedback devices
- `embossed`—For paged Braille printers
- `handheld`—For handheld devices with limited screen size and bandwidth
- `print`—For printed material and documents viewed on screen in Print Preview mode
- `projection`—For projected presentations
- `screen`—For color computer screens
- `tty`—For devices that use a fixed-pitch character grid (such as terminal, teletype, or handheld devices with limited displays)
- `tv`—For television-type devices, which are typically low resolution and color, with a limited capability to scroll

Perhaps the most interesting of these media is the `aural` type, for web pages that can be read aloud or otherwise listened to. Clearly, the architects of CSS envision a web with a much broader reach most people currently think of when designing pages primarily for computer screens. Although you probably don't need to worry too much about aural web page design just yet, it serves as a good heads-up for what you might need to accommodate if you choose a career in web design.

The good news about stylesheets as applied to other media is that they don't require you to learn anything new. Okay, maybe in the case of aural web pages you'll need to learn a few new tricks, but for now, you can use the same style properties you've already learned to create print-specific stylesheets. The trick is knowing how to apply a stylesheet for a particular medium.

As you recall, the `<link />` tag is used to link an external stylesheet to a web page. This tag supports an attribute named `media` that specifies the name of the medium to which the stylesheet applies. By default, this attribute is set to `all`, which means that an external stylesheet will be used for all media if you don't specify otherwise. The other acceptable attribute values correspond to the list of media provided in the previous list.

Establishing a print-specific stylesheet for a web page involves using two `<link />` tags, one for the printer and one for each remaining medium. The following code handles this task:

```
<link rel="stylesheet" type="text/css" href="standard.css" media="all" />
<link rel="stylesheet" type="text/css" href="for_print.css" media="print" />
```

In this example, two stylesheets are linked into a web page. The first sheet targets all media by setting the `media` attribute to `all`. If you did nothing else, the `standard.css` stylesheet would apply to all media. However, the presence of the second stylesheet results in the `for_print.css` stylesheet being used to print the page.

You can specify multiple media types in a single `<link />` tag by separating the types with a comma, like this:

```
<link rel="stylesheet" type="text/css" href="for_pp.css"
      media="print, projector" />
```

This code results in the `for_pp.css` stylesheet applying solely to the `print` and `projector` media types, nothing else.

Designing a Stylesheet for Print Pages

Using the recommended list of modifications required for a print-friendly web page, it's time to take a stab at creating a print-friendly stylesheet. Let's first look at a page that is displayed using a normal (screen) stylesheet (see Figure 20.3).

This figure reveals how the page looks in a normal web browser. In reality, this page isn't too far from being print-ready, but it could still benefit from some improvements.

The following changes can help make this web page more print-friendly:

► Change the color of all text to black.

► Remove link formatting (bold and color).

► Stack the two player information sections vertically because they are unlikely to fit horizontally on the printed page.

► Remove the contact link entirely.

NOTE

You can also use the `@import` command to link media-specific stylesheets. For example, the following code works just like the previous `<link />` code:

```
@import url(standard.css) all;
@import url(for_print.css)
print;
```

CAUTION

You might have been tempted to specify `media="screen"` in the first linked stylesheet in the previous code. Although this would work for viewing the page in a normal web browser, it would cause problems if a user viewed the page using a handheld browser or any of the other types of media. In other words, a stylesheet applies only to the specific media types mentioned in the `media` attribute, nothing more.

FIGURE 20.3
A CSS-styled page as viewed in a normal web browser.

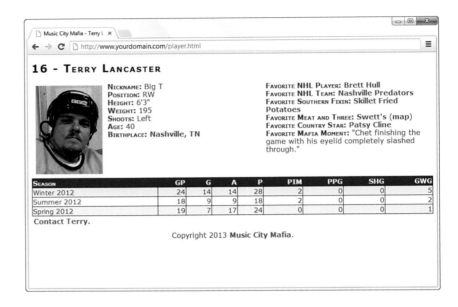

The first two changes to the normal stylesheet are straightforward; they primarily involve changing or undoing existing styles. The third change, however, requires a bit of thought. Because you know that printed pages are a fixed size, you should use absolute positioning for all the elements on the printed page. This makes placing the content sections exactly where you want them much easier. Finally, the last item on the list is very easy to accommodate: Simply set the `display` style property of the `contact` element to `none`.

Listing 20.1 shows the CSS code for the `player_print.css` stylesheet, which incorporates these changes into a stylesheet that is perfectly suited for printing hockey player pages.

LISTING 20.1   CSS Code for the Print-Specific Hockey Player Stylesheet

```
body {
    font-family:Verdana, Arial;
    font-size:12pt;
    color: #000000;
}

h1 {
    font-size:18pt;
    font-weight:bold;
    font-variant:small-caps;
    letter-spacing:2px;
    position:absolute;
    left:0in;
```

```
  top:0in;
}

img {
  position:absolute;
  left:0in;
  top:0.5in;
}

footer {
  position:absolute;
  text-align:left;
  left:0in;
  top:9in;
}

a, a:link, a:visited {
  color: #000000;
  font-weight:normal;
  text-decoration:none;
}

div {
  padding:3px;
}

div.player_info {
  position:absolute;
  left:1.75in;
  top:0.5in;
}

div.player_favorites {
  position:absolute;
  left:1.75in;
  top:2in;
}

div.contact {
  display:none;
}

.label {
  font-weight:bold;
  font-variant:small-caps;
}

table, tr, td {
  border: 1px solid black;
  border-collapse: collapse;
}

table.stats {
  width:100%;
  text-align:right;
  font-size:11pt;
```

```
    border: 1px solid black;
    border-collapse: collapse;
    position:absolute;
    left:0in;
    top:4in;
}

thead {
    font-variant:small-caps;
    background-color: #000000;
    color:white;
}

tr.light {
    background-color: #ffffff;
}

tr.dark {
    background-color: #eeeeee;
}

th.season, td.season {
    text-align:left;
}
```

NOTE

In Listing 20.1, a left margin of 0in is used in some instances. You might find that your browser needs *some* margin; otherwise, it will cut off the content. If that is the case, just adjust it to 0.1in or 0.25in or some other value—you should still get the point of the placement.

Probably the biggest difference in this code is how it uses inches (in) as the unit of measure for all the absolute positioning that takes place via CSS. This makes sense when you consider that we think of printed pages in terms of inches, not pixels. If you study the code carefully, you'll notice that the text is all black, all special style formatting has been removed from the links, and content sections are now absolutely positioned (so that they appear exactly where you want them to appear on the single sheet of paper).

Viewing a Web Page in Print Preview

Figure 20.4 shows the print-friendly version of a hockey player page as it appears in a browser's Print Preview window.

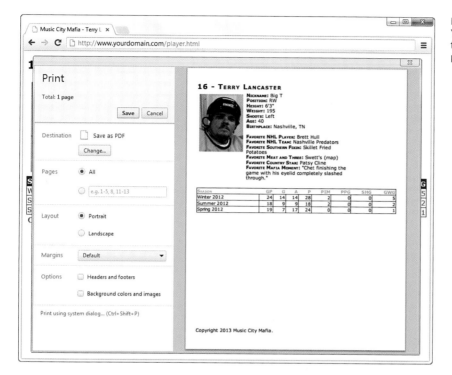

FIGURE 20.4
You can use Print Preview to view the print-friendly version of a web page before you print it.

Just for good measure, Figure 20.5 shows the full printed page (as a PDF); the print preview was accurate!

NOTE

Adobe's virtual printer can be used to "print" the hockey player web page to a PDF document. You might also find PDF converters such as DoPDF (www.dopdf.com) that work for you at a lower cost than the Adobe Acrobat software. Printing to a PDF effectively creates a version of the print-friendly web page in a format that can be easily shared electronically for printing.

To learn more about Acrobat, visit http://www.adobe.com/products/acrobat.html.

FIGURE 20.5
The hockey player page was converted to a PDF document by printing it (saving it) as an Adobe PDF.

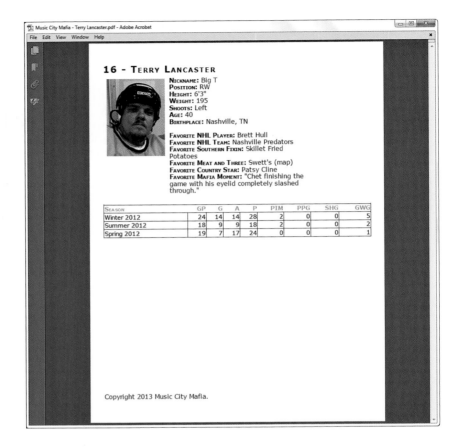

Summary

This chapter focused on a practical application of CSS that solves a common need: printing web pages. You began the chapter by learning what exactly constitutes a print-friendly web page. From there, you learned about the mechanism built into CSS that allows a page to distinguish between the media in which it is being rendered, and then you learned how to select a stylesheet accordingly.

Finally, you created a print-specific stylesheet that was used to style a page just for printing. Although most users prefer to view a page on a large computer screen instead of reading it on paper, sometimes a printed web page is a necessity. Be sure to give your web page visitors the utmost in flexibility by offering print-friendly pages.

Q&A

Q. Can I use the `media` **attribute of the** `<link />` **tag to create a stylesheet specifically for viewing a web page on a handheld device?**

A. Yes. By setting the `media` attribute of the `<link />` tag to `handheld`, you specifically target handheld devices with a stylesheet. However, some devices do not interpret this appropriately or consistently, which is why many designers use the `screen` attribute with additional queries to determine the width and thus layout.

Q. Do I still need to provide printer icons on my pages so that they can be printed?

A. No, that is a handy visual cue, but not a required one. The linked stylesheet technique you learned about in this hour allows you to support print-friendly web pages without any special links on the page. However, if you want to enable the user to view a print-friendly version of a page in a browser, you can link to another version of the page that uses the print-specific stylesheet as its main (browser) stylesheet. Or you can provide some "fine print" on the page that instructs the user to use the browser's Print Preview feature to view the print-friendly version of the page.

Workshop

The Workshop contains quiz questions and activities to help you solidify your understanding of the material covered. Try to answer all questions before looking at the "Answers" section that follows.

Quiz

1. Does having a button to a print-friendly page mean the page is actually print-friendly?

2. What happens to an external stylesheet that is linked to a page without any `media` attribute specified?

3. How do you link a stylesheet named `freestyle.css` to a page so that it applies only when the page is viewed on a television?

Answers

1. No—you still have to link to a page with a specific stylesheet applied to the content so that it appears print-friendly.

2. The `media` attribute assumes its default value of `all`, which causes the stylesheet to target all media types.

3. Use the following in the `<head>` section of your HTML:

```
<link rel="stylesheet" type="text/css" href="freestyle.css"
media="tv" />
```

Exercises

▶ Create a print-friendly stylesheet for a page that has a fair number of colors and images. Be sure to add an extra `<link />` tag to the page that links in the print-specific stylesheet.

▶ If you're feeling really ambitious, try using the `handheld` value of the `<link />` tag's `media` attribute to create a handheld-specific version of one of your web pages. The concept is the same as when creating a print-friendly page, except that, in this case, you're dealing with an extremely constrained screen size instead of a printed page. You can test the page by publishing it and then opening it on a mobile phone or handheld browser.

Understanding Dynamic Websites and HTML5 Applications

The term *dynamic* means something active or something that motivates another person to become active. When talking about websites, a dynamic website is one that incorporates interactivity into its functionality and design, but also motivates a user to take an action—read more, purchase a product, and so on. In this hour, you learn about the different types of interactivity that can make a site dynamic, including information about both server-side and client-side scripting (as well as some practical examples of the latter).

I've mentioned client-side scripting elsewhere in this book, and you used a little of it in Hour 18, "Using Mouse Actions to Modify Text Display," when you used event attributes and JavaScript to change the styles of particular elements—that is called manipulating the Document Object Model (DOM). You do a bit more of that type of manipulation in this hour. Specifically, after learning about the different technologies, you use JavaScript to display a random quote upon page-load and swap images based on user interaction. Finally, having learned at least the keywords and the basic concept of putting together the HTML, CSS, and JavaScript pieces together, you're introduced to the possibilities that exist when creating HTML5 applications.

WHAT YOU'LL LEARN IN THIS HOUR:

▶ How to conceptualize different types of dynamic content

▶ How to include JavaScript in your HTML

▶ How to display randomized text with JavaScript

▶ How to change images using JavaScript and user events

▶ How to begin thinking ahead to putting all the pieces together to create HTML5 applications

Understanding the Different Types of Scripting

In web development, two different types of scripting exist: server side and client side. Both types of scripting—which is, in fact, a form of computer programming—are beyond the scope of this book. However, they are not *too* far beyond this book. Two very useful and popular books in the *Sams Teach Yourself* series are natural extensions of this one: *Sams Teach Yourself PHP, MySQL and Apache All-in-One* (for server-side scripting) and *Sams Teach Yourself JavaScript in 24 Hours* (for client-side scripting).

Server-side scripting refers to scripts that run on the web server, which then sends results to your web browser. If you have ever submitted a form at a website (which includes using a search engine), you have experienced the results of a server-side script. Some popular (and relatively easy-to-learn) server-side scripting languages include the following (to learn more, visit the websites listed):

▶ **PHP (PHP: Hypertext Preprocessor)**—http://www.php.net/

▶ **Ruby**—http://www.ruby-lang.org/

▶ **Python**—http://www.python.org/

▶ **Perl**—http://www.perl.org/

On the other hand, *client-side scripting* refers to scripts that run within your web browser—no interaction with a web server is required for the scripts to run. By far the most popular client-side scripting language is *JavaScript*. For several years, research has shown that more than 98 percent of all web browsers have JavaScript enabled.

Another client-side scripting language is Microsoft's *VBScript (Visual Basic Scripting Edition)*. This language is available only with the Microsoft Internet Explorer web browser and, therefore, should not be used unless you are very sure that users will access your site with that web browser (such as in a closed corporate environment). Given a desire to reach the largest possible audience, this hour assumes the use of JavaScript for client-side scripting; the coding examples in this lesson are all JavaScript.

Including JavaScript in HTML

JavaScript code can live in one of two places within your files:

▶ In its own file with a `.js` extension

▶ Directly in your HTML files

External files are often used for script libraries (code you can reuse throughout many pages), while code that appears directly in the HTML

TIP

Despite its name, JavaScript is not a derivation of or any other close relative to the object-oriented programming language called Java. Released by Sun Microsystems in 1995, Java is closely related to the server-side scripting language JSP. JavaScript was created by Netscape Communications, also in 1995, and given the name to indicate a similarity in appearance to Java but not a direct connection with it.

files tends to achieve functionality specific to those individual pages. Regardless of where your JavaScript lives, your browser learns of its existence through the use of the `<script></script>` tag pair.

When you store your JavaScript in external files, it is referenced in this manner:

```
<script type="text/javascript" src="/path/to/script.js"></script>
```

These `<script></script>` tags are typically placed between the `<head></head>` tags because, strictly speaking, they are not content that belongs in the `<body>` of the page. Instead, the `<script>` tag makes available a set of JavaScript functions or other information that the rest of the page can then use. However, you can also just encapsulate your JavaScript functions or code snippets with the `<script>` tag and place them anywhere in the page, as needed. Listing 21.1 shows an example of a JavaScript snippet placed in the `<body>` of an HTML document.

NOTE

It is also quite common to find scripts loaded at the bottom of your page, just before the close of the `<body>` element. This ensures that your pages render without waiting to load the script. However, you cannot use this method of loading scripts if you also use your scripts to write content out to the page—it would just write it at the end, which is likely not your intention.

LISTING 21.1   Using JavaScript to Print Some Text

```
<!DOCTYPE html>

<html lang="en">
  <head>
    <title>JavaScript Example</title>
  </head>

  <body>
    <h1>JavaScript Example</h1>
    <p>This text is HTML.</p>
    <script type="text/javascript">
    <!-- Hide the script from old browsers
    document.write('<p>This text comes from JavaScript.</p>');
    // Stop hiding the script -->
    </script>
  </body>
</html>
```

Between the `<script></script>` tags is a single JavaScript command that outputs the following HTML:

```
<p>This text comes from JavaScript.</p>
```

When the browser renders this HTML page, it sees the JavaScript between the `<script></script>` tags, stops for a millisecond to execute the command, and then returns to rendering the output that now includes the HTML output from the JavaScript command. Figure 21.1

TIP

You might have noticed these two lines in Listing 21.1:

```
<!-- Hide the script from old browsers
// Stop hiding the script -->
```

This is an HTML comment. Anything between the `<!--` start and `-->` end will be visible in the source code but will not be rendered by the browser. In this case, JavaScript code is surrounded by HTML comments, on the off chance that your visitor is running a very old web browser or has JavaScript turned off. These days, nearly all browsers use or ignore JavaScript appropriately, but there's no harm in commenting it out for very old browsers or screenreaders that do not handle JavaScript at all.

shows that this page appears as any other HTML page appears. It's an HTML page, but only a small part of the HTML comes from a JavaScript command.

FIGURE 21.1
The output of a JavaScript snippet looks like any other output.

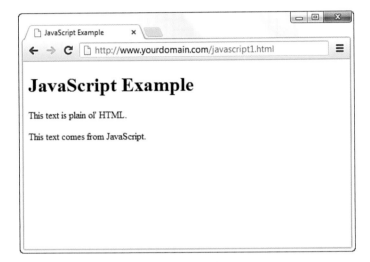

Displaying Random Content

You can use JavaScript to display something different each time a page loads. Maybe you have a collection of text or images that you find interesting enough to include in your pages.

I'm a sucker for a good quote. If you're like me, or plenty of other people creating personal websites, you might find it fun to incorporate an ever-changing quote into your web pages. To create a page with a quote that changes each time the page loads, you must first gather all your quotes, along with their respective sources. You then place these quotes into a JavaScript *array*, which is a special type of storage unit in programming languages that is handy for holding lists of items.

After the quotes are loaded into an array, the JavaScript used to pluck out a quote at random is fairly simple (we explain it momentarily). You've already seen the snippet that will print the output to your HTML page.

Listing 21.2 contains the complete HTML and JavaScript code for a web page that displays a random quote each time it loads.

LISTING 21.2   A Random Quote Web Page

```html
<!DOCTYPE html>

<html lang="en">
  <head>
    <title>Quotable Quotes</title>

    <script type="text/javascript">
      <!-- Hide the script from old browsers
      function getQuote() {
        // Create the arrays
        quotes = new Array(4);
        sources = new Array(4);

        // Initialize the arrays with quotes
        quotes[0] = "When I was a boy of 14, my father was so " +
        "ignorant...but when I got to be 21, I was astonished " +
        "at how much he had learned in 7 years.";
        sources[0] = "Mark Twain";

        quotes[1] = "Everybody is ignorant. Only on different " +
        "subjects.";
        sources[1] = "Will Rogers";

        quotes[2] = "They say such nice things about people at " +
        "their funerals that it makes me sad that I'm going to " +
        "miss mine by just a few days.";
        sources[2] = "Garrison Keillor";

        quotes[3] = "What's another word for thesaurus?";
        sources[3] = "Steven Wright";

        // Get a random index into the arrays
        i = Math.floor(Math.random() * quotes.length);

        // Write out the quote as HTML
        document.write("<p style='background-color: #ffb6c1' >\"");
        document.write(quotes[i] + "\"");
        document.write("<em>- " + sources[i] + "</em>");
        document.write("</p>");
      }
      // Stop hiding the script -->
    </script>
  </head>

  <body>
    <h1>Quotable Quotes</h1>
    <p>Following is a random quotable quote. To see a new quote just
    reload this page.</p>
    <script type="text/javascript">
      <!-- Hide the script from old browsers
      getQuote();
```

```
     // Stop hiding the script -->
   </script>
  </body>
</html>
```

Although this code looks kind of long, a lot of it consists of just the four quotes available for display on the page.

The large number of lines between the first set of `<script></script>` tags is creating a function called `getQuote()`. After a function is defined, it can be called in other places in the same page, which you see later in the code. Note that if the function existed in an external file, the function could be called from all your pages.

If you look closely at the code, you will see some lines like this:

```
// Create the arrays
```

and

```
// Initialize the arrays with quotes
```

These are code comments. A developer uses these types of comments to leave notes in the code so that anyone reading it has an idea of what the code is doing in that particular place. After the first comment about creating the arrays, you can see that two arrays are created— one called `quotes` and one called `sources`, each containing four elements:

```
quotes = new Array(4);
sources = new Array(4);
```

After the second comment (about initializing the arrays with quotes), four items are added to the arrays. Let's look closely at one of them, the first quote by Mark Twain:

```
quotes[0] = "When I was a boy of 14, my father was so " +
"ignorant...but when I got to be 21, I was astonished at " +
"how much he had learned in 7 years.";
sources[0] = "Mark Twain";
```

You already know that the arrays are named quotes and sources. But the variables to which values are assigned (in this instance) are called `quotes[0]` and `sources[0]`. Because quotes and sources are arrays, the items in the array each have their own position. When using arrays, the first item in the array is not in slot #1—it is in slot #0. In other words, you begin counting at 0 instead of 1, which is typical in programming—just file that away as an interesting and useful note for the future (or a good trivia answer). Therefore, the text of the first quote (a value) is assigned to `quotes[0]` (a variable). Similarly, the text of the first source is assigned to `source[0]`.

Text strings are enclosed in quotation marks. However, in JavaScript, a line break indicates an end of a command, so the following would cause problems in the code:

```
quotes[0] = "When I was a boy of 14, my father was so
ignorant...but when I got to be 21, I was astonished at
how much he had learned in 7 years.";
```

Therefore, you see that the string is built as a series of strings enclosed in quotation marks, with a plus sign (+) connecting the strings (this plus sign is called a *concatenation operator*).

The next chunk of code definitely looks the most like programming; this line is generating a random number and assigning that value to a variable called `i`:

```
i = Math.floor(Math.random() * quotes.length);
```

But you can't just pick any random number—the purpose of the random number is to determine which of the quotes and sources should be printed, and there are only four quotes. So this line of JavaScript does the following:

- Uses `Math.random()` to get a random number between 0 and 1. For example, 0.5482749 might be a result of `Math.random()`.

- Multiplies the random number by the length of the quotes array, which is currently 4; the length of the array is the number of elements in the array. If the random number is 0.5482749 (as shown previously), multiplying that by 4 results in 2.1930996.

- Uses `Math.floor()` to round the result down to the nearest whole number. In other words, 2.1930996 turns into 2.

- Assigns the variable `i` a value of `2` (for example).

The rest of the function should look familiar, with a few exceptions. First, as you learned earlier this hour, `document.write()` is used to write HTML that the browser then renders. Next, the strings are separated to clearly indicate when something needs to be handled differently, such as escaping the quotation marks with a backslash when they should be printed literally (\) or when the value of a variable is substituted. The actual quote and source that is printed is the one that matches `quotes[i]` and `sources[i]`, where i is the number determined by the mathematical functions noted previously.

But the act of simply writing the function doesn't mean that any output will be created. Further on in the HTML, you can see `getQuote();` between two `<script></script>` tags—that is how the function is called. Wherever that function call is made, that is where the output of the function will be placed. In this example, the output displays below a paragraph that introduces the quotation.

Figure 21.2 shows the Quotable Quotes page as it appears when loaded in a web browser. When the page reloads, there is a one-in-four chance that a different quote displays—it is random, after all!

FIGURE 21.2
The Quotable Quotes page displays a random quote each time it is loaded.

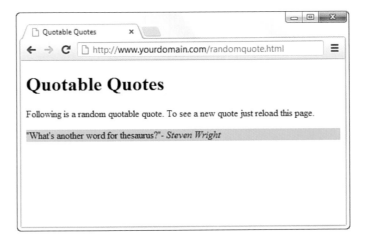

Keep in mind that you can easily modify this page to include your own quotes or other text that you want to display randomly. You can also increase the number of quotes available for display by adding more entries in the `quotes` and `sources` arrays in the code. And of course, you can modify the HTML output and style it however you'd like.

If you use the Quotable Quotes page as a starting point, you can easily alter the script and create your own interesting variation on the idea. And if you make mistakes along the way, so be it. The trick to getting past mistakes in script code is to be patient and carefully analyze the code you've entered. You can always remove code to simplify a script until you get it working, and then add new code one piece at a time to make sure each piece works.

Understanding the Document Object Model

This section could also be called "The Least You Need to Know About the Document Object Model to Begin Working with It and Learning More in the Future," but that would make for a terrible section title even if it is true. As you've read, client-side interactivity using JavaScript typically takes the form of manipulating the Document Object Model (DOM) in some way. The DOM is the invisible structure of all documents—not the HTML structure or the way in which you apply semantic formatting, but a sort of overall framework or container. If this description seems vague, that's because it is; it's not a tangible object.

The overall container object is called the `document`. Any container that you create within the document, that you've given an ID, can be referenced by that ID. For example, if you have a `<div>` with an ID called `wrapper`, then in the DOM, that element is referenced as follows:

```
document.wrapper
```

Recall that, in Hour 18, you changed the visibility of a specific element by changing something in the `style` object associated with it. Similarly, if you wanted to access the `background-color` style of the `<div>` with an ID called `wrapper` (to then do something with it), it would be referred to as follows:

```
document.wrapper.style.background-color
```

To change the value of that style to something else, perhaps based on an interactive user event, use the following to change the color to white:

```
document.wrapper.style.background-color="#ffffff"
```

The DOM is the framework behind your ability to refer to elements and their associated objects in this way. Obviously, this is a brief overview of something quite complicated, but at least you can now begin to grasp what this document-dot-something business is all about. To learn a lot more about the DOM, visit the World Wide Web Consortium information about the DOM at http://www.w3.org/DOM/.

Changing Images Based on User Interaction

Hour 18 introduced you to the different types of user interaction events, such as onclick, onmouseover, and onmouseout. In that hour, you invoked changes in text based on user interaction; in this section, you see an example of a visible type of interaction that is both practical and dynamic.

Figure 21.3 shows a page that contains one large image with some text next to it, and three small images farther down the page. If you look closely at the list of small images, you might notice that the first small image is, in fact, a smaller version of the large image that is displayed. This is a common display for a type of small gallery, such as one that you might see in an online catalog, in which an item has a description and a few alternate views of the product. Although close-up images of the details of products are important to the potential buyer, using several large images on a page becomes unwieldy from both a display and bandwidth point of view, so this type of gallery view is a popular way to display alternative images. I don't personally have products to sell, but I do have pictures of big trees that I can use as an example (see Figure 21.3).

FIGURE 21.3
An informational page with a main image and alternative images ready to click and view.

The large image on the page is called using this `<img/>` tag:

```
<img
   id="large_photo"
   style="border: 1px solid black; margin-right: 13px;"
   src="mariposa_large_1.jpg"
   alt="large photo" />
```

The `style`, `src`, and `alt` attributes should all make sense to you at this stage of the game. Additionally, as you can see, this image is given an ID of `large_photo`. Therefore, this image exists in the DOM as `document.images['large_photo']`—images are referred to by their ID. This is important because a bit of JavaScript functionality enables us to dynamically change the value of `document.images['large_image'].src`, which is the source (`src`) of the image.

The following code snippet creates the third small image in the group of three images shown at the bottom of Figure 21.3. The `onclick` event indicates that when the user clicks on this small image, the value of `document.images['large_image'].src`—the large image slot—is filled with the path to a matching large image.

```
<a href="#"
   onclick="javascript:document.images['large_photo'].src = 'mariposa_
   large_1.jpg'">
<img
   style="border: 1px solid black; margin-right: 3px;"
   src="mariposa_small_1.jpg"
   alt="photo #1" /></a>
```

Figure 21.4 shows the same page, but not reloaded by the user. The slot for the large image is filled by a different image when the user clicks on the third of the smaller images at the bottom of the page.

FIGURE 21.4
The large image is replaced when the user clicks on a smaller one.

Thinking Ahead to Developing HTML5 Applications

I'm not going to lie—there's a pretty big difference between a basic website built with HTML and CSS, and advanced applications that use some of the advanced features of HTML5. But it's important to your understanding of HTML, the language of the web, to have some idea of just how far you can extend it (it's pretty far, as it turns out). Beyond basic markup, HTML5 extends to include APIs (application programming interfaces) for complex applications, beginning with the native integration of audio and video elements, as you learned in previous lessons, and going all the way to built-in offline storage mechanisms that allow full-blown applications to be accessed and run (and data stored on the client side) even without a network connection.

Although HTML5 is incredibly rich, the creation of highly interactive HTML5 websites and applications—including mobile applications—doesn't happen in isolation. Interactivity comes when HTML5 is paired with a client-side language such as JavaScript, which then reaches back into the server and talks to a server-side language (such as PHP, Ruby, Python, and so on) through a persistent connection called a *web socket.* With this connection open and talking to some server-side code that is (for example) talking to a database or performing some calculation, the browser can relay a bundle of information that is additionally processed by JavaScript and finally rendered in HTML5. Be it a video game, a word processing program, or an email or Twitter client, just to name a few popular types of HTML5 applications, the combination of the advanced features of HTML5 plus JavaScript— and, specifically, the feature-rich JavaScript libraries such as jQuery (jquery.com)—really makes the opportunities limitless when it comes to application creation.

The depth of the technologies involved in HTML5 application creation is beyond the scope of this basic book, but the foundation you should have in standards-compliant HTML5 and CSS3 will serve you well if you begin to think outside the box of a basic website. To learn more about HTML5 application creation, take a look at *Sams Teach Yourself HTML5 Mobile Application Development in 24 Hours* for an introduction to some of the core features. Throughout *this* book, you get a solid foundation in the basics of HTML5. I am confident that, with additional instruction, you can take the next step and begin to learn and build basic interactions in an HTML5 application.

Summary

In this hour, you learned about the differences between server-side scripting and client-side scripting, and you learned how to include JavaScript in your HTML files to add a little interactivity to your websites. You also learned how to use the JavaScript `document.write()` method to display random quotes upon page load. Finally, you learned a bit about the Document Object Model.

By applying the knowledge you've gained from previous hours, you've learned how to use client-side scripting to make images on a web page respond to mouse movements. None of these tasks requires much in the way of programming skills, but they might inspire you to learn more about JavaScript or a server-side programming language so that you can give your pages more complex interactive features, including taking a step into the world of creating HTML5 applications.

Q&A

Q. **If I want to use the random quote script from this lesson, but I want to have a library of a lot of quotes, do I have to put all the quotes in each page?**

A. Yes. Each item in the array must be there. This is where you can begin to see a bit of a tipping point between something that can be client side and something that is better dealt with on the server side. If you have a true library of random quotations and only one is presented at any given time, it's probably best to store those items in a database table and use a little piece of server-side scripting to connect to that database, retrieve the text, and print it on the page. Alternately, you can always continue to carry all the quotes with you in JavaScript, but you should at least put that JavaScript function into a different file that can be maintained separately from the text.

Q. **I've seen some online catalogs that display a large image in what looks to be a layer on top of the website content—I can see the regular website content underneath it, but the focus is on the large image. How is that done?**

A. The description sounds like an effect created by a JavaScript library called Lightbox. The Lightbox library enables you to display an image, or a gallery of images, in a layer that is placed over your site content. This is a very popular library used to show the details of large images or just a set of images deemed important enough to showcase "above" the content. The library is freely available from its creator at http://lokeshdhakar.com/projects/lightbox/. To install and use it, follow the instructions included with the software; you will be able to integrate it into your site using the knowledge you've gained in this book so far.

Workshop

The Workshop contains quiz questions and activities to help you solidify your understanding of the material covered. Try to answer all questions before looking at the "Answers" section that follows.

Quiz

1. You've made a picture of a button and named it `button.gif`. You've also made a simple GIF animation of the button so that it flashes green and white. You've named that GIF `flashing.gif`. What HTML and JavaScript code can you use to make the button flash whenever a user moves the mouse pointer over it and also link to a page named `gohere.html` when a user clicks the button?

2. How can you modify the code you wrote for Question 1 so that the button flashes when a user moves the mouse over it and continues flashing even if the user then moves the mouse away from it?

3. What does the plus sign mean in the following context?

```
document.write('This is a text string ' + 'that I have created.');
```

Answers

1. Your code might look something like this:

```
<a href="gohere.html"
onmouseover="javascript:document.images['flasher'].src=
'flashing.gif'"
onmouseout="javascript:document.images['flasher'].src='button.gif'">
<img src="button.gif" id="flasher" style="border-style:none" /></a>
```

2. Your code might look something like this:

```
<a href="gohere.html"
onmouseover="javascript:document.images['flasher'].src=
'flashing.gif'">
<img src="button.gif" id="flasher" style="border-style:none" /></a>
```

3. The plus sign (+) joins two strings together.

Exercises

▶ Do you have any pages that would look flashier or be easier to understand if the navigation icons or other images changed when the mouse passed over them? If so, try creating some highlighted versions of the images, and try modifying your own page using the information presented in this hour.

▶ You can display random images—such as graphical banners or advertisements—in the same way you learned to display random content using JavaScript earlier in this chapter. Instead of printing text, just print the `<img/>` tag for the images you want to display.

Working with Web-Based Forms

To this point, pretty much everything in this book has focused on getting information out to others. But you can also use your web pages to gather information from the people who read them.

Web forms enable you to receive feedback, orders, or other information from the users who visit your web pages. If you've ever used a search engine such as Google, Yahoo!, or Bing, you're familiar with HTML forms—those single-field entry forms with one button that, when pressed, gives you all the information you are looking for and then some. Product order forms are also an extremely popular use of forms; if you've ordered anything from Amazon.com or purchased something from an eBay seller, you've used forms. In this chapter, you learn how to create your own forms, but you learn only how to create the front end of those forms. Working with the back end of forms requires knowledge of a programming language and is beyond the scope of this book.

How HTML Forms Work

An HTML form is part of a web page that includes areas where users can enter information to be sent back to you, to another email address that you specify, to a database that you manage, or to another system altogether, such as a third-party management system for your forms such as Salesforce.com.

Before you learn the HTML tags that are used to make your own forms, you should at least conceptually understand how the information from those forms makes its way back to you. The actual behind-the-scenes (the *server-side* or *back-end*) process requires knowledge of at least

WHAT YOU'LL LEARN IN THIS HOUR:

▶ How HTML forms work
▶ How to create the front end of an HTML form
▶ How to name pieces of form data
▶ How to include hidden data in forms
▶ How to choose the correct form input controls for the situation
▶ How to submit form data
▶ How to validate form data
▶ Sending form results by email

NOTE

PHP is the most popular server-side programming language; it's supported by any web hosting provider worth its salt. You can learn more about PHP at http://www.php.net/, or you can just dive right in to learning this programming language (plus database interactivity) from the ground up in *Sams Teach Yourself PHP, Apache, and MySQL All-in-One* (ISBN: 0672335433). Although several other books on PHP and related technologies are available, I am partial to this one because I wrote it. It is geared toward absolute beginners with PHP or any other programming language.

NOTE

There is a way to send form data without a server-side script, and you'll learn about that method—which uses a mailto link in the action attribute of the <form>—later in this hour. But as you try that, be aware that it can produce inconsistent results; individual web browsers, as well as personal security settings, can cause that action to respond differently than you intended.

one programming language—or at least the ability to follow specific instructions when using someone else's server-side script to handle the form input. At that point in the process, you should either work with someone who has the technical knowledge or learn the basics on your own. Simple form processing is not difficult, and your web hosting provider likely has several back-end scripts that you can use with minimal customization.

Forms include a button for the user to submit the form; that button can be an image that you create yourself or a standard HTML form button that is created when a form <input> tag is created and given a type value of submit. When someone clicks a form submission button, all the information typed in the form is sent to a URL that you specify in the action attribute of the <form> tag. That URL should point to a specific script that will process your form, sending the form contents via email or performing another step in an interactive process (such as requesting results from a search engine or placing items in an online shopping cart).

When you start thinking about doing more with form content than simply emailing results to yourself, you need additional technical knowledge. For example, if you want to create an online store that accepts credit cards and processes transactions, there are some well-established practices for doing so, all geared toward ensuring the security of your customers' data. That is not an operation that you'll want to enter into lightly; you'll need more knowledge than this book provides.

Before you put a form online, you should look in the user guide for your web hosting provider to see what it offers in the way of form-processing scripts. You are likely to find a readily available Perl or PHP script that you can use with only minimal configuration.

Creating a Form

Every form must begin with a <form> tag, which can be located anywhere in the body of the HTML document. The <form> tag typically has three attributes: name, method, and action:

```
<form name="my_form" method="post" action="myprocessingscript.php">
```

The most common method is post, which sends the form entry results as a document. In some situations, you need to use method="get", which submits the results as part of the URL query string instead. For example, `get` is sometimes used when submitting queries to search engines from a web form. Because you're not yet an expert on forms, just use `post` unless your web hosting provider's documentation tells you to do otherwise.

The `action` attribute specifies the address for sending the form data. You have two options here:

▶ You can type the location of a form-processing program or script on a web server, and the form data will then be sent to that program. This is by far the most common scenario.

▶ You can type `mailto:` followed by your email address, and the form data will be sent directly to you whenever someone fills out the form. However, this approach is completely dependent on the user's computer being properly configured with an email client. People accessing your site from a public computer without an email client will be left out in the cold.

```
<form name="my_form" method="post" action="mailto:me@mysite.com">
```

The form created in Listing 22.1 and shown in Figure 22.1 includes just about every type of user input component you can currently use in HTML forms in modern browsers. Refer to this figure and listing as you read the following explanations of each type of input element.

NOTE

HTML5 has undergone many improvements and additions for creating forms and form elements, but as of this writing, not all of them can be used in ways you expect. The good news is that even if you use an input type in your form that an older browser doesn't technically support, it will still display a usable generic input field. Overall, this hour discusses only the input types you can be confident using. To stay up to date on browser support for new form-related elements and attributes, check out "Can I Use..." at http://caniuse.com/#feat=forms, which aggregates information about browser support for HTML5 and CSS3.

FIGURE 22.1
The code in Listing 22.1 uses
many common HTML form
elements.

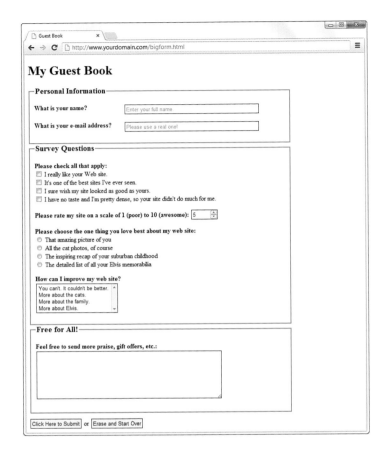

LISTING 22.1   A Form with Various User-Input Components

```
<!DOCTYPE html>

<html lang="en">
  <head>
    <title>Guest Book</title>

    <style type="text/css">

      fieldset {
         width: 75%;
         border: 2px solid #ff0000;
      }

      legend {
         font-weight: bold;
         font-size: 125%;
      }
```

```
        label.question  {
            width: 225px;
            float: left;
            text-align: left;
            font-weight: bold;
        }

        span.question  {
            font-weight: bold;
        }

        input, textarea, select {
            border: 1px solid #000;
            padding: 3px;
        }

        #buttons {
            margin-top: 12px;
        }

    </style>
</head>
<body>
    <h1>My Guest Book</h1>
    <form name="gbForm" method="post" action="URL_to_script">

    <fieldset>
        <legend>Personal Information</legend>

        <p><label class="question" for="the_name">What is your
        name?</label>
        <input type="text" id="the_name" name="the_name"
              placeholder="Enter your full name."
              size="50" required autofocus /></p>

        <p><label class="question" for="the_email">What is your e-mail
              address?</label>
        <input type="email" id="the_email" name="the_email"
              placeholder="Please use a real one!"
              size="50" required /></p>
    </fieldset>

    <fieldset>
        <legend>Survey Questions</legend>

        <p><span class="question">Please check all that apply:</span><br/>
        <input type="checkbox" id="like_it" name="some_statements[]"
              value="I really like your Web site." />
        <label for="like_it">I really like your Web site.</label><br/>
        <input type="checkbox" id="the_best" name="some_statements[]"
              value="It's one of the best sites I've ever seen" />
        <label for="the_best">It's one of the  best sites I've ever
              seen.</label><br/>
```

```
<input type="checkbox" id="jealous" name="some_statements[]"
       value="I sure wish my site looked as good as yours." />
<label for="jealous">I sure wish my site looked as good as
       yours.</label><br/>
<input type="checkbox" id="no_taste" name="some_statements[]"
       value="I have no taste and I'm pretty dense, so your site
       didn't do much for me." />
<label for="no_taste">I have no taste and I'm pretty dense, so your
       site didn't do much for me.</label></p>

<p><label for="choose_scale"><span class="question">Please rate my
       site on a scale of 1 (poor) to 10 (awesome):</span></label>
<input type="number" id="choose_scale" name="choose_scale"
       min="0" max="10" step="1" value="5"/></p>

<p><span class="question">Please choose the one thing you love best
       about my web site:</span><br/>
<input type="radio" id="the_picture" name="best_thing"
       value="me" />
<label for="the_picture">That amazing picture of you</label><br/>
<input type="radio" id="the_cats" name="best_thing"
       value="cats" />
<label for="the_cats">All the cat photos, of course</label><br/>
<input type="radio" id="the_story" name="best_thing"
       value="childhood story" />
<label for="the_story">The inspiring recap of your suburban
       childhood</label><br/>
<input type="radio" id="the_treasures" name="best_thing"
       value="Elvis treasures" />
<label for="the_treasures">The detailed list of all your Elvis
       memorabilia</label></p>

<p><label for="how_improve"><span class="question">How can I
       improve my web site?</span></label><br/>
 <select id="how_improve" name="how_improve" size="4" multiple>
       <option value="You can't. It couldn't be better.">You can't.
       It couldn't be better.</option>
       <option value="More about the cats.">More about the
       cats.</option>
       <option value="More about the family.">More about the
       family.</option>
       <option value="More about Elvis.">More about Elvis.</option>
  </select></p>

</fieldset>

<fieldset>
  <legend>Free for All!</legend>
  <p><label for="message"><span class="question">Feel free to send
  more praise, gift offers, etc.:</span></label>
  <textarea id="message" name="message" rows="7" cols="55">
  </textarea></p>
</fieldset>
```

```
    <div id="buttons">
      <input type="submit" value="Click Here to Submit" /> or
      <input type="reset" value="Erase and Start Over" />
    </div>

    </form>
  </body>
</html>
```

The code in Listing 22.1 uses a `<form>` tag that contains quite a few `<input />` tags. Each `<input />` tag corresponds to a specific user input component, such as a check box or radio button. The input, select, and text area elements contain borders in the stylesheet, so it is easy to see the outline of the elements in the form. Keep in mind that you can apply all sorts of CSS to those elements.

The next few sections dig into the `<input />` tag and other form-related tags in detail.

Accepting Text Input

To ask the user for a specific piece of information within a form, use the `<input />` tag. Although the tag does not explicitly need to appear between the `<form>` and `</form>` tags, it is good practice and makes your code easier to follow. You can place `<input />` elements anywhere on the page in relation to text, images, and other HTML tags. For example, to ask for someone's name, you could type the following text followed immediately by an `<input />` field:

```
<p><label class="question" for="the_name">What is your name?</label>
<input type="text" id="the_name" name="the_name"
       placeholder="Enter your full name."
       size="50" required autofocus /></p>
```

The `type` attribute indicates what type of form element to display—a simple, one-line text entry box, in this case. (Each element type is discussed individually in this hour.) In this example, note the use of the `placeholder`, `required`, and `autofocus` attributes. You'll learn about the `required` attribute later in this hour; the `autofocus` attribute automatically focuses the user's cursor in this text field as soon as the browser renders the form. A form can have only one `autofocus` field. The `placeholder` attribute enables you to define some text that appears in the text box but disappears when you begin to type. Using this

TIP

If you want the user to enter text without the text being displayed on the screen, you can use `<input type="password" />` instead of `<input_type="text" />`. Asterisks (***) are then displayed in place of the text the user types. The `size`, `maxlength`, and `name` attributes work exactly the same for `type="password"` as they do for `type="text"`. Keep in mind that this technique of hiding a password provides only visual protection; no encryption or other protection is associated with the password being transmitted.

attribute, you can give the user a bit more guidance in completing your form.

The `size` attribute indicates approximately how many characters wide the text input box should be. If you are using a proportionally spaced font, the width of the input will vary depending on what the user enters. If the input is too long to fit in the box, most web browsers automatically scroll the text to the left.

The `maxlength` attribute determines the number of characters the user is allowed to type into the text box. If a user tries to type beyond the specified length, the extra characters won't appear. You can specify a length that is longer, shorter, or the same as the physical size of the text box. The `size` and `maxlength` attributes are used only for those input fields meant for text values, such as `type="text"`, `type="email"`, `type="URL"`, and `type="tel"`, but not check boxes and radio buttons since those have fixed sizes.

Naming Each Piece of Form Data

No matter what type an input element is, you must give a name to the data it gathers. You can use any name you like for each input item, as long as each one on the form is different (except in the case of radio buttons and check boxes, discussed later in this chapter). When the form is processed by a back-end script, each data item is identified by name. This name becomes a variable, which is filled with a value. The value is either what the user typed in the form or the value associated with the element the user selected.

NOTE

Form-processing scripts are oversimplified here, for the sake of explanation within the scope of this book. The exact appearance (or name) of the variables made available to your processing script depends on the programming language of that script. But conceptually, it's valid to say that the name of the input element becomes the name of the variable, and the value of the input element becomes that variable's value on the back end.

For example, if a user enters Jane Doe in the text box defined previously, a variable is sent to the form-processing script; the variable is `user_name`, and the value of the variable is Jane Doe. Form-processing scripts work with these types of variable names and values.

To use this text field (or others) in JavaScript, remember that the text object uses the `name` attribute; you refer to the value of the field in the previous snippet as follows:

```
document.formname.user_name.value
```

Labeling Each Piece of Form Data

Labeling your form data is not the same as using a `name` or `id` attribute to identify the form element for later use. Instead, the `<label></label>` tag pair surrounds text that acts as a sort of caption for a form element. A form element `<label>` provides additional context for the element, which is especially important for screen reader software.

You can see two different examples in Listing 22.1. First, you can see the `<label>` surrounding the first question a user is asked (What is your name?). The use of the `for` attribute ties this label to the `<input />` element with the same `id` (in this case, `the_name`):

```
<p><label class="question" for="the_name">What is your name?</label>
<input type="text" id="the_name" name="the_name"
       placeholder="Enter your full name."
       size="50" required autofocus /></p>
```

A screen reader would read to the user, "What is your name?" and then also say "text box" to alert the user it to complete the text field with the appropriate information. In another example from Listing 22.1, you see the use of `<label>` to surround different options in a check box list (and also a list of radio buttons, later in the listing):

```
<p><span class="question">Please check all that apply:</span><br/>
<input type="checkbox" id="like_it" name="some_statements[]"
       value="I really like your Web site." />
<label for="like_it">I really like your Web site.</label><br/>
<input type="checkbox" id="the_best" name="some_statements[]"
       value="It's one of the best sites I've ever seen" />
<label for="the_best">It's one of the  best sites I've ever
       seen.</label><br/>
<input type="checkbox" id="jealous" name="some_statements[]"
       value="I sure wish my site looked as good as yours." />
<label for="jealous">I sure wish my site looked as good as
       yours.</label><br/>
<input type="checkbox" id="no_taste" name="some_statements[]"
       value="I have no taste and I'm pretty dense, so your site
       didn't do much for me." />
<label for="no_taste">I have no taste and I'm pretty dense, so your
       site didn't do much for me.</label></p>
```

In this situation, the screen reader would read the text surrounded by the `<label>` tag, followed by "check box," to alert the user to choose one of the given options. Labels should be used for all form elements and can be styled using CSS in the same manner as other container elements—the styling does not affect the screen reader, but it does help with layout aesthetics and readability.

Grouping Form Elements

In Listing 22.1, you can see the use of the `<fieldset>` and `<legend>` element three different times, to create three different groups of form fields. The `<fieldset>` element does just that—it surrounds groups of form elements to provide additional context for the user, whether they are accessing it directly in a web browser or with the aid of screen reader software. The `<fieldset>` element just defines the grouping; the `<legend>` element contains the text that will display or be read aloud to describe this grouping, such as the following from Listing 22.1:

```
<fieldset>
    <legend>Personal Information</legend>
    <p><label class="question" for="the_name">What is your name?</label>
    <input type="text" id="the_name" name="the_name"
        placeholder="Enter your full name."
        size="50" required autofocus /></p>
...
</fieldset>
```

In this situation, when the screen reader reads the `<label>` associated with a form element, as you learned in the previous section, it also appends the `<legend>` text, such as "Personal Information. What is your name? Text box." The `<fieldset>` and `<legend>` elements can be styled using CSS, so the visual cue of the grouped elements can easily be made visible in a web browser (as you saw previously in Figure 22.1).

Including Hidden Data in Forms

Want to send certain data items to the server script that processes a form, but don't want the user to see those data items? Use an `<input />` tag with a `type="hidden"` attribute. This attribute has no effect on the display; it just adds any name and value you specify to the form results when they are submitted.

If you are using a form-processing script provided by your web hosting provider, you might be directed to use this attribute to tell a script where to email the form results. For example, including the following code emails the results to me@mysite.com after the form is submitted:

```
<input type="hidden" name="mailto" value="me@mysite.com" />
```

You sometimes see scripts using hidden input elements to carry additional data that might be useful when you receive the results of the form submission; some examples of hidden form fields include an email address and a subject for the email. If you are using a script provided by your web hosting provider, consult the documentation provided with that script for additional details about potential required hidden fields.

Exploring Form Input Controls

Various input controls are available for retrieving information from the user. You've already seen one text-entry option; the next few sections introduce you to most of the remaining form-input options you can use to design forms.

Check Boxes

Besides the text field, one of the simplest input type is a *check box*, which appears as a small square. Users can click check boxes to select or deselect one or more items in a group. For example, the check boxes listed in Listing 22.1 display after text that reads "Please check all that apply," implying that the user could indeed check all that apply.

The HTML for the check boxes in Listing 22.1 shows that the value of the name attribute is the same for all of them:

```
<p><span class="question">Please check all that apply:</span><br/>
<input type="checkbox" id="like_it" name="some_statements[]"
    value="I really like your Web site." />
<label for="like_it">I really like your Web site.</label><br/>
<input type="checkbox" id="the_best" name="some_statements[]"
    value="It's one of the best sites I've ever seen" />
<label for="the_best">It's one of the  best sites I've ever
    seen.</label><br/>
<input type="checkbox" id="jealous" name="some_statements[]"
    value="I sure wish my site looked as good as yours." />
<label for="jealous">I sure wish my site looked as good as
    yours.</label><br/>
<input type="checkbox" id="no_taste" name="some_statements[]"
    value="I have no taste and I'm pretty dense, so your site
    didn't do much for me." />
<label for="no_taste">I have no taste and I'm pretty dense, so your
    site didn't do much for me.</label></p>
```

The use of the brackets in the name attribute ([]) indicates to the back-end processing script that a series of values will be placed into this one variable instead of using just one value (well, it might be just one value if the user selects only one check box). If a user selects the first check box, the text string I really like your Web site. is placed in

TIP

If you find that the label for an input element is displayed too close to the element, just add a space between the close of the `<input />` tag and the start of the label text, like this:

```
<input type="checkbox"
name="mini" /> <label>Mini
Piano Stool</label>
```

the `website_response[]` bucket. If the user selects the third check box, the text string `I sure wish my site looked as good as yours.` also is put into the `website_response[]` bucket. The processing script then works with that variable as an array of data rather just a single entry.

However, you might see groups of check boxes that do use individual names for the variables in the group. For example, the following is another way of writing the check box group:

```
<p><span class="question">Please check all that apply:</span><br/>
<input type="checkbox" id="like_it" name="liked_site" value="yes"
     value="I really like your Web site." />
<label for="like_it">I really like your Web site.</label><br/>
<input type="checkbox" id="the_best" name="best_site" value="yes"
     value="It's one of the best sites I've ever seen" />
<label for="the_best">It's one of the  best sites I've ever
     seen.</label><br/>
<input type="checkbox" id="jealous" name="my_site_sucks" value="yes"
     value="I sure wish my site looked as good as yours." />
<label for="jealous">I sure wish my site looked as good as
     yours.</label><br/>
<input type="checkbox" id="no_taste" name="am_dense" value="yes"
     value="I have no taste and I'm pretty dense, so your site
     didn't do much for me." />
<label for="no_taste">I have no taste and I'm pretty dense, so your
     site didn't do much for me.</label></p>
```

In this second list of check boxes, the variable name of the first check box is `"liked_site"` and the value (if checked) is `"yes"` when handled by a back-end processing script.

If you want a check box to be checked by default when the web browser renders the form, include the `checked` attribute. For example, the following code creates two check boxes, and the first is checked by default:

```
<input type="checkbox" id="like_it" name="liked_site" value="yes"
     value="I really like your Web site." checked />
<label for="like_it">I really like your Web site.</label><br/>
<input type="checkbox" id="the_best" name="best_site" value="yes"
     value="It's one of the best sites I've ever seen" />
```

The check box labeled `I really like your site.` is checked by default in this example. The user must click the check box to uncheck it and thus indicate they have another opinion of your site. The check box marked `One of the best I've seen.` is unchecked to begin with, so the user must click it to turn it on. Check boxes that are not selected do not appear in the form output.

Radio Buttons

Radio buttons, for which only one choice can be selected at a time, are almost as simple to implement as check boxes. The simplest use of a radio button is for yes/no questions or for voting when only one candidate can be selected.

To create a radio button, use `type="radio"` and give each option its own `<input />` tag. Use the same `name` for all the radio buttons in a group, but don't use the `[]` that you used with the check box, because you don't have to accommodate multiple answers:

```
<input type="radio" id="vote_yes" name="vote" value="yes" checked />
<label for="vote_yes">Yes</label> <br />
<input type="radio" id="vote_no" name="vote" value="no" />
<label for="vote_no">No</label>
```

The `value` can be any name or code you choose. If you include the `checked` attribute, that button is selected by default. No more than one radio button with the same `name` can be checked.

When designing your form and choosing between check boxes and radio buttons, ask yourself whether the question being asked or implied that could be answered in only one way. If so, use a radio button.

NOTE

Radio buttons are named for their similarity to the buttons on old push-button radios. Those buttons used a mechanical arrangement so that when you pushed one button in, the others popped out.

Selection Lists

Both *scrolling lists* and *pull-down pick lists* are created with the `<select>` tag. You use this tag together with the `<option>` tag, as the following example shows (taken from Listing 22.1):

```
<p><label for="how_improve"><span class="question">How can I
    improve my web site?</span></label><br/>
<select id="how_improve" name="how_improve" size="4" multiple>
    <option value="You can't. It couldn't be better.">You can't.
        It couldn't be better.</option>
    <option value="More about the cats.">More about the cats.</option>
    <option value="More about the family.">More about the
        family.</option>
    <option value="More about Elvis.">More about Elvis.</option>
</select></p>
```

Unlike the `text` input type that you learned about briefly in a previous section, the `size` attribute here determines how many items show at once on the selection list. If `size="2"` were used in the preceding code, only the first two options would be visible and a scrollbar would

If you leave out the `size` attribute or specify `size="1"`, the list creates a simple drop-down pick list. Pick lists don't allow for multiple choices; they are logically equivalent to a group of radio buttons. The following example shows another way to choose `yes` or `no` for a question:

```
<select name="vote">
  <option value="yes">Yes
  </option>
  <option value="no">No
  </option>
</select>
```

appear next to the list so the user could scroll down to see the third and fourth options.

Including the `multiple` attribute enables users to select more than one option at a time; the `selected` attribute makes an option initially selected by default. When the form is submitted, the text specified in the `value` attribute for each option accompanies the selected option.

No HTML tags other than `<option>` and `</option>` should appear between the `<select>` and `</select>` tags, with the exception of the `<optgroup>` tag (not shown in Listing 22.1). The use of `<optgroup>`, as in the following snippet, enables you to create groups of options (that's where the name `optgroup` comes from) with a label that shows up in the list but can't be selected as an "answer" to the form field. For example, this snippet:

```
<select name="grades">
    <optgroup label="Good Grades">
        <option value="A">A</option>
        <option value="B">B</option>
    </optgroup>
    <optgroup label="Average Grades">
        <option value="C">C</option>
    </optgroup>
    <optgroup label="Bad Grades">
        <option value="D">D</option>
        <option value="F">F</option>
    </optgroup>
</select>
```

produces a drop-down list that looks like this:

```
Good Grades
    A
    B
Average Grades
    C
Bad Grades
    D
    F
```

In this situation, only A, B, C, D, and F are selectable, but the `<optgroup>` labels are visible.

Text Fields, Text Areas, and Other Input Types

The `<input type="text">` attribute mentioned earlier this chapter allows the user to enter only a single line of text. When you want to allow multiple lines of text in a single input item, use the `<textarea>` and `</textarea>` tags to create a text area instead of just a text field. Any text you include between these two tags is displayed as the default entry in that box. Here's the example from Listing 22.1:

```
<textarea id="message"  name="message" rows="7" cols="55">Your
      message here.</textarea>
```

As you probably guessed, the `rows` and `cols` attributes control the number of rows and columns of text that fit in the input box. The `cols` attribute is a little less exact than `rows` and approximates the number of characters that fit in a row of text. Text area boxes do have a scrollbar, however, so the user can enter more text than what fits in the display area.

Let's turn back to the basic `<input />` element for a minute, however, because HTML5 provides many more `type` options for input than simply "text," such as built-in date pickers. The downside is that not all browsers fully support many of those options (such as the built-in date picker). Here are a few of the different input types (some new, some not) that *are* fully supported but that we haven't discussed in any detail in this lesson:

► `type="email"`—Appears as a regular text field, but when form validation is used, the built-in validator checks that it is a well-formed email address. Some mobile devices display relevant keys (the @ sign, for example) by default instead of requiring additional user interactions.

► `type="file"`—Opens a dialog box to enable you to search for a file on your computer to upload.

► `type="number"`—Instead of creating a `<select>` list with `<option>` tags for each number, this type enables you to specify a `min` and `max` value, and the `step` between numbers, to automatically generate a list on the browser side. You can see this in use in Listing 22.1.

► `type="range"`—Much like the `number` type just covered, this type enables you to specify a `min` and `max` value and the step-between numbers, but in this case, it appears as a horizontal slider.

▶ `type="search"`—Appears as a regular text field, but with additional controls sometimes used to allow the user to clear the search box using an x or similar character.

▶ `type="url"`—Appears as a regular text field, but when form validation is used, the built-in validator checks that it is a well-formed URL. Some mobile devices display relevant keys (the `.com` virtual key, for instance) by default instead of requiring additional user interactions.

You can stay up to date with the status of these and other `<input>` types using the chart at https://developer.mozilla.org/en-US/docs/Web/HTML/Element/input.

Using HTML5 Form Validation

Many features in HTML5 have made web developers very happy people. One of the simplest yet most life-changing might be the inclusion of form validation. Before HTML5 form validation existed, we had to create convoluted JavaScript-based form validation, which caused headaches for everyone involved.

But no more! HTML5 validates forms by default, unless you use the `novalidate` attribute in the `<form>` element. Of course, if you do not use the `required` attribute in any form fields themselves, there's nothing to validate. As you learned in a previous section, not only are fields validated for content (any content at all)—they are validated according to the type that they are. For example, in Listing 22.1, we have a required field for an email address:

```
<p><label class="question" for="the_email">What is your e-mail
    address?</label>
<input type="email" id="the_email" name="the_email"
    placeholder="Please use a real one!"
    size="50" required /></p>
```

In Figures 22.2 and 22.3, you can see that the form automatically validates for the presence of content, but then also slaps you on the wrists when you try to enter a junk string in the field instead of an email address.

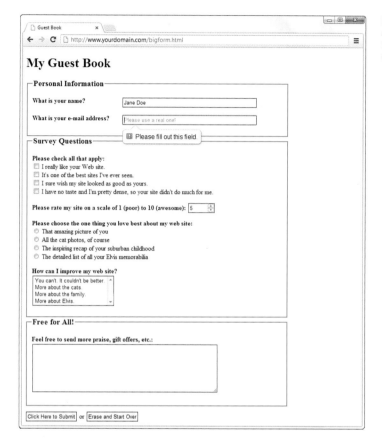

FIGURE 22.2
Attempting to submit a form with
no content in a required field
causes a validation error.

You can use the `pattern` attribute of the `<input />` field to specify your
own pattern-matching requirements. The `pattern` attribute uses regular
expressions, which is a large enough topic to warrant its own book.
But consider a little example. If you want to ensure that your `<input />`
element contains only numbers and letters (no special characters), you
could use the following:

```
<input type="text" id="the_text" name="the_text"
    placeholder="Please enter only letters and numbers!"
    size="50" pattern="[a-z,A-Z,0-9]" required />
```

The pattern here says that if the field contains any letter between `a`
and `z`, letter between `A` and `Z` (case matters), and number `0` and `9`, it's
valid. To learn more about regular expressions without buying an
entire book, take a look at the online tutorial at http://regexone.com/.

NOTE

Validation of email addresses
begins and ends with it simply
looking like an email address.
This sort of pattern matching
is really the only type of
"validation" that you can do
with email addresses, short
of a time-consuming back-end
processing script.

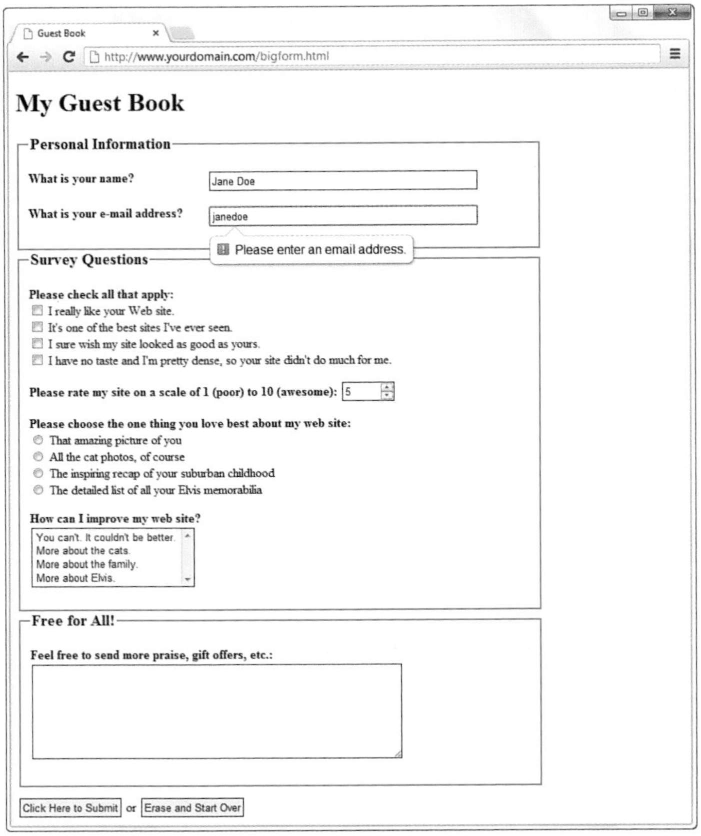

FIGURE 22.3
Attempting to submit a form with badly formed content in a field expecting an email address causes a validation error.

Submitting Form Data

Forms typically include a button that submits the form data to a script on the server or invokes a JavaScript action. You can put any label you like on the Submit button with the `value` attribute:

```
<input type="submit" value="Place My Order Now!" />
```

Unless you change the style using CSS, a gray button is sized to fit the label you put in the `value` attribute. When the user clicks it, all data items on the form are sent to the email address or script specified in the form's `action` attribute.

You can also include a Reset button that clears all entries on the form so that users can start over if they change their minds or make mistakes. Use the following:

```
<input type="reset" value="Clear This Form and Start Over" />
```

If the standard Submit and Reset buttons look a little bland to you, remember that you can style them using CSS. If that's not good enough, you'll be glad to know that there's an easy way to substitute your own graphics for these buttons. To use an image of your choice for a Submit button, use the following:

```
<input type="image" src="button.gif" alt="Order Now!" />
```

The `button.gif` image displays on the page, and the form also is submitted when a user clicks the `button.gif` image. You can include any attributes normally used with the `<img />` tag, such as `alt` and `style`.

The form element also includes a generic button type. When using `type="button"` in the `<input />` tag, you get a button that performs no action on its own but can have an action assigned to it using a JavaScript event handler (such as `onclick`). However, because you need JavaScript interaction for that, it's best to stick with the `submit`, `rest`, or `image` types, or use the actual `<button>` element (in IE 9 and greater), which has `type` attributes of `submit` and `rest` and allows for slightly more flexibility in styling than the `<input>` elements of the same `type`.

Summary

This hour demonstrated how to create HTML forms, which allow your visitors to provide information to you when they are hooked up to a back-end processing script (which is outside the scope of this book).

You learned about all the major form elements, including a little about how form-processing scripts interpret the names and value attributes of those elements. When you are ready to try a back-end form-processing script, you'll be well versed in the front-end details.

We stopped short of doing anything in-depth with that information because form handling requires an external script to process that form. However, there is plenty to do to set up a form that looks and acts just the way you want it to, including form validation, so you have a lot to practice before taking that next step into form interactivity.

Table 22.1 summarizes the HTML tags and attributes covered in this chapter.

TABLE 22.1   HTML Tags and Attributes Covered in Chapter 22

Tag/Attribute	Function
`<form>...</form>`	Indicates an input form.
Attributes	
`action="scripturl"`	Gives the address of the script to process this form input.
`method="post/get"`	Indicates how the form input will be sent to the server. Normally set to `post` rather than `get`.
`<label>...</label>`	Provides information for the form element to which it is associated.
`<fieldset>...</fieldset>`	Groups a set of related form elements.
`<legend>...</legend>`	Provides a label to a set of related form elements.
`<input />`	An input element for a form.
Attributes	
`type="controltype"`	Gives the type for this input widget. Some possible values are `checkbox`, `hidden`, `radio`, `reset`, `submit`, `text`, and `image`, among others.
`name="name"`	Gives the unique name of this item, as passed to the script.
`value="value"`	The default value for a text or hidden item. For a check box or radio button, it's the value to be submitted with the form. For reset or submit buttons, it's the label for the button itself.
`src="imageurl"`	Shows the source file for an image.
`checked`	Used for check boxes and radio buttons. Indicates that this item is checked.
`autofocus`	Puts focus on the element when the form is loaded.
`required`	Indicates that the field should be validated for content, according to type (where appropriate).
`pattern="pattern"`	Indicates that the content of this field should be validated against this regular expression.
`size="width"`	Specifies the width, in characters, of a text input region.
`maxlength="maxlength"`	Specifies the maximum number of characters that can be entered into a text region.

`<textarea>...</textarea>`	Indicates a multiline text entry form element. Default text can be included.
Attributes	
`name="name"`	Specifies the name to be passed to the script.
`rows="numrows"`	Specifies the number of rows this text area displays.
`cols="numchars"`	Specifies the number of columns (characters) this text area displays.
`autofocus`	Puts focus on the element when the form is loaded.
`required`	Indicates that the field should be validated for content according to type (where appropriate).
`pattern="pattern"`	Indicates that the content of this field should be validated against this regular expression.
`<select>...</select>`	Creates a menu or scrolling list of possible items.
Attributes	
`name="name"`	Shows the name that is passed to the script.
`size="numelements"`	The number of elements to display. If `size` is indicated, the selection becomes a scrolling list. If no `size` is given, the selection is a drop-down pick list.
`multiple`	Allows multiple selections from the list.
`required`	Indicates that the field should be validated for a selection.
`<optgroup>...</optgroup>`	Indicates a grouping of `<option>` elements.
Attributes	
`label="label"`	Provides a label for the group.
`<option>...</option>`	Indicates a possible item within a `<select>` element.
Attributes	
`selected`	With this attribute included, the `<option>` is selected by default in the list.
`value="value"`	Specifies the value to submit if this `<option>` is selected when the form is submitted.

Q&A

Q. Is there any way to create a large number of text fields without dealing with different names for all of them?

A. Yes. If you use the same name for several elements in the form, their objects form an array. For example, if you defined 20 text fields with the name `member`, you could refer to them as `member[0]` through `member[19]`. This also works with other types of form elements.

Q. If HTML5 contains form validation, do I ever have to worry about validation again?

A. Yes, you do. Although HTML5 form validation is awesome, you should still validate the form information that is sent to you on the back end. Back-end processing is outside the scope of the book, but as a rule, you should never trust any user input—always check it before performing an action that uses it (especially when interacting with a database).

Workshop

The Workshop contains quiz questions and activities to help you solidify your understanding of the material covered. Try to answer all questions before looking at the "Answers" section that follows.

Quiz

1. What HTML code do you use to create a guestbook form that asks someone for his or her name and gender? Assume that you have a form-processing script set up at `/scripts/formscript` and that you need to include the following hidden input element to tell the script where to send the form results:

   ```
   <input type="hidden" name="mailto" value="you@yoursite.com" />
   ```

2. If you created an image named `submit.gif`, how would you use it as the Submit button for the form you created in Question 1?

3. Which of these attributes of a `<form>` tag determines where the data will be sent?

   a. `action`

   b. `method`

   c. `name`

Answers

1. You use HTML code similar to the following (with the appropriate DOCTYPE and other structural markup, of course):

```
<form name="form1" method="post" action="/scripts/formscript">
<input type="hidden" name="mailto" value="you@yoursite.com" />
<p><label for="name">Your Name:</label>
<input type="text" id="name" name="name" size="50" /></p>
<p>Your Gender:
<input type="radio" id="male" name="gender"
     value="male" /> <label for="male">male</label>
<input type="radio" id="female" name="gender"
     value="female" /> <label for="female">female</label>
<input type="radio" id="go_away" name="gender"
     value="mind your business" />
     <label for="go_away">mind your business</label></p>
<p><input type="submit" value="Submit Form" /></p>
</form>
```

2. Replace the following code:

```
<input type="submit" value="Submit Form" />
```

with this code:

```
<input type="image" src="submit.gif" />
```

3. a. The `action` attribute determines where the data is sent.

Exercises

▶ Create a form using all the different types of input elements and selection lists to make sure you understand how each of them works.

▶ Learn a little bit about regular expressions, and implement some custom validation using the `pattern` attribute.

▶ Investigate the form-handling options at your web hosting provider, and use a script that the web hosting provider made available to you to process the form you created in the previous exercise.

HOUR 23
Organizing and Managing a Website

The bulk of this book has led you through the design and creation of your own web content, from text to graphics and multimedia. Along the way, I've noted some of the ways you can think about the lifecycle of that content—but in this hour, you learn how to look at your work as a whole.

This hour shows you how to think about organizing and presenting multiple web pages so that visitors will be able to navigate among them without confusion. You'll also learn ways to make your website memorable enough to visit again and again. Web developers use the term *sticky* to describe pages that people don't want to leave. Hopefully this chapter helps you make your websites downright gooey!

Because websites can be (and usually should be) updated frequently, it's essential to create pages that can be easily maintained. This hour shows you how to add comments and other documentation to your pages so that you—or anyone else on your staff—can understand and modify your pages. It also introduces you to version control so that you can innovate individually or as part of a team without overwriting work that you might want to have saved.

WHAT YOU'LL LEARN IN THIS HOUR:

▶ How to determine whether one page is enough to handle all your content

▶ How to organize a simple site

▶ How to organize a larger site

▶ How to write maintainable code

▶ How to get started with version control

By this point in the book, you should have enough HTML and CSS knowledge to produce most of your website. You probably have created a number of pages already, and perhaps even published them online.

As you proceed through this hour, think about how your pages are organized now and how you can improve that organization. Have you used comments in your HTML or created a document for future website maintainers regarding your content organization? If not, now is a good time to start. Along the way, don't be surprised if you decide to do a redesign that involves changing almost all your pages—the results are likely to be well worth the effort!

When One Page Is Enough

Building and organizing an attractive and effective website doesn't always need to be a complex task. If you are creating a web presence for a single entity (such as a local event) that requires only a brief amount of very specific information, you can effectively present that information on a single page without a lot of flashy graphics. In fact, there are several positive features to a single-page web presence:

▶ All the information on the site downloads quicker than on more extensive sites.

▶ The whole site can be printed on paper with a single print command, even if it is several paper pages long.

▶ Visitors can easily save the site on their hard drives for future reference, especially if it uses a minimum of graphics.

▶ Links between different parts of the same page usually respond more quickly than links to other pages.

Figure 23.1 shows the first part of a web page that serves its intended audience better as a single lengthy page than it would as a multipage site. The page begins, as most introductory pages should, with a succinct explanation of what the page is about and who would want to read it. A detailed table of contents allows visitors to skip directly to the section containing the material they find most interesting. If this "page" were printed, it would contain about six paper pages' worth of text about driving traffic to websites—something a visitor might think about printing and reading later, perhaps while also taking notes.

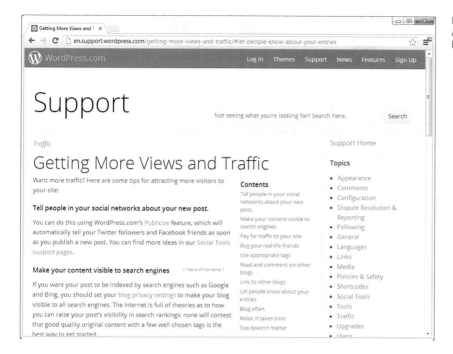

FIGURE 23.1
A good table of contents can make long pages easier to navigate.

When pages contain a table of contents to separate sections of information, it is also common for each short section to contain a link back up to the table of contents so that navigating around the page feels much the same as navigating around a multipage site. Because the contents of these types of longer pages are intended as a handy reference, visitors will definitely prefer the convenience of bookmarking or saving a single page instead of having to save 8 or 10 separate pages. The most common examples of single-page information websites are encompassed within Wikipedia, at www.wikipedia.org. If you consider each entry full of rich content to be its own "site," the single-page sites within Wikipedia—with their own tables of contents— represent millions of printed pages.

Having experienced many beautiful and effective graphical layouts online, you might be tempted to forget that a good, old-fashioned outline is often the clearest and most efficient way to organize long web pages full of text-based content within a site. This is especially true with the influx of single-page interfaces (also called single-page *applications*) that attempt to bring all the interactivity of desktop applications into a web browsing experience. These applications are often built using HTML and JavaScript frameworks and include significant visual design elements; in fact, these sites are often used to publish design portfolios rather than the type of text-based content that I'm using here.

Organizing a Simple Site

With the exception of the aforementioned special cases of single-page applications and portfolio sites, single-page websites tend to serve as merely "coming soon" or placeholder purposes. If you spend any time at all on the web, you'll quickly learn that most companies and individuals serve their readers better by dividing their site into short, quick-read pages surrounded by graphical navigation that allows them to gather almost all the information they could want within a few clicks. Furthermore, using multiple pages instead of a series of very long pages minimizes scrolling on the page, which can be especially bothersome for visitors who are using mobile devices to view the full site or who have relatively low-resolution monitors (less than 800×600).

The fundamental goal of a website is to make the individual or organization visible on the Internet, but also—and more important—to act as a portal to the information within the site itself. The main page of a site should give the user enough information to provide a clear picture of the organization, as well as traditional contact information and an email address to submit questions or feedback. It should also provide clear pathways into the highly structured information within other pages in the site. The main page shown in Figure 23.2 provides examples of all these good features: basic information, contact information, and paths to information for multiple audiences.

One of the most common mistakes beginning website developers make is creating pages that look fundamentally different than other pages on the site. An equally serious mistake is using the same publicly available clip art that thousands of other web authors are also using. Remember that, on the Internet, one click can take you around the world. The only way to make your pages memorable and recognizable as a cohesive site is to make all your pages adhere to a unique, unmistakable visual theme. In other words, strive for uniqueness when compared to other websites, yet uniformity within the site itself.

TIP

Regardless of how large your site is, it's a good idea to carefully organize your resources. For example, placing the images for your web pages in a separate folder named `images` is one step toward organization. Similarly, if you have files that are available for download, place them in a folder called `downloads`. This makes it much easier to keep track of web page resources based on their particular types (HTML pages, PNG images, and so on). Additionally, if you organize your site into sections, such as Company, Products, Press, and so on, put the individual pages into similarly named directories (`company`, `products`, `press`, and so on), for the same organizational reasons.

FIGURE 23.2
This university main page uses a
basic design, minimal but useful
graphics, and a clear structure to
entice users to explore for more
information.

As an example of how uniformity can help make a site more cohesive,
think about large, popular sites you might have visited, such as
ESPN.com. If you visit the MLB section at ESPN.com (see Figure 23.3)
and then visit the NFL section (see Figure 23.4), you'll notice a very
similar structure.

FIGURE 23.3
The MLB section at ESPN.com.

In both examples, you see navigation elements at the top of the page (including some subnavigation elements), a large area in the middle of the page for the featured item graphic, a rectangle on the right side containing links to top stories, and a set of secondary rectangles under the primary image leading readers to additional stories. The only difference between the MLB section and the NFL section is the color scheme: The MLB section is part of a predominantly blue color scheme, whereas the NFL section is predominantly green. However, in both sections, you know that if you want to read the popular news stories, you look to the right of the page. If you want to navigate to another section in the site or to the site's main page, you look to a navigational element at the top left of the page.

The presence of consistent design and organizational elements helps ensure that your users will be able to navigate throughout your content with confidence. From a maintenance perspective, the consistent structural template enables you to reuse pieces of the underlying code. This type of code reuse typically happens through dynamic server-side programming outside the scope of this book, but in general, it means that instead of copying and pasting the same HTML, CSS, and JavaScript over and over, that client-side code exists in only one place and is applied dynamically to the content. Therefore, instead of making changes to thousands of files to make a background change from blue to green, for example, you would need to make a change only once.

FIGURE 23.4
The NFL section at ESPN.com.

Organizing a Larger Site

For complex sites, sophisticated layout and graphics can help organize and improve the looks of your site when used consistently throughout all your pages. To see how you can make aesthetics and organization work hand in hand, let's look at examples of navigation (and, thus, underlying organization) for a few sites that present a large volume of information to several different audiences.

Figure 23.5 shows the main page of Amazon.com, specifically with the side navigation selected. Amazon is in the business of selling products, plain and simple. Therefore, it makes sense for Amazon to show product categories as the main navigational elements.

FIGURE 23.5
Amazon.com shows product categories as primary navigation elements.

Although Amazon is in the business of selling products, it still has to provide information regarding who it is, how to contact it, and other ancillary yet important information to enhance the business-to-consumer relationship. Links to this sort of information appear in the footer, or bottom portion, of the Amazon.com website—outside the viewing area of this screenshot. When creating your site template, you must determine the most important content areas and how to organize that content; also remember to provide users with basic information—especially if that information will enhance your image and make users feel as if you value what they have to say.

The next example is of a secondary page within the Peet's Coffee & Tea website (www.peets.com). All the pages in the Peet's website follow one of the common types of presenting navigation and subnavigation: a horizontal strip for main navigation, with secondary elements for that section placed in a vertical column on the left. As Figure 23.6 shows, the section the user is currently browsing (Community) is highlighted in the main navigation (through a subtle font color change), as is the specific page in the secondary navigation (using a background color change for the element). These types of visual indicators help users orient themselves within the site. Using a visual indicator is a useful tactic because your users might arrive at a page via a search engine or by a link from another website. After your users arrive, you want them to feel at home—or at least feel as if they know where they are in relation to your site.

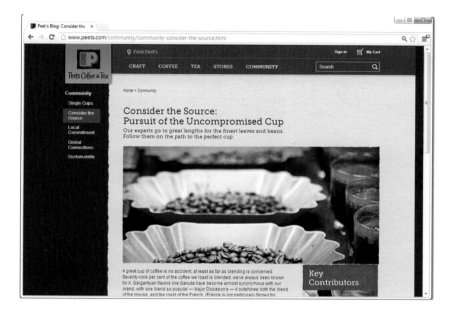

FIGURE 23.6
This Peet's Coffee & Tea secondary page shows a main navigation element selected with secondary navigation on the left side of the page.

As you can see by the different main navigation elements—Craft, Coffee, Tea, Stores, and Community—the Peet's website has to serve the needs of many different types of people who come to the website for many different reasons. As you organize your own site content, determine the information that is most important to you, as well as the information that is most important to your users, and create a navigation scheme that finds a happy medium between the two.

Figure 23.7 shows another example of a navigation style, this time with a twist on the standard top navigation/left side navigation scheme. In this example, the left side navigation (the secondary navigation, in this case) also appears in a drop-down menu under the main navigation (refer to Hour 17 for information on how to do something like this). Hovering the mouse over any of the other main navigation elements shows similar menus. This scheme gives users an entire site map at their fingertips because they can reach any place in the site within one click of any other page.

FIGURE 23.7
The BAWSI.org website shows
subnavigation attached to each
main navigation element.

Also notice that the Overview link in the side navigation window is styled a bit differently—with heavier purple text—than the other links in the window, indicating to visitors what page they are on. This visual detail, similar to what you saw on the Peet's site, is an unobtrusive way to give users a sense of where they are within the current navigational scheme.

You can choose among many different types of navigation styles and ways of indicating to users where they are and where they might want to go next. Keep in mind the following fact: Studies have repeatedly shown that people become confused and annoyed when presented with more than seven choices at a time, and people feel most comfortable with five or fewer choices. Therefore, you should avoid presenting more than five links (either in a list or as graphical icons) next to one another, if at all possible—and definitely avoid presenting more than seven at once. Amazon.com gets a pass here because it is an Internet superstore, and users expect a lot of "departments" in which to shop when they get there. But when you need to present more than seven links in a navigation list, break them into multiple lists with a separate heading for each of the five to seven items.

It will also help your readers navigate your site without confusion if you avoid putting any page more than two (or, at most, three) links away from the main page. You should also always send readers back to a main category page (or the home page) after they've read a subsidiary page. In other words, try to design somewhat of a flat link structure in which most pages are no more than one or two links deep. You don't want visitors to have to rely heavily, if at all, on their browsers' Back buttons to navigate your site.

Writing Maintainable Code

If you've done any coding before reading this book, you already know how important it is to write code that can be maintained—that is, you or someone else should be able look at your code later and not be utterly confused by it. The challenge is to make your code as immediately understandable as possible. A time will come when you'll look back on a page that you wrote, and you won't have a clue what you were thinking or why you wrote the code the way you did. Fortunately, there is a way to combat this problem of apparent memory loss.

Documenting Code with Comments

Whenever you develop an HTML page or CSS snippet, keep in mind that you or someone else will almost certainly need to make changes to it someday. Simple text web pages are usually easy to read and revise, but complex pages with graphics, tables, and other layout tricks can be quite difficult to decipher.

To see what I'm talking about, visit just about any page in a web browser and view its source code. Using Internet Explorer, right-click any page and select View Source. Using Chrome or Firefox, right-click any page and select View Page Source. You might see a jumbled bunch of code that is tough to decipher as pure HTML. This might be because content management software systems have generated the markup dynamically, or it might be because its human maintainer has not paid attention to structure, ease of reading, code commenting,

NOTE

To include comments in a stylesheet, begin comments with /* and end them with */ (your commented code should be between these characters).

The HTML <!-- and --> comment syntax does not work properly in stylesheets.

and other methods for making the code readable by humans. For the sake of maintaining your own pages, I encourage you to impose a little more order on your HTML markup and stylesheet entries. The same goes for any JavaScript you might write in the future: Proper indentation is your (and your future development partner's) friend.

As you have seen in several different lessons throughout this book, you can enclose comments to yourself or your coauthors using the HTML beginning and ending comment syntax: `<!--` and `-->`. These comments will not appear on the web page when viewed with a browser but can be read by anyone who examines the HTML code in a text editor or via the web browser's View Source (or View Page Source) function. The following example provides a little refresher just to show you how a comment is coded:

```
<!-- This image needs to be updated daily. -->
<img src="headline.jpg" alt="Today's Headline" />
```

As this code reveals, the comment just before the `<img />` tag provides a clue to how the image is used. Anyone who reads this code knows immediately that this is an image that must be updated every day. Web browsers completely ignore the text in the comment.

TIP

One handy use of comments is to hide parts of a web page that are currently under construction. Instead of making the text and graphics visible and explaining that they're under construction, you can hide them from view entirely with some carefully placed opening and closing comment indicators around the HTML that you do not want to appear. This is a great way to work on portions of a page gradually and show only the end result to the world when you're finished.

▼ TRY IT YOURSELF

Commenting Your Code

It will be well worth your time now to go through all the web pages and stylesheets you've created so far and add any comments that you or others might find helpful when revising them in the future. Here's what to do:

1. Insert a comment explaining any fancy formatting or layout techniques before the tags that make it happen.

2. Use a comment just before an `<img />` tag to briefly describe any important graphic whose function isn't obvious from the `alt` message.

3. Consider using a comment (or several comments) to summarize how the cells of a `<table>` are supposed to align.

4. If you use hexadecimal color codes (such as `<div style="color: #8040B0">`), insert a comment indicating what the color actually is (bluish-purple).

5. Indent your comments to help them stand out and make both the comments and the HTML or CSS easier to read. Don't forget to use indentation in the HTML, CSS, and JavaScript itself to make it more readable, too, as we discuss in the next section.

Indenting Code for Clarity

I have a confession. Throughout the book, I've been carefully indoctrinating you into an HTML code development style without really letting on. It's time to spill the beans. You've no doubt noticed a consistent pattern with respect to the indentation of all the HTML code in the book. More specifically, each child tag is indented to the right two spaces from its parent tag. Furthermore, content within a tag that spans more than one line is indented within the tag.

The best way to learn the value of indentation is to see some HTML code without it. You know how the song goes—"You don't know what you've got 'til it's gone." Anyway, here's a very simple table coded without any indentation:

```
<table><tr><td>Cell One</td><td>Cell Two</td></tr>
<tr><td>Cell Three</td><td>Cell Four</td></tr></table>
```

Not only is there no indentation, but there also is no delineation between rows and columns within the table. Now compare this code with the following code, which describes the same table:

```
<table>
  <tr>
    <td>Cell One</td>
    <td>Cell Two</td>
  </tr>
  <tr>
    <td>Cell Three</td>
    <td>Cell Four</td>
  </tr>
</table>
```

This heavily indented code makes it plainly obvious how the rows and columns are divided up via `<tr>` and `<td>` tags.

Consistent indentation might even be more important than comments when it comes to making your HTML code understandable and maintainable. And you don't have to buy into this specific indentation strategy. If you'd rather use three or four spaces instead of two, that's fine. And if you want to tighten things up a bit and not indent content within a tag, that also works. The main point to take from this section is that it's important to develop a coding style of your own and then ruthlessly stick to it.

TIP

If you work with other people (or plan to) in developing web pages, consider getting together as a group to formulate a consistent coding style. That way, everyone is on the same page—pun intended.

Thinking About Version Control

If you've ever used Google Docs, you have encountered a form of version control; in Google Docs, Google automatically saves revisions of your work as you are typing. This is different than simply automatically saving your work (although it does that, too) because you can revert to any revision along the way. You might have encountered this concept when using popular blog-authoring software such as Blogger or WordPress, or even when editing wikis—both of these also enable users to revise their work without overwriting, and thus deleting for all time, their previous work.

You might be wondering, "Well, what does that have to do with HTML or CSS? You're talking about documents." The answer is simple: Just as you might want to revert to a previous edition of an article or letter, you might want to revert to a previous edition of your HTML or CSS. This could be because you followed a good idea to the end, but your markup just proved untenable and you don't want to start over entirely—you just want to back up to a certain point along your revision path.

Version control involves more than just revision history. When you start using version control systems to maintain your code, you will hear terms like these:

▶ **Commit/check in and check out**—When you put an object into the code repository, you are committing that file; when you check out a file, you are grabbing it from the repository (where all the current and historical versions are stored) and working on it until you are ready to commit or check in the file again.

▶ **Branch**—The files you have under version control can branch or fork at any point, thus creating two or more development paths. Suppose you want to try some new display layouts or form interactivity, but you don't want an existing site to appear modified in any way. You might have started with one master set of files but then forked this set of files for the new site, continuing to develop them independently. If you continued developing the original set of files, that would be working with the *trunk*.

▶ **Change/diff**—This is just the term (you can say change or diff) for a modification made under version control. You might also hear *diff* used as a verb, as in "I diffed the files," to refer to the action of comparing two versions of an object (there is an underlying UNIX command called `diff`).

▶ **Fork**—When you find an open source GitHub repository that you want to use as the basis for your own work (or that you want to contribute to), you *fork* the repository to then create a copy of it that you can work on at your own pace. From the forked repository, you can *push* commits to your own version, *fetch* changes from the original repository, and issue *pull requests* to the owner of the original if you would like to contribute your changes to the original repository that you forked.

You will hear many more terms than just these few listed here, but if you can conceptualize the repository, the (local) working copy, and the process of checking in and checking out files, you are well on your way to implementing version control for your digital objects.

Using a Version Control System

Several different version control systems are available for use, some free and open source, and some proprietary. The two most popular systems are Subversion (subversion.apache.org) and Git (git-scm.com). If you have a web hosting service that enables you to install Subversion, you can create your own repository and use a Subversion client to connect to it.

An increasingly popular tool is Git, which is a decentralized approach to version control and also offers numerous tools and hosting options for users who want to get started with a repository but don't necessarily want, need, or understand all the extra installation and maintenance overhead that goes with it. One such hosting option for Git repositories is GitHub (github.com). It allows users to create accounts and then store and maintain as many code repositories for free as they would like (as long as they are open source), while also providing paid solutions for users who want to maintain private code repositories.

For anyone wanting to get started with version control, I recommend Git and GitHub for relative ease of use and free, cross-platform tools. The GitHub Help site is a great place to start: See http://help.github.com/. An added benefit of the already-free GitHub account is the capability to use Gist (gist.github.com) to share code snippets (or whole pages) with others (those snippets themselves are Git repositories and, thus, are versioned and forkable in their own right). GitHub repositories, including Gists, are also excellent ways to get started with version control of your work.

Using HTML and CSS Frameworks

If you use a content management system (CMS) such as Wordpress (www.wordpress.org) or Drupal (www.drupal.org) to power your website, you will end up using a presentation template designed for one of those systems—but what about the people who do *not* want to use a CMS but *would* like a starting point for an advanced HTML and CSS presentation? Over the last few years, the web development world has seen the rise of HTML and CSS (or "front-end") frameworks, which can help solve this problem. Many of these frameworks are open source and available for download or forking from GitHub repositories. These frameworks often also include advanced JavaScript functionality, but don't let that scare you—numerous examples and documentation help guide you through the initial stages of your work.

I recommend three popular front-end frameworks:

▶ **Bootstrap**—Developed internally by engineers at Twitter, this framework is open source software for anyone who wants to use it to get started with modern design elements. Learn more at http://getbootstrap.com/, which includes a simple "Get Started" section that explains what is included and how to use it.

▶ **Foundation**—Another open source framework, Foundation emphasizes responsive design so that people with all different kinds of devices, from desktops to phones, can enjoy and use your website. Learn more at http://foundation.zurb.com/, which includes an extensive "Getting Started" section that details the components of the display templates you can use.

▶ **HTML5 Boilerplate**—One of the leanest frameworks out there, this might be the most useful for beginners because it provides the basics of what you need without overwhelming you with the possibilities. Learn more at http://html5boilerplate.com/, and see the documentation maintained within the GitHub repository.

Although front-end frameworks can be incredibly useful for speeding up some of the foundational work of web development, you run the risk of falling into the "cookie cutter" trap, in which your site looks like all the others out there (at least, the ones using the same framework). However, with a little creativity, you can avoid that trap.

Summary

This hour gave you examples and explanations to help you organize your web pages into a coherent site that is informative, attractive, and easy to navigate. Web users have become quite savvy and expect well-designed websites, and they will quickly abandon your site if they experience a poor design that is difficult to navigate.

This hour also discussed the importance of making your code easy to maintain by adding comments and indentation. Comments are important not only as a reminder for you when you revisit code later, but also as instructions if someone else inherits your code. Indentation might seem like an aesthetic issue, but it can help you quickly analyze and understand the structure of a web page at a glance.

Because you likely will soon need code-management tools either for yourself or for yourself and other developers in your group, this lesson introduced you to a few concepts of version control. Version control enables you to innovate without losing your solid, production-quality work and also provides more opportunities for other developers to work within your code base.

Finally, you learned a little bit about HTML and CSS frameworks, of which there are many. These frameworks can help you speed up your web development project by giving you templates that already contain modern and validated markup.

Q&A

Q. Won't adding a lot of comments and spaces make my pages load slower when someone views them?

A. The size of a little extra text in your pages is negligible when compared to other, chunkier web page resources (such as images and multimedia). Besides, slower dial-up modem connections typically do a decent job of compressing text when transmitting it, so adding spaces to format your HTML doesn't usually change the transfer time. You'd have to type hundreds of comment words to cause even 1 extra second of delay in loading a page. Also keep in mind that, with the broadband connections (cable, DSL, and so on) that many people use, text travels extremely fast. The graphics are the components that slow pages down, so although you need to optimize your images as best you can, you can use text comments freely. You can also learn more about the concept of "minifying" your HTML and CSS (and JavaScript, too) at https://developers.google.com/speed/docs/best-practices/payload?hl=fr#MinifyHTML.

Q. Using version control seems like overkill for my tiny personal website. Do I have to use it?

A. Of course not—websites of any type, personal or otherwise, are not required to be under version control or other backup systems. However, most people have experienced some data loss or website crash, so if you don't use version control, I highly recommend at least performing some sort of automated backup of your files to an external system. By "external system," I mean any external drive, whether a physical drive attached to your computer or a cloud-based backup service such as Dropbox (www.dropbox.com).

Workshop

The Workshop contains quiz questions and activities to help you solidify your understanding of the material covered. Try to answer all questions before looking at the "Answers" section that follows.

Quiz

1. What are three ways to ensure that all your pages form a single cohesive website?

2. What two types of information should you always include in your home page?

3. You want to say to future editors of a web page, "Don't change this image of me. It's my only chance at immortality." But you don't want users who view the page to see that message. How can you do this?

Answers

1. Use consistent background, colors, fonts, and styles. Repeat the same link words or graphics on the top of the page that the link leads to. Repeat the same small header, buttons, or other elements on every page of the site.

2. Use enough identifying information that users can immediately see the name of the site and understand what it is about. Also, whatever the most important message is that you want to convey to your intended audience, state it directly and concisely. Whether it's your mission statement or a trademarked marketing slogan, make sure that it is in plain view here.

3. Put the following comment immediately before the `<img />` tag:

```
<!-- Don't change this image of me.
     It's my only chance at immortality. -->
```

Exercises

▶ Grab a pencil (the oldfangled kind) and sketch out your website as a bunch of little rectangles with arrows between them. Sketch a rough overview of what each page will look like by putting squiggles where the text goes and doodles where the images go. Each arrow should start at a doodle icon that corresponds to the navigation button for the page the arrow leads to. Even if you have the latest whiz-bang website-management tools (which are often more work to use than just creating the site itself), sketching your site by hand gives you a much more intuitive grasp of which pages on your site will be easy to get to and how the layout of adjacent pages will work together—all before you invest time in writing the actual HTML to connect the pages. Believe it or not, I still sketch out websites like this when I'm first designing them. Sometimes you can't beat a pencil and paper!

▶ Open the HTML files that make up your current website, and check them all for comments and code indentation. Are there areas in which the code needs to be explained to anyone who might look at it in the future? If so, add explanatory comments.

Is it difficult for you to tell the hierarchy of your code—is it difficult to see headings and sections? If so, indent your HTML so that the structure matches the hierarchy and thus enables you to jump quickly to the section you need to edit.

▶ Create an account at GitHub, and create a repository for your personal website or other code-based project. From this point forward, keep your repository in sync with your work on your personal computer by committing your changes to the GitHub repository.

Helping People Find Your Web Pages

Your web pages are ultimately only as useful as they are accessible—if no one can find your pages, your hard work in creating a useful architecture, providing interesting content, and coding them correctly will be for naught. The additional HTML tags you'll discover in this hour won't make any visible difference in your web pages, but they are extremely important because they will help your audience more easily find your web pages.

For most website creators, this might be the easiest—but most important—hour in the book. You'll learn how to add elements to your pages and how to construct your site architecture to increase the possibility that search engines will return links to your site when someone searches for words related to your topic or company; this is called *search engine optimization* (SEO).

Contrary to what you might hear from companies who try to sell search engine optimization services to you, no magic secrets guarantee that you'll be at the top of every list of search results. However, you can follow a set of *free* best practices on your own to make sure your site is as easy to find as possible.

Publicizing Your Website

Presumably, you want your website to attract someone's attention, or you wouldn't bother to create it in the first place. If you are placing your pages only on a local network or corporate intranet, or if you are distributing your site exclusively on removable storage media, helping users find your pages might not be much of a problem. But if you are adding the content of your website to the billions of other pages of content indexed by search engines, bringing your intended audience to your site is a very big challenge indeed.

To tackle this problem, you need a basic understanding of how most people decide which pages to look at. People become aware of your website in three basic ways:

▶ Somebody tells them about it and gives them the address; they enter that address directly into their web browser.

▶ They follow a link to your site from someone else's site, from an aggregator and recommendation service such as Digg or Reddit, or from a link or mention on a social networking site such as Facebook, Twitter, or Google+.

▶ They find your site indexed in the databases that power the Google, Bing, or Yahoo! search engines (among others).

You can increase your website traffic with a little time and effort. To increase the number of people who hear about you through word-of-mouth, well, use your mouth—and every other channel of communication available to you. If you have an existing contact database or mailing list, announce your website to those people. Add the site address to your business cards or company literature. If you have the money, go buy TV and radio ads broadcasting your Internet address. In short, do the marketing thing. Good old-fashioned word-of-mouth marketing is still the best thing going, even on the Internet—we just have more tools available to us online.

Increasing the number of incoming links to your site from other sites is also pretty straightforward—although that doesn't mean it isn't a lot of work. If there are specialized directories on your topic, either online or in print, be sure you are listed in them. Participate in social networking, including the implementation of Facebook and Google+ pages (if applicable) for your service or business. Create a Twitter account to broadcast news and connect with customers—again, if that is applicable to your online presence. Go into the spaces where your customers might be, such as blogs that comment on your particular topic of interest, and participate in those communities. That's not to say that you should find a forum on your topic or service and spam its users with links to your site. Act as an expert in your given field, offering advice and recommendations along with your own site URL. There's not much I can say in this hour to help you with that, except to go out and do it.

The main thing I can help you with is making sure search engines can gather and index your content correctly. It's a fair assumption that if your content isn't in Google's databases, you're in trouble.

Search engines are basically huge databases that index as much content on the Internet as possible—including videos and other rich media. They use automated processing to search sites, using programs called *robots* or *spiders* to search pages for content and build the databases. After the content is indexed, the search applications themselves use highly sophisticated techniques of ranking pages to determine which content to display first, second, third, and so on when a user enters a search term.

When the search engine processes a user query, it looks for content that contains the key words and phrases that the user is looking for. But it's not a simple match, as in "If this page contains this phrase, return it as a result," because content is ranked according to frequency and context of the keywords and phrases, as well as the number of links from other sites that lend credibility to it. This lesson teaches you a few ways to ensure that your content appears appropriately in the search engine, based on the content and context you provide.

NOTE

A very popular, high-traffic, and well-respected site (because of its accuracy and added value) for tips for interacting in social networking spaces, especially for the business user, is Mashable (www.mashable.com).

Listing Your Pages with the Major Search Sites

If you want users to find your pages, you absolutely must submit a request to each of the major search sites to index your pages. Even though search engines index web content automatically, this is the best way to ensure that your site has a presence on their sites. Each of these sites has a form to fill out with the URL address, a brief description of the site, and, in some cases, a category or list of keywords with which your listing should be associated. These forms are easy to fill out; you can easily complete all of them in an hour, with time left over to list yourself at one or two specialized directories you might have found as well. (How do you find the specialized directories? Through the major search sites, of course!)

Before You List Your Pages

But wait! Before you rush off this minute to submit your listing requests, read the rest of this hour. Otherwise, you'll have a very serious problem, and you will have already lost your best opportunity to solve it.

To see what I mean, imagine this scenario: You publish a page selling automatic cockroach flatteners. I am an Internet user who has a roach problem, and I'm allergic to bug spray. I open my laptop, brush the roaches off the keyboard, log on to my favorite search site, and enter "cockroach" as a search term. The search engine promptly presents me with a list of the first 10 out of 10,400,000 web pages containing the word "cockroach." You have submitted your listing request, so you know that your page is somewhere on that list.

Did I mention that I'm rich? And did I mention that two roaches are mating on my foot? You even offer same-day delivery in my area. Do you want your page to be number 3 on the list or number 8,542? Okay, now you understand the problem. Just getting listed in a search engine isn't enough—you need to leverage your content and work your way up the rankings.

TIP

Some sites provide one form that automatically submits itself to all the major search engines, plus several minor search engines. These sites—such as www.scrubtheweb.com, www.submitexpress.com, and www.hypersubmit.com—are popular examples of sites that attempt to sell you a premium service that lists you in many other directories and indexes as well. Depending on your target audience, these services might or might not be of value, but I strongly recommend that you go directly to the major search sites listed previously in this hour, and any others applicable to your site, and use their own forms to submit your requests to be listed. That way, you can be sure to answer the questions (which are slightly different at every site) accurately, and you will know exactly how your site listing will appear in each search engine.

Even though listing with the major search engines is easy and quick, it can be a bit confusing: Each search engine uses different terminology to identify where you should click to register your pages. The following list might save you some frustration; it includes the addresses of some popular search engines that will include your site for free, along with the exact wording of the link you should click to register:

▶ **Google**—Visit https://www.google.com/webmasters/tools/submit-url, enter the address of your site, and then enter the squiggly verification text, called a CAPTCHA (or completely automated public turing test to tell computers and humans apart) shown on the page. Then click the Submit button to add your site to Google.

▶ **Bing (and a bonus listing with Yahoo!)**—Visit http://www.bing.com/toolbox/submit-site-url to sign in; then enter the verification text, enter the address of your site, and click the Submit URL button. You get a bonus listing with Yahoo! when you submit to Bing, because if you go to Yahoo's own Submit Your Site page at http://search.yahoo.com/info/submit.html, it redirects to the Bing submission form.

Providing Hints for Search Engines

Fact: You can do absolutely nothing to guarantee that your site will appear in the top 10 search results for a particular word or phrase in any major search engine (short of buying ad space from the search site, that is). After all, if there were such guarantees, why couldn't everyone else who wants to be number 1 on the list do it, too? What you can do is avoid being last on the list and give yourself as good a chance as anyone else of being first; this is called search engine optimization (SEO), or optimizing the content and structure of your pages so that search engines will favor your pages over others.

Each search engine uses a different method for determining which pages are likely to be most relevant and should therefore be sorted to the top of a search result list. You don't need to get too hung up on the differences, though, because they all use some combination of the same basic criteria. The following list includes almost everything any search engine considers when trying to evaluate which pages best match one or more keywords:

- ▶ Do your titles naturally include useful keywords in the `<title>` tag of the page?

- ▶ Does the body content naturally contain keywords that a user would search for?

- ▶ Do keywords appear in a concise description in a `<meta />` tag in the page?

- ▶ Does your site make use of semantic elements such as `<section>`, `<article>`, `<header>`, and `<nav>`, which makes it even easier to apply meaning to your content?

- ▶ Does important text appear in `numbered level` headings in the page?

- ▶ Do you use good descriptions in the names of image files and `alt` text for images in the page?

- ▶ How many other pages within the website link to the page?

- ▶ How many other pages in other websites link to the page? How many other pages link to those pages?

- ▶ How many times have users chosen this page from a previous search list result?

Clearly, the most important thing you can do to improve your position is to consider the keywords your intended audience is most likely to enter. Don't concern yourself with common, single-word searches such as "food"; the lists they generate are usually so long that trying to make it to the top is like playing the lottery. Focus instead on uncommon words and two- or three-word combinations that are most

NOTE

Some overeager web page authors put dozens or even hundreds of repetitions of the same word on their pages, sometimes in small print or a hard-to-see color, just to get the search engines to position that page at the top of the list whenever users search for that word. This practice is called *search engine spamming*.

Don't be tempted to try this sort of thing—all the major search engines are aware of this practice and immediately delete any page from their database that sets off a spam detector by repeating the same word or group of words in a suspicious pattern. It's still fine (and quite beneficial) to have several occurrences of important search words on a page, in the natural course of your content. Make sure, however, that you use those words in normal sentences or phrases—then the spam police will leave you alone.

likely to indicate relevance to your topic (for instance, "Southern home-style cooking" instead of simply "food"). Make sure that those terms and phrases occur several times on your page, and be certain to put the most important ones in the `<title>` tag and the first heading or introductory paragraph.

Of all the search engine evaluation criteria just listed, the use of `<meta />` tags is probably the least understood. Some people rave about `<meta />` tags, as if using them could instantly move you to the top of every search list. Other people dismiss `<meta />` tags as ineffective and useless. Neither of these extremes is true.

A `<meta />` *tag* is a general-purpose tag you can put in the `<head>` portion of any document to specify some information about the page that doesn't belong in the `<body>` text. Most major search engines look at `<meta />` tags to get a short description of your page and some keywords to identify what your page is about. For example, your automatic cockroach flattener order form might include the following two tags:

```
<meta   name="description"
        content="Order the SuperSquish cockroach flattener." />
<meta   name="keywords"
        content="cockroach,roaches,kill,squish,supersquish" />
```

The first tag in this example ensures that the search engine has an accurate description of the page to present on its search results list (if that's how they do it, and several do). The second `<meta />` tag may slightly increase your page's ranking on the list whenever any of your specified keywords are included in a search query, if the search engine uses this type of tag in their algorithm.

Always include `<meta />` tags with `name="description"` and `name="keywords"` attributes in any page that you want a search engine to index. Doing so might not have a dramatic effect on your position in search lists, and not all search engines look for `<meta />` tags, but it can only help. Exercise caution and restraint, though—use description and keyword tags judiciously and naturally, and do not stuff them full of every word you can think of.

To give you a concrete example of how to improve search engine results, consider the page in Listing 24.1.

This page *should* be easy to find because it deals with a specific topic and includes several occurrences of some uncommon technical terms for which users interested in this subject would be likely to search. However, you can do several things to improve the chances of this page appearing high on a search engine results list.

LISTING 24.1   A Page That Will Have Little Visibility During an Internet Site Search

```
<!DOCTYPE html>

<html lang="en">
  <head>
    <title>Fractal Central</title>
  </head>

  <body>
    <header style="text-align:center">
      <img  src="fractalaccent.gif" alt="a fractal" />
    </header>
    <div style="width:133px; float:left; padding:6px;
                text-align:center; border-width:4px;
                border-style:ridge">
      Discover the latest software, books and more at our
      online store.<br />
      <a href="orderform.html"><img src="orderform.gif"
        alt="Order Form" style="border-style:none" /></a>
    </div>
    <div style="float:left; padding:6px">
      <h2>A Comprehensive Guide to the<br />
      Art and Science of Chaos and Complexity</h2>
      <p>What's that? You say you're hearing about
      "fractals" and "chaos" all over the place, but still
      aren't too sure what they are? How about a quick
      summary of some key concepts:</p>
      <ol>
        <li>Even the simplest systems become deeply
        complex and richly beautiful when a process is
        "iterated" over and over, using the results
        of each step as the starting point of the next.
        This is how Nature creates a magnificently
        detailed 300-foot redwood tree from a seed
        the size of your fingernail.</li>
        <li>Most "iterated systems" are easily simulated
        on computers, but only a few are predictable and
        controllable. Why? Because a tiny influence, like
        a "butterfly flapping its wings," can be strangely
        amplified to have major consequences such as
        completely changing tomorrow's weather in a distant
        part of the world.</li>
        <li>Fractals can be magnified forever without loss
        of detail, so mathematics that relies on straight
        lines is useless with them. However, they give us
        a new concept called "fractal dimension" which
        can measure the texture and complexity of anything
```

```
        from coastlines to storm clouds.</li>
        <li>While fractals win prizes at graphics shows,
        their chaotic patterns pop up in every branch of
        science. Physicists find beautiful artwork coming
        out of their plotters. "Strange attractors" with
        fractal turbulence appear in celestial mechanics.
        Biologists diagnose "dynamical diseases" when
        fractal rhythms fall out of sync. Even pure
        mathematicians go on tour with dazzling videos of their
        research.</li>
      </ol>
      <p>Think all these folks may be on to something?</p>
    </div>
    <div style="text-align:center">
      <a href="http://netletter.com/nonsense/">
        <img src="findout.gif" alt="Find Out More"
            style="border-style:none" /></a>
    </div>
  </body>
</html>
```

Now compare the page in Listing 24.1 with the changes made to the page in Listing 24.2. The two pages look almost the same, but to search robots and search engines, these two pages appear quite different. The following list summarizes what was changed in the page and how those changes affected indexing:

▶ Important search terms were added to the `<title>` tag and the first heading on the page. The original page didn't even include the word *fractal* in either of these two key positions.

▶ `<meta />` tags were added to assist search engines with a description and keywords.

▶ The headline was given a higher value.

▶ Semantic tags were used to apply additional meaning to the content through its structure.

▶ A very descriptive `alt` attribute was added to the first `<img />` tag. Not all search engines read and index `alt` text, but some do.

▶ The quotation marks around technical terms (such as `"fractal"` and `"iterated"`) were removed because some search engines consider `"fractal"` to be a different word than `fractal`. The quotation marks were replaced with the character entity `&quot;`, which search robots simply disregard.

▶ The keyword *fractal* was added twice to the text in the order form box.

It is impossible to quantify how much more frequently users searching for information on fractals and chaos were able to find the page shown in Listing 24.2 versus the page shown in Listing 24.1, but it's a sure bet that the changes only improved the page's visibility to search engines. As is often the case, the improvements made for the benefit of the search spiders probably made the page's subject easier for humans to recognize and understand as well. This makes optimizing a page for search engines a win–win effort.

LISTING 24.2   An Improvement on the Page in Listing 24.1

```html
<!DOCTYPE html>

<html lang="en">
  <head>
    <title>Fractal Central: A Guide to Fractals, Chaos,
           and Complexity</title>
    <meta name="description" content="A comprehensive guide
          to fractal geometry, chaos science and complexity
          theory." />
    <meta name="keywords"  content="fractal,fractals,chaos
          science,chaos theory,fractal geometry,complexity,
          complexity theory" />
  </head>

  <body>
    <header style="text-align:center">
      <img  src="fractalaccent.gif" alt="Fractal Central: A
          Guide to Fractals, Chaos, and Complexity " />
    </header>
    <section>
    <div style="width:133px; float:left; padding:6px;
                text-align:center; border-width:4px;
                border-style:ridge">
      Discover the latest fractal software, books and
      more at the  <strong>Fractal
      Central</strong> online store <br />
      <a href="orderform.html"><img src="orderform.gif"
        alt="Order Form" style="border-style:none" /></a>
    </div>
      <header>
      <h1>A Comprehensive Guide to the<br />
      Art and Science of Chaos and Complexity</h1>
      </header>
      <p>What's that? You say you're hearing about
      &quot;fractals&quot; and &quot;chaos&quot; all
      over the place, but still aren't too sure what
      they are? How about a quick summary of some key
      concepts:</p>
      <ol>
        <li>Even the simplest systems become deeply
        complex and richly beautiful when a process is
```

```
&quot;iterated&quot; over and over, using the
Results of each step as the starting point of
the next. This is how Nature creates a magnificently
detailed 300-foot redwood tree from a seed
the size of your fingernail.</li>
<li>Most &quot;iterated systems&quot; are easily
simulated on computers, but only a few are predictable
and controllable. Why? Because a tiny influence, like
a &quot;butterfly flapping its wings, &quot; can be
strangely amplified to have major consequences such as
completely changing tomorrow's weather in a distant
part of the world.</li>
<li>Fractals can be magnified forever without loss
of detail, so mathematics that relies on straight
lines is useless with them. However, they give us
a new concept called &quot;fractal dimension&quot;
which can measure the texture and complexity of
anything from coastlines to storm clouds.</li>
<li>While fractals win prizes at graphics shows,
their chaotic patterns pop up in every branch of
science. Physicists find beautiful artwork coming
out of their plotters. &quot;Strange attractors&quot;
with fractal turbulence appear in celestial mechanics.
Biologists diagnose &quot;dynamical diseases&quot;
when fractal rhythms fall out of sync. Even pure
mathematicians go on tour with dazzling videos of their
research.</li>
  </ol>
  <p>Think all these folks may be on to something?</p>
</section>
<footer style="text-align:center">
  <a href="http://netletter.com/nonsense/">
     <img src="findout.gif" alt="Find Out More"
         style="border-style:none" /></a>
</footer>
</body>
</html>
```

These changes go a long way toward making the content of this site more likely to be appropriately indexed. In addition to having good, indexed content, remember that the quality of content—as well as the number of other sites linking to yours—is important as well.

Additional Tips for Search Engine Optimization

The most important tip I can give you regarding search engine optimization is to not pay an SEO company to perform your SEO tasks if that company promises specific results for you. If a company promises that your site will be the number-one result in a Google search, run for the hills and take your checkbook with you—no one can promise that because the search algorithms have so many variables that the top result might change several times over the course of a given week. That is not to say that all SEO companies are scam artists. Some legitimate site content and architect consultants who perform SEO tasks get lumped in with the spammers who send unsolicited email, such as this:

```
"Dear google.com, I visited your website and noticed that you are not
 listed in most of the major search engines and directories..."
```

This sample email is used as an example in Google's own guidelines for webmasters, along with the note to "reserve the same skepticism for unsolicited email about search engines as you do for burn fat at night diet pills or requests to help transfer funds from deposed dictators." Yes, someone actually sent Google a spam email about how to increase their search ranking—in Google. For more good advice from Google, visit http://www.google.com/webmasters/.

Here are some additional actions you can take, for free, to optimize your content for search engines:

▶ Use accurate page titles. Your titles should be brief but descriptive and unique. Do not try to stuff your titles with keywords.

▶ Create human-friendly URLs, such as those with words in them that users can easily remember. It is a lot easier to remember—and it's easier for search engines to index in a relevant way—a URL such as http://www.mycompany.com/products/super_widget.html than something like http://www.mycompany.com?c=p&id=4&id=49f8sd7345fea.

▶ Create URLs that reflect your directory structure. This assumes that you have a directory structure in the first place, which you should.

▶ When possible, use text—not graphical elements—for navigation.

▶ If you have content several levels deep, use a breadcrumb trail so that users can find their way back home. A breadcrumb trail also gives search engines more words to index. For example, if you are looking at a recipe for biscuits in the Southern Cooking category of a food-related website, the breadcrumb trail for this particular page might look like this:

Home > Southern Cooking > Recipes > Biscuits

▶ Within the content of your page, use semantic elements and numbered level headings (`<h1>`, `<h2>`, `<h3>`) appropriately.

In addition to providing rich and useful content for your users, you should follow these tips to increase your site's prominence in page rankings.

Summary

This hour covered some extremely important territory by exploring how to provide hints to search engines (such as Google and Bing) so that users can find your pages more easily. You also saw an example of the HTML behind a perfectly reasonable web page *redone* to make it more search engine friendly. Finally, you learned a few more tips to optimize the indexing of your site overall.

Table 24.1 lists the tags and attributes covered in this hour.

TABLE 24.1   HTML Tags and Attributes Covered in Hour 24

Tag/Attribute	Function
`<meta />`	Indicates meta-information about this document (information about the document itself). Most commonly used to add a page description and to designate keywords. Used in the document `<head>`.
Attributes	
`name="name"`	Can be used to specify which type of information about the document is in the `content` attribute. For example, `name="keywords"` means that keywords for the page are in `content`.
`content="value"`	The actual message or value for the information specified in `name`. For example, you could see a list of keywords in the `content` attribute.

Q&A

Q. I have a lot of pages in my site. Do I need to fill out a separate form for each page at each search site?

A. No. If you submit just your home page (which is presumably linked to all the other pages), the search spiders will crawl through all the links on the page (and all the links on the linked pages, and so on) until they have indexed all the pages on your site.

Q. I submitted a request to be listed with a search engine, but when I search for my page, my page doesn't come up—not even when I enter my company's unique name. What can I do?

A. Most of the big search engines offer a form you can fill out to instantly check whether a specific address is included in their database. If you find that it isn't included, you can submit another request form. Sometimes it takes days or even weeks for the spiders to get around to indexing your pages after you submit a request.

Q. When I put keywords in a `<meta />` tag, do I need to include every possible variation of spelling and capitalization?

A. Don't worry about capitalization; almost all searches are entered in all lowercase letters. Do include any obvious variations or common spelling errors as separate keywords. Although this is simple in concept, more advanced strategies available when it comes to manipulating the `<meta />` tag than I've been able to cover in this hour. Visit http://en.wikipedia.org/wiki/Meta_element for good information on the various attributes of this tag, how to use it, and when it might be ignored.

Q. I've heard that I can use the `<meta />` tag to make a page automatically reload itself every few seconds or minutes. Is this true?

A. Yes, but there's no point in doing that unless you have some sort of program or script set up on your web server to provide new information on the page. However, for usability reasons, the W3C and users in general frown on the use of `<meta />` to refresh content.

Workshop

The Workshop contains quiz questions and activities to help you solidify your understanding of the material covered. Try to answer all questions before looking at the "Answers" section that follows.

Quiz

1. If you publish a page about puppy adoption, how can you help make sure that the page can be found by users who enter "puppy," "dog," and "adoption" at all the major Internet search sites?

2. Suppose you decide to paste your keywords hundreds of times in your HTML code, using a white font on a white background so that your readers cannot see them. How do search engine spiders deal with this?

3. Is it better to throw all your content in one directory or to organize it into several directories?

Answers

1. Make sure that *puppy*, *dog*, and *adoption* all occur frequently on your main page (as they probably already do), and title your page something along the lines of Puppy Dog Adoption. While you're at it, put the following `<meta />` tags in the `<head>` portion of the page:

   ```
   <meta name="description"
   content="dog adoption information and services" />
   <meta name="keywords" content="puppy, dog, adoption" />
   ```

   Publish your page online, and then visit the site submittal page for each major search engine (listed earlier in the hour) to fill out the site submission forms.

2. Search engine spiders ignore the duplications, and possibly blacklist you from their index and label you as a spammer.

3. Definitely organize your content into directories. This makes maintenance of your content easier and also gives you the opportunity to both create human-readable URLs with directory structures that make sense and create a navigational breadcrumb trail.

Exercises

▶ You've reached the end of the book. If you have a site that is ready for the world to see, review the content and structure for the best possible optimizations—and then submit the address to all the major search engines.

INDEX

X - Y - Z

FREE
Online Edition

 Safari
Books Online

Your purchase of *Sams Teach Yourself HTML and CSS in 24 Hours* includes access to a free online edition for 45 days through the **Safari Books Online** subscription service. Nearly every Sams book is available online through **Safari Books Online**, along with thousands of books and videos from publishers such as Addison-Wesley Professional, Cisco Press, Exam Cram, IBM Press, O'Reilly Media, Prentice Hall, Que, and VMware Press.

Safari Books Online is a digital library providing searchable, on-demand access to thousands of technology, digital media, and professional development books and videos from leading publishers. With one monthly or yearly subscription price, you get unlimited access to learning tools and information on topics including mobile app and software development, tips and tricks on using your favorite gadgets, networking, project management, graphic design, and much more.

Activate your FREE Online Edition at
informit.com/safarifree

STEP 1: Enter the coupon code: HUNMPEH.

STEP 2: New Safari users, complete the brief registration form.
Safari subscribers, just log in.

If you have difficulty registering on Safari or accessing the online edition,
please e-mail customer-service@safaribooksonline.com